Contents

CONTENTS

PART 4
There Shall Be No Night

BELIEVABLE LIES

BELIEVABLE LIES

The Misfits
Who Fought Churchill's
Secret Propaganda War

TERRY STIASTNY

WH ALLEN

UK | USA | Canada | Ireland | Australia
India | New Zealand | South Africa

WH Allen is part of the Penguin Random House group of companies
whose addresses can be found at global.penguinrandomhouse.com

Penguin Random House UK
One Embassy Gardens, 8 Viaduct Gardens, London SW11 7BW

penguin.co.uk
global.penguinrandomhouse.com

First published by WH Allen in 2025

1

Typeset in 13.4/15.5pt Garamond MT Pro by Six Red Marbles UK, Thetford, Norfolk.
Printed and bound in Great Britain by Clays Ltd, Elcograf S.p.A.

The authorised representative in the EEA is Penguin Random House Ireland,
Morrison Chambers, 32 Nassau Street, Dublin D02 YH68

A CIP catalogue record for this book is available from the British Library

Hardback ISBN 9780753559833
Trade Paperback ISBN 9780753559840

Penguin Random House is committed to a sustainable future
for our business, our readers and our planet. This book is made
from Forest Stewardship Council® certified paper.

For Veronica Stiastny
and in memory of
Norbert Stiastny
(1943–2020)
my parents

Cast of Characters

THE POLITICAL WARRIORS

Robert Bruce Lockhart – author, journalist, diplomat. Director-general of the Political Warfare Executive (PWE), 1941–1945

Richard Crossman – philosopher, journalist, aspiring Labour MP. Head of German section of the PWE, later working for US-led Psychological Warfare Bureau

Denis 'Tom' Sefton Delmer – former *Daily Express* Berlin correspondent, in charge of black propaganda for the German section of the PWE

Elisabeth Barker – BBC producer who moved to work for the Balkan section of the PWE, becoming head of the section, 1941–1944

Rex Leeper – head of the Political Intelligence Department, 1938. Head of SO1 propaganda section, 1940–1941. Director of the 'Country' HQ of the PWE, 1941–1943

Ralph Murray – BBC journalist 1934–1939. Worked for SO1 at Woburn. Head of Balkan section of the PWE 1941–1942. PWE representative to Greek government-in-exile from 1943

Brigadier Dallas Brooks – deputy director-general (military) of the PWE, in charge of liaison with military

Freddy Voigt – former *Manchester Guardian* correspondent in Berlin. Worked on propaganda radio, 1940–1941

Peter Ritchie Calder – director of plans at the PWE

THE POLITICIANS

Winston Churchill – prime minister, 1940–1945

Brendan Bracken – Conservative MP, confidant of Churchill. Minister of information, 1941–1945

Hugh Dalton – Labour MP. Minister of economic warfare, 1940–1942

Anthony Eden – Conservative MP. Foreign secretary, 1940–1945

Clement Attlee – leader of the Labour Party. Deputy prime minister, 1942–1945

Sir Stafford Cripps – lord privy seal, 1942

Alfred Duff Cooper – Conservative MP. Minister of information, 1940–1941

Max Aitken, Lord Beaverbrook – owner of the *Daily Express*. Minister of aircraft production, 1940; minister of supply, 1941

THE CIVIL SERVANTS

Sir Alexander 'Alec' Cadogan – permanent under-secretary, Foreign Office

Desmond Morton – prime minister's personal assistant, 1940–1945

John 'Jock' Colville – prime minister's assistant private secretary

Sir Robert Vansittart – chief diplomatic adviser to the British government, 1938–1941. Member of House of Lords from 1941

THE MILITARY

Air Marshal Sir Arthur 'Bomber' Harris – head of Bomber Command

Fitzroy Maclean – head of British military mission to Tito in Yugoslavia

Donald McLachlan – worked for the Naval Intelligence Division; collaborated closely with Delmer's black radio

THE BBC

Noel Newsome – BBC European news editor, then director of European broadcasts, 1941–1944

Douglas Ritchie – BBC assistant European news editor; voice of 'Colonel Britton' in propaganda broadcasts; later assistant director, European broadcasts, 1941–1944

Ivone Kirkpatrick – diplomat, BBC adviser on foreign affairs, liaison with government

THE AMERICANS

Franklin D. Roosevelt – president of the United States, 1933–1945

General Dwight D. Eisenhower – commander-in-chief, Allied Forces HQ

General Walter Bedell Smith – chief of staff to Eisenhower

General Robert McClure – chief of information and censorship section, Allied Forces HQ, 1942–1944; chief of Psychological Warfare Division, SHAEF, from April 1944

C.D. Jackson – deputy chief, Psychological Warfare Branch, AFHQ, 1943–1944; deputy chief, Psychological Warfare Division, SHAEF, 1944–1945

THE INTERNATIONAL LEADERS

Charles de Gaulle – leader of Free French in exile

Edvard Beneš – exiled president of Czechoslovakia, leader of government-in-exile

Josip Broz 'Tito' – leader of Partisans in Yugoslavia

Draža Mihailović – leader of Serb Četniks in Yugoslavia

THE OTHER HALVES

Isabel Delmer – artist, wife of Tom Delmer, illustrator of propaganda leaflets

Zita Crossman – wife of Richard Crossman, occasional broadcaster on the BBC

Moura Budberg – friend and former lover of Robert Bruce Lockhart, suspected of espionage

Mauricette Murray – multilingual Austrian wife of Ralph Murray

Introduction
The Boys in the Back Room

Late in the morning of 1 September 1939, a young intelligence officer received orders by telegram. The messages, sent both to his north London home and office, told him: 'Mobilize today, 7pm.'[1] Germany had invaded Poland and war was imminent. The twenty-seven-year-old, who had been working in intelligence for less than six months, knew what he had to do. His instructions told him to report at the Sugar Loaf Hotel in Dunstable and to ask for Mr Gibbs-Smith. If he found that the gentleman was not there, he should stay put and await orders. 'Do not,' the instructions insisted, 'make enquiries of anybody.' Robert Walmsley set off for Dunstable, a market town around thirty miles north of London, in his ancient Morris, bought for £15 from the proceeds of his secret work. He'd been told to bring along a suitcase containing clothes for a fortnight, including soap and towels, his gas-mask, and sandwiches for one meal. He was not the only one on his way.[2]

Vernon Bartlett, a prolific journalist and the defiantly independent MP for Bridgwater, was also driving to Dunstable. He had expected the roads out of London to be crowded with evacuees fleeing the capital, but he found the route so empty of traffic that he was an hour early and had time for a nap before his rendezvous. Bartlett pulled up in a country lane and asked a farmer to wake him after three-quarters of an hour.

At the appointed time, Bartlett reached the Sugar Loaf on Dunstable High Street, a redbrick Georgian coaching inn with a white portico. Inside, he gave the receptionist the code word. The receptionist was unflustered. 'You're another of the cloak-and-dagger boys?' he asked wryly. 'You'll find them all in the back room.'

On entering, Bartlett found a dozen or so of his friends clustered around a large map.[3] The map was not, as he might have expected, of Germany, but of nearby Woburn Abbey and its grounds. Bartlett, Walmsley and their future colleagues were to work at the abbey in a secret government department producing British wartime propaganda to the enemy. They started with little, equipped only with a couple of typewriters, a box of pins and a few pencils.[4] The map was to protect the sensibilities of their reluctant host, the eighty-one-year-old Duke of Bedford; it showed the recruits how to enter and leave the grounds without walking in front of his windows. The duke had only accepted the 'dreadful temporary civil servants' to avoid being 'afflicted with evacuee children from the East End of London'.[5] These dreadful civil servants, once they reached the abbey, were required to sign the Official Secrets Act – if they hadn't already – before they could begin to discover more about what their wartime role would be.

Woburn Abbey was referred to throughout the war as the Country HQ, often shortened to just 'the Country'. From its initial country base within the grounds of Woburn, the organisation spread out into the surrounding countryside, creating a 'hush-hush village' populated by an eccentric mixture of journalists, politicians, intelligence officers, authors, advertisers, artists and forgers. While many were British, among their number were émigrés and refugees from across occupied Europe who wanted to help liberate their homelands.

Robert Bruce Lockhart arrived at Woburn a week after the outbreak of war. He was met at Dunstable station by his new boss, Rex Leeper, a career diplomat and a longtime friend. Bruce Lockhart, at fifty-two, was a well-known personality, both in London society and in the media. As the British envoy to the Bolsheviks during the Russian Revolution, accused of plotting the overthrow of the nascent communist state, he had been imprisoned in the Kremlin before being released in a prisoner exchange in 1918. His 1932 book about his Russian exploits had been turned into a film, *British Agent*, two years later, starring Leslie Howard as the hero, modelled on Bruce Lockhart himself.[6] Leeper had helped to broker his freedom. Bruce Lockhart had agreed to work alongside Leeper in Woburn, responsible for the section dealing with propaganda to central Europe and the Balkans. Bruce Lockhart's career had always been colourful; a proud Scot, he had spent time in Berlin, Paris and Malaya before his Russian adventures. During the 1930s, he had lived in Prague and travelled in eastern Europe, working variously as a diplomat, banker, journalist and author. Bruce Lockhart's overspending – and his inability to keep up with it – was often a spur for him to change careers. This job was conventional by comparison; his responsibilities were to prepare memos for the Foreign Office and compile a summary of intelligence on the countries in his region.[7]

Sir Robert Bruce Lockhart, February 1943

On his first day, Bruce Lockhart strolled around Woburn's abundant grounds with Leeper. Safe from the threat of the bombs that many people expected to hit London imminently, he was nonetheless concerned that an intelligence department would not be able to 'function efficiently fifty miles away from the centre of all intelligence'. But Woburn, if far from the action, was outwardly a beautiful place to be. The 'pleasantly undulating' landscape was 'like paradise parks', he observed, with 'smooth grass rides between the great oaks'. The grounds were full of pheasant and partridge, and fat, sleek hares nibbled at the lawns.[8] There were larger specimens of wildlife too: Père David's deer, rheas, llamas and even rare European bison. They were not all as tame as they seemed; in the autumn, the deer could be ferocious. Thomas Barman, who worked on propaganda to Scandinavia, recalled an awful morning when two colleagues on Home Guard duty 'had spent the whole of the night crouching in a ditch, sheltering from deer that had become fiercely bellicose in the rutting season'. His colleagues went about armed with sticks after that.[9]

The grounds at Woburn may have been well-stocked, as was the bar, but the living conditions for the staff were less luxurious. Bruce Lockhart was at first housed in a villa called Foxgrove, in an attic room with not even a chest of drawers for his clothes. For a man who had once been locked up in a Moscow cell, it should not, perhaps, have seemed all that bad. He recounted that, soon after his arrival, he plunged into, what, for him, was a fairly frequent mood of despair; 'a gradual declension to pessimism ending in a night of gloom'. Bruce Lockhart was a man who thrived on being at the centre of a busy social milieu and he did not see himself fitting in to a 'circle of intellectuals', as just 'a cog in a bureaucratic machine'. He divided his time between a busy social life in London, and Woburn, where he claimed, by contrast, to live a 'regime of ascetic simplicity'. He was probably protesting rather much about his part-time asceticism; along with his debts, Bruce Lockhart had a complex love life and was dependent on alcohol, particularly his favourite Scotch whisky.

His colleagues likewise complained; Bartlett moaned that his billet was 'a grubby room inherited from a stable boy whose chamber pot had not been emptied and whose tooth glass sported cobwebs'. These were nonetheless not great deprivations for wartime, and the rations made up for the accommodation. Although work sometimes went on until the early hours, there was 'an excellent small bar' open, where staff could enjoy 'five sherries or a reasonable bottle of claret for half a crown'.

It was almost inevitable that a department largely composed of journalists, politicians and others for whom gossip was a stock in trade was hard to keep a secret for long. Many of these people had known each other long before the war. In December 1939, a reporter for the *Daily Express* wrote that villagers near Woburn had seen 'truck-loads of printing machinery', 'big Lyons catering vans' and 'a fleet of Daimler cars' – counting up to twenty-eight luxury cars in one day – arriving at the abbey, bringing 'mysterious occupants', including 'professors and all' to the grounds. 'Girl typists' were travelling to work in luxury while the Duke of Bedford himself was reduced to driving a Ford. In a remarkably well-crafted quote, one villager whispered in confidence to the reporter, 'There must be something big happening up there. What they are doing is a secret, but it may win the war.'

The reporter, an M. Lacey, seemed unusually well-informed, saying that a hundred to a hundred and fifty employees were working at the abbey for the Ministry of Information. Lacey's villagers also managed to recognise some of the secret visitors, including 'Sir Campbell Stuart, chief of the Enemy Propaganda Dept., Mr Noël Coward and Mr Vernon Bartlett MP', who were not guests of the duke but officials of the Information Department. Bartlett, finding himself frustrated and hopeless at keeping secrets, had already left the team.

These quotes have the air of an invention – Bedfordshire villagers might well have recognised Noël Coward, but probably not the head of British propaganda or a new MP – and it's more likely that Lacey had information from inside the abbey, which was now populated by many who had worked for the *Daily Express*. Robert Bruce Lockhart himself was a close friend of the paper's owner, Lord Beaverbrook. Noël Coward, who had indeed visited and was directed to the gates by some kindly villagers, said that the secret headquarters would have been 'fairly easy to find by any German agent with the faintest enterprise'.[10] Lacey made a 'guess' in the final line of his report: 'I should say that the work being done at Woburn Abbey is that of printing leaflets for Germans to read.'[11] This was clearly an educated guess: it's precisely what they were doing.

The article, though, was censored before it got to press. The Ministry of Information's censors were outraged at this clear breach of security, stamping the reporter's copy 'Not to be Published'. It was deemed such a serious leak that the director-general of the press bureau at the ministry phoned Lord Beaverbrook's office himself to tell the proprietor that the article 'gave information of value to the enemy' and to say that the Service in question was a Secret Service, carried out for the Foreign Office.[12] Beaverbrook, who had himself worked in propaganda during the first war, was probably well aware of this.

This is the story of the key members of the propaganda team, how they came to work in political warfare, the contributions that they made and how they changed the course of the war. Even as they argued about the ethics of the nation speaking the truth to other nations – or not – these people were not always telling the truth about themselves in their own lives. Robert Bruce Lockhart, the man who had once attempted to bring down the Russian Revolution, was the elder statesman of the group. As director-general of what would become the Political Warfare Executive, or PWE, he needed all his diplomatic skills to liaise between ministers and his often-troublesome crew.

Richard Crossman was a young man in a hurry. At thirty-two, he had already begun several brilliant careers: as a philosopher, a journalist and an aspiring Labour MP. He had travelled through Germany and reported for radio on his experiences there. He was always up for a debate, though he sometimes came across too forcefully. Crossman had great insight into how propaganda could work effectively, but he also loved to break the rules and defy his superiors, right the way to the top of government.

Denis Sefton Delmer, the former Berlin correspondent for the *Daily Express*, was a man of equally forceful views and a cavalier attitude. He had grown up in Germany and reported on the Nazis' rise to power. Delmer believed that much bending of the truth, exaggeration and downright lies could be justified in the service of defeating Germany. If there were limits, he was prepared to push at them and sometimes overstep them, though in a different way from Crossman.

Brendan Bracken was Churchill's confidant and a supreme networker who became minister of information. A man with a tenuous relationship with the truth in his own life, he was put in charge of propaganda policy and was prone to fighting with his ministerial counterparts as well as his underlings.

Women also took key roles in the organisation: there were not only boys in the back rooms of Woburn but girls too. Elisabeth Barker, recruited from the BBC where she had been an early foreign affairs producer, would eventually run her own section. She, too, had secrets to keep both professionally and personally.

Some believed that this was a brilliant team which came to organise propaganda on so 'clever and vast a scale' that it 'saved the lives of hundreds of thousands of people' by shortening the course of the war.[13] More often than not, though, the team was riven with conflicts that were both political and deeply personal. While we often have the misleading impression that, during wartime, politics as usual took a back seat, huge rows between individuals and about the conduct of policy persisted. Sometimes these escalated into feuds, with government ministers barely on speaking terms with one another, and maligning and briefing against each other in a scarcely concealed way.

During the Second World War, Britain produced fake news. It believed that it was doing so with a political, a military, and even a moral purpose. The British government, in doing this, wanted to undermine the morale of their opponents and to cause confusion. The counter-argument, which was frequently made at the time, was that spreading deliberately untrue stories also jeopardised Britain's reputation for telling the truth in the longer term. At key points in the war, there were heated discussions about whether the government should allow statements to be put out – even by senior ministers or claiming to be from foreign governments – that they knew to be lies. It was also argued that this was purely an expedient in wartime, that total warfare called for 'black' propaganda which could not be justified in times of peace.

Black propaganda was the most secret part of the work and it took many forms. Delmer, the man who was instrumental in creating this, called it 'a new weapon of psychological warfare' that he believed was needed to undermine morale in Germany and the rest of occupied Europe.[14] The organisation began to work on the deliberate spreading of untrue stories towards the end of 1939. At first, these were referred to as 'sibs' – from the Latin *sibillare*, meaning hiss or whisper – or just as whispers. These were rumours that could be dropped into news stories, designed to spread by word of mouth in occupied countries. But without the co-operation of the BBC or the means to put their own radio stations on air, these rumours could not spread far. The relationship with the BBC in the early days did not get far either, with some calling it an 'organisational disaster'. The Ministry of Information tried, at first, to instruct the BBC to broadcast long, dull, official messages in full and to wait before broadcasting recent news. This approach couldn't hold.[15]

Black propaganda would use the newest technology available: radio was central to its reach. Under Delmer, the Political Warfare Executive created a network of 'black' radio stations that broadcast into Europe, purporting to be the voices of disgruntled and formerly loyal supporters of the Axis regimes, as well as those of opposition or resistance movements. In fact, they were based not in Berlin, Rome or the Balkans, but in Aspley Guise and Milton Bryan, villages around Woburn, and the voices broadcasting were those of exiles, refugees and, later, prisoners of war from across Europe.

Muriel Spark, hired to work on black propaganda by Delmer later in the war, called what she worked on 'subtle and deadly anti-Nazi propaganda', and she set out their method: 'Detailed truth with believable lies'.[16] Black propaganda relied on accurate intelligence on conditions within occupied Europe so that stories could be constructed that were based as far as possible in reality. Delmer developed a clear view of how this should work: 'We must never lie by accident, or through slovenliness, only deliberately.'[17]

Many of Delmer's colleagues doubted that what he was doing was justified or helpful. Black propaganda was deniable – great lengths were taken to make sure the real source of it remained secret – but many argued that the better way to influence enemy forces was to tell them the truths their own leaders hid from them. This was referred to as 'white' propaganda and was broadcast on official outlets by the BBC.

This book looks at how the small, eccentric team developed its skills and its organisation over the course of the war. They started in a period of defeat, where they could do little but watch and wait, and where political control over what they were doing was divided. As the fortunes of war began to turn, once Britain had headed off the existential threat of invasion and began to plan ahead for the counter-attacks in North Africa and on the European mainland, the rows about who controlled propaganda intensified. Once Allied forces were on the ground, propaganda found a clearer purpose: to act as a way of changing the hearts and minds of their enemies in battle, as well as those of the people that the Allies hoped to liberate. Lives were at stake and their messages had to be clearer and more precise. That didn't mean they were always in agreement – arguments about what propaganda should say and to whom went all the way to the top of the Allied governments. Nor did black propaganda completely end with the war; it was revived, with some reservations but with many of the same staff, during the Cold War.

This is not a study of how British propaganda worked at home, but rather an exploration of how Britain projected itself to the outside world. I have also looked more at the work of the secret black propaganda stations than at the BBC's foreign-language broadcasts. Political warfare created the voice of Britain and its Allies – even if in heavy disguise – to the Axis countries and the nations they occupied. Some of that reach was determined by technology – broadcasting directly beyond Europe or to Asia was technically difficult – and some by politics as well. There were no broadcasts aimed at the Soviet Union, for instance.

The secret propaganda department was known, at first, as the Political Intelligence Department. That would remain its public cover name for the duration of the war. In its first year, the department was known to those working for it as Electra House, or EH, after its London base on the Embankment. Electra House was answerable to the newly created Ministry of Information but was financed by the secret vote, which meant that its funds weren't scrutinised and its existence kept secret, with the Foreign Office controlling its expenditure.[18] In July 1940, as Churchill's new government took charge, it became part of the Special Operations Executive, or SOE. The SOE was initially an organisation of two halves: the half that would become better known was SO2, which was tasked with sabotage and underground operations in hostile territory, and SO1, the section that dealt with propaganda to occupied and enemy countries. In September 1941, the organisation's name changed again, this time to the Political Warfare Executive. Each change of title reflected a ministerial battle over who was in control of propaganda and what they wanted it to achieve.

This confusion of acronyms was matched by the initial uncertainty about what British propaganda to enemy countries was really doing, especially as the war began. At first confined to Woburn Abbey's outbuildings – the riding school and the indoor tennis court – the propaganda operation lacked direction. The atmosphere was described as one of 'bustling amateurishness' and 'complete ineffectualness'.[19] Part of the problem was political: the British government was waiting and watching. There was no clear leadership in terms of propaganda, as in much else in the conduct of the war. Many of the new recruits to propaganda had opposed the government's policy of appeasement towards Germany before the war began and they were itching to run a more aggressive campaign of warfare by words than the government would let them.

It was partly down to personnel. Britain was still running a propaganda operation in the same way and with the same people as it had done at the end of the First World War. Electra House, which had been set up in March 1938, was still trading on the glories of twenty years earlier. Sir Campbell Stuart, the head of Electra House, had, during the Great War,

been the deputy to Lord Northcliffe, who had run operations. Stuart had written a book, *Secrets of Crewe House*, sub-
titled 'The Story of a Famous Campaign', which gave away
some of those wartime secrets.[20] In the last year of that war,
Britain and its allies had dropped millions of leaflets over the
German lines, telling the German soldiers 'the truth which
was being concealed from them by their leaders'.[21] It was a
haphazard process, though, with the leaflets being sent out
in unmanned propaganda balloons and dropped via a timed
fuse. They were dependent on the wind blowing in the right
direction to reach the Germans on the front. German soldiers
were told, for example, that if they surrendered, they would be
well treated as prisoners of war and were promised American
rations, including beef, white bread, potatoes and coffee.[22]
British propaganda to enemy countries in the first war had
been widely praised, though some thought it had been given
too much credit for its effect on German morale.

The bureaucratic machinery of propaganda was untried:
the new Ministry of Information had been created in the
week that war was declared and was only clumsily finding its
way. Members of Parliament immediately began to criticise its
work in informing the public at home. They were given little
information about what propaganda to the enemy involved,
but Parliament was told about the first leaflets dropped over
Germany. Six million copies of a message to the German
people were dropped by aircraft on the night of 3 September,
the day that Britain entered the war. The Germans were told
that their own government's 'iron censorship' had imprisoned
their minds in a concentration camp. But Britain's message,
despite the state of war, was still one of possible peace.
The leaflets said, 'We also desire peace and are prepared to
conclude it with any peace-loving government in Germany.'[23]

Germany, at this time, was far ahead of Britain in terms
of creating and broadcasting its own domestic propaganda,
with Joseph Goebbels quick to spot the potential of the

new technology of radio. Within months of taking power in 1933, the Nazi regime was both supplying cheap radio sets and talking of radio as the 'eighth great power'. Centralised control of both the medium and the message meant that the German government was able to provide, in Goebbels's words, radio that reached the people and also reached across borders. A democracy would never be able to exert such extensive control over what it was broadcasting.

What was once the back room of the Sugar Loaf Hotel in Dunstable – today the Old Sugar Loaf Inn – is now the 'Sugar Lounge', a bar with blue fairy lights and a glitter ball. On a weekday morning in July 2022, it was only occupied by a few drinkers playing fruit machines and would have made an unlikely location for a secret rendezvous for official recruits. I had gone to see what we could still learn about the hush-hush village and its occupants. It was only a few days since Boris Johnson had resigned as prime minister and I could not escape the sense that, even at a time of huge international crises, politicians continued to feud, to lie and to accuse one another of lying, and to live double lives in public and private. Politicians, journalists, and government officials were not so different during the Second World War; the difference is that now we can learn, far more quickly and with less secrecy and deference, what is going on. They had lived under the threat of dictatorship, bombing and invasion; we had been living, during the pandemic, under severe restrictions on our lives and the threat of disease and death. In a political context, the claims and counter-claims of 'fake news' were being constantly traded and deliberate disinformation was more widespread than it had ever been. The political warriors of Woburn would have recognised all of this, even if the technology available to us might have bewildered them at first. I was drawn to learn more about what these fascinating characters really did and find out the truths that they often tried, in many ways, to hide.

The story of British political warfare has only been partially told. It has been full of half-truths and evasions. As with many secret wartime departments, the PWE staff were not supposed to speak in public about their work. Many of them, as we have already seen, had trouble abiding by those rules. Even the official history of the PWE, commissioned for internal use immediately after the war, was not made public for more than fifty years. The man assigned to write it, David Garnett, the novelist and critic known to his Bloomsbury Group friends as 'Bunny', had worked at the PWE for part of the war. Even for a man who had lived among the Bohemian atmosphere of Bloomsbury and spent time in neo-pagan groups, he felt that 'the atmosphere of Woburn Abbey was one of the strangest that the writer has ever experienced'. Garnett felt 'there was more than a touch of madness about it'.[24] Some of those who worked for the organisation published their own accounts in the years after the war: Bruce Lockhart was able to tell part of the story as early as 1947, but was heavily constrained in what he could publish. Delmer, too, wrote his own vivid but idiosyncratic recollections almost twenty years later.

A more substantial reckoning would have to wait until the release of government files in the 1970s but, even then, some files remained classified for decades longer, particularly those which relate to the security services. I have been able to get some more documents released under Freedom of Information requests. Debates about the history of the PWE and those involved in its work were sometimes conducted through the letters pages of newspapers, where grudges that had been borne for thirty years could finally be aired. Some collections of diaries and letters, such as those of Bruce Lockhart and Beaverbrook, and other collections of personal papers, have proved extremely helpful in showing what the participants thought about their work at the time.

There are many papers that simply no longer exist: some of the PWE's files were destroyed at the end of the war, and Brendan Bracken ordered that all of his personal papers be burned within twenty-four hours of his death, in 1958.[25] There were many people whose stories I wanted to give their rightful place in the narrative, whose contributions had been overlooked or only fleetingly written into previous versions of the secret histories of the PWE. Although Bruce Lockhart often praised the many women who worked with him, he was not able to name them at the time he wrote. Fewer of the women wrote about their own experiences in the wartime organisation.

The exiles, refugees and prisoners of war who were the voices of British propaganda were also largely uncredited for their work. At the time, this was a matter of necessity. For people who had been involved in resistance to the Nazi regime before the war, adopting false names had been essential to their survival and their escapes from occupied Europe. When they broadcast on British radio, particularly on the secret 'black' stations, it was vital that their real identities were not known. It would have given away the fact that these were not genuine German, or other opposition, stations and undermined the whole project of black propaganda. If German authorities were able to put real names to those voices, this would also have had repercussions for any of their families or contacts who had remained in Germany. Some exiles adopted a second layer of false names for their broadcasts and, if they remained in Britain after the war, they often took on new, Anglicised names to go with their adopted nationality. Those who returned to post-war Germany did not tend to discuss their wartime work. In accounts like Delmer's, the exiles were given (his own) pseudonyms. With time and access to recently declassified files, I have been able to peel away some of these layers of identities to find out more about the real people beneath them.

This is a story of characters who, often brilliant, but also often troubled, played a key part in the war. Even if they were not fighting on the front lines, their roles in the back room of British propaganda had an influence far beyond their secret rooms and villages.

PART I
Bright Ineffectual Angels

I

The Prima Donna

Richard Crossman never failed to make an impression on anyone who met him. Whether that impression was good or bad was another matter. At Woburn Abbey, he was a powerful presence, both physically and intellectually. One male colleague, while claiming to find Crossman's personality 'dominant and overbearing', still seemed somehow drawn to him, writing that 'he generally wore tweeds or some rough material that emphasised his height and breadth just as fur increases the size of some great bear. His heavy face, his full lips, his untidy mass of hair, were like the characters of some mountain owing its power and beauty to some inner principle of mass rather than to the outward forms of order.'[1]

Crossman was a brilliant young man, but possibly all too aware of that. In his careers to date, he had often made a shining start but swiftly come into conflict with colleagues and superiors. He was quick to learn new things, but also quick to jeopardise his own position through a blithe disregard for the rules and for what was expected of him. Somehow, he usually got away with it.

What made Crossman so valuable as a propagandist was the combination of all the talents that he used in his various careers: he had the analytical, intellectual skills of an Oxford don and was a journalist and a broadcaster who could communicate clearly. He had spent time in Germany and knew the country and the language.

His love of politics both got him into trouble and sometimes helped him get out of it again. He was argumentative and often persuasive. He thrived when he was thrown into a crisis and had to react fast. He struggled when he came up against equally intransigent opposing views or institutions. Crossman was clear-sighted about the strengths and failings of British propaganda. He loved a good argument for its own sake; though he was not a habitual liar, he enjoyed the process of debate so much that often he didn't seem to care which side he was arguing for.

When the war began, Crossman was juggling several jobs at once, as was his habit. He was broadcasting talks on the BBC, writing for the *New Statesman*, where he was the assistant editor, and had been given a job at the Ministry of Information as a liaison officer in the publicity section. He found the ministry boring, a waste of time and a place where nothing happened, despite it offering him a salary of £750 a year.[2] He wrote letters home to his wife during meetings in stuffy rooms. He only lasted six weeks, however, before resigning and going back to journalism.[3] It would take a change of government to bring Crossman into political warfare.

When Churchill took over from Neville Chamberlain as prime minister in May 1940, he appointed many more Labour ministers to senior positions. Among them was Hugh Dalton, who became minister of economic warfare. He was in charge of international economic matters, aiming to prevent the Axis from getting hold of raw materials through blockades and other means. Dalton was also given responsibility for sabotage and subversion. Churchill's instruction to him was famously to 'set Europe ablaze', both through propaganda and direct action against the enemy. At this turning point in the war, when the new prime minister warned that 'without victory, there is no survival', subversion and propaganda were meant to go hand in hand. Richard Crossman, a Labour activist with that knowledge of Germany, would have seemed an ideal

Richard Crossman, the young man in a hurry, 1940

recruit for Dalton. The pair had known each other since at least 1936 and had corresponded about Crossman's search for a Labour nomination to stand for Parliament.[4] Many of those who came to work on political warfare were part of the same network of friends who had followed events in Germany through the 1930s, from their student days onwards. Crossman, though, managed to come highly recommended, even by people whose political views did not chime with his own. Quintin Hogg, the Conservative MP who had fought the Oxford by-election of 1938 on a pro-Munich Agreement platform, seems to have put in a good word for him with the War Office.[5] So did Denis Sefton Delmer.[6]

From the outset, Crossman didn't hold back in his views on propaganda policy, even before he had formally been appointed to a senior job. When Robert Bruce Lockhart first met him, at a weekly Woburn propaganda meeting in mid-1940, he quickly realised that Crossman had 'remarkable qualities for this kind of work'. On the positive side, 'he was full of ideas, had great driving force, and in a crisis could work at immense speed'. But this brilliance, which some saw as arrogance, had its problems, as Bruce Lockhart noted. 'Not even his greatest enemy could say that he lacked self-confidence. On the contrary he was full of it and was inclined to go ahead on his own initiative without reference to me or to anyone else.'[7]

Crossman's reputation for brilliance, but also for often being insufferable, was present from an early age. When he arrived at New College, Oxford as a scholar from his public school, Winchester, he quickly became well known – and just as quickly divided opinion. The third child of six, his father was a barrister and later a judge. Stafford Crossman was a stern and conventional man, and Dick's willingness to be open to new ideas seems to have come from his mother, Helen, who, Crossman said, taught him to argue and to question everything.[8] His student contemporaries described him variously as an aesthete, a rugby player and an intellectual bully. He had also acquired the nickname which would follow him throughout his political career: 'double-Crossman'.

He was undoubtedly clever: on graduating from Oxford with a First in 1930, he was offered a fellowship, teaching philosophy, by his college. The college suggested, however, that Crossman should spend a year abroad before taking up the job. That year changed the course of his life.[9] He himself called it a 'seminal year'. It seems unlikely that Dick Crossman, always eager for new worlds to conquer, would ever have remained contentedly an Oxford philosophy don for the rest of his working life, but travelling to Germany at the beginning of the 1930s changed the way he saw the world. He had visited either Germany or Austria almost every year since he was fourteen, but this time things were different.

When Crossman arrived in Frankfurt in October 1930, Germany had just experienced a 'political earthquake'.[10] A month earlier, the Nazi Party had made a breakthrough at the latest elections, leaping from 12 to 107 seats in the Reichstag, and Hitler had held rallies that tens of thousands attended. The election itself was marked by violence. Near Berlin, on the eve of the poll, forty-eight people were injured when National Socialists attacked a Socialist meeting, in a battle which involved the use of beer mugs, chair legs and table legs.[11] The Nazis in turn were attacked by communists waiting outside. On election day itself, the *Manchester Guardian* reported, there were shootings and riots, and bottles of sulphuric acid being thrown about. 'Lorries crowded with partisans, waving bright flags,' the paper's correspondent wrote, 'tear up and down.'[12] In Berlin, Nazi lorries turned up at the communist headquarters and, in the resulting fights, one man was shot dead and several injured.[13]

Crossman was staying in Frankfurt with Justizrat Fuld, an eminent judge, who was Jewish, while he learned German and studied philosophy.[14] Although his first interests involved watching opera, politics intruded dramatically. In his first few days in Frankfurt, Crossman went to see the first performance of a new Kurt Weill opera – *The Rise and Fall of the City of Mahagonny*, written by Weill and Brecht. The performance, he said, was interrupted by a shower of stink-bombs from the gallery. The opera's performances were regularly disrupted by Nazi sympathisers, who hated the radical production by a Jewish composer and a Marxist writer. Outside the opera house, as he walked through the centre of the city, Crossman was 'passed by a gigantic torchlit procession of strenuous, sweating Nazis'.[15] This, he wrote, was his introduction to modern politics.

In Berlin the following spring, he became even more closely aware of events. Crossman encountered a man who in his own way was an extremely successful propagandist. Willi Münzenberg was a communist member of the Reichstag always keen to meet impressionable young visitors, whom he hoped to persuade to support the communist cause.

Crossman always maintained that he was not impressed with Münzenberg's communism, let alone converted to it, despite the German's invitation to join the revolution. However, he did spend a good deal of time around Münzenberg, even, for a while, living in his Berlin flat. Crossman told the story later that Münzenberg had offered him money, giving him a twenty-mark gold piece on the day that the pound was devalued in September 1931 with the observation, 'You'll need this. There will be bread riots in London before long.'[16]

If he wasn't convinced by the need for a communist revolution, Crossman's encounters with Münzenberg changed his life in another way. While he was in Berlin, he fell in love. Even though most of Crossman's early romantic relationships at Oxford had been with men, when he met Erika Glück, he became, one profile wrote, 'flamboyantly heterosexual'.[17] She had been born Erika Landsberg in Nuremberg in 1906, and she was Jewish. Crossman himself had been unsure of much about her and his biographers would be unclear about her original name or her real age.[18] They met through Münzenberg whom Erika worked with, though she denied reports that she had been the communist's mistress. Erika had, though, already been married twice, the first time when she was only seventeen, the second two years later. She had a daughter from her first marriage.

When Crossman returned to Oxford in 1931 to take up his teaching job, Erika came with him. The arrival of a twice-divorced German communist was always likely to cause scandal, both in the university and in Crossman's family. Her first visit to the family home, at Christmas 1931, was a disaster. Erika collapsed and the doctor was called. What at first seemed to be a mystery illness turned out to be the result of her drug use; Erika was addicted to morphine.[19] This would have explained some of her eccentric behaviour. Crossman's parents threw Erika out of the house and refused to attend their son's forthcoming wedding. Crossman's Oxford contemporaries circulated ribald, even obscene, rumours about the couple. Nonetheless, they were married at Oxford register office in July 1932.[20]

Although the couple briefly seemed happy, the relationship did not last; by the end of the year, Erika had fled to Germany. Crossman's short-lived marriage and his search for his absent wife meant he had to return to Germany under the new Nazi regime. As he told an interviewer years later, 'I had to chase around Europe to serve a warrant on her and get divorced. For a young Oxford don, that was expensive and I took up journalism to pay for it.'[21]

The events Crossman witnessed and reported on in Germany in the 1930s were key to forming his views of Germany, and of propaganda, during the war. He travelled there in the summer of 1933, after the Nazi takeover, and again the following year. In particular, his BBC reports of the period would often be cited by his political critics as evidence that he had sympathy for the Nazi regime. This was something Crossman strenuously denied; he maintained that his early views had changed well before the war. In 1947, he wrote that when visiting Germany in 1934, all his friends in Frankfurt or Berlin had fled or gone underground.[22] As he told the *Sunday Times* in 1969, 'I went back to Germany in 1934, and I couldn't find half my friends, and I couldn't understand why. It had never occurred to me before that half my friends were Jews.'[23] This was a remarkable oversight given the fact that he also had a Jewish ex-wife and distant Jewish cousins.

What started as a passing interest in German politics at the beginning of the decade had become his area of expertise by the end of it. No doubt Crossman's early views, those of a new graduate in his early twenties, had been naive. As he learned more about what happened to opponents of the regime, these views became more sophisticated.

In his first talk on the BBC, Crossman reported on a labour camp in Schleswig-Holstein, which he had visited in

April 1934. His first impressions of the camp were 'by no means reassuring';[24] he found the uniforms and military ethos disconcerting. In this first broadcast, the twenty-six-year-old Crossman seemed aware of what he called 'a paradox certainly, a danger – perhaps'. He believed that the camp's organisation was 'efficient' and was prepared to believe that its young residents might be genuine in their professed desire for peace, but he certainly expressed his reservations as to what might be to come. 'The revolt of youth has been drilled and disciplined into a conscript army,' Crossman said. 'The rebels against law and militarism now march only too often under the command of old officers, and click their heels like any hardened veteran.'

Crossman's pursuit of both his divorce and his new career in journalism were a distraction from his main job as a tutor of philosophy and ancient history. Although his colleague, the philosopher Isaiah Berlin, believed Crossman was a marvellous, lively and provocative tutor, he also thought that Crossman was clearly bored by academic philosophy.[25] Berlin had come to distrust his colleague deeply – on both a personal and a political level. He believed that Crossman had a 'ferocious, nihilistic streak',[26] and that he was someone who was prepared to lie and break promises in pursuit of his political ends. To Berlin, 'all [Crossman] was really interested in was Germany, German politics, himself, Plato as a fascist'. Berlin also saw too much admiration in Crossman's early view of Germany, even calling him a 'left-wing Nazi', arguing that Crossman's lack of fundamental beliefs, love of power and his dislike of 'a sort of peaceful honest decent dreary civil service' led him to admire the 'hearty, vulgar' aspects of 'young men singing songs'.[27]

By 1934, Dick Crossman had found Erika. According to the divorce petition which he filed in May that year, she had been living with a man called Peter Niels Heller in Vienna for three months. When the papers were filed, though, she was staying at a sanatorium in Bayreuth, the Kurhaus Main-schloss.[28] This was a luxurious modern facility, popular with Jewish patients, which accommodated up to twenty-four guests suffering from nervous conditions.[29] Erika was possibly being treated there for her addiction. By 1935, the divorce was granted on the grounds of her adultery.

On 30 June 1934, the Night of the Long Knives, when Hitler had leaders of the SA, the Nazi Party's paramilitary wing, shot or arrested, Crossman heard the news of the killings while in Heidelberg. He listened to Hitler's speech on the radio in a cafe that evening. From there, he headed to Munich where the murders had happened, before travelling to Berlin in order to be able to broadcast; the only radio circuit available was at the German radio headquarters in the capital. While he began his live ten-minute talk with the 'bare fact' of what had happened, Crossman's description of German reactions made it less clear whether he was just an impartial reporter or endorsing what he saw. His fellow cafe patrons in Heidelberg, he reported, had applauded briefly and expressed the view that SA leader Ernst Röhm had been no good, before changing the subject. Crossman made the contrast with Britain in an analogy, asking his listeners to imagine that the prime minister had landed in Edinburgh and ordered the trial and execution of eight of his closest allies in a day. Crossman reported a man in a Munich cafe telling him that 'the scoundrels are dead now and out of the way'.[30] Crossman described the events as 'a personal triumph for Hitler', who could now declare any rival 'an outlaw and a scoundrel' as he decreed. His detached description left room for the interpretation that he was fascinated, rather than appalled, by this seizure of complete power. This talk would be held against him – and even raised in Parliament – by his critics during the war.

Crossman also neglected to point out that the people he met in German cafes might be reluctant to tell their genuine feelings to a visiting British academic and journalist, even if they had opposed the regime's actions. Crossman did know, though, the extent of censorship and control of government propaganda that the Nazi regime had introduced, and he was made vividly aware of it in the next few weeks.

Crossman was due to give another talk on 'The German Scene' on 24 July, again from Berlin. This time, he was interrupted and ultimately did not make it on air. He was told it was due to a technical fault, but Crossman wasn't convinced. He wrote to the BBC's Head of Talks, Charles Siepmann, the next day. His letter was written in pencil from Nuremberg station at six-thirty on Wednesday morning, as Crossman returned to Bavaria. He apologised to Siepmann that 'England missed my lovely voice last night'. It was a typically flippant beginning to a letter describing a serious situation. 'An SS man came in just as I was about to start,' Crossman wrote, informing Siepmann that he spent a 'richly humorous' hour and a half with the Propaganda ministry, 'explaining myself away' and telling the official what he wanted to hear. 'Finally, I told him the BBC was his only friend in England and that I was so pro-Nazi that no Englishman would speak to me.'[31] Again, this was Crossman trying to exert his powers of persuasion in order to be allowed to broadcast, and it seemed to have worked. The propaganda official relented, gave his permission for Crossman to speak and rang both the German Foreign Office and the radio station to allow the talk to go ahead. Some technical fault between Berlin and London, however, meant that Crossman's talk wasn't heard in his own voice.

In his script, Crossman did discuss the nature of German public opinion and the reaction to Röhm's killing in more depth. Goebbels's official had told him that his broadcast, if it had been made by a German, would have been considered 'high treason', as it gave voice to the doubts of some Germans that Hitler's leadership was right. Crossman wrote: 'Many Germans feel that if the Leadership Principle can produce in a year and a half a state of affairs in which such violent remedies were necessary, the Leadership Principle itself must be modified.'

Crossman wrote pieces about Germany for the *Spectator* and the *Economist* in 1934 and, the following year, contributed to the *New Statesman*. He published his first book, *Plato To-Day*, in 1937. It was based on a series of talks which he'd given on the BBC in 1936, titled 'If Plato lived again' – although BBC managers had criticised some of Crossman's talks as using the BBC as 'a medium for the ventilation of his own views and doctrines'.[32] Crossman later described Plato's *Republic* as 'a handbook for aspiring dictators'. His book was a popularising attempt to bring Greek philosophy into the era of fascism and communism where, Crossman thought, 'we, too, are standing on the edge of the abyss, and philosophy has become a matter of life and death instead of a matter for polite discussion'.[33]

By the time his book was published, Crossman's academic career was also on the edge of the abyss because of another scandal in his private life. After he had filed for divorce from Erika, he was involved in relationships with both Resi, the German cook who worked for him in Oxford, and Zita Baker, the wife of another Oxford don. He invited Mrs Baker to join him at the BBC studios in London when he was broadcasting one of his early talks on Germany. This tangled love life did not go down well with Crossman's college, not least because Zita's husband also taught there. Although Crossman wasn't mentioned in the resulting divorce case, even though he and Zita planned to marry, his fellowship at New College was rescinded and Crossman left academia.[34]

He had been pursuing a political career, but would not become a full-time politician until after the war. Already the leader of the Labour group on Oxford City Council, Crossman stood for Parliament at the West Birmingham by-election in April 1937. He lost, but reduced the Tory majority by around four thousand votes. Zita, herself a Labour activist, was advised to take a back seat during the campaign while her divorce was going through. By the end of the year, Crossman had been selected for a more winnable seat in Coventry, where Zita helped cultivate his prospective constituency.

Dick and Zita married in London in December 1937, and the couple were left searching for new jobs and somewhere to live. They were soon effectively living over the shop, in a Holborn flat above the offices of the *New Statesman*, where Crossman became assistant editor. Crossman's second marriage was a close partnership and seemed much happier than his first. He and Zita often worked together, including at the *New Statesman*. She also broadcast on the BBC during the war, particularly in the aftermath of the bombing of Coventry. In August 1940, Ormond Wilson of the BBC wrote to her saying 'we liked [your talk] very much, and we want you to do some more'.[35] She suggested that her talks go out under the name of Zita Nanson, her mother's surname.

Robert Walmsley, working alongside Crossman during the war, was not sure that Crossman had many friends, with the exception of Zita, 'of whom, alone among humanity, he spoke with any kindness'. Walmsley had thought better of a clause in that sentence which he blacked out of his memoir – the crossed-out section seems to say that her 'attractions were not superficial'.[36]

When Crossman arrived at Woburn as head of the German section in August 1940, he felt, for the first time in his life, completely happy.[37] Like many of his colleagues in political intelligence, however, he was not as good as he should have been at keeping secrets and nearly blew things even before arriving. The department's security services were told that Crossman had been heard 'proclaiming in some public waiting room that he had been asked to help in controlling the German broadcasts of the BBC but that he was damned if he would take £1,000 a year for sitting on his behind and making suggestions which the BBC ignored'.[38]

At the same time as working on the secret side of propaganda, Crossman would continue his overt work, broadcasting to Germany for the BBC. This required a degree of doublethink. He described the complexities of this dual role: 'My left hand knew what my right hand was doing, but my right hand, the BBC, had no notion of what my left hand was doing.'[39]

Hugh Dalton was well aware that Crossman was someone who could be difficult to manage. He wrote: 'Not everyone liked him or trusted his judgement. Nor did all his seniors find him an easy subordinate.' Even in August 1940, Dalton had already observed that Crossman had taken a dislike to some of his colleagues, such as the diplomat Rex Leeper, who was in day-to-day charge of political intelligence. But Dalton believed that Crossman's talents outweighed these difficulties. He wrote to Crossman on 23 August in an attempt to impress on him the need for diplomacy. 'I am confident that you will now show, not only your habitual virtues of intelligence, energy and courage, but also those more difficult gifts of conciliation, tact and discretion.'[40] That was never going to be easy.

At the time that Crossman arrived at Woburn, SO1, the department in charge of subversive foreign propaganda, was beginning to conduct its first experiments in broadcasting to the enemy. The covert radio stations, which pretended to be coming from within Europe, went by the code names of 'research units', or RUs. One of the big questions they had to decide was who their audience should be. For Crossman and Dalton, both Labour politicians, the most promising target was socialists and German working people more broadly, whom they thought would be most receptive to hearing – and possibly acting on – resistance to the Nazi regime.

The first RU that was set up, in May 1940, however, had taken a different tack. Das Wahre Deutschland (The True Germany) went on air on the 26th. It also seems to have been described as Hier Spricht Deutschland (Germany Speaking) after its opening announcement. Freddy Voigt, the former *Manchester Guardian* correspondent in Berlin, was in charge of the station. He was working with German exiles who had fled the country, including Carl Spiecker and Hans Albert Kluthe. Spiecker was a liberal politician and former government spokesman in the Weimar Republic who had left Germany in 1933. He had run some fledgling opposition radio stations first in Paris and later on a ship in the Channel. Kluthe, who became the main voice of Hier Spricht Deutschland, was a liberal journalist, also writing under the name of 'Walter Westphal', who had left for England in 1936. The station was influenced by their liberal and Christian political views. The three men 'hoped to find their public among the nationalistically- and conservatively-minded bourgeoisie. Their assignment was to make it clear to these circles that one could not be a true German and a Nazi at the same time.'[41]

Crossman and Dalton both also believed that they should be appealing to opponents of the regime, but they based their views of Germany on very different ideas to those of Voigt. They believed the best way to oppose the Nazi regime was to encourage resistance from what remained of the German left, and from the workers. Their German friends and contacts were mainly socialist and communist exiles who had fled to Britain. Over the summer of 1940, Crossman and his fellow Labour German expert, Patrick Gordon Walker, were in regular contact with left-wing Germans in London. In July, Crossman and Gordon Walker held a meeting to discuss setting up what they called a 'Bureau for subversive work'.[42] In August, Gordon Walker met some of Crossman's contacts to continue the discussions, including Baron Hellmut von Rauschenplat, a socialist who adopted the name of Fritz Eberhard, Walter Auerbach and Hilde Meisel Olday. This group seemed to have the aim of encouraging resistance and sabotage, as well as making propaganda. The government, though, seemed unclear about it what it wanted them to do: Crossman said that the Foreign Office was trying to make the subversive bureaux into purely advisory bodies. A month later, the subversive project seemed to be off: Freddy Voigt told Gordon Walker that the Bureau was closed, that he was doing only propaganda work and other projects had been abandoned. The security service, MI5, had rejected Gordon Walker and others from secret work.[43]

But within a fortnight, another project was under way, with the same team assembled to work on a new research unit, with Crossman in charge: the Sender der Europäische Revolution – the European Revolution station. These programmes went on air on 7 October 1940. MI5 had overcome its objections to the employment of some of the members of staff, even those who belonged to the Neu Beginnen (New Beginnings) group, a left-wing German opposition group, many of whom held communist and Marxist views. At first, there had been concerns from the security services that they were too radical, but as an MI5 officer explained later in the war, 'nearly all the German and Austrian political refugees in this country are Socialists, and most of them belong to the Continental Marxist school. If, therefore, one was to have a ban on all refugees who hold "anti-Capitalist" or "anti-Imperialist" views, PWE would be hard put to it to find German and Austrian collaborators.'[44] As long as they were '100% in favour of the defeat of Germany' and weren't pursuing political aims opposed to those of Britain, the security services were happy, even if some British politicians weren't. Many of the new émigré recruits, including husband and wife Paul and Evelyn Anderson, and another couple, Waldemar and Juliana von Knoeringen, were regular broadcasters on the station.

Not much is known about what the European Revolution programmes sounded like, but Fritz Eberhard said that he broadcast every day, with programmes running four times each evening, each twenty minutes long, before the top of the hour.[45] The tone of the station was aimed at inciting a socialist revolt against the German regime. Through his contacts who had been forced to emigrate, Crossman knew that inciting resistance was dangerous for all involved – and most dangerous for those who remained in Germany, in the absence of any meaningful support from outside.

One of Crossman's passionate beliefs at the start of the war was that 'there was a big, good Germany that could be appealed to. I know there were many in Germany who did not like the regime, but if you appealed to them as *traitors*, they did not take the propaganda. They were much more content to overhear you talking to a Nazi. If a democrat overheard you scoring off a Nazi he could enjoy it without feeling that he was a traitor, whereas if he heard you appealing to him direct, he often switched off his set.'[46]

Whether there was such a good Germany distinct from, and in opposition to, the Nazi regime was one of the big debates that resounded throughout the war. Politicians and diplomats drew competing conclusions about how to persuade the German people to listen to them.

Crossman clearly took to his work in the noble surroundings of Woburn. Newly happy and increasingly confident, he enjoyed the process of chairing meetings and making decisions. His intelligence colleague Robert Walmsley watched how he worked with a combination of awe and scepticism. 'His easy mastery in the Chair, his careful flattery of the weak, his anxious enquiry for the views of all who might feel affronted if ignored, and even his smart crack with the truncheon when some buffoon raised his head, all these seemed somehow to be part of a performance on some gigantic stage.' Perhaps Walmsley hadn't encountered many aspiring politicians before. He felt, though, that this brilliance 'did not convert but daze'.[47]

Thomas Barman, the propagandist to the Nordic countries who had run afraid of the deer at Woburn, believed Crossman wasn't just someone who stirred up hornets' nests, but was 'a hornet's nest all to himself'. He, too, found that Crossman's disputatious nature wasn't the best way to make allies, observing 'he does not mind contradicting even those friends and admirers who are most disposed to agree with him, even if this means making enemies of them'.[48]

At the beginning of the war, Crossman's ambition had long been evident, but his colleagues found his politics harder to pin down. Rex Leeper, the Foreign Office diplomat who was in charge of early political warfare, half-joked in 1940: 'There goes a future Prime Minister of England – Conservative of course!'[49] This was a jibe at Crossman's opportunism, but it was perhaps his ability to argue a case, whatever his personal beliefs or lack of them – combined with his fluency and speed of writing – that helped to make him so talented at propaganda.

At Robert Bruce Lockhart's first meeting with Crossman, he spotted the younger man as a future star. 'Every good propagandist is like a prima donna and must be given a reasonable amount of latitude,' Bruce Lockhart observed. The trouble was that when Crossman arrived at Woburn, he found another man, Freddy Voigt, who saw himself as the main expert on Germany. Voigt, who was forty-eight, had longer and more direct experience of the country. When Crossman arrived, he was treading on Voigt's toes. They had very different ideas about what made effective propaganda and what the tone of broadcasters should be. This was an argument not just about style but about substance, rooted in different beliefs.

The rivals' views of Germany, the nature of its people and how they should be addressed in British propaganda were soon to erupt into bitter rows. Similar feuds persisted throughout Crossman's time in political warfare, his willingness to pursue his own line testing his colleagues' patience to the utmost.

2

The Hush-Hush Village

Dawn Edge stands along a narrow lane that leads away from the village hall in Aspley Guise in Bedford-shire, not far from Woburn Abbey. The house is at the top of a curving drive that is lined with tall pine trees. One of its wartime residents described it as 'a slightly rambling low-rise edifice in the Palladian style'.[1] When Richard and Zita Crossman moved there in July 1940, it was not just a home but also a workplace. They would share their new house with a variety of German émigrés who had also been recruited to work on propaganda. At first, the Crossmans had been travelling between London and the Country HQ, but in September 1940, their London flat above the *New Statesman* offices in Holborn was hit in the Blitz. The couple had luckily been away from London at the time of the raid, but returned home to find that the firefighters were unable to save it. The flat was burnt out.[2]

These days, Aspley Guise is a busy village, where commuter traffic rushes through along the main road. The village shops have closed and only a couple of pubs survive. During the war, it became known as the 'hush-hush village', where many of the large houses, set away from the roads, were requisitioned for secret workers. Dawn Edge and others – like The Rookery, Larchfield and substantial old rectories, sheltered by trees – were occupied by a multinational community which had to live largely in hiding. The inhabitants were not allowed to associate with others beyond their home – even those who were also working for the secret organisation – or to tell potentially inquisitive local neighbours what they were doing there.

'We were fortunate,' Crossman said, 'that we started our psychological warfare in a period of abysmal defeat. In 1940 and 1941, the only thing we could do was tell the truth, and we got an immense amount of good-will in Germany by admitting defeat.'[3] France had fallen and Dunkirk had been evacuated, and while Britain had resisted invasion as the Battle of Britain was fought overhead, the country did not have much to offer the rest of the world beyond the 'good and reasonable hopes of final victory' which Churchill evoked in his 'finest hour' speech. Crossman's double life working on both overt and covert propaganda meant he spent half the week in London, working on the 'white' propaganda of the BBC's German Service, and half in the country, overseeing the shadier services that were not publicly acknowledged.

These early Freedom Stations were broadcasting what could be described as 'grey' propaganda: their work was secret in that it was not broadcast over the official British channels of the BBC and their programmes made out that they were coming from within occupied Europe. To that extent, they were not completely honest with their listeners. They were hoping to appeal to small, defined sections of the occupied populations. The earliest RUs were experimental and did not yet have the full energy behind them that would come later in the war. They were limited in what they could broadcast and how far the reach of their programmes went; they were only transmitted on short wave and they could be easily jammed.

The first stations broadcast to Germany and France. There were four French stations, the first two of which began broad-casting in November 1940 from Woburn. Radio Travail – the Workers' Radio – was aimed at socialists and trade unionists; Radio Inconnue – Radio Unknown – was 'Rabelaisian' and vulgar in its language, aimed at 'the man in the streets'. Radio

Inconnue was bourgeois, strongly anti-Vichy, wasn't averse to spreading conspiracy theories about those in charge in France and later discouraged French people from working for the German occupiers.[4]

The two stations that followed were Radio Catholique, whose presenter was a priest from Lille, a Capitaine Lagrave, who encouraged his listeners to pray with him and, later, Radio Gaulle, also sometimes known as Radio France, which supported the Free French.[5]

By October 1940, the organisation employed 152 staff, of which 90 were working on the main functions and the other 62 were 'messengers, maintenance staff, drivers, household domestics and cleaners'.[6] The numbers of staff and radio stations were to expand quickly.

An Italian Freedom Station, Radio Italia, also went on air in November 1940, with its initial recordings made in a Woburn onion shed.[7] Balkan stations would follow in 1941. Ten 'different flavours' of radio stations were set up during the first year that RUs operated.[8] Running the secret houses that functioned as family homes as well as workplaces and radio newsrooms was a huge logistical and diplomatic headache.

Dawn Edge, the Crossman household, was headed by Zita Crossman. The houses were run using the terminology of the British boarding school, to the extent that the person in charge of each unit was referred to as a 'housemaster', their accompanying wives as 'housemistress' or 'matron'. Some senior staff were allowed to bring their wives and families with them to live in the country, despite the requirement for secrecy. The women were expected to help run the household, even if they also had professional work on the radio stations. The residents ate together and they had local staff, including cooks and gardeners. Among the early residents of Dawn Edge were Paul and Evelyn Anderson, Fritz Eberhard and the other staff of the European Revolution station. They would later be joined by an Austrian priest, Father Elmar Eisenberger, the journalist

Hans Bermann and others. A new young recruit described being dropped off by a driver at the house and having to summon the residents from their lunch to answer the door before joining them in the dining room. Zita Crossman was at the head of the table and her fellow diners discussed horticulture and the care and breeding of poultry.[9]

Each household was supposed to be oblivious to the existence of the others. Making sure that the staff of RUs who held and broadcast deeply opposed political views didn't run into one another involved a high level of subterfuge. Edward Halliday, who in peacetime was a portrait painter, interior designer and broadcaster, but who during the war supervised the output of the Freedom Stations, explained that whether they were allowed to meet or to share houses depended on who they were and what they believed. So, for instance, the RU which supported de Gaulle, which had the codename of station F4, had to be kept 'not only separate from but ignorant of the French Socialist RU', Radio Travail. The young de Gaulle-supporting soldiers who worked on F4, however, could live in the same house as the religious Catholic station, 'whose French priest was their comrade and ministered to their spiritual needs in a chapel converted from a bedroom'.[10]

Halliday said there were two reasons for this segregation. Firstly, it was so that each set of broadcasters could remain in the misguided belief that they were unique, and that the British government was supporting only their part of the cause. Secondly, this was in order to prevent 'conscious or unconscious copying of technique', so that the stations did not begin to sound alike. Even when two stations were deemed able to cohabit, that didn't guarantee they would get along. The broadcasters on Radio Travail and Radio Inconnue lived uncomfortably in the same rectory and fell out over whether to eat in the dining room or the kitchen, something British colleagues put down to class divisions.[11]

As with a boarding school, there were strict rules on what the residents of the houses in Aspley Guise and the surrounding villages were allowed to do and where they were allowed to go. They were not to fraternise with the permanent English residents of the village, apart from those who worked in their houses. They weren't even supposed to answer the door: 'Enquiries from neighbours or callers should be discouraged, but when a reply is unavoidable, it should be stated that the house is in Government occupation and the residents are engaged in research work for HMG.' The inhabitants were not allowed to visit local pubs or the Bedford Arms near the abbey at Woburn, nor could they make telephone calls or send telegrams without permission. They were also banned from going to church, hence the reliance on émigré priests. Any letters had to travel via a post office box address in London, rather than be posted locally.[12] Their ability to shop was likewise restricted; staff were told not to use sweet ration cards or clothing coupons within ten miles of their house, raising the question, since they were limited in how far they could travel, of how they bought these items at all.[13]

The residents' main job was to write and produce the radio programmes which they hoped would come across as genuine resistance stations within occupied Europe. They were giving the illusion of being broadcast from 'lonely cottages in the Ardennes, of transmitters disguised in motorvans or hidden in the forests of central Europe'.[14] Of course, they were really working in the villas and rectories of Bedfordshire. The native speakers worked under the direction of British staff, who would check and censor the scripts.

At this stage of the war, most of the Freedom Stations' broadcasts had to be pre-recorded. The only exceptions were where late breaking news meant permission could be given for live broadcasts. Being pre-recorded made them easier to censor, as it was possible to check that each item corresponded with the approved script. It also allowed for rewrites and retakes. The disadvantage, though, was the risk of it being revealed that they weren't live. As Halliday correctly observed, 'it is inconceivable that a genuine "Freedom Station", operating in enemy or enemy-occupied country perhaps from a coal mine or in the attic of a hut in the woods under most difficult conditions and in continual fear of discovery by the Gestapo, could be equipped with recording gear'.

The programmes made by each Freedom Station were recorded onto fragile 16-inch glass discs, at 33⅓ revolutions per minute, which gave them a little more than twelve minutes of usable time on each disc. The discs were breakable and had to be transported with great care. When they were played out, if the glass disc skipped or stuck, or there were repeats or retakes in the recording, the glitch would make it clear that the station was not what it claimed to be. There were, fortunately, few occasions on which this happened.

The programmes were transmitted from a studio known as 'Simpson', which was based in Wavendon Tower, near Milton Keynes. This was a former manor house which held four recording studios, one located in the old billiard room. It was about five miles from the secret houses, a time-consuming and often risky journey in wartime conditions, even with a 'selected team of drivers chosen for their integrity and knowledge of the countryside'. In bad weather, Halliday reported, snow and fog made journeys difficult. The glass discs holding the recordings were carefully packed into specially made boxes and the RU teams were driven to Simpson on a schedule that was supposed to bring them to the studio half an hour before they were due on air. It wasn't only the weather that threatened the careful planning. Sometimes the teams were simply late to their recording deadlines.

The RU teams were accompanied to the studio by their supervising 'housemaster' to act as censor and make sure nothing unauthorised went on air. In the summer of 1941, a sudden shortage of records due to problems getting the discs across the Atlantic meant that programmes had to be transmitted live, a situation which made the logistics even more complicated. The secrecy around the rival teams of broadcasters extended to their journeys to and from the studios. They were not allowed to arrive at the studios on foot and the comings and goings of the cars were carefully timed to ensure that they didn't accidentally meet.

On one occasion at least, this planning went disastrously wrong. A late breaking news story had happened and, Halliday related, the F1 station team had gone back to their studio to re-record some material to bring it up to date. However, when they returned, another station was hard at work, 'declaiming their de Gaullist case in a studio next to the Billiards Room' while their compatriots were listening to a playback of their programme. Halliday recalled, 'Though all studios were supposed to be sound-proof, the open fire-place of the Billiards Room had a thin back wall and through this the French Socialists heard the Opposition giving voice.' The Radio Travail team were so outraged to hear the opposing political views coming through the back of the fireplace that they 'resigned in a body on the spot'. They blamed Britain – 'yet another example, they said, of "Perfide Albion"'.[15]

This story, while it might have been amusing in hindsight, illustrates a deeper political problem that beset propaganda to enemy countries in the early part of the war. Allowing a variety of Freedom Stations to proliferate meant that several disparate messages were going out to as many potential audiences. The messages that were being put out from Britain were fragmented and unclear. They may have been saying what a variety of opponents of the European regimes wanted to hear, but they didn't give a clear idea, however disguised, about what Britain wanted to happen and how the course of the war might go.

Hugh Dalton, the minister of economic warfare, bounded into the debate with his typical blend of enthusiasm and insensitivity. His department had been given charge of secret broadcasts as part of his responsibility for subversion and sabotage, but he did not have total political control. Dalton loved what he called his 'Black Life' – a reference to the covert aspects of his ministerial job. He was proud of the Freedom Stations and particularly keen that they should urge Europe's workers to oppose the Germans, but was seemingly unaware of how dangerous this could be. In his wartime memoir, Dalton wrote: 'The Germans were often completely foxed by these stations. I remember, for instance, a most amusing account of a house-to-house search carried out by German troops in heavy boots in Bucharest to locate a Rumanian Freedom Station operating from Woburn.'[16] Being raided by German troops was doubtless not remotely amusing, and probably life-threatening, to the people in Romania who were wrongly suspected of broadcasting an opposition radio station.

Dalton and his wife had, in fact, had a German refugee from Danzig, George Wagner, living in their London flat for several months, but didn't seem to have absorbed the risks people opposing the Nazis had run. Wagner, who also worked at Woburn, called Dalton a new broom who 'didn't half sweep' – someone who was keen to reform the operation. The minister was working with 'ferocious intensity' as he got to grips with his new job, staying in his office until the early hours of the morning and existing on little sleep, catching a few hours in a bunk in the ministry's basement.[17] But Dalton's way of approaching people could be deliberately rude.[18]

While some in politics called him 'Dr Dynamo', others resented his weekend visits to Country HQ. Dalton was a tall man with a loud voice and a habit of speaking to people as though he were addressing a public meeting. 'He was a great booming bully,' Thomas Barman thought, 'and even at breakfast time his manner was horribly hearty. He used to dress himself in a sort of heavy white jersey, as worn by the best goal-keepers, and call for volunteers to go for a walk with him of a Sunday morning.'[19]

Dalton's enthusiasm for exercise – and his wearing of sports kit – was unusual for its time and his long walks, occasionally even runs, were how he cleared his head. He would break into jogs as he paced the bounds of Woburn's parks, often accompanied by his principal private secretary, Hugh Gaitskell, who operated as his political eyes and ears as well as his running companion. Dalton did, however, realise that these forced jogs weren't entirely popular with the 'volunteers', particularly after dinner, brandy and cigars on a Saturday night, observing, 'some responded better than others to this form of recreation'.[20]

Dalton found that those he was in charge of at Woburn weren't all as dynamic as he was; they were a 'mixed lot', temperamental and full of personal rivalries. In July 1940, Rex Leeper took over from Sir Campbell Stuart, the man who had run Electra House on First World War lines. Although Leeper, too, was an old hand at propaganda and had also been working on political intelligence since the end of that war, he was now put in charge of a new department. The Special Operations Executive, which had been set up at Churchill's instigation, initially had two sections. SO1 was in charge of psychological warfare, which would include propaganda and secret foreign broadcasts. The other half, SO2, was concerned with sabotage and direct action against the enemy. Political control of both rested with Dalton's Ministry of Economic Warfare. Leeper had moved from his initial Woburn job with the Foreign Office to take charge of SO1. He was an old-school diplomat who looked the part, 'tall and spare with the thoughtful, concentrated face of some old-time papal secretary'.[21] As head of the Foreign Office's News Department during the 1930s, he had been an opponent of both communism and appeasement. Delmer acknowledged that Leeper had 'one of the subtlest political brains'. Some in Whitehall, though, were quick to coin a nickname for his department – 'Leeper's sleepers' – implying that they did too little. Their minister thought this wasn't always true. 'Most of them were continually active,' Dalton wrote, 'and some were sleepless prima donnas.'[22]

Leeper himself, though, found Dalton excessively keen. In September 1940, Leeper was already complaining that his new ministerial boss was 'driving him mad'. Dalton had objected to Leeper sending out documents without his approval and then foisted his own junior officials on him as weekend house-guests. The minister was also pulling Leeper up on his working hours. Writing in annoyance that he wasn't at his desk, Dalton noted 'it is now quarter past three, and you have not returned from luncheon. I, on the other hand, have to go back to the country.'[23]

This criticism didn't put Leeper off having another long lunch with Robert Bruce Lockhart to vent his frustrations. The two men had known each other for decades; one of Leeper's earliest Foreign Office jobs had been to negotiate the prisoner swap in which Bruce Lockhart, jailed in the Kremlin, was exchanged for the Russian revolutionary Maxim Litvinov. Leeper was despairing of the situation, telling Bruce Lockhart it was 'impossible' to work in London and that 'the whole show would collapse and he would sink with it'. Bruce Lockhart detected that part of Leeper's concern was driven by fear. Leeper was much happier – in 'rapturous delight', even – when he was told the next week that he could be based in Woburn. 'For days he has been scared by the bombing and he does not care if people say he is running away or not.'

Bruce Lockhart was less fearful of the bombing. During a daytime air raid in September, he was working in his 'sunless and miserably furnished' office in Lansdowne House, on Berkeley Square in Mayfair, where he complained that he lacked both a secretary and an armchair, when the sirens sounded and the staff were told to take shelter below ground.

During the raid, a sixteen-year-old Czech girl arrived at the office with a personal message to Bruce Lockhart from Edvard Beneš, the exiled Czech leader. Bruce Lockhart had a second job, as British minister or representative to the Czech government-in-exile. The young messenger was untroubled by the air raids; 'she had walked from Grosvenor Place to Berkeley Square and, bomb or no bomb, would walk back.'[24] Bruce Lockhart remained below ground for lunch at one of his favourite restaurants and 'both drank and spent too much' before going back to work. He felt ashamed that the young girl had braved the danger while he sheltered in safety. From that point on, he insisted that work didn't have to stop for air raids.

Life below ground continued after work. The Lansdowne Club was just around the corner from the Political Intelligence Department's London offices and it became their regular haunt. Although Bruce Lockhart would have protested that he worked until nine at night, he and his colleagues would then go down to the club where they ate, drank and danced to the accompaniment of show tunes. By ten, the bar would be crowded. During the Blitz, they would often listen to Jerome Kern's 'All the Things You Are', played, Bruce Lockhart recalled, by a 'tall, pale consumptive-looking saxophonist' with a plaintive voice.[25] Like the Mayfair and the Ritz, which also had basement clubs of 'gilded squalor', they would find officers, officials, American correspondents and 'occasional ministers' around the tables. Music and alcohol blurred the noise of the bombs. Even if Dalton would not have been pleased by their work ethic or their propensity to gossip, these clubs were somewhere that they could talk about what was supposedly secret work among people who were in similar worlds. The Lansdowne, for Bruce Lockhart, was almost a workplace, where 'nearly everyone was a war-worker', and 'at dinner we met officials from other departments and discussed our common problems'. It was perhaps no wonder, then, that in 1940, Hugh Dalton wrote that there was 'much too much quack, quack going on', particularly in the restaurants and clubs of the West End, which allowed people to overhear conversations and make intelligent guesses, whereby 'gossip is continually embellished'.[26]

Bruce Lockhart had a close call, however, on the night of heavy bombing which hit London on 14 October. Already bombed out of his London flat, he was living at the East India and Sports Club on St James's Square. That evening, he was dining with his close colleague Dallas Brooks, just around the corner at the United Services Club on Pall Mall, when a bomb struck the building. The Carlton Club, further down the street and popular with Conservative ministers and MPs, was destroyed in the same raid, though there were no fatalities. Bruce Lockhart was thrown from his chair by the blast and got to his feet to see the only man left standing in the room, a naval captain holding a full glass of port. The captain enquired whether Bruce Lockhart had been hurt. On hearing that he hadn't, the captain drained his glass, observing, 'Thank God that didn't spill.' Inspired by this display of military sang-froid, Bruce Lockhart and Brooks picked their way through fires in the streets in search of more to drink, ending up back at the Lansdowne.

Despite Dalton's best efforts and the change of policy that had come with the new government in May, British propaganda was still becalmed. Partly this was to do with the state of the war. Britain had successfully defended itself against the German air attacks of the Battle of Britain and was still living under the regular onslaughts of the Blitz, but there was little prospect of further progress in the short term. 'In that autumn of 1940 the propaganda situation was almost tragic,' Bruce Lockhart wrote. 'There was an abundance of real talent at Woburn but the inability of propaganda to disturb the tide of German military successes did not increase the department's prestige, although at the time the task was, in fact, hopeless.'[27]

Bruce Lockhart wrote in his diary at the end of the year about the divergence of views between the propagandists and the ministers and others who supervised them. 'One curious feature of this Woburn organisation (which includes many freaks, some genuine antiques, several fakes and a few geniuses) is the almost universal contempt for the professional politician including the ministers. Yet the ministers preen themselves, pout and patronise as if they were making a tremendous impression on everyone.'[28]

Bruce Lockhart loved to lunch, dine and gossip with civil servants and others, such as Max Beaverbrook, the newspaper proprietor and now a minister himself. He had written to Dalton ten days earlier to complain that he was being underused, emphasising his own long experience. 'I have a wider, longer and more varied personal knowledge of European countries and leading personalities than most people, and my first-hand experience of revolutionary movements is, I think, unique.' Bruce Lockhart told Dalton that he felt he was wasting his time in producing reports that duplicated other work. Dalton reassured Bruce Lockhart about his position, but a shift in the Cabinet just before Christmas was more significant: Anthony Eden returned as foreign secretary to replace Lord Halifax.

Eden had resigned from that role in 1938 after he had disagreed with Chamberlain's foreign policy, not wanting to enter into talks with Mussolini's Italy. He brought knowledge, a facility with languages and a certain personal flair. Eden was also someone who was senior – and confident – enough to be able to argue with Churchill about policy when he thought it was necessary. Rex Leeper and Bruce Lockhart welcomed his return, Leeper telling his friends that he was excited about it. The Foreign Office had a responsibility for propaganda in that it was supposed to make sure that the messages which were being put out from Britain were in line with the country's overall policy, and Eden, as a political heavyweight, was able to intervene and ultimately be a deciding voice in some key arguments. But before he got his feet under the desk, there were still some fundamental disagreements about what Britain's message to her enemy, Germany, should be.

Sir Robert Vansittart's series of talks on the BBC in November 1940 revived the debate about what British propaganda could or should attempt to do at a point when the war was still largely defensive. Vansittart was one of the influential figures who believed that Britain's view of Germany was not nearly harsh enough. He was a diplomat of long experience and also literary talent – as a young man, he had written a play in French which was performed in Paris for six weeks. Since 1938, Vansittart had been the government's chief diplomatic adviser, and at the time of his broadcasts and his book, he described himself as 'a working diplomatist with his coat off'. It was controversial for a serving diplomat to speak and write so publicly, and his argument was uncompromising.

His radio talks were published in a book, *Black Record: Germans Past and Present*, early the following year. Vansittart's distrust of Germany dated back to his first visits to the country as a student at the turn of the century, where he had experienced intense Anglophobia, loathed the culture of duelling which was prevalent among German students, and 'learnt what it was like to be really hated'. Working with German prisoners of war in the First World War had confirmed him in his views. In his talks, he traced German aggression back to Roman times, and throughout history, comparing the country to a 'butcher-bird' that struck out with unprovoked aggression. Germans, he said, were characterised by 'envy, self-pity and cruelty'. The individuals who opposed such actions, he argued, had been few and far between, and had never managed to tip the balance against German aggression. It was wrong to believe that there was 'an effective element of kindly and learned old gentlemen and of sweet pig-tailed maidens'. Those individuals, Vansittart believed, would never make the difference. 'There have been bright ineffectual angels in Germany,' he wrote, 'but those who have suffered from Germany throughout the years know only that they have always been ineffectual, and so we must consider them, till the question is answered whether the Night of the Dark Ages is to descend upon the world, or the "Night of Long Knives" upon the Nazis.' The collective, Vansittart claimed, would always override the individual. 'The *German* is often a moral creature; the *Germans* never; and it is the *Germans* who count.'[29]

Richard Crossman, as we have seen, was most often on the side of those bright ineffectual angels. It would have followed from Vansittart's argument that there was no point in appealing to the better natures of individual Germans in propaganda, as they could never achieve what Britain wanted them to. The publication of Vansittart's talks in early 1941 had prompted debate about the issue and there were questions in Parliament about whether a serving diplomat should make such interventions. Crossman, wary of letting Vansittart's arguments lead the agenda, addressed them in a long memo, entitled 'On the use of the motifs of fear, guilt and hate in our propaganda to Germany'.[30]

Crossman did not accept the premise that fear, guilt or hate currently had no place in British propaganda at all. On the contrary, he said that they were present, but in different proportions. To base British broadcasting in hatred, in the same way that German propaganda attacked Britain, he argued, was to play into Hitler and Goebbels's hands. It would reinforce the German claims that Britain hated Germany. 'Will German morale be lowered,' he asked rhetorically, 'by what Germans will feel to be the reiteration of British hatred for them as a nation?' Crossman posed a further question: 'Is the aim of our propaganda simply to demoralise all Germans or is it to keep alive and enlarge oppositional groups?'[31] If the Allies gave up on encouraging opposition, he maintained, the result would be to drive any potential opposition 'willy nilly into the Communist party', because they would search for someone promising an alternative future and see no difference between the Soviet Union and the British. He did not believe that propaganda alone could 'drive a wedge' between the regime and the people, but that it 'can only keep alive and intensify such differences as already exist'. It was essential to continue to provide the German people with the awareness that another world existed beyond the regime, 'a world not dominated by the methods of greed, hate and brutality'.

Crossman mustered practical arguments in his cause, arguments which he would maintain throughout the conflict: firstly, that encouraging the internal opposition could shorten the war, and secondly, that propaganda had to be backed by the imminent threat of military force and the desire to win. In his memo, he typed these points underlined for emphasis: 'By creating a body of opinion in Germany which definitely prefers a British victory, we may well be able to spare ourselves a long period of war.' It was too soon, he stated, to switch to an outright policy of terrifying potential German listeners. 'Terror propaganda produces precisely the opposite result to that intended if it is not accompanied by an equivalent military effort or at least an equivalent military threat.'

He concluded in his proposals for action that 'while retaining our present line, we should stiffen and toughen it wherever possible. We need not only ideals and principles, but a will to victory, and this must be clear in every bulletin.'

This was Crossman's call to action, but he had an opponent on Vansittart's side of the argument who was running the other German Freedom Station. Freddy Voigt loved argument and controversy just as much as Crossman did, and he had a good claim to know Germany more deeply. Born in London to German parents who had become British, and having served as a British conscript soldier in the First World War, Frederick Voigt had been the *Manchester Guardian*'s correspondent in Berlin from 1920 until he was expelled by the Nazi regime as it came to power. Voigt did not seem at first sight like an intimidating figure. His *Guardian* colleagues remembered him as 'tall of build, fragile-looking and nervous in manner, shortsighted, with a trick of smiling from the mouth downwards'.[32] He was also 'a brilliant talker, an outstanding linguist, and a man of great personal courage'.[33]

Even after Voigt had been expelled from Germany, the Nazis pursued him, because they hated his critical reporting, which he continued from Paris. Late in 1933, the Gestapo attempted to assassinate him on French soil.[34] Voigt, like Crossman, had been a regular contributor to the BBC on Germany. In 1937, the corporation described him as having broadcast for the past three years and being the BBC's 'No. 1 authority on European affairs', though some at the BBC found him tiresome.[35]

Voigt's politics had shifted as a result of his experiences in Germany. Having originally been on the left, he despaired of what he saw as the left's failure to oppose Hitler successfully, and moved towards a more conservative view that was based in Christian theology. He retained, a former colleague believed, 'an idealism which through all his radical changes of philosophy remained undaunted'.[36] He left the *Guardian* and joined the Department for Enemy Propaganda in February 1940 as an adviser on Germany, telling the BBC that he was working about twelve hours a day at one of the 'hush! hush! places'. His new philosophy was reflected in the character of Hier Spricht Deutschland, which used exiles of centrist and liberal views as its broadcasters.

Although Voigt and Crossman agreed that the BBC should provide straight, hard and truthful news, and resist all attempts to move it towards untrue 'black' propaganda, there was little else they found in common. Robert Walmsley, who sat in on the weekly meetings with Voigt, Crossman and others, remembered that those meetings 'often degenerated into long tirades by Voigt against the methods of British propaganda'.[37]

In March 1941, Voigt's first Freedom Station was closed down, with its last broadcast on 15 March. It was seen as being dull, with little news and too much commentary. One of its main broadcasters had also become ill. There were already plans underway to replace it with a darker, cruder type of station, one which emulated Lord Haw-Haw's broadcasts from Germany to Britain.[38] These anonymous broadcasts by William Joyce – the American-born fascist known as Haw-Haw – began with the words 'Germany calling . . .' and had gained a receptive audience in Britain during the early months of the war. They seemed to combine humour, mockery of the authorities and misinformation, giving listeners a sense of hearing something illicit.

When Voigt's house and team were disbanded, he was furious. He was not going to go quietly. He resigned on 7 April 1941 and sent Valentine Williams – the former thriller-writer who had served as Campbell Stuart's deputy – a fifty-two-page resignation memo, telling his former boss everything that he thought was wrong with British propaganda to the enemy. While some of Voigt's criticisms were undoubtedly valid, his way of putting them meant that those who read his angry document were bound to resist what it said.

His first charge was that British propaganda was wrong to address the opposition inside Germany. This was work addressed to 'a non-existent Germany, to a fairy-tale realm that is wholly unrelated to the Third Empire with which we are at war'.[39] Voigt said they should not assume that the kind of opposition that had existed in 1933 was still present; rather, that the Germans had been exposed to years of domestic propaganda to convince them that the regime was right and that it was Britain which had attacked Germany. He believed that exiles who had left the country in the early 1930s had become out of touch with the current feeling within their homeland.

Voigt also said that it was counter-productive to suggest that Britain was on the side of the German people while at the same time attacking them. 'We are at war with the German nation as a whole and our propaganda must be addressed to that nation as a whole,' he wrote. 'Our war-aim is to defeat the German nation by breaking their armed might. If, in our propaganda, we say we are not fighting the German "people", we shall pass for hypocrites, because the German "people" who are being bombed and blockaded <u>know</u> that we are fighting them. Our assurances to the contrary will only tend to confirm them in this knowledge.' Rather, Voigt said, British propaganda should say that it was confronting German militarism and aiming to bring about German defeat.

Few who were working on propaganda at that time would have disagreed with Voigt that it was too diffuse, too varied and produced a large amount of work that had little measurable result. It was probably fair of him to say that the estimates of about a million Germans listening to foreign stations were 'purely conjectural'; there was no accurate way to measure this, given that listening to foreign broadcasts was illegal and punishable.

Voigt's phrasing, though, was typically uncompromising. Telling his colleagues that 'there is no conclusive evidence that our propaganda has had the slightest effect on the Germans or is in any way contributing towards their ultimate defeat' was perhaps not the most diplomatic way of putting things. But, as *The Times* remembered after Voigt's death, 'controversy he enjoyed and the fiercer the battle the better he liked it'. In this, at least, Voigt and Crossman were highly similar, which is probably why they came into such conflict.

Freddy Voigt's misgivings about the tone of voice of British propaganda were similar to those that Denis Sefton Delmer expressed when he joined the organisation, replacing him. Both believed that relying too much on the voices and the concerns of émigrés was a mistake. They risked being out of date and out of touch, as well as sharing a worldview that was different from that of Germans who had remained behind. According to Robert Walmsley, though, Voigt came to the opposite conclusion to that of Delmer, noting that Voigt was 'totally unsympathetic to the idea of anything but the whitest of white propaganda and seemed unable to distinguish between propaganda to different audiences'.[40]

Voigt's answer was that England (he generally used this term rather than 'Britain') should be voicing its own authentic view of the world. 'Our propaganda should, above all, be English in character. It should be the voice of England.' It should have, he continued, 'the character, the content, the might, the force and the quality' of the nation. It was less clear what Voigt liked than what he disliked. His aversions included the exaggeration, cheapness, frivolity and sneering that he detected in many broadcasts. It was essential, he believed, that England's propaganda should be based in truthfulness and integrity, not just in straight news but also in talks and features.

Voigt wanted a shift in the political slant to represent a broader range of English opinion. 'The Left is much too conspicuous in our propaganda. England is liberal and conservative as well as socialist.' He also perceived the broadcasts as showing a 'complete lack of insight into German working-class life'.

In terms of organisation, Voigt suggested that propaganda should be better planned – something that many would have agreed with. He also felt that it was essential to move the centre of operations from the country back to London, where again he would have been in agreement with Bruce

Lockhart and others. His argument for moving away from Woburn was not just one of practicality but also of sentiment. Voigt believed that people who were living and working through the Blitz would have a greater direct understanding of the war than those living in the peaceful seclusion of the country. He called it 'the uplifting grandeur of the harsh realities that have become part of everyday life in London', which he contrasted with the 'pettiness of the unreality that prevails at CHQ' (Country Headquarters).

Nor did Voigt like the use of German exiles on air, suggesting that their influence was 'considerable' and 'almost entirely harmful'. He thought the broadcasters should be replaced with English announcers. The novelist Thomas Mann, in particular, despite his great reputation, should be axed: 'To exploit the well-earned literary fame of an old man, who has become mentally warped by insult and exile and has lost all sense of proportion, in this manner, is nothing less than a disgraceful stunt.'

What was wrong with British propaganda, Voigt concluded, was that it was too favourable to Germany. 'The principal contention of this memorandum is that our propaganda to Germany is, in a last analysis, pro-German. Such a defect must, of course, be fatal.' He contrasted this with propaganda to France, which he saw as 'animated by the spirit of combat and patriotism' and having 'character'.

The reaction to Voigt's memo among his former colleagues was to interpret it as a personal attack on Dick Crossman. Crossman did not reply on his own behalf, but it was left to a colleague, Con O'Neill, to respond, a week after Voigt's memo was received. Since Crossman had personally asked for O'Neill to be recruited as an assistant, it's likely he was expressing Crossman's own views.[41] O'Neill was a young diplomat who had resigned from the Foreign Office over Chamberlain's policy of appeasement before the war and he accepted that the German section would in fact have agreed with many of the substantive points about their output that Voigt was making. He observed that 'the strange thing about this whole controversy is that there is in fact little disagreement on our side with the brilliant analysis of the German position contained in Mr Voigt's paper'. The section believed, on the contrary, that there was much they could do better.

But O'Neill wasn't going to accept Voigt's attacks unquestioningly, hitting back by saying 'he is engaged, it is clear, in total warfare against the Department; and he uses all available weapons'. He then proceeded to dismantle Voigt's argument, questioning his premises and his conclusions. O'Neill argued that Voigt made 'assumptions as large and baseless as those he imputes to us', that he ignored evidence and juggled with definitions. Finally, he maintained, Voigt's argument rested on a contradiction. Voigt was making two contradictory assertions, that propaganda 'produces no effect whatever in Germany', while at the same time, 'it does incalculable damage to our cause'.

It was clear to Robert Bruce Lockhart that although 'every good propagandist is like a prima donna and must be given a reasonable amount of latitude', this situation could not go on with two divas. 'As it is virtually impossible to have two prima donnas on the stage at the same time, it is equally impossible to have two experts on the same country in the same organisation.'[42] Voigt was the one who had to go, with, so Bruce Lockhart wrote, 'hurt feelings and considerable bitterness'.

Bruce Lockhart's view was that Crossman stayed because he was the better propagandist, but it was also the case that he was the better politician. Crossman had political backing from Hugh Dalton, and Dalton was more favourable to the left-of-centre view that propaganda should appeal to the workers within Germany. Dalton, however, was beginning to come under political pressure himself.

Voigt, despite his resignation, was not going to let his grievances go. He may not have had ministerial protection, but he had friends who would be persuaded of his views, and the questions he raised would flare up again, the next time in public.

3

Warfare by Words

As Elisabeth Barker waited in the lobby of Broadcasting House on 18 June 1940, she was looking out for her guest, a French general. She did not know what he would look like. Nor did she know how significant this guest would become, or how important this broadcast would be. Not many people in Britain yet knew much about Charles de Gaulle at all. The first thing the thirty-year-old BBC producer noticed about him was his height. Although she was tall herself, the general was 'immensely tall'. The next thing she noticed was his boots. Her eye travelled up de Gaulle's long frame to his face, which was 'strange, and in its way impressive, but far from handsome'. When Barker later read a comparison of Charles de Gaulle's appearance to that of a dinosaur, she agreed it was an excellent description.[1]

She escorted de Gaulle to the radio studio for his broadcast. The talk had been cleared at the highest levels: the Ministry of Information had told the BBC that they should expect their distinguished guest, while Churchill and the War Cabinet had cleared his broadcast and his script did not need to be censored. In the studio, de Gaulle gave the impression that he could not see anything around him except for the microphone.[2] Barker was impressed further by de Gaulle's delivery. 'He had a very deep voice,' she recalled, and 'he declaimed the broadcast in a style which I should think would have been suitable for a Racine tragedy.'

This talk, broadcast at 10pm in London, was later known as the famous 'Appeal' to the French people. As France fell to the German invasion, de Gaulle had shuttled between London and France, by plane and by boat, having resigned as the under-secretary for defence in the French government. On 17 June, he had left France for what would be the last time until he was able to return in victory. Heading into exile was an enormous and risky step. As Julian Jackson describes it, 'de Gaulle left France to defend what he later called his "*idea* of France"',[3] as opposed to Pétain's claim to be representing the soil of France. The eighty-four-year-old Marshal Pétain had just become head of the gov-ernment of what remained of France, and was surrendering. One of de Gaulle's first tasks in creating this idea of France, as he saw it, was to 'raise his colours' and he saw the radio as the ideal means of communication. His broadcast was to be a response to Pétain's call for an armistice. He had only a few minutes to tell the French nation that they should not give up.

The appeal was full of rhetorical questions and flour-ishes. 'But has the last word been said? Must hope vanish? Is the defeat final? No!' de Gaulle declaimed. 'France is not alone,' he repeated three times. The general called on French officers, soldiers and anyone with military expertise to join him in Britain. 'Whatever happens, the flame of the French resistance must not be extinguished and will not be extin-guished.' Concluding, de Gaulle said that he would broadcast again the next day.

The symbolism of this broadcast and those that succeeded it was huge; it helped to create de Gaulle as a leader of the nation. Many French people would know his voice long before they knew what he looked like.[4] At the time, though, neither the BBC nor the few people who heard the original broadcast realised quite how significant a historical moment this was. Had the corporation done so, it would probably not have been left to a fairly junior female producer to take charge of it. Only subsequently did it become clear how powerful a

General Charles de Gaulle returns to the BBC for another broadcast, 30 October 1941

piece of propaganda this broadcast was. It represented clear resistance to Germany and, by being broadcast on the BBC, showed that Britain stood alongside an alternative vision of France. However, as with Britain's own propaganda, allowing foreign leaders to broadcast was often beset with problems and political arguments.

Elisabeth Barker carried on working late into the night translating de Gaulle's French into English so that the text of the appeal could be sent out to news agencies like the Press Association, a job that she found 'terrifying' in case she wasn't able to do justice to the classical style of the original.

De Gaulle returned to the BBC the next day, hoping to make a new statement as he had promised. Instead of being shown into a studio, he was ushered into the office of the director-general, Frederick Ogilvie. Ogilvie had told Barker's boss, Leonard Miall, that he would like to offer the general a drink and shake his hand. Miall and Barker were invited to join them. As de Gaulle sipped his drink, he asked Miall whether his appeal had been recorded. Miall had to tell de Gaulle that it hadn't. There was an understandable reason for the omission: 18 June was also the day that Churchill made his 'finest hour' speech. This, too, was a repeat of sorts. Churchill spoke first to the House of Commons, just before four in the afternoon.[5] Because the proceedings of Parliament weren't allowed to be broadcast, Churchill had to make his speech again for the airwaves. All the BBC's recording channels, of which there were only about six at the time, were used to make copies of his resonant performance. So there were no channels available to record the words of a then fairly obscure French general.

When he was informed of this, de Gaulle was furious. There was, Miall recalled with British understatement, 'quite a scene' and he described himself as having been 'the first British recipient of the famous de Gaulle temper'. It was a temper that British political leaders would experience often during the war.

The BBC at first was more concerned with correct appearances. Rather than being praised for her important work, Elisabeth Barker was rebuked by Sir Stephen Tallents, the controller of overseas services and former controller of public relations, once he realised that the general was important. He told her off for not having worn stockings when greeting the eminent guest.[6]

Very few listeners actually heard de Gaulle's original broadcast. The BBC had only broadcast in French for the first time in September 1938, as a response to the Munich crisis, in order to relay Chamberlain's speech where he said Germany's attempt to annex part of Czechoslovakia was 'a quarrel in a faraway country between people of whom we know nothing'. The introductory words, *'Ici Londres'*, that would become so familiar during the war, were not yet well-known. There were as yet few listeners in France who would know how to find the BBC, even if they had been able to tune in. And, as it turned out, there was no copy of the broadcast that could be played out again.

Radio was a new and revolutionary technology: the BBC had only existed for twelve years when Elisabeth Barker started work there in 1934; Broadcasting House was a building not yet three years old. The BBC's news department itself was brand-new: until 1934, the corporation had not provided its own news bulletins but relied on news copy from agencies like Reuters. The newspaper proprietors were so anxious about competition from radio that they managed to have the BBC stopped from broadcasting any news at all before the evening.

To be in at the start of such a new project must have been exciting. Foreign news services were an even more recent innovation: the BBC broadcast in Arabic from 1938 and started talks in French, German and Italian that year. By 1944, the European Service would be making programmes in sixteen different languages.[7] In terms of using the national broadcaster for international propaganda, Britain started from behind Germany. Although the BBC liked to think of itself as being at arm's length from the government, during wartime it accepted censorship and directives about what should and should not be broadcast. As with more covert propaganda, the process of government control was complex and often unclear.

Dealing with the swirl of European leaders and would-be leaders who made London their base during the war required not just the production skills to put them on air, to make sure they spoke fluently and were recorded clearly, but it also required a level of diplomacy and negotiation at a high political level. Often, the message that the foreign leaders wanted to put out would not be what the British government wanted them to say. De Gaulle's broadcasts were frequently a case in point. On a subsequent occasion, de Gaulle arrived unannounced at Broadcasting House expecting to give another talk. By this time, the BBC had been told that they should not put the general on air unless both the Foreign Office and the Ministry of Information were in agreement. There were five minutes to go before the news and de Gaulle stood waiting in the Broadcasting House reception room, surrounded by his entourage of French officers. Elisabeth Barker had to run to a phone box in the lobby and put a call through first to the Foreign Office duty clerk, and then to Sir Robert Vansittart, the government's chief diplomatic adviser, who was at his country house in Buckinghamshire. In the meantime, the agreement from the Ministry of Information came through and an official there agreed to take responsibility for any fallout from the de Gaulle talk. De Gaulle duly spoke again.

Barker clearly had diplomatic skills that suited her to these tricky negotiations. Over the next year, she dealt not only with the French but also with the Czechs, Poles and Yugoslavs in exile in London. Barker would become one of the most senior women in British political warfare. She moved from working on the BBC's own efforts at white propaganda, which aimed to encourage resistance in occupied Europe, to working directly for the government. Not only did she know the politics of central Europe and the Balkans, and an array of European languages, but she managed to get along well with people of a wide range of political views and form lasting friendships with them. She also, unlike many of her male colleagues, managed to be both discreet and modest about her work and her achievements. Those qualities, though, make her story harder to find. Even when she wrote about the history of the times, Barker was reluctant to put herself at the centre of it.

'There was always something distinguished and distinctive about Elisa,' her college friend Margaret Bottrall wrote. 'She had, and kept, the look of a Chartres angel, long and thin, with an expression of sweetness and good humour.' It was not recorded whether General de Gaulle noted this resemblance to a French cathedral statue. This angelic appearance was matched by her brightness. 'Nor did she ever lose the

Elisabeth Barker, BBC producer turned political warrior, at the BBC in 1952

intellectual energy and responsiveness that characterised her as a young woman,'[8] Bottrall said.

Elisabeth Barker was born in Oxford in 1910, the daughter of Ernest Barker, then a lecturer in modern history at St John's College and a political theorist, and his wife Emily. She was the youngest of three siblings, with a brother, Arthur, and a sister, Margaret. Her peaceful childhood in north Oxford, where she loved climbing trees in the family's Park Town garden, was interrupted when Elisabeth was ten and they moved to London. Three years afterwards, her mother died and her father later remarried. Elisabeth returned to Oxford at seventeen for university, arriving at Lady Margaret Hall to read Greats as the senior scholar of her year in 1927.

Leaving Oxford in 1931 with a Second, which she called a 'respectable though far from brilliant degree', Barker soon set off for central Europe, where her brother Arthur had become the *Times* correspondent. She said that she 'drove his car around for two years', but she seems to have done more than that, acquiring a good knowledge of several European languages and acting as a journalistic fixer. Arthur Barker was based in Vienna and the two travelled together through much of eastern Europe and the Balkans. These were turbulent years in the region, as in Germany to the north, with economic crisis and civil unrest. By the beginning of 1934, Austria was on the brink of civil war. This time was the foundation of Elisabeth Barker's career.

She may have been inspired to become a foreign correspondent in her own right, but on returning home, getting a foot in the door, for a young woman, was still difficult, despite her family connections. Her father, Ernest, by then professor of political science at Cambridge, was a famous, self-made networker – so much so that he became the model for Anthony Powell's Sillery in *A Dance to the Music of Time*, the gossipy, ever-networking Oxford don who enjoyed helping to propel his students and friends to positions of influence.[9] Powell had been taught by Barker on the 'politico-military course' at Cambridge during the war and said the cheerful, if egotistical, professor had the 'sense of a career open to talents, which had brought him where he was'.[10] Although Professor Barker was prepared to use his network to help his children, it was harder for him to pull strings for his daughter than for his son.

Ernest contacted his friend Sir John Reith, the first director-general of the BBC. There was a job for his daughter, but she was told that 'there was no possibility of my entering the BBC on anything but a clerical level'. Many of the men who joined the fledgling news service as sub-editors were younger and less experienced than her. Barker joined the BBC in 1934 as a shorthand typist and clerk in the news department, where her first job was to help create the News Information service. The job at that time consisted largely of 'cutting up newspapers, and filing the cuttings into boxes and answering queries from news staff'. It was a service whose filing cabinets and envelopes of yellowing newspaper clippings persisted until at least the 1990s.

Once she had joined the BBC, though, Barker was able to progress through the new branch of the organisation. She created a pronunciation index for unfamiliar names and places – something that survives to this day as the pronunciation unit. Within a couple of years, the BBC had begun to hire its own reporters and correspondents, and with this move came new opportunities. The *Foreign Report* programme was an early attempt at putting contributors in foreign countries live on air, and the weekly programme, which went out on Sunday evenings after the news, was fraught with all the glitches that live broadcasting always entails. Ralph Murray, another Oxford graduate who had spent time in Vienna, and had been the BBC's reporter at the League of Nations in Geneva, was in charge of the programme. Barker was hired to work with him and the two of them alone put out the twenty-minute broadcast. With characteristic modesty, she described herself as 'a sort of dogsbody'. She was still, however, underpaid relative to her male colleagues. Any man doing the job, she observed, would have to have been paid more. Again, she did more than she gave herself credit for: when Murray travelled abroad to report, which he did more often as the crises in Europe of the late 1930s escalated, Barker was in sole charge of the show. Ralph Murray broadcast live from Austria during the *Anschluss* of March 1938 and travelled to the Sudetenland after the Munich Agreement that September.

When war broke out, Barker and many of her colleagues moved in to live in the 'very pleasant' Langham Hotel on Portland Place, just across the road from Broadcasting House. The hotel's residents in September 1939, as listed in the government register that was used to allocate ID cards and ration books, were BBC typists and telephonists, engineers and announcers, sub-editors and journalists. Broadcasting, during the early days of the phoney war, was in an uneasy lull.[11] Wartime conditions meant there could be no live links from foreign capitals and *Foreign Report* went off air. Barker found herself having to rewrite dull announcements from the Ministry of Information instead.

Her whole career was nearly derailed by a personal clash with her boss. The BBC's fifty-year-old news editor, R.T. Clark, was a Glaswegian and an old Fleet Street hand. He had a robust view of what the BBC's role should be during the war, telling staff in September 1939 that 'the only way to strengthen the morale of the people whose morale is worth strengthening is to tell them the truth and nothing but the truth, even if the truth is horrible'.[12] This, however, wasn't why Barker fell out with him – rather, it was because she complained that Clark decided to promote a 'charming young secretary' over the heads of older women in the department. Barker declined to go into details even forty years later, but her implication was clear. She told her boss that this promotion was causing 'trouble in the lower ranks', but he took her protest in standing up for other women as a sign of 'rebellion or even mutiny' and threatened to exile her to the BBC Monitoring Service, outside London.

A more friendly boss, Leonard Miall, the head of European News Talks, intervened to get her career back on track, but even then he was nearly blocked, saying that he had 'great difficulty in persuading the powers that be' to allow her appointment. Despite her journalistic experience in central Europe and in London, and her facility with French and some central European languages, there was still huge reluctance to give Barker a suitable job. One of those standing in her way was her own brother, Arthur, who by this point had moved from *The Times* to the BBC as overseas news editor, and was apparently concerned that it might look like nepotism to promote his sister. Arthur Barker was described by one of his other BBC colleagues, Noel Newsome, as a 'strange, scholarly, dreamy character',[13] who seemed to Newsome to be 'utterly unsuited' for the 'extremely tough job' that he would find himself in once the war began.

Eventually, Barker was found a job working particularly on talks in Czech and other languages, where her contributors included Jan Masaryk, the future Czechoslovak foreign minister and a star broadcaster, who had fluent English dotted with American slang, and Edvard Beneš, the exiled president. In a post-war job application, Barker described her language proficiency as having good German and French, 'fair' Czech and some Russian and Serbo-Croat. She also worked with the Polish language services.[14] This was how she came to be the person waiting to greet General de Gaulle in June 1940.

As the Blitz began, working at Broadcasting House became much more dangerous and the building was hit by bombs twice in the early days of the attacks. The first time was in October 1940, when a 550lb high-explosive bomb hit Portland Place and killed seven members of staff, as well as destroying the BBC's phone switchboard and damaging the music library. The newsreader, Bruce Belfrage, continued to read his bulletin as the explosion detonated outside. Under the continued threat of bombing, the European Service moved down from its second-floor offices to a 'crowded and uncomfortable' basement.[15] When the second bomb landed, in December 1940, Barker was working in the basement, standing outside the Polish translators' room. A parachute mine descended slowly over Portland Place before its canopy caught on a lamp post near the Langham Hotel. When it exploded, it left a huge crater in the street and killed one police officer who had been on duty. Barker and her colleagues kept broadcasting until about an hour and a half after the explosion, when the basement began to flood and they were evacuated. She and her secretary, against orders, returned to an office to rescue their precious recordings of interviews which hadn't yet been broadcast.

After this second blast, the European Service was moved to the Maida Vale studios, housed in a converted roller-skating rink, which although it may have been further from the centre of London and was perhaps a less likely target, did not seem much safer. They worked in 'draughty whitewashed cellars' just below ground level, with no air-raid shelters. Noel Newsome, the European news editor, was horrified by how several hundred of his colleagues were made to work and protested. 'The hall had been partitioned into tiny offices and we were packed into those pens like cattle in a market which might at any moment become a slaughterhouse.'[16] The most frightening thing, for both Barker and Alan Bullock, the historian, who had joined the European Service in September 1940, was working beneath the glass roof of the former roller rink, which offered little protection against bombs or shrapnel. According to Bullock, 'even a journey to the canteen in search of the turkey sandwiches and coffee on which we lived was a matter of some danger'.[17] For Barker, the frustrations of the canteen included not only the danger of sitting beneath the glass roof – where occasionally the mood was lightened by someone playing the studio's grand piano – but the likelihood that an air-raid siren would sound and the canteen would suddenly be closed before she had reached the front of the queue for food.

It was an intense working environment and the pressures and dangers of war made it more so. Bullock wrote after the war: 'We worked together in two or three adjoining rooms; knew each other well; lived, slept, ate and talked our job.' There were some compensations. Barker was sometimes given gifts by contributors that were hard to come by during wartime: on one occasion, a case of French rosé from an actress who had been voicing morale-boosting talks for French soldiers; on another, a dozen bottles of Fortnum & Mason's gin from

Jan Masaryk. The journalists would be driven home through the bombings in an armoured bus, one of the few times they felt safe. On one night that the City of London was bombed, Barker saw that 'the whole of the sky in the east was red'. In March 1941, the European News Service was moved again, this time to Bush House on the Aldwych, just off the Strand. The BBC had to negotiate with the Air Ministry for scarce office space in the building. But while they were away from the fragile glass roof of Maida Vale, the working conditions were still difficult and often dangerous. By now, they were feeling the effects of the war close to home, and the BBC was beginning to turn its attention to how it might more consistently influence the war further abroad.

It was the creation of the BBC's 'V Campaign' which led Barker into her role in propaganda. The V Campaign began with a broadcast in January 1941. Listeners to the BBC in Belgium were urged to carry out small acts of resistance or sabotage, such as painting or chalking V symbols on walls in public places. The campaign was the invention of an émigré Belgian BBC producer, Victor de Laveleye, 'a fairly tall, handsome man, with thick grey hair and a thin, almost hawk-like face'.[18] He chose the letter because it worked in both French – *Victoire*, victory – and in Flemish – *Vrijheid*, meaning freedom. The idea soon caught on not only in Belgium, but also in France and in the Netherlands, reinforced by further BBC broadcasts over the next few months. A thirty-six-year-old BBC editor, Douglas Ritchie, became the voice of the campaign as it developed, taking on the persona of 'Colonel Britton', who broadcast at midnight every Friday, urging resistance to the occupations, his words used again in broadcasts to Europe the following day. His voice was well-spoken and calm, almost soothing, telling his listeners that the night was their friend and the V was their sign. The V symbol became a musical signal as well. The three dots and a dash of a V in Morse code, represented by the opening notes of Beethoven's

Fifth Symphony, were regularly used in broadcasts from June onwards. The musical V became the recognisable identity of the European Service from that time onwards.

The V Campaign was one of British propaganda's best-known creations, and the V symbol itself would survive in the public imagination long after the war was over. At first, it was a BBC initiative alone. As the government began to get to grips with how best to use propaganda assertively, the rival government ministries wanted to assert more control over what the BBC might be telling the populations of occupied Europe to do on Britain's behalf.

The European Service and its staff had a close call on the night of 10 May 1941, the worst night of the Blitz. That night, the bombs hit many of Britain's most important institutions, including the Houses of Parliament and Westminster Abbey. St Clement Danes church, just across the road on the Strand from Bush House, was directly hit by an incendiary bomb which penetrated the church's lead-covered roof and exploded within the roof space. Not wanting to leave Bush House during the raid to go home, Elisabeth Barker and her secretary found what seemed to be a relatively safe place to sleep, deep underground in the building. They were woken suddenly in the middle of the night by a furious engineer who tripped over the two women. The engineer told them, 'This is where the emergency transmitter is', so they were kicked out of their hiding place in order that the transmitter could be switched on and broadcasting could continue.

St Clement Danes church was completely destroyed by the resulting fire, which burnt so fiercely that the fire brigade could not save the building. Once the all-clear was sounded, Barker and her secretary emerged into the morning, the destruction a strange contrast with the brightness of the day; 'a beautiful May morning and there were all the burnt leaves of hymn books from St Clement Danes coming down like sort of black smoke'.

Just over two weeks later, the V Campaign was put on a more formal footing. A committee was set up to manage how it would work and what its messages would be. Barker attended the first meeting of the committee at Bush House on 26 May. Then working for the BBC's Balkan section, she was moving into a position with influence over the BBC's white propaganda. The V Committee was a joint committee of the BBC and government; the Ministry of Economic Warfare sent a representative who was really from the secret SO1.

The BBC was clear that it was broadcasting propaganda and that the government would have a say in this. The first function of the V Committee, it was agreed at the meeting, was 'to broadcast propaganda of such a kind as to create the frame of mind in which our listeners will feel themselves part of a great army'.[19] They then planned to instruct this army to do things which were good for its own morale and bad for that of the Germans. They knew, though, that they had to proceed cautiously, so as to 'avoid causing alarm'.

There were, however, fundamental questions to be addressed about what the ultimate aim of this 'army' should be. Noel Newsome, the BBC's European news editor, raised an essential question in one of the V Committee meetings about what it was they were trying to do. 'Was London to be regarded as assuming direction and leadership in provoking resistance in the occupied territories?' he asked. 'Or was this resistance to be presented as a spontaneous reaction of Europe against the Germans?'[20] If it was the former, the governments in exile would also want some say in the matter. A spontaneous reaction might have been welcome news in London, but without any direction or defence, it was a dangerous project for the BBC's listeners to be involved in.

Some reservations were raised about the campaign within the BBC itself, and Barker was one of those who urged caution. 'Mentality and methods of resistance vary a great deal from country to country,' she wrote to Douglas Ritchie in early May 1941, even before the V Committee had started its formal work.[21] She suggested instead starting small, with individual 'exercises' that were targeted at particular countries and might already be happening there. Building up a 'European consciousness', she suggested, was risky. 'If we try to rush the "European consciousness"', she wrote, 'we might well fail, or at the most produce something rather artificial which might not stand up to the strain.'

By the summer of 1941, the V Campaign had come to wider attention. This culminated in a message from Churchill, delivered by Colonel Britton on 20 July, where he told listeners across Europe that the V sign was 'the symbol of the unconquerable will of the occupied territories', urging the audience that if they refused to collaborate with the invader, his 'cause will perish and that Europe will be liberated'.[22] The Germans noticed the effects of the campaign and, in response, tried to claim the V symbol for their own, playing out Beethoven from the radio stations they controlled and insisting over the airwaves that the V stood for Viktoria and represented German victory. Both the German government's official spokesman on the air, Hans Fritzsche, and Lord Haw-Haw (aka William Joyce), who broadcast from Germany in English, protested that the V symbol was Germany's invention. The symbol, Fritzsche said in July, had 'spread like an avalanche' across Europe.[23] Throughout the propaganda war, a response from the enemy was taken as a sign of a campaign's success. If they felt it necessary to respond, British propaganda had clearly found an audience who were listening and perhaps acting.

MPs had heard of the broadcasts too and wanted to discuss them in Parliament. Edgar Granville, a Liberal National MP, thought that the V movement 'may be the best opportunity we have had of smashing the Goebbels propaganda machine on the Continent'. He urged the Ministry of Information to work together with the Russians and Allied governments to give the V Campaign their support. Ernest Thurtle, the minister responding, was lukewarm in his reply, not promising any co-ordinated response from the government and saying only that the ministry was 'fully sympathetic' to the campaign and that it 'regards the V campaign as a sort of "Lift up your heart" signal to the oppressed peoples of Europe'.[24] He stopped short of saying that the government was encouraging people to resist.

This chimed with a sense that Colonel Britton, in July, had perhaps gone too far. At the V Committee's meeting on 21 July, after both Churchill and Britton had exhorted the V campaign, some members said that, in future, the colonel's talks should be 'less dramatic in tone and substance', less directed towards exciting an emotional response from listeners and instead suggesting small, practical tasks for them. An extraordinary meeting of the committee the following day heard concerns that previous policy had been not to create tension, 'raise false expectations' or lead people to expect dramatic action.

Subsequent broadcasts suggested more passive forms of resistance, which were intended to make life more difficult for the occupying German forces. In September 1941, the V Campaign promoted a 'Go Slow' day, using the symbol of a tortoise. Colonel Britton advised his listeners to get up late and take things deliberately easy. 'Eat your breakfast slowly. Walk slowly. Talk a lot and do little. Ask a lot of questions and don't listen to the answers. Tell your employer you want more money. And if you're asked to do something, do it wrong. Go slow in everything you do. This is your duty as a patriot.'[25] Intelligence reports that were passed on to the BBC suggested that the tortoise campaign was well-received by workers in Czechoslovakia, who scrawled tortoises on their factory walls, perhaps in the spirit of the fictional Czech anti-hero, the Good Soldier Švejk – the Austro-Hungarian soldier who specialised in dumb insolence.[26] Nonetheless, in Europe under German occupation, even these things could be dangerous for those who tried them. Britain was still far from being able to support any resistance movements directly.

While the V Campaign was well-known, it also divided opinion. The MP for Keighley, Ivor Thomas, in his book *Warfare by Words*, called it 'the one really brilliant idea that has emerged in British propaganda during the war'.[27] Thomas, who spent a year working at Woburn, held many grudges against his former colleagues there and was generally critical of the operation of propaganda during the early years of the war. Richard Crossman believed, in typically forthright and contrary manner, that the V Campaign, 'one of the early successes of British political warfare . . . was a catastrophe'.[28] It was successful, he argued, in that it reached a large number of people and induced them to act. It was disastrous because that call to action was not backed up by the imminent prospect of military force. Any invasion and second front was still years away. 'It created false hopes among our friends,' Crossman said. 'It made many of them do risky things and pay the penalty.'

In the heat of the sweltering summer of 1941, Robert Bruce Lockhart visited the BBC's basement offices to listen to the French programme. 'Conditions in which staff – especially editorial – work are terrible', he wrote in his diary. 'Forty to fifty feet below ground. No air-conditioning, too little space, and very indifferent ventilation.'[29] In Elisabeth Barker's recollection, the sweaty conditions that day had been deliberately exacerbated – there had been air-conditioning, but a member of staff had switched it off to make a point, so that the 'high-ups' would make representations that they needed more space and air. When the minister for economic warfare, Hugh Dalton, made another visit with Bruce Lockhart in September, he was even more appalled, calling the office the BBC's 'underground slum' and saying 'it is a *frightful* Hole of Calcutta; no ventilation and two dozen people in one not very large room'.[30] Dalton, who was given a rare headache from the stuffy newsroom, made representations to have the European Service moved. Accommodation aside, it was clear that at this key point in the war, the government wanted to establish more control over the overt, white propaganda that the BBC was putting out.

At the same time, Bruce Lockhart was attempting to recruit new staff from the BBC to work on the secret side of propaganda. Ralph Murray had joined the Woburn operation from the BBC early in the war, starting out as the second in command of the Balkans section.[31] He was charged with 'development of all forms of subversive propaganda' to his region. As the network of Freedom Stations expanded, they needed more experienced radio staff working with them, as well as people who understood the occupied nations. Elisabeth Barker could clearly do both. On 15 July, Murray wrote to Bruce Lockhart to ask for his help. There were plans to set up an underground radio station broadcasting to the Czechs, to supplement those already broadcasting to other countries. Barker was evidently well thought of among the Czechoslovaks in exile. Murray wrote to say that he had been speaking with a Dr D – presumably Dr Prokop Drtina, the private secretary to Edvard Beneš, the Czech president-in-exile. The Czechs, according to Murray, were 'warmly in favour of Miss B dealing with them over the question of the RU'. If Bruce Lockhart were discussing the question of a Czech RU with Beneš, Murray continued, 'I imagine he would have no objection if he knew his two officers were in favour.' Since Bruce Lockhart had a dual role in both propaganda and as the British representative to the Czech government, he was well-placed to influence this. Ralph Murray clearly thought Bruce Lockhart could also pull strings at the top of the BBC and asked him to take up Barker's recruitment with the director-general, Frederick Ogilvie. 'I do not know when you may see your way to asking Ogilvie whether he can release the lady

concerned; I hope very much he can on your personal intervention, because there is practically speaking no-one who
could handle the matter and be incidentally so useful.'[32] Soon,
Barker would escape the BBC's stuffy basement for the darker
side of propaganda in the greener surroundings of Woburn.

4

The Shooting War in Whitehall

Like so many successful politicians, Brendan Bracken
had the ability to make those he met feel like the centre
of the world, even if only for a minute. Bracken was
an unmistakeable presence. When he swept up to his fellow
Conservative MP Edward Spears in the lobby of the House
of Commons on 21 May 1940, Spears was immediately both
flattered and overwhelmed. 'Large, bespectacled, with shrewd
slit eyes in ambush behind thick lenses, a mass of red hair, the
thickness, shape and density of a wire mop, fitted on top of
his face like moss on a flat square stone, he caught me up in
the lobby, put his arm through mine, and giving the impression he was going on with a conversation, that is, a Brendan
conversation, a one-sided affair, something started 10 minutes
earlier which you were supposed to know the beginning of,
however recently scooped into the flow of words projected
as if under pressure through pursed lips, he said, as if he had
been listening to the voice of my spleen: "Winston has an
idea of making use of you. He has something important in
mind."' [1]

Although Brendan Bracken was instantly recognisable,
what exactly he did was harder to pin down. Spears wasn't even
sure what Bracken's job was, but knew that he worked closely
with the newly appointed prime minister, Winston Churchill,
who had only been in office for about ten days. Bracken fired
a barrage of compliments at Spears and followed up with a
rattle of questions about the state of French politics as the

country was about to collapse in defeat. Spears was still trying to formulate his answers when Bracken moved on to the next person he needed to talk to. 'His arm was locked into that of someone ahead, his conversation was going on in the same tone and at the same tempo with the new man who had been swept into it as I had been. The muffled resonance of his voice was in my ear, the bulky confidence he exuded was with me long after he had gone.'

Although Bracken himself might have been elusive, on this occasion his promise of an important job came good. This encounter was typical of the way he operated as a political fixer, a quality which made him indispensable to Churchill. Everyone knew who Brendan Bracken was; he, in turn, seemed to know everyone who mattered. Bracken, according to others who worked with Churchill, had an exhaustive knowledge of almost everyone in public life. Jock Colville, who was Churchill's young assistant private secretary, explained Bracken's popularity and his usefulness as being down to his friendliness, his pretended ruthlessness – Colville and others thought Bracken was not as ruthless as he claimed to be – and his 'ungrasping' nature, as well as his huge propensity to network.[2]

Bracken hadn't come by his network as many others in public life at that time had – through his family, school or university. He had acquired it through effort and assiduous study. He made a point of learning the names and backgrounds of potential appointees to countless official jobs, whether in politics, the Church or academia. Ronald Tree, a longstanding friend of his, was awed by Bracken's capacity for teaching himself. 'A life-long sufferer from insomnia, he was a prodigious reader, and having a retentive memory, had an encyclopaedic knowledge on many subjects, but particularly of the houses and churches of Britain.'[3]

Bracken's defining political relationship was with Winston Churchill. The two men first met when Bracken was only twenty-two, through J.L. Garvin, the editor of the *Observer*, who had taken Bracken under his wing. In 1923, Churchill, then forty-eight, had hit a low point politically, losing ministerial office and his parliamentary seat at the November 1922 election. Bracken believed, correctly, that his career would rise again. In his biographer Andrew Boyle's account, Bracken wrote to his mother that he had 'decided to hitch onto a political star – the name of the star is Winston Churchill'.[4] Bracken cultivated this friendship, in part, by being ever-present. He would turn up at the Churchills' London home in Sussex Square, and at Chartwell in Kent, where Churchill's wife Clementine commented that he 'appeared to arrive with the furniture – and he never left'.[5] He was described as one of Churchill's 'faithful chelas' – the followers of a guru. Bracken was there, often late at night, when Churchill wanted someone to drink with and to talk to, particularly when he was suffering with depression. Bracken won the seat of North Paddington in 1929 by just 500 votes and established himself as a Conservative MP.

In March 1939, Bracken wrote to his friend Lord Beaverbrook suggesting that he would join the armed forces in the event of war, explaining that 'as I am what is called an able-bodied man my duty in times of war must be to go off with the soldiers'.[6] That would have been unlikely for the ungainly and short-sighted Bracken, who was nearly forty – and he admitted he would have made an incompetent warrior. Instead, he stayed in politics and tied himself even more closely to Churchill.

When Churchill came back into government, Bracken was at his side as parliamentary private secretary. He may have made many political friends, but this didn't make him popular within the Conservative Party with the supporters of Chamberlain and appeasement. Some of them downright despised him. Nancy Dugdale, wife of the MP Thomas Dugdale, wrote to her husband bemoaning that 'reptile satellites' like Bracken would join the government and 'ooze into jobs they are utterly unfitted for'.[7] She passed on a gossipy conversation where the participants made insinuations about Bracken's appointment, 'for what services rendered heaven knows'.[8]

But when Churchill wanted to promote Bracken to become a member of the Privy Council, he was willing to defend him against resistance from the highest levels of the state. Being appointed a Privy Counsellor would mean that Bracken had access to the most important and confidential information in government. The foreign secretary, Lord Halifax, went so far as to raise objections to the appointment with the king. Halifax felt Bracken hadn't earned the privilege. Churchill wrote to the king defending Bracken as one of his loyal supporters. He explained that had Bracken 'joined the ranks of the time-servers and careerists . . . I have no doubt he would have attained high office'.[9] This was a clear sideswipe at those who, like Halifax, had formed part of the Chamberlain government. The royal household backed down.

One of Bracken's many useful skills was resolving a crisis. On 14 October 1940, as Robert Bruce Lockhart was picking his way through the debris of St James's in search of a consoling whisky, Bracken, according to one account, was putting on a tin hat in Westminster and venturing through the blackout to Downing Street to inspect the bomb damage there. Churchill recalled a 'providential impulse' that had occurred to him as he was being served dinner that led him to tell his cook, Mrs Landemare, and other servants to get into the air-raid shelter shortly before the bomb hit. The huge plate-glass window of the Number 10 kitchen was shattered in a blast about three minutes later.[10] That bomb landed on Treasury Green – what is now the Downing Street Garden – where three civil servants who were on Home Guard duty in the bomb shelter there were killed. Churchill wrote that they were 'buried under tons of brick rubble'. The Treasury, then immediately behind

Downing Street, was also struck in the blast, which caused serious damage to the building.[11]

Once Bracken was on the scene, he reportedly acted with 'instinctive compassion' for the casualties, found out about their lives and their families, then contacted the bereaved families of the low-paid, married men and organised generous pensions from the Treasury.[12] But there's little other evidence for this story, which casts Bracken in a sympathetic light. In another version, he was unlikely to have been at his own house to hear the bombs fall, since in September 1940 he had 'closed up his window-shattered home in Lord North Street', sent his servants and his possessions to a house in rural Wiltshire, and moved himself into 10 Downing Street.[13] Churchill doesn't mention Bracken's presence in his account of the evening – but then Churchill omits any mention of him by name in that volume of his book, even though Bracken was often at his side.

Jock Colville did recall him having been present in Downing Street in the aftermath of a bombing, but that was on a separate occasion, two days later, when the two men inspected the basement and refuges at Number 11. On 17 October, Colville recorded that four members of the Home Guard had been killed at the Treasury, calling it a 'second hit within four days in almost the same place'.[14] Colville and Bracken, discussing this, agreed that it was only a question of days before Number 10 fell a victim to a similar hit. It's possible, of course, that those recording their memories of this intense time confused these incidents, but the story is never as simple, with Bracken, as in the first telling.

While Bracken could be helpful to those in his circle, he was also reluctant to let a feud go once he had begun it. He came into conflict with Hugh Dalton almost as soon as the two men were both in positions of power. Bracken disliked Dalton intensely; the feeling was mutual. Dalton constantly suspected Churchill's friends and allies, whom he referred to as the 'Camarilla' – a word derived from the Spanish for a scheming group of courtiers – of briefing against him. His suspicions were often right. Bracken, as a key member of that court, was someone that Dalton frequently ran up against.

One of the reasons they came into conflict was Bracken's love of getting his preferred people into key jobs. Dalton liked to do the same thing and they rarely agreed on the choice. The pair bumped heads with each other in part because they had certain similarities. They were both effusive, loud and physically large presences – welcome to some, deeply irritating to others. But they came from very different backgrounds, both socially and politically. Bracken was a self-created and self-made Tory; Dalton came from a comfortable background – a father in the Church, educated at Eton and Cambridge – but was a socialist. Dalton's biographer Ben Pimlott noted the similarities between the two. 'Bracken was a genial bully, a bestower of cruel nicknames, a fixer, a climber (not a social but an "important-person" climber, according to one friend)'.[15] Dalton, too, was seen as bullying.

The arguments between the two men often happened in the full view of colleagues. In November 1940, they squared off against each other outside the Cabinet Room in 10 Downing Street. This row had been brewing since September, when Dalton decided to demote Major Lawrence Grand from his position as the head of Section D, SOE's intelligence forerunner, where he was charged with developing plans for sabotage. Major Grand, a suave, elegant, moustachioed figure, may have 'exuded an air of mystery' from his headquarters in the St Ermin's Hotel, but Dalton believed he was disloyal and dishonest.[16] Grand claimed that he had the backing of influential figures and wanted his case to be raised at Cabinet level. Bracken was one of those who had supported Grand. When he ran into Dalton, Bracken exclaimed: 'There is that great brute who, like his friend Mr Bevin, tramples all opposition in the mud. He has no liberal sentiments at all!' Bracken then wound up Dalton further, telling him that rumours were going around that Dalton's treatment of Grand had been an outrage and threatening to tell Churchill this. Dalton, who rarely failed to take Bracken's bait, retorted: 'Whatever I have been, I have never been a Liberal!'[17] Despite having been so irritated, Dalton felt, with his habitual vanity, that he had the better of Bracken and had come across as a 'strong man'.

In the same November week that Dalton faced off against Bracken outside Cabinet, he was also picking a fight with Alfred Duff Cooper, the minister of information. Dalton accused Duff Cooper's department of 'poaching' and stealing his leaflets. What he meant was that Duff Cooper had been discussing plans to drop leaflets over France with the foreign secretary, without Dalton's knowledge. This became a fundamental disagreement about which ministry should take charge of propaganda, an issue that was raised with the prime minister.[18] Leaflets to be dropped abroad, Dalton maintained, were his department's responsibility. He was even more keen to retain control over radio broadcasting, something he thought was more important to the propaganda war.

In December, Desmond Morton, the PM's aide, who had listened to both sides, summed up the argument. On the one hand, 'Dr Dalton suggests that he should take over all broadcasting to enemy countries, since he already controls *secret* broadcasts and leaflets.' Duff Cooper's contention was precisely the opposite: that 'all foreign propaganda whether directed to enemy or neutral countries and whether conducted by radio, leaflets, the Press or through any other means should be controlled by one Department only'.[19] Duff Cooper, of course, believed that department should be the Ministry of Information, and the Ministry of Economic Warfare should just be left with projects for bribery or sabotage.

Previous ministers of information had come and gone quickly during the course of the war. Duff Cooper, an urbane and charming man with a taste for the high life – he was often described as a 'bon viveur' due to his taste for wine, women and gambling – had been given the job in the incoming Churchill administration in the expectation that his reputation as an 'excellent speaker and an effective broadcaster' would see him through.[20] Duff Cooper was, however, finding the job challenging. Dalton himself admitted, with some understatement, that his relations with Duff Cooper were 'sometimes rough', while those with Bracken were 'often stormy'.[21]

This wasn't just an administrative squabble. The reason the argument crossed the prime minister's desk was that it was a row about the political control of British propaganda.

Since Dalton and the Ministry of Economic Warfare still had responsibility for sabotage and for operations behind enemy lines, lives were at stake as well. Dalton's biographer, Ben Pimlott, pointed out the contrast. Whereas, he said, for SO2, 'the shooting war was in the field', for SO1, the propaganda side of operations, that shooting war was in Whitehall. No-one may actually have died in Westminster as a result, but the fighting was nonetheless vicious.

Churchill's adviser Desmond Morton tended to agree with Duff Cooper's suggestion that the Ministry of Information should take charge, but politically this was a tricky argument, and Dalton was going to fight for his territory. Any decision which shifted the balance of responsibility between a Labour Cabinet minister, Dalton, and a Conservative one, Duff Cooper, was likely to cause ructions in Cabinet.

Churchill decided to delegate handling the row, asking Sir John Anderson, the lord president of the council, who was in charge of a key Cabinet committee, to look into the dispute.[22] At this point, Anderson essentially left it to the squabbling pair to attempt to sort things out between themselves. As he wrote later, 'the two ministers believed that it would be possible for them to reconcile their differences'. This meant there was a temporary lull in the fighting in the new year of 1941, but Anderson's was a false hope. Desmond

Morton confided in Robert Bruce Lockhart about the prime minister's attitude to the dispute. Churchill, Morton said, 'liked Duff but knew he had failed' as minister of information and didn't wish to see him, but Dalton bored him – 'and no man wants to see bores'.[23] It was little surprise, then, that the PM held the two at arm's length.

Dalton's next skirmish, this time with Brendan Bracken, began in the faded splendour of the Carlton Grill. The Grill was the basement restaurant of a hotel on the corner of Haymarket and Pall Mall, near Trafalgar Square, where Auguste Escoffier had once been the chef. The hotel had been damaged by bombing a couple of months earlier and its guest rooms closed, but the restaurant remained popular in the political world. On 20 February 1941, Dalton wrote in his diary that he had heard that some 'not flattering' things had been said about him at a recent lunch party. 'Someone had complained,' he wrote, 'that I am sometimes too assertive in the Cabinet.'[24] In the margin, he elaborated: 'Bracken had been abusing me loudly in the Carlton Grill at lunch.' Bracken's fellow diners were Rex Fletcher and Tommy Davies. Fletcher was a Labour MP and former naval officer, and Davies was an intelligence officer responsible for training SOE agents. Bracken shouldn't have been surprised, then, that his conversation immediately got back to Dalton. Dalton went straight to see the Labour leader Clement Attlee that afternoon to complain about what he saw as 'anti-Labour intrigue'.

But this wasn't enough for Dalton; he wanted to find out more. He had Fletcher over to dinner, plied him with drink until he was 'rather tight', and got him to sign an account of Bracken's conversation that Davies had helpfully written down. Fletcher suspected Bracken, in Dalton's version, of being 'violently' anti-Labour. Although Attlee raised the issue with Churchill, and the prime minister was, Attlee told Dalton, 'very angry' and had told Bracken off, Bracken was undeterred.

The simmering anger between Dalton and Duff Cooper boiled over again just six weeks later. The two ministers' criticisms of each other flared up when the Ministry of Information asked whether leaflets dropped abroad could be made public. Dalton insisted that his department was secret, and so were its leaflets. Duff Cooper aggravated the situation, in Dalton's view, by saying that the creation of the Country House – Woburn – was 'a profound error'. He felt the occupants of the secret Country HQ weren't co-operating with the Ministry of Information and that his senior civil servant was 'obliged to make a weekly pilgrimage into the country' to talk to his counterparts, with little result.[25]

The suggestion that the Woburn operation was a mistake was a threat to Dalton, who hit back. It was Duff Cooper's ministry which was uncooperative, he believed. But if Duff Cooper had complaints about the Ministry of Economic Warfare, Dalton argued, he should bring those directly to him as the minister and not rely on officials. The back and forth of letters between the ministers continued for a week, with each man needling his opposite number still further.

Pushed again by Dalton to say directly, rather than through civil servants, what his problem was with SO 1's propaganda, Duff Cooper let loose. Dalton's leaflets, he wrote, were 'utterly deplorable . . . One is a revolting picture of a dead child, who might for all we know just as well be a German child killed inadvertently by the RAF as a child of any other country. The picture itself is disgusting and the reproduction of it suggests a thoroughly macabre and Hunnish mentality.'[26]

Duff Cooper insisted that 'pictures of horror and stories of atrocities are not good propaganda'. Ever since the First World War, British propaganda had often been criticised for relying too much on tales of German atrocities which were sometimes untrue. Many believed that this had contributed to resentment and hatred within Germany after the war. Dalton responded that such leaflets were good for attacking German morale and that, in any case, he had Churchill's support, writing: 'The Prime Minister has instructed me to do our leaflet work in close concert with him.'[27]

In Duff Cooper's letter complaining about the use of atrocities as propaganda, he gave a glimpse of his underlying grievances. It wasn't just the nature of Dalton's leaflets or the existence of Woburn. He said that in future, broadcasts to Germany 'shall all be directed from this Ministry'.

This was the crux of the dispute: Duff Cooper wanted the Ministry of Information to have complete control over broadcasts in German and in other languages. Dalton was equally determined that secret broadcasts, which included the RUs and black propaganda, should be run by the Ministry of Economic Warfare, together with other forms of subversion. He believed that secret operations could not be run effectively by a department whose main task was publicity. It was clear that, whoever was in charge of the Ministry of Information, Dalton would want to retain the secret territory of his 'black life'.

Dalton found it 'impossible' that Duff Cooper wanted to create his own German section within the Ministry of Information to rival that at Woburn. Worse, Duff Cooper wanted to hire Freddy Voigt, Crossman's nemesis, to work in his ministry. Dalton wrote back that he doubted whether Duff Cooper 'would find Voigt very satisfactory', but said he wouldn't put his reasons for that belief in writing. Crossman, however, he said, was 'first class', and Dalton was insistent that, as one of his 'personal selections', it was essential that Crossman stayed with his own department.

This kind of internal feuding clearly wasn't sustainable. As the war of words escalated between the two ministers, one civil servant at the Ministry of Information warned the Privy Council Office, which dealt with government disagreements: 'I ought to let you know that things are boiling up between my Minister and the Minister of Economic Warfare.' Cooper and

Dalton were summoned to a meeting with Sir John Anderson, the lord president of the council, on 16 May, in order for him to bash their heads together. Dalton was warned ahead of the meeting not to lose his temper with Duff Cooper, even if the other minister did so first.[28]

In the week before that meeting, the war seemed very close to Westminster. Squabbles between ministers might have seemed less important, but Dalton, with his usual arrogance, continued to pursue his rivalries and seemed little concerned for the sufferings of others. On the weekend of 10–11 May, he returned from Woburn to witness the aftermath of the bombing of the Houses of Parliament. Smoke was still hanging in the air, the streets 'full of broken glass and charred bits of paper'. On the Sunday afternoon, Dalton went to look at the devastation of the Commons chamber, which was completely gutted. What had once been the entrance to the Members' Lobby was open to the sky, 'a great mass of broken bricks, twisted iron and charred bits of wood'. He recorded: 'I clamber about among the rubble with my nose full of the smell of burnt wood, and watch firemen still leisurely playing their hoses on some smoking debris. The Members' lavatory in the old Aye Lobby is still intact. Therefore, as a last gesture, I enter and relieve nature. Then we depart.'[29]

Dalton had called in to check on his flat in Carlisle Mansions, just behind Westminster Cathedral. His home had narrowly escaped a direct hit, but nearby buildings had been struck. He remarked offhandedly that 'an incendiary bomb has burned out the top flat immediately opposite mine. This will improve my view.' He showed a striking lack of concern for the safety of his wife, Ruth, who had been staying in the fourth-floor flat alone.[30] Although the couple had increasingly been living separate lives, Dalton did not even think to ask about his wife, with friends reporting instead that he had been more worried about the safety of his new suits. Ruth took this as final confirmation that Hugh scarcely noticed her existence, and although it took her several months to leave him and London for war work elsewhere, the couple did not live together again for the rest of the war.

As Dalton was tramping through the ruins of the Houses of Parliament, he had not yet had word of the series of bizarre and unexplained events taking place in Scotland and the English countryside which would have an unexpected impact on the direction of British propaganda.

5

This Strange Bird of Good Omen

The weekend of 10–11 May 1941 saw a full moon. In London, that meant it was one of the heaviest periods of bombing of the Blitz, during which the capital was severely hit, with 1,400 Londoners losing their lives. For Winston Churchill, the prospect of a moonlit weekend meant that he would leave Downing Street for the relative safety of Ditchley Park, an eighteenth-century Palladian mansion in Oxfordshire. The house was owned by the Anglo-American Conservative MP Ronnie Tree and his wife Nancy. The prime minister first invited himself to stay for certain weekends 'when the moon was high' in November 1940. Tree recalled the PM investing the phrase with 'mystery and poetry'.[1] Tree was a junior minister to Duff Cooper at the Ministry of Information and could hardly refuse to host his political superiors. The Oxfordshire countryside was deemed to be far safer for Churchill on days when a clear sky and a bright moon made London more vulnerable to bombing; the location of the prime minister's country residence at Chequers in Buckinghamshire was too well known and an obvious target.

Although the Trees were used to playing host to prominent guests from politics and society, having bought their twenty-four-bedroom house with three thousand acres of land in 1933, accommodating the wartime prime minister required both hospitality and security on a different scale. Churchill came with an entourage of friends, family and staff: secretaries set to work and a phone system and scrambler were put in, while a company of local light infantry was posted around the house. Brendan Bracken would almost always be among the group. Tree had the idea of organising for films to be screened at the house and he was able to arrange for the Ministry of Information's film unit to send both a recent film and an operator to show it.

Even though there was a frenzy of activity around Churchill's arrival, the prime minister himself was far less active on these weekends. On reaching the country late on a Friday afternoon, he would have a drink – either a whisky or a cup of tea – before retiring to bed until it was time for dinner. Only after dinner and champagne would Churchill hit his stride, staying up until the early hours drinking and talking, as Tree recalled, 'having exhausted his entourage, who had not, like him, had an afternoon's sleep'. The following day, Churchill would eat a cooked breakfast in bed, but not get up until lunchtime, instead reading newspapers or working on his ministerial boxes. The same pattern would be repeated on both Sunday and Monday. Churchill would almost never go outdoors, only walking around the house's Italian garden on one or two occasions. But on this weekend, Churchill's usual leisurely routine was disturbed not by the flights of bombers, but by news of an unexpected visitor to the country.

His assistant private secretary, Jock Colville, had remained in London and was on duty on Sunday. Walking through the city after the air raids, Colville observed that what 'should have been a perfect May morning' was marred by a low cloud of smoke over the town and 'because a warehouse full of paper had been among the night's casualties, small flakes of paper were falling from heaven for all the world as if it were snowing'.[2] It was the same scene that Elisabeth Barker had observed a little further east as she emerged from Bush House to witness the destruction of St Clement Danes, and the same that Hugh Dalton had seen. Colville made his way past the burning House of Commons, through the devastation of

Whitehall. He was astonished that Downing Street had not 'collapsed like a pack of cards'. Colville attended a service at St Faith's chapel in Westminster Abbey, which was crowded with worshippers, even though the abbey had itself been hit.

In the late morning, Colville went to the Foreign Office, expecting to catch up on gossip with Anthony Eden's private secretary, Nicholas Lawford, Colville's counterpart.[3] When Colville arrived, his friend Lawford was on the phone. He heard him tell the caller that Colville should hear what he had to say. Before handing over the phone, Lawford held his hand over the receiver and explained:

'This may be a lunatic. He says he is the Duke of Hamilton, that something extraordinary has happened, that he is about to fly down from Scotland to Northolt and that he wants to be met there by Alec Cadogan and the Prime Minister's Secretary.'[4]

Lawford, not sure whether his mystery caller was insane, was reluctant to bother his boss, Sir Alec Cadogan, the most senior civil servant in the Foreign Office, on what was one of Cadogan's first days off in months. Lawford said that the person who claimed to be the duke had mentioned that the series of events unfolding was like an E. Phillips Oppenheim thriller. E. Phillips Oppenheim was an extraordinarily prolific thriller-writer, whose books included spies, mistaken identities and doppelgängers. By coincidence, as he woke from a broken night's sleep, disturbed by the crash of bombs, Colville had just been thinking about a similar recent book by Peter Fleming, in which the author imagined Hitler flying into London. 'Has somebody arrived?' Colville asked the man on the phone. There was a long pause before the presumed duke said 'Yes' and asked Colville to meet him at Northolt.

Eventually, the man on the phone managed to convince the officials that he was, in fact, the Duke of Hamilton. The duke remembered the conversation as a 'tremendous argument' during which he was disbelieved, put off and told that he should not, as a low-ranking member of the RAF, 'a mere Wing Commander', be trying to reach the head of the Foreign Office on a Sunday morning. Cadogan, Hamilton was told, was 'an extremely busy man' who might possibly see him the next day.[5]

Once the officials were satisfied that they were in fact speaking to the Duke of Hamilton and not an impostor, Colville decided that he should tell the prime minister at Ditchley. Colville still didn't know who had arrived, as Hamilton had refused to tell him. When Churchill asked him 'It can't be Hitler?' Colville replied that he imagined not.

The Duke of Hamilton had been on RAF duty at Turnhouse airbase near Edinburgh late on Saturday night when he was first alerted to the mysterious visitor. He was told that a German pilot had bailed out of his aircraft over the west of Scotland and had been aiming to land at Hamilton's estate, Dungavel House. By Sunday morning, the pilot was in the hands of the Glasgow police and insisting that he needed to speak to the duke. The pilot gave his name to the police as Captain Horn. After driving to Glasgow to meet the captive, Hamilton resolved to fly to London to inform the prime minister. By late afternoon, someone had decided it was worth disturbing Sir Alec Cadogan's Sunday at his cottage and called to tell him that Hamilton was flying south from Scotland.

At this point, recollections of the exact sequence of events begin to differ. In Churchill's account, he was brought the news by Brendan Bracken. They had been watching a Marx Brothers comedy in a darkened sitting room at Ditchley when the film was interrupted by a phone call. Told that the matter was of 'Cabinet importance', he sent Bracken to answer the phone. Bracken returned, saying: 'This is going to amaze you – Rudolf Hess has landed by parachute in Scotland.'[6] Churchill was unmoved, reportedly muttering, 'Hess or no Hess, I'm going to watch the Marx Brothers.'

This was a remarkably sanguine reaction for a prime minister who had just been told that one of the most senior men in Nazi Germany might have landed in his own country. Rudolf Hess was nominally the third in charge of Germany – after Hitler and Hermann Goering, the head of the Luftwaffe – and was deputy leader of the party and deputy führer. He had been one of Hitler's earliest and closest supporters. If true, this was significant.

The Duke of Hamilton remembered it differently, having just flown down through Blitz skies and already exhausted.[7] When he landed at Kidlington airfield in Oxfordshire, it was dark and he was driven to Ditchley, about twelve miles away, to be greeted by a 'very pompous and smart butler'. The duke was scruffy and exhausted. 'My appearance could be better imagined than described when I tell you that I had had no sleep, or practically no sleep, for four nights and had just finished a rather arduous journey from Scotland to Southern England.'[8]

Shown into the dining room to meet the prime minister and his other gentlemen guests at dinner, Hamilton found Churchill was taking the whole issue rather flippantly. 'The Prime Minister was in tremendous form. He was cracking jokes the whole time and ordered me in a rather light-hearted fashion – "Now, come and tell us this funny story of yours." I told him that I thought I had better give him the information in private.' Hamilton explained the situation to Churchill and Sir Archibald Sinclair, the secretary of state for air, who was also present. One version had Churchill indignant at being disturbed by what he believed to be a 'cock-and-bull' account.

The first and most pressing problem was whether the uninvited German visitor was really who he claimed to be. According to Ivone Kirkpatrick, who met the pilot over the next few days, 'Captain Horn' had declared, once Hamilton was ushered in to see him in a Glasgow hospital, 'I am Reichsminister Hess'. Hamilton said that since he had never met Hess, he could not know. 'Hess' believed that he could prove who he really was.

'He opened a pocket-book and extracted from its folds a snapshot of himself with a small boy on his knee. "There you are," he said triumphantly, "you can see that this is a picture of me." Hamilton replied that he could see that the photograph was indeed a picture of the prisoner, but that he had no evidence that it was a picture of Hess. "I never thought of that," said Captain Horn in a dejected tone.'[9]

Hamilton showed the picture to Churchill and Sinclair. Although they agreed that the photo did resemble Hess, neither minister could be absolutely sure. Hamilton wrote: 'I had taken pictures from the prisoner's wallet and assured him that those were portraits of the German whom I had interviewed in the morning but whether the man was Hess or not was still very uncertain.'

Hamilton was cut short, as in his recollection, the prime minister was still 'somewhat impatient' to see his Marx Brothers film. Once the film was finished, Hamilton had to repeat his story, this time in greater detail. He was put up at Ditchley for the night. The other weekend guests were, officially at least, told little of what was going on. All that Nancy Tree, the hostess, knew was that the Duke of Hamilton had been a guest on Sunday night. She had been mystified; all Churchill would say was that 'truth is sometimes stranger than fiction'.

The foreign secretary, Anthony Eden, was brought into the secret on Sunday night and, on Monday morning, Churchill returned with Hamilton to Downing Street. The search was on for someone who could definitively identify Hess, if Captain Horn was who he claimed to be. Despite Hess's importance in Germany, few in Britain had met him face to face.

Hamilton had to repeat his story several times in meetings at Downing Street and the Foreign Office. While the officials needed urgently to find someone who knew Hess, at the same time they didn't want the secret of the landing to spread around Whitehall. As Eden was on his way into Cabinet, he asked Alec Cadogan whether he knew anyone who would be able to recognise Hess, to rule out the man being an impostor or a deliberately planted doppelgänger.

Cadogan made a call to Ivone Kirkpatrick at the BBC. Kirkpatrick was a diplomat who had plenty of experience in propaganda. A First World War veteran, he had been shot twice at Gallipoli as he fought his way up Kiretch Tepe ridge and was so close to death that he was given the last rites. He had just survived another near-death experience, closer to home: a couple of months earlier, he had been hit by a car which mounted the pavement in St James's Street and ran him over. After a month off work, Kirkpatrick had begun a new job at the BBC, where he had been appointed foreign affairs adviser, the corporation's liaison with the government. Friends called him a brave and forthright man, with 'the wiry resilience of the physically diminutive', who was 'quick-witted and sure-footed like a mountain animal'.[10] Kirkpatrick knew Germany well. After a posting in Rome at the start of the 1930s, he had moved to Berlin in 1933. As head of chancery at the British Embassy, he had built up good contacts in the country. Most importantly, he had met Rudolf Hess.

Cadogan's first question to Kirkpatrick was whether he knew Hess. Kirkpatrick said that he did. Cadogan's second question seemed stranger: 'he then enquired whether I would recognise him with certainty if I saw him. This seemed to me an odd question, but I assured Cadogan that I knew Hess well and could not possibly fail to recognise him if I saw him.'[11] Kirkpatrick was summoned to the Foreign Office, where Cadogan repeated his questions face-to-face. After Cabinet, the foreign secretary Anthony Eden wanted to meet Kirkpatrick. He wanted to know who the man was, but also told Kirkpatrick not to get involved in any long discussions with him. The instructions were to identify the prisoner, report the identification and take note of any statement that the purported Hess might make. Kirkpatrick started to have a few qualms about being taken in by a hoaxer. Cadogan also consulted 'C', the head of the Secret Intelligence Service, about sending Kirkpatrick to Scotland. C, Sir Stewart Menzies, agreed he should go.[12]

The next problem was getting to Scotland to see the prisoner. All of the arrangements were taking a long time. Hamilton recalled Kirkpatrick's sardonic tone at the meeting in the afternoon; after Kirkpatrick had mentioned that Hess was the third most powerful man in Germany, he suggested that 'Mr Eden, being the third most powerful man in Britain, could get us an aeroplane so that the Foreign Office man and myself could go to Scotland and identify the man's identity completely'.[13]

The plane that was eventually found was a slow one that couldn't reach Turnhouse (then a military base, now the modern-day Edinburgh Airport) without refuelling. It was after five in the afternoon before they flew from Hendon and, battling headwinds, didn't reach Edinburgh until 9.40 at night, almost forty-eight hours since the supposed Hess had landed. Kirkpatrick and Hamilton had just sat down to eat a steak when Eden phoned them at the airport, insisting they had to leave immediately and couldn't have even twenty minutes to eat their dinner.

This sudden urgency was because the news was out. While Kirkpatrick and Hamilton were in the air, German radio had announced that Hess was missing. It reported that he had taken a plane without permission as he had been banned from flying due to 'an illness of some years' standing'. The German statement said that Hess had shown 'mental disorder' and that it was 'feared that he was a victim of hallucinations' – but it insisted that his departure would have no effect on the continuance of the war. A report based on this was also broadcast on the BBC news.

By 10.45 that evening, Eden had a copy of the German announcement. He and Cadogan went to see Churchill in the Cabinet War Rooms to discuss what the British government should say in reply. Cadogan was exasperated: Churchill's proposed text said that Hess had come 'in the name of humanity'. 'This won't do,' Cadogan wrote in his diary the next evening, having started out saying that 'in all the years I have kept this beastly diary I have never been so hard pressed'. Churchill's statement wouldn't do, he thought, because it 'looks like a peace offer, and we may want to run the line that he has quarrelled with Hitler'.

Having got lost in the dark on the way, it was midnight before Kirkpatrick and Hamilton arrived at Buchanan Castle, the military hospital where the pilot was held. They found the prisoner in a servant's bedroom beneath the eaves, where he was sleeping in grey flannel military-issue pyjamas on an iron bedstead. When Kirkpatrick and Hamilton woke him, he recognised the former 'after a moment of dazed uncertainty'. If Kirkpatrick still had any residual doubt that this was really Hess, it was dispelled when Hess drew out his packet of manuscript notes and, in Hamilton's description, 'launched immediately into a harangue in German'.

The harangue was still going on an hour later when Eden had a call put through to ask whether Kirkpatrick could identify Hess. He left the room to tell the foreign secretary that he was sure they had the right man. Hess still didn't stop talking. He kept up his tirade until about four in the morning, interrupted occasionally by Kirkpatrick who was trying to establish what he actually wanted. Hess claimed that his aim was to convince the British government of 'the inevitability of a German victory' and to bring about a peace by negotiation. When Hess eventually stopped his monologue, Kirkpatrick and Hamilton retired and finally managed to get something to eat — a plate of scrambled eggs.

At twenty past eleven on Monday night, Downing Street put out its statement on Hess's landing; Tuesday morning's *Times* ran the statement in full.[14] The statement set out how Hess's Messerschmitt had crossed into Scotland and crashed near Glasgow, saying that he had brought photographs of himself that were 'deemed to be' of Hess, and that 'an officer of the Foreign Office who was closely acquainted with Hess before the war had been sent up by aeroplane to see him in hospital'. An update beneath the statement added: 'At 2 o'clock this morning the Ministry of Information stated that the identity of the man who landed from a Messerschmitt in Scotland as Rudolf Hess has now been established beyond all possible doubt.' *Times* readers could also learn about Hess's background, the German statement on his departure and some local colour from the paper's correspondent in Glasgow. The reporter had interviewed the ploughman, David McLean, who had found the unarmed but injured Hess and taken him to his farmhouse while waiting to hand his captive over to the Home Guard. McLean told reporters that Hess 'refused tea but asked for a drink of water'.

The story was running in the papers just as prominently as the bombing of Westminster over the weekend. The German government, however, had given a far more extensive statement – no matter how much more misleading – than the British had done. The news, and the details, had spread so quickly in fact that Ivone Kirkpatrick, while settling down to his 4am breakfast at Buchanan Castle, was told that the BBC had turned up asking for an interview. 'A BBC recording van arrived at the castle door and demanded alternatively a recording by Hess or one by myself. It was sad not to be able to reward such enterprise.'

In Germany, Goebbels was initially worried about what Britain might say in response – and what Rudolf Hess might have told them. Privately, he had his own criticisms of the statement that had been put out over German radio announcing Hess's flight. If he was as deluded as the statement suggested, Goebbels wondered, would people not wonder why he had been allowed to remain the führer's deputy?[15] Over the next few days, as the British government declined to say much more about what had happened, Goebbels became less anxious.

The Ministry of Information, however, was keen to get Britain's version of events into the news. Ronald Tree's view was that Britain had failed to take advantage of a huge propaganda opportunity because of the delay in getting to Hess. 'There was considerable criticism in Britain that we had missed what could have been one of the great propaganda coups of the war. There was a simple reason why we failed to make it so; it was impossible at a few hours' notice to find anyone who could identify Hess.'

It wasn't quite as simple as Tree suggested. There was also disagreement at the top of government as to whether, and how, to exploit Hess as part of British propaganda to Germany. It would be better, the propagandists believed, to give more information about Hess and to suggest that he had fled to Britain because he believed Germany could no longer win the war. Suggestions that he had come to pursue peace, or that he had come because he was not in his right mind, were less helpful for Britain.

Harold Nicolson, the parliamentary secretary at the Ministry of Information, shared the opinion that Hess's escape was an enormously precious propaganda gift to Britain. In a memo on the Tuesday, he wrote: 'Whatever value Hess may be as a prisoner of war, he is fifty times more value as a propaganda-carrier. He ought to be our bird before he is anyone else's bird. And we will have to think very hard and long, and consult all concerned, as to how on earth we are to treat this strange bird of good omen who has dropped into our midst.'[16]

The ministry's internal discussions were becoming more frantic as time went by and they couldn't satisfy the journalists' appetite for news. Nicolson said that he had consulted Rex Leeper, Noel Newsome at the BBC, Valentine Williams of SO1 and William Ridsdale, the head of the news department at the Foreign Office, and that they had largely agreed on the line to take. They agreed to focus on four points: 'a) Hess is sane b) Exposure of German facts and ridicule of same c) details regarding Hess' hospital life d) Quotations from the Minister's speech today and the Prime Minister's reply in the House.'

The agreement on a common line, Nicolson thought, was more 'due to luck and the native intelligence of those concerned' than to good staff work. But he argued that the line wouldn't hold for much longer: journalists could be 'held on the bedchamber stories' – urged to write colourful details about Hess's treatment in Scotland – for only about twelve hours more, 'but after that we must put out something regarding the attitude of the Government to this exile'.

The ministry officials weren't able to handle the story in the way they normally would, by dealing directly with journalists, because it was so politically and militarily sensitive. Every decision had to be referred to the highest levels and this took up even more time. When the Ministry of Information asked for still and newsreel pictures of Hess to be taken, in order to prove that he was in captivity in Britain, the response from the War Office was 'Don't be fools, this is a Cabinet matter.'[17] The ministry was insistent that the photos had to show both Hess and his Scottish surroundings, for the avoidance of doubt. A handwritten note in the file mentions that Duff Cooper, Anthony Eden and Cyril Radcliffe, the most senior civil servant at the Ministry of Information, were to see the PM that afternoon, on Wednesday the 14th, and photographs would be discussed.

As the minister of information, Duff Cooper wrote to Churchill accordingly on Thursday, setting out what he wanted: 'I should like to have your approval of sending a photographer to Scotland to take some pictures of the Deputy Führer. Whether it might prove desirable to publish pictures or no can be decided later, but I do not think it can do any harm to have the pictures in our possession.' He said that the photographer would be instructed 'not to present the subject in too flattering a light'. He added another reason that photos of Hess might come in useful. 'Incidentally, if he were to escape, an unlikely but not impossible occurrence, recent pictures of him might be of great value.' However, by 18 June, Duff Cooper told Parliament that no such photos had yet been taken.

The prime minister had made only a passingly brief mention of Hess in the House, despite the eagerness of MPs to ask questions about the German's arrival. The Commons was forced to meet in Church House on Tuesday the 13th, because the Commons Chamber in the Houses of Parliament had been completely destroyed by the bombing – but the press was not allowed to report where debates were taking place. Hugh Dalton found Church House a 'miserable annexe' where MPs were in a terrible mood. The prime minister's answers to the questions were gnomic at best; Churchill wouldn't be drawn on Hess's reasons for his arrival or his state of mind, saying only that he would make a statement in the near future.[18] Pressed by one MP on whether the minister of information would handle this piece of news with 'skill and imagination', Churchill replied that he had been with Duff Cooper until 'a very late hour' the previous night, but noted that 'this is one of these cases where imagination is somewhat baffled by the facts as they present themselves'.

Alec Cadogan at the Foreign Office was growing ever more frustrated by both his workload and the indecision of his political masters. 'Hess is the bane of my life and all my time is wasted,' he complained in his diary. On the evening of Wednesday the 14th, he had gone to Downing Street for a meeting with Churchill, Eden, Duff Cooper and Stewart

Menzies of the Secret Intelligence Service. Churchill dictated a statement that he wanted to give to Parliament, but again Cadogan thought he had it all wrong. '*How* slow he is,' the civil servant huffed in private. Churchill wanted to talk about Hess's peace proposals, but Cadogan protested that this corresponded exactly to the German version of events and said that 'Hitler would heave sigh of relief. *And the German people.*' That day, German international radio had put out more statements on Hess, saying that he had wanted to warn the British people and 'at the eleventh hour persuade them to make peace'.[19] These further statements were being widely reported. Cadogan did not believe the German people would think Hess a traitor; he wanted them instead to *fear* that he was. Churchill and Duff Cooper did not listen ('PM and that ass Duff brushed me aside'), though Eden, who had left the meeting early, agreed with him. So did Max Beaverbrook, who had dined with Churchill, as Cadogan heard in a call after midnight. Churchill, in a bad temper, decided to postpone his Commons statement.

As the prime minister's advisers attempted to manage the news, gossip about Hess was spreading quickly and not always accurately around government circles and beyond. The first Robert Bruce Lockhart had heard, even as Kirkpatrick was on his way to Scotland on the night of Monday 12th, was that 'Rudolf Hess disappears from aeroplane. Apparently suicide as a result of madness.'[20] The next day he had heard more, saying that there was 'immense excitement' over Hess, who he had heard came to Scotland 'either to escape the wrath of the Gestapo or to see the Duke of Hamilton about peace – probably the second'. Bruce Lockhart thought that Kirkpatrick was the wrong person to send to see Hess, believing the diplomat to have 'no knowledge or understanding of psychology'.

Meanwhile, Hugh Dalton heard the rumours from his assistant at the Ministry of Economic Warfare, Gladwyn Jebb.

In his diary, Dalton wrote: 'Gladwyn says he has overheard, but must not repeat to me, who was the "Scottish personality" whom Hess said he had come to see.' Hoping to tempt Jebb into giving the game away, Dalton suggested a couple of possible names. Was it Lord Brocket or the Duke of Buccleugh? Jebb didn't rise to the bait, even when Dalton said he would spread rumours about who it might be.[21]

Dalton didn't have to go far to find the answer. Outside the ministry, he ran into David Bowes-Lyon, the Queen's brother, who also worked there, and Malcolm McCorquodale, a Conservative MP. McCorquodale told Dalton that he'd heard on the grapevine that it was the Duke of Hamilton who Hess had come to see. 'He knows this from a man who travelled down by the night train to see Andrew Duncan and who heard it from people who were standing drinks to the ploughman who picked Hess up.' Andrew Duncan was the minister of supply and one of McCorquodale's fellow Conservative MPs. This kind of careless talk among MPs and ministers, even in the street outside government buildings, showed that it would be impossible to keep the story secret.

Bruce Lockhart's view was that Churchill was hesitating because he hoped to obtain valuable military information out of Hess. He observed that the prime minister 'has taken complete control. No ammunition for the propagandists.' This was a source of frustration for the propagandists who wanted to know – and to be allowed to say – more. Bruce Lockhart also noted that 'Valentine Williams and Sefton Delmer not allowed to go to Glasgow'.

Denis Sefton Delmer knew Rudolf Hess, after all. He had been the first British journalist to interview Hitler before he took power and had many contacts among the Nazi regime. 'Tom' Delmer, as he was usually known, had only just signed the Official Secrets Act at Woburn, but even as a new recruit, he already had strong ideas about how propaganda should be run. It's perhaps no surprise that the Cabinet and their advisers picked the safe, diplomatic choice of Ivone Kirk-patrick rather than the outspoken and eccentric journalist as their first emissary to Hess. Delmer, however, believed that the whole affair had been 'amateurish' in its handling. He described the 'amazed chagrin'[22] of Dick Crossman that Winston Churchill was giving the BBC no chance to exploit Hess's escape further. Delmer put Churchill's reluctance down to him possibly believing that a 'Peace Party' could seize on the idea that Hess wanted peace. Delmer thought that if not himself, then a senior figure from the government should be sent to Hess, and that Hess should be given a truth drug to get him to reveal his real intentions. He also argued that Max Beaverbrook, the newspaper proprietor and government minister, who had also met Hess before, should be one of those to talk to him. Beaverbrook was eventually sent, but not until several weeks later.

By Thursday, MPs were demanding more answers about Hess from the prime minister, but they still weren't getting very far. Vyvyan Adams asked why Britain hadn't put out an announcement before midnight on the day that Hess was apprehended, allowing Germany to issue its own statement first. In fact, Downing Street *had* put out its initial statement shortly before midnight. Not satisfied with Churchill's first answer, he asked again whether the prime minister considered it 'unfortunate' that forty-eight hours had been allowed to elapse, 'during which the enemy were enabled to issue an entirely deceitful version'. Churchill's reply was that the delay was 'not unfortunate, and if it had been unfortunate, it would have been unavoidable'. He put this down to the delay in getting someone to Scotland and said that he himself hadn't believed the first reports on Sunday night.[23]

MPs referred to reports regarding the Duke of Hamilton: that morning's *Times* had reported that Hess remembered meeting Hamilton at the Berlin Olympics in 1936, which was why he had chosen him, and ran extensive details from the

Press Association which reporters had heard from the Scottish farm workers who had looked after Hess on his landing. Hess had told them about 'the great distress' that prevailed among the people of Germany over the bombing of towns by the RAF, and claimed to share Hamilton's interests in skiing and flying. The rumours that had been circulating around Westminster had now reached the public. The duke's name was now in the public domain and questions were being asked as to why exactly Hess wanted to talk to him. Hamilton denied that he had been in touch with Hess.

Churchill had also, intentionally or not, provoked another argument with one of his ministers. During earlier questions, he had been asked to specify precisely which minister was responsible for propaganda: was it the minister of information or the minister of economic warfare? The prime minister was again reluctant to set out who was in charge of exactly what, saying instead that he would direct questions to the appropriate minister. He added, probably by way of a joke, 'if it falls between the two, I shall be glad to serve the House'. This quip went down extremely badly with Hugh Dalton, who detected a 'frightful gaffe' by Churchill and was upset that the prime minister never seemed to acknowledge that Dalton had any responsibility over propaganda.

In the absence of a line from the government as a whole, individual ministers' statements around the country were noted by the newspapers. Herbert Morrison, the Labour home secretary, had some lively analogies for an audience in his Hackney constituency on the weekend after Hess's landing. He said the 'gangster' Hess would stay in British hands, calling him a 'brutal thug'. 'Whether he is Rat No.1 or a Trojan horse, or just a baby panda over here in the vain hope of finding innocents to play with, the main thing is that he is caged.'[24]

The absence of a clear agreement as to whether Hess might be rat, Trojan horse or baby panda persisted. According to Cadogan, by the Monday, a week after Hess's arrival had first been discussed at Cabinet, ministers could still not agree on a public statement. 'PM still hankering after his stupid statement about Hess,' Cadogan wrote in his diary. 'Insisted on reading it with great gusto to the Cabinet.' But fortunately, from Cadogan's point of view, 'they were *unanimous* against it, and I think he has dropped the idea'.

The Ministry of Information did agree to put out one intentionally misleading statement via the Foreign Office. With speculation swirling that Hess had been in contact with the Duke of Hamilton before his flight, they admitted that he had written to Hamilton some months earlier. However, the exact details given were untrue. Hess's letter had been intercepted by the security services, but the statement said that Hamilton had voluntarily handed it over. It was believed that this false statement was 'less likely to give rise to suspicion' of Hamilton's conduct.[25]

Hess himself was in an ever more distressed state. On 15 June, he made his first attempt at suicide by throwing himself down the stairs at the house codenamed 'Camp Z' where he had been moved – Mytchett Place in Surrey. He survived with a broken leg and pelvis. The SIS relayed information on Hess's mental state to the officials. The psychiatrists sent to monitor Hess were agreed that he was paranoid, delusional and convinced that he was being poisoned.

A month after Hess's arrival, the situation was still not resolved. No statement had yet been made and the propagandists were continuing to push for a clearer, public line on what the British government was thinking and doing about Hess. On 19 June, MPs discussed the Hess case in an adjournment debate, many of them asking why they hadn't heard more from the government. The Labour MP Sydney Silverman asked his colleagues to consider how the German government would have handled things if the deputy leader of the British government had 'landed by parachute at Berchtesgaden'. Silverman claimed that 'the Germans would have made much better use of that for their purposes than we have made of this sensational event for ours'.[26] Some MPs repeated wild rumours about Hess, including the suggestion that he was being held at Chequers. Responding for the government, the junior Foreign Office minister Rab Butler flatly said that he had nothing to add beyond the fact that Hess was being treated as a prisoner of war. There was clearly some political pressure for the government to go further in its response, partly because ministers like Morrison were speaking outside the House and rumours were still spreading.

Con O'Neill, who had deputised for Crossman in the row with Freddy Voigt in April, had been asked to write a report making recommendations on how the Hess case could be used in propaganda, both white and black. 'Propaganda about Hess can be overt or covert,' reported O'Neill. 'If covert it can take the form of whispers or secret broadcasting. Whispers have made, and no doubt will continue to make, great use of the case.'[27] In O'Neill's view, it did not matter that those whispers might be various and inconsistent. He argued that the best theme which those rumours could play on was that 'Hess came because he knew that Germany could not win the war'. The problem with using Hess in covert propaganda, however, was clear. 'Secret broadcasting is at a heavy disadvantage in dealing with the Hess case – save as a good purveyor of whispers – because the legend of the "Research Units" is that they operate abroad, and in the nature of the case the best information about Hess has to come from England.'

O'Neill thought it would be more effective to use the Hess case in acknowledged British white propaganda, but in order to make the most of it, there needed to be a supply of fresh news about the affair. Journalists were running out of things to write and speculation would only take them so far. As O'Neill wrote, 'the few facts already published have been sucked quite dry, and no more flesh can be got off these bones'.

He thought the answer was for someone senior – the foreign secretary or the prime minister – to make a public statement to the House of Commons. O'Neill had also drawn up a suggested statement that either of them could make. He wanted this to be consistent, as far as possible, with the truth. But, crucially, O'Neill was not suggesting that the senior minister should tell Parliament the *full* truth.

'The undiluted truth about the Hess case does not make good propaganda,' O'Neill stated baldly. The propaganda line that had been set out in earlier weeks consisted of four propositions: that Hess was sane; that he had given the British important information on various subjects; that he was anxious for peace because he had lost his confidence in German victory; and that he was 'not an idealist or a refugee, but a Nazi who has lost his nerve and his faith in Hitler'. This was the line which had evolved through the BBC and the Ministry of Information in the first days after Hess's landing. O'Neill admitted that 'none of this is true'.

He defended his suggestion that ministers should make a fundamentally misleading and untrue statement. 'It may be repugnant and disagreeable to distort the truth. But if we are to use the case of Hess to inflict the maximum damage on the morale of the enemy, made specially vulnerable by this episode, I think we must do so. The important thing is, not to distort the truth in a way that can be detected.'

O'Neill had several further suggestions about how Hess could be used in active propaganda, including the idea that the German's own words from a letter written to his son could be broadcast, or even that Hess could be recorded making his case for peace and told – again untruthfully – that his broadcast would be heard by British audiences.

His superiors though were quick to question whether any of this was a good idea. Responding to the report, Alec Cadogan remained 'doubtful' whether there should be any public statement on Hess.[28] He felt that the current silence was succeeding in making the Germans uncomfortable, but at the same time Cadogan didn't want to let the Germans 'forget the whole episode comfortably'. His view was that the affair was still best discussed via covert propaganda, through Freedom Stations and 'whispers'. He had two major objections to official statements in Britain: firstly, that they would be likely to provoke controversy at home; secondly, that Germany might be able to disprove what Hess was telling the British, which would backfire. Further, if Hess were telling his interrogators any German state secrets, it would be best not to let the enemy know what they were. Cadogan concluded that although he agreed it was important to keep the episode alive, it was best to 'keep Germany guessing'.

It was left to Eden to draw a firm political conclusion, which he did in red ink at the bottom of Cadogan's minute. Although O'Neill's report was 'a capable production', he could not accept its conclusions. Eden wrote: 'It does, however, involve a statement by the Foreign Secretary (or Prime Minister) that is admittedly wide of the truth. I should not be willing to make such a statement, despite its possible immediate advantages.'

This was a point of principle for Eden: he was not prepared to lie to Parliament, even in the interests of Britain's war aims. Intentionally misleading Parliament was then, as now, a resigning matter, and this was a line that Eden would not, at that time, contemplate crossing.

Cadogan seems to have reconsidered a little after he was informed by Ivone Kirkpatrick about the difficulties of using the Hess case on the Freedom Stations, which were limited by pretending to be located within Germany. Cadogan aimed to damp down the Hess story domestically while boosting it internationally, believing it 'essential that Hess should not drop out of the news altogether'.[29] But he was also concerned about the rumours spreading in the United States that there was something 'phony' about the Hess affair, which could be dangerous. No statement, however, came, whether along O'Neill's lines or any other.

Even by the end of the year, no senior minister had made any official statement on Hess. As late as November, when MPs asked about the captive, they were told by Clement Attlee that the prime minister would make a statement on the subject when he considered it necessary.[30]

In the Hess affair, the perceived need for secrecy and the absence of clear statements from the government allowed rumour and eventually conspiracy to take the place of genuine information. There was some truth in the claims that it had taken time to get Hess's identity confirmed – and it would have been very bad news for British propaganda to have announced that Hess had landed if 'Captain Horn' had turned out to be someone else – but the political indecision at the top of government meant that those pushing for more clear answers to be given to the public were left frustrated. At the same time, though, work was already underway to develop a new way of reaching listeners in enemy countries, with a completely different approach, where rumours would be deliberately spread in order to sow confusion.

The Hess affair was an accidental turning point in British propaganda. Duff Cooper's position as minister of information was already precarious. He was ill with flu in mid-May and had been convalescing at his home in Bognor, putting him at a distance from events. He was also unhappy with his job and many, including Lord Beaverbrook, were unhappy with the role of the Ministry of Information overall. Duff Cooper had been facing criticism on the domestic propaganda front as well and even described his own ministry as 'a misbegotten freak'. He tried to defend his position for a while, even threatening to resign if he wasn't given a place in the War Cabinet, but in the event, he was pushed.[31] Churchill now saw a job that his confidant Brendan Bracken, with his experience in newspapers, might be able to do instead. Propagandists saw the importance of reacting quickly to unexpected events and the opportunities that shifts in the fortunes of war could provide. There was also a growing realisation that the 'rumours' and 'whispers', which had been used as the basis for covert propaganda, were not being pushed effectively enough. These too were about to be put on a more professional and systematic footing. Tom Delmer had just been introduced to this secret world and he was pushing at an opening door.

PART 2

Freaks, Antiques, Fakes and Geniuses

6

Propaganda in Battledress

Tom Delmer, a man who believed his own myth as the 'genius' of black propaganda, was, in Muriel Spark's phrase, a man 'far too big for the room'. He was a huge physical presence, 'immensely large and fat with a black beard'.[1] The beard was a wartime affectation, but he had always been a man who loved good food and wine. His friends described a gregarious man, 'helped by a genial and Rabelaisian nature and by a Falstaffian corpulence which so easily became the subject of confidences'.[2]

Delmer had been trying to get himself hired for cloak-and-dagger wartime work ever since he returned to London from Europe in July 1940. He had been allowed to broadcast talks on the BBC in German, but there were objections to his working on covert propaganda. Piecing together what Delmer really did, compared with what he said he did, can be as difficult as it is with some of his other colleagues. Delmer, by and large, preferred a good story to the truth – which is exactly what he was hired to provide.

On 10 October 1940, he and his artist wife, Isabel, were living in a flat in Lincoln's Inn, on the top floor of 9 Stone Buildings. Delmer had good connections in London: among the 'small and select' group of guests he invited to dinner that evening were Prince Bernhard of the Netherlands, Ian Fleming and Leonard Ingrams. Fleming, in uniform, was working for naval intelligence, while Ingrams worked on political warfare for the Ministry of Economic Warfare. The dinner party was interrupted by the sound of an 'end-of-the-world' explosion, just as Prince Bernhard was enjoying his last brandy. The party, however, continued, even though the building had been hit. In Delmer's telling, 'we lit some candles and continued to gossip and drink champagne as if nothing had happened'. Images of the building after the blast show the front of 9 Stone Buildings was largely blown away and the interior floors hugely damaged.[3] They stayed until an irate local air-raid warden shouted at the remaining guests 'to cease your disgusting orgy and come down immediately, the building is about to collapse'.[4] They went to the Savoy to carry on drinking and talking, despite suspicious neighbours apparently having reported them to the police for 'speaking foreign languages'. Delmer's wife, Isabel, told a similar version of the story, adding that she returned to the flat to rescue a portrait of herself.

A few weeks later, in November 1940, Delmer was writing letters from Lansdowne House, the London base of the Political Intelligence Department, writing a reference for the nightclub owner Leon Dajou, a friend from his Berlin and Paris days who had also fled to London and wanted to join the armed forces.[5] It's not clear, though, whether Delmer had any official role in secret propaganda at that point. The couple seem also to have spent some time living at Lansdowne House after their Lincoln's Inn home was bombed. Tom Delmer had become a regular contributor on the BBC, responding in German to the propaganda broadcast by the regime's Hans Fritzsche, alternating with Crossman and Voigt. Delmer also provided information to the SIS while he was sent on assignment to Lisbon for the *Daily Express* at the end of 1940. In Lisbon, he got in touch with his émigré German contacts who were hoping to escape to Britain.

Getting a formal job, though, was harder. Delmer was told that he had been rejected for more substantial secret work on security grounds. He believed that the security services had declined to hire him partly because he had been born in Germany. It's more likely, though, that their questions arose from his reporting and his contacts within the Nazi regime. As far back as 1932, MI5 had filed away mentions of Delmer, including reported criticisms of his apparent closeness to Nazi politicians.

Even when he landed at Chivenor aerodrome near Barnstaple, returning from Portugal at the end of January 1941, his arrival was reported to the security services as potentially suspicious, because he was reluctant to tell officials much about his visit to Lisbon. An internal MI5 memo of 10 February shows that the intelligence services' doubts about Delmer had been overcome, partly with a quiet word from his friend and Blitz dinner-party guest, Leonard Ingrams. Ingrams had rung up a Mr White at MI5 to persuade him. 'Mr Ingrams said that they were very anxious to employ DELMER and that as he had known him for many years, felt that he could clear him of any possible suspicion attaching to him.' The author of the memo continued, explaining how the path was now clear: 'The fact was that SIS had some doubts of his reliability, but I understand they have now withdrawn their objections to his employment, and DELMER may therefore be cleared by us for the post for which he is applying.'[6] MI5 noted, after their checks, that there was 'nothing recorded to his detriment'.

Delmer's knowledge of Germany and his colloquial fluency in the language came from his childhood. He had been born in Berlin in 1904, the son of an Australian professor, Frederick Sefton Delmer, who taught English language and literature at Berlin University, and his wife Mabel. He spent his childhood in Berlin and claimed to have spoken only German until he was five years old, when he was sent back to Australia to stay with relatives and learned English. The family was uprooted from Germany by the outbreak of war in 1914. Professor Delmer was interned at the start of the war, but the family was later able to leave for England.

Arriving in London in 1917, the younger Delmer transformed himself into an English schoolboy, attending St Paul's School and then winning a scholarship to study Modern History at Lincoln College, Oxford. At university, he was a sportsman; college photographs show him with his rowing eights and as part of a coxless four. He has deep-set eyes and a sardonic smile, his mouth turned up at one corner. Even though in later life he was 'bald, large and untidy in appearance', he was described as 'very handsome as a young man'; the photos taken after his rowing regattas bear out his good looks. Delmer switched subjects after two years, from History to German – which no doubt came relatively easily given his fluency – and obtained a Second in 1927. In his autobiography, he mentions the scholarship but not the subsequent change of course. His parents had returned to Germany by

Denis 'Tom' Sefton Delmer, seated left, in his Lincoln College rowing four, 1924

1923; when he arrived at Oxford, his family address was given as Lietzenburger Strasse 1, near the Tiergarten and the Berlin Zoo.[7] After university, he returned to stay with his parents.

A meeting with Max Beaverbrook at the Adlon Hotel in Berlin in 1927 secured Delmer his foot in the door of journalism. After a detour via the *Daily Express*'s Brussels bureau, he soon returned to Berlin as the paper's correspondent. Back in his home city, he was in his journalistic element. 'Berlin in 1928 had just about everything which the editor of a popular daily yearns for,' he wrote. 'Sex, murder, political intrigue, money, mystery and bloodshed. Particularly bloodshed.'[8]

Political intrigue got Delmer some of his biggest stories. He first interviewed Hitler in Munich in 1931, when the future leader had seemed to him a 'rather ordinary fellow', resembling an 'ex-soldier travelling salesman', distinguished from others like him only by his passion, volubility and concentration. He met Ernst Röhm, the leader of the SA who would be killed in the 1934 Night of the Long Knives, spending an evening with him at a Berlin drag bar. Delmer covered the Reichstag fire, but later refused to believe that the Nazis had instigated the fire for their own ends. His views of Germany, as expressed in his books and later articles, tend towards the strange and conspiratorial, particularly when looking at events in the country after the war.

He left Germany for Paris in 1934. In Delmer's own words, he 'could see that being on good terms with the Nazis while they were in opposition was one thing, being friends with them while they were in power and acting the way they were was another'.[9]

It was in Paris that he met Isabel Nicholas. On that much, Delmer's version of the story and that of his future wife agree. Isabel had been given a letter of introduction to him by an *Express* colleague. In Delmer's story, they met by chance, on the terrace of the Dome cafe in Montparnasse, and he recognised her instantly. In Isabel's story, she had phoned him and arranged to meet, crossing the Pont Neuf on the Seine to visit his apartment. Isabel was an artist who had not long arrived in the country and, at twenty-two, was eight years younger than Delmer. She had been working as an assistant and a model for the sculptor Jacob Epstein after leaving the Royal Academy of Art without finishing her degree. She had also been in a relationship with the married artist and had given birth to his child. Isabel gave up the baby to Epstein and his wife, Margaret.[10]

The rest of their story likewise comes in different versions: in Tom's tale, he had already fallen in love with Isabel – or at least an image of her – before they met, and known that he would marry her. He had seen a sculpture of Isabel, made by Epstein, exhibited in the Tate. Tom perceived Isabel as an exotic, living version of the bronze bust that he first saw in the gallery, with 'high cheekbones and slanting Nefertiti eyes'. Even though when she first spoke, he didn't like her voice, writing that she had a 'larynx of tin', he claimed to have fallen for 'the girl of the bronze'. Whether he was in love with the real woman or with the artist's image which someone else had created is another matter. Isabel was a model for many artists: she was painted by André Derain and by Pablo Picasso. One of Derain's portraits of Isabel, painted in 1936, captures her dark, curly hair, her red lips and her distinctive brown eyes with their catlike shape.

Although Isabel moved into Delmer's flat on the Rue de Castiglione, near the Place Vendôme, in 1935, they did not officially marry until September 1936. Delmer was constantly travelling across Europe as the pre-war crises erupted; to the Saarland, and to report on the Spanish Civil War. Although Isabel occasionally accompanied him, including to war zones such as Spain, they spent much time apart from each other. Delmer himself had possibly been having an affair with fellow war correspondent Virginia Cowles in Spain; she was certainly among the journalists, also including Ernest Hemingway and Martha Gellhorn, who gathered in his rooms at the Hotel Florida in Madrid, where they would share ham, sardines, beer and whisky at parties that went on until the early hours of the morning.[11] Isabel began a double life: on the right bank, with Delmer, and on the left bank, with her artist friends in Montparnasse.

Their relationship began to drift apart. Isabel's life became a double one in another sense. In 1935, she had met the Swiss sculptor Alberto Giacometti. They would see each other every day, at five in the afternoon. Within a few months, Isabel was modelling for him. This was clearly a deep and lasting affair. She was the model for many of his works, her long slender torso influencing the distinctive shape of his female figures. Isabel clearly faced a hard choice as to whether to leave Giacometti behind in Europe as the war closed in, repeatedly leaving the continent's mainland and then returning on several occasions before she finally departed with Delmer, on the overcrowded SS *Madura* from near Bordeaux, after the fall of France.

This is not the story that Delmer told. The way he wrote of his relationship with Isabel reveals the methods that he used both in propaganda and in his own life story. The heightened detail, the precise descriptions of food and particularly drink, the exaggerated charms of beautiful women – all serve to make the story more lurid and enticing, while at the same time, obscuring the more difficult, less romantic truth. Delmer puts into practice what he told others to do when he was working on propaganda: to use the 'sharp and vivid' style of 'his side of Fleet Street' – what we'd these days call tabloid journalism – and to use the appeal of the significant human story to make the tale seem more personal. In his books, every character has a short, evocative pen-portrait, every scene is set with atmosphere and description. It just isn't always true.

When Isabel wrote her story, she was writing it for herself, a handwritten manuscript in a sketch book, and it was never published. Delmer was writing for an audience.

It was probably February 1941 when he was whisked up to Woburn in a 'vast Daimler', not knowing his destination. He described this as being soon after his return from Lisbon, being made to sign the Official Secrets Act before allowed onto the grounds. Delmer claimed that Beaverbrook, his former boss, offered to make up the disparity between his government salary and what he would have earned at the *Express* in cash and shares, but this didn't happen. Delmer was as dismayed as Robert Bruce Lockhart had been by the shabby office he found waiting for him in London, which provided him with in and out trays, official stationery and a PO Box address, but 'no real work'. He seems to have spent a couple of months with little to do before suitable work was found.

In the spring of 1941, plans were already underway to create a new, right-wing RU radio station to broadcast material of a 'crude, direct and low-class character'.[12] The station was to be a response to German propaganda to Britain, which intelligence suggested was popular because it used vulgar language that listeners would never have heard on the BBC. German stations such as Workers' Challenge told British audiences that government ministers like Churchill, Bevin and Attlee were a 'filthy, lousy gang who have betrayed you and exploited you'. Ernest Bevin was accused of being a 'bloody rat' who sat in his office while telling others to work '84 blinking hours a week'.[13]

The British response was the real beginning of 'black propaganda'. In April, it was noted in the minutes of the German section's weekly meeting that the new station would 'specialise in black propaganda'.[14] Delmer wanted it to appeal to a new audience. He had been arguing that the BBC's talks to Germany were 'terrible', that they sounded like 'émigrés talking to émigrés', like 'Maida Vale calling Hampstead' rather than 'London calling Berlin'. The BBC, he thought, had got itself into 'a bad and unprofitable groove'. Although Delmer was happy to make his regular broadcasts, he didn't believe they made much difference to a German audience, describing them as 'the dry and dreary business of debating with the Nazis over the ether, an exercise of which the BBC with its flock of would-be MPs was over-fond'. He agreed with Freddy Voigt, whose station had been closed down, that broadcasts run predominantly by left-of-centre émigrés did not chime with current conditions in Germany. 'They were addressed not to the mass of Germans who supported Hitler and his war of aggression, but to the infinitesimal few who wanted to lose it.'

Instead, Delmer argued, broadcasts into Germany that really wanted to appeal to their audience should undermine Hitler 'not by opposing him, but by pretending to be all for him and his war'.[15] So he proposed to create a station hosted by a character who played the part of a disaffected former army officer, someone who been a Nazi supporter initially but was now disillusioned by the regime. Like the other 'research units', this new station would give the impression that it was coming from an undisclosed location within Germany. The new level of 'trickery and deception' entailed in black propaganda was 'outside what it was possible or desirable for the BBC to undertake'.

At the end of April 1941, Delmer's appointment to run this new station was being discussed by Crossman and Rex Leeper.[16] A week later, Delmer was in place at Woburn and 'choosing the necessary team', while officials tried to find them suitable accommodation.[17] On 12 May, two days after Hess's landing in Scotland, Tom and Isabel moved into Larchfield, a 'discreet redbricked' house in Aspley Guise. Larchfield was both their home – and that of the many German refugees who worked alongside them – and the initial codename for

Delmer's radio station. In a weekly report for the German section, the character of LF, short for Larchfield, was set out: 'LF's objective is subversive. It will spread disturbing and disruptive news to induce Germans to distrust and disobey their Government, not so much from highminded political motives as from ordinary human weakness (for which, however, highminded political excuses can be supplied).'[18]

The report set out how this would work. The station was not attempting to provide its listeners with a political campaign, rather, they were 'intended to feel that they are eavesdropping on the private wireless service of a secret organisation, whose members know its political programme. By listening to LF's news, the listener picks up that the members are anti-communists who previously supported Hitler but are now appalled at the corruption, profiteering, place-hunting, clique rivalries, etc, which the party has instituted, and appalled at the left swing that is accompanying the Hitler-Stalin understanding, which will give to party bureaucrats even greater power.'[19]

Crossman and Delmer were now jointly in charge of Woburn's German propaganda section, with Crossman reporting to the Ministry of Information for BBC work and Delmer answerable to SO1 for the secret side of the work.[20]

The new station, which would be known to its listeners by the callsign Gustav Siegfried Eins, went on air for the first time on 23 May. Its identity used the German signalling alphabet for 'G' and 'S', with the '1' suggesting that there were other such channels, though the letters did not stand for anything in particular. Its presenter was named only as 'Der Chef' – The Chief. In his book *Black Boomerang*, Delmer gave him the name of Paul Sanders, a Berlin 'detective story writer', who had 'a sallow face, watchful observant eyes and the aristocratic hawk nose'. His voice was, to Delmer, 'virile and resonant with just that slight trace of a Berlin drawl'.[21] In fact, Der Chef's real name was Peter Secklmann, who also used the pen name of Peter Motram.[22] He was a thirty-nine-year-old émigré, originally from Berlin, who had worked in Paris for a news agency after leaving Germany and described himself as a writer and literary agent.[23] He arrived in Britain to stay in early 1937.[24]

Delmer decided that since no senior German official appeared without an adjutant, The Chief needed an assistant.[25] His initial sidekick on the programme was Johannes Reinholz, a conservative German émigré journalist who also scripted the talks.[26] Later, the role of The Sergeant was taken over by Frank Lynder.[27]

The programmes were still recorded rather than live. Only a few minutes of Der Chef's broadcasts survive, a recorded item from 1943, but the format of the GS1 pieces was similar from the outset. After the thin sound of a piano theme tune, it begins, 'Achtung, Achtung, hier Gustav Siegfried Eins. Es spricht Der Chef' – The Chief is speaking. The Chief's target on this occasion was the German operation in Sicily. He accused the German commander of the Hermann Goering Division, General Paul Conrath, who he said had been calling for the defence of Catania in Sicily to the very last breath, of not being in Sicily at all. Der Chef repeats himself several times to make his point: the man who has promised to defend Catania, who believes Catania to be so important for the whole of Italy, is defending Catania from Berlin.[28]

The repetition served a dual purpose: both to drive the point home to the listeners and to make sure that soldiers or others listening over crackly short-wave radio with poor reception could hear it if they missed it the first time. The broader aim was to spread the rumour that German generals were abandoning their soldiers to fight while themselves remaining in relative safety. In the case of Conrath, this was deliberate disinformation, as although he often lost contact with his forces on the ground by radio, he was at least in Sicily at the time of the battles in July.[29] Der Chef also maintained that another German general had been commanding his forces from the safety of the French Riviera.

From the first broadcast, Der Chef used deliberately coarse language, aimed at appealing to German troops on the ground. Charles Roetter, one of the émigrés who worked with Delmer, said Der Chef 'used the foulest and most obscene language that has been transmitted over the airwaves before or since'.

Roetter said that Der Chef's signature tune was a musical response to the theme of the official German propaganda station, Deutschlandsender.[30] Where the German radio introduced itself with an eighteenth-century song – used as the sound of the bells of Potsdam's garrison church, whose lyrics meant 'truth and probity' – Delmer responded with the next line, which would have had the words 'until your cool grave'. Roetter described the tune broadcast by GS1 as 'played on what seemed to be a cracked piano in some primitive front line trench'.[31] His description, from the broadcast that survives, is accurate.

Der Chef's first broadcast also didn't announce that it was a new programme. The implication instead was that it was a series that had been going on for some time, in order, Roetter suggested, 'to cause the greatest possible confusion in Germany's security services and the maximum amount of recrimination inside Nazi monitoring organisations'.

Der Chef was allowed to exploit Hess's landing in a way that regular white propaganda and BBC broadcasts had not been able to do. Secklmann's character derided Hess as 'among the clique of cranks, megalomaniacs, string-pullers and parlour Bolsheviks'[32] around Hitler. He blamed these, in particular Himmler, rather than the führer himself, for allowing Hess to escape, and supported the generals who, in Der Chef's view, weren't able to get close to the leader to tell him the truth. He signed off with the assurance that he would repeat his broadcast, 'all being well', every hour at seven minutes to the hour.

Since at this point, the transmissions were only on short-wave radio, it's unclear how many of the intended audience were able to hear them. Many German listeners only had the most basic of radio sets. The brown Bakelite *Volksempfänger*, or 'People's Receivers', which had been launched in 1933 as a cheap way to allow more people access to the radio – of course, in order that they could hear German government propaganda – could only tune in to a limited number of stations, not including short wave. That was deliberate, in order to make sure German listeners weren't getting access to foreign news and opinion. Some in the military, though, were able to receive short wave; later RU stations would focus primarily on serving German military personnel to influence their morale. Of course, even for those who found a way to listen to foreign radio, it was still illegal and dangerous.

Delmer's interest in black propaganda was not confined to radio. His first attempt at creating fake news was on a very small, bespoke scale, but it 'backfired viciously', by his own admission. Although he had been unleashed on Hess's escape via Der Chef's tirade on GS1, Delmer also wanted to influence Hess's interrogation directly. The initial plan was to create a fake page, at least, purporting to be from the German newspaper the *Völkischer Beobachter*, the longstanding Nazi party mouthpiece. This proved too complicated, and only a short paragraph on a page was produced, denying supposed claims about Hess's family. 'Stories in the foreign press to the effect that Hess's wife and 4-year-old son are in the custody of the Gestapo are the malicious inventions of enemy propaganda. At the present time Frau Hess and her son are in a mental hospital in Thuringia.'[33] The idea that Hess's family had been taken into an institution was obviously designed to upset and destabilise him.

There was also another fake article, supposedly from an English newspaper. According to Ellic Howe, a printer who was an expert in typefaces and who was recruited to create fake documents for Delmer later that year, this article was a forgery of the *Daily Telegraph* and repeated the claim, from different sources, that Hess's son was mentally ill. Howe pointed out that this wasn't what Delmer had said; in Delmer's version of events, the fake English newspaper story said that Hess had been given truth drugs. Where the plan went wrong, for Delmer, was that Hess, on reading that he might have been secretly administered truth drugs, demanded to have all of his food tasted before he ate it. This is undoubtedly the better story, but Howe said that he had seen copies of the fake *Telegraph* and knew where they were printed and by whom. Whatever Delmer's articles did in fact suggest, it didn't help in the interrogation of Hess, who was already in a fragile state.

Even if this creation of fake print news was a failure, it would not deter Delmer from trying again. As the war went on, black operations grew in scope to include leaflets, booklets and other forgeries, such as ration cards and stamps. Isabel used her artistic training to work on producing some of the images that were used.

In early June, Delmer arrived for the first of his regular meetings in the 'stately ballroom' at Woburn Abbey to find himself surrounded by 'a motley of university dons, advertising men, diplomats, motor salesmen, journalists and officers from the services'.[34] Accompanying them were political aides like Hugh Gaitskell, then still carrying Hugh Dalton's ministerial bag. One of the biggest secrets that Delmer and his colleagues learned at the meeting was that Hitler was only a few weeks away from attacking Russia, which would lead to a massive change in direction of the war. Delmer believed that GS1's line on the invasion should be to applaud and support it. He would use the chance to attack Nazi party officials for their greed, spreading rumours, for instance, that the wives of senior party figures were stocking up on clothing at the expense of the average family. The attack on Russia, Delmer claimed, was the making of Der Chef, turning him into 'an entirely plausible figure'.

Over the course of the war, Delmer's black propaganda became both more sophisticated and more targeted. Further research into conditions in Germany and access to additional information about the state of the war and of the civilian population allowed the 'black' stations to refer more precisely to conditions on the ground and therefore sound more authentic. In August 1941, Delmer listed the stories that his station had been working on in a slightly chaotic manner, a typed document full of corrections that described the rumours he had been putting out. It included a story on how chocolate supplies for German troops had been stolen; 'filthy black market dealers', GS1 claimed, 'had sold it to Jews'. There was more deliberate misinformation giving a fake coded message about a steamer crossing the Baltic, which Delmer hoped would cause the authorities to waste time trying to figure out its meaning. He followed this with a naval story complaining about the bad quality of recruits for the navy. New recruits, The Chief complained, were being diverted to bomb disposal work. The station said that 'the son of one of our comrades had been killed digging out a British time bomb'. Delmer noted that the 'harrowing and realistic' details for this episode had been supplied by his corporal, who had worked on bomb disposal in a Pioneer Corps.[35] He was beginning to develop the themes that he would later elaborate further: food, disease and corruption among the Nazi party elite were the topics he thought would strike the greatest chords with listeners among the German forces.

Three months into its operation, Delmer's RU station was outgrowing its home at Larchfield and it was suggested that Delmer and his team should move to The Rookery, also in Aspley Guise (and referred to by its acronym of RAG).[36] Once installed there, Delmer continued his usual fast pace of work, offering hospitality to his colleagues and a few permitted visitors, such as Robert Walmsley. Many of Delmer's propaganda 'lines', Walmsley remembered, 'first saw the light over the remains of his cellar at RAG'. Delmer, the intelligence officer wrote, 'was not only an indefatigable but an unceasing worker, and after dinner, from nine until one or two in the morning . . . discussions on new projects and new themes were broken only by intervals of listening to his own station or even to rival ones'.[37] Delmer displayed, Walmsley thought, 'complete singleness of purpose and untiring application to work'. Walmsley was an undoubted fan, writing that 'Delmer was the nearest thing to a genius which PWE produced. In fact, in his particular line he was a genius.'[38]

'Squatting on his vast settee' at The Rookery, Delmer would go over a paragraph of a talk 'literally dozens of times, muttering crossly to himself as he did so', before sending its author back to rewrite their work. This process could take hours. Sometimes, Delmer would break off with a new thought. 'Stopping, in the middle of a sentence, a worried wrinkle would appear on his large brow, and, retrieving at least one of his shoes and giving his braceless trousers a heave, he would stump rapidly out of the room to impart a new brilliant idea to one of his writers, probably by that time in bed.' But according to Walmsley, he was more congenial to work with than Crossman. Delmer was someone 'who created vastly more than Crossman ever did, whose mind ranged in fields where Crossman never felt at home, and who had a far wider range of opposition to overcome, made friends of those who might have stood in his path'.

Although Delmer was sceptical of the propaganda abilities of many of the German and other refugees already in

Tom Delmer responding to German propaganda broadcasts on the BBC, September 1941

Britain, he believed there were excellent refugees to be used 'if you knew where to find them'. In some cases, he did know, wanting to bring over his own contacts whom he had met in Berlin, Paris or Spain before the war. Many of those who left Europe as the war spread had had dramatic escapes. In some cases, they were helped by the British authorities to reach the country.

When a man travelling on a Czech passport under the name of Mikulas Bedam disembarked from the SS *Sobo* in Liverpool on 13 July 1941, he stated the purpose of his journey to British officials as 'to escape from Nazis'. It was a short, bald statement of what had been a long and difficult voyage. The man was forty-three years old, five foot ten, with fair hair and blue eyes. In a passport photo from one of his variety of passports, he looks distinguished, with round, owlish glasses, a straight, prominent nose and a thin-lipped mouth. His real name was Ernst Adam and he was German, a First World War veteran who had taught commerce at a university. Adam, an active trade unionist and communist, was imprisoned by the Nazis for three months for anti-government political activities in 1933. His father collapsed during a 'severe interrogation' by the Gestapo and died as a result. Ernst fled the country for Paris, where he worked as a newspaper correspondent for the Telegraf-Orient news agency and the Taylor-Prior press agency, providing news for central European papers. Adam then left Paris for Spain, where he became the chief of staff for the Republicans' 47th Division. He got to know Delmer both in Madrid and in Paris.[39] Returning to Paris in June 1938, Adam went back to journalism.

What made Adam so potentially useful to Delmer and his colleagues was that he already had experience of running a black propaganda radio station. In the record of Adam's interrogation on his arrival, he told his questioner that he 'formulated the news for the "Free German Station" which although generally believed to be broadcasting inside Germany was operated from Paris'.[40] This station was run by Willi Münzenberg, the German communist activist who had later split with the party. Münzenberg had met both Delmer and Crossman in Berlin in the early 1930s. Adam had started working for the French ministry of propaganda, which organised the radio station, at the outbreak of war, using a Spanish passport. However, once the French government realised that Adam was in fact originally German, he was interned in January 1940, only being allowed to leave the country again after the German invasion.

His escape from occupied Europe was dangerous. From Paris, Adam made his way to Marseille, where he obtained a Czech passport, then onwards via Perpignan to Spain and then to Portugal. Once he reached Portugal in September 1940, he made contact with the British authorities and 'did confidential work for the British' in Lisbon. 'The British

Embassy in Lisbon,' it was noted, 'is aware of the nature of this work.' In Adam's record from 'British Passport Control' in Lisbon – usually a cover name for MI6 – he gives Denis Sefton Delmer of the *Daily Express* as a reference. Delmer clearly had enough influence with the secret services that he could make sure that certain of his friends were able to escape Europe and reach Britain. While Delmer was in Portugal at the end of 1940 and supplying information to MI6, he was also back in touch with Adam. Questioned on arrival in Liverpool, Adam said that in Lisbon he had been 'introduced to various gentlemen who came from England, but whose names he does not know, but whom he helped by giving information about various matters'.

Some of the information he gave the British secret services was about a German actor and film producer, now also in Lisbon, whom he suspected of being a Gestapo agent. Adam spoke to MI6's informant, along with Babette Gross, the widow of Willi Münzenberg, who had died in unexplained circumstances trying to escape France in June 1940.[41] They accused the man of working also for the Soviet GPU as well as both the German and French secret services. This kind of information was potentially valuable, even if their British interviewer didn't seem entirely convinced.

Getting Ernst Adam first to Britain and then to Woburn, however, wasn't straightforward. Delmer's friend, Leonard Ingrams, rang a Captain Liddell in Lisbon, who appears to have been in MI6, in late May 1941, to ask that Adam be brought to Britain to work for Electra House. Adam had been planning to leave for the Belgian Congo, but a few days before his departure, he was 'visited by a man calling himself Captain Shaw', who asked him if he was still keen to come to Britain.[42] He was; none of his attempts to gain a visa, even with official requests from the Ministry of Information and others, had yet been successful.

Captain Liddell drove Adam to Olhão, a fishing port on the southern Algarve coast, where he put him on a small sailing boat, 'manned by a Portuguese', and sent him to Gibraltar. Armed with a letter from the British Embassy, Adam was then put aboard the naval cruiser HMS *London*. This ship was supposed to take him to London, but was diverted to search for the German battleship *Bismarck* in the Atlantic. After ten days at sea, Adam found himself further south than he had started, ashore in Bathurst – the present-day Banjul in Gambia – waiting to take ship again. His next port of call was Freetown in Sierra Leone, via the warship HMS *Woodruff*. At last, with another letter of recommendation to add to his growing collection, saying that he was 'urgently required' by the government in London, Ernst Adam boarded the SS *Sobo*, destined for Liverpool.

Almost two months after his journey began, Adam reached Britain on 13 July, but even then his arrival was not easy. There was a flurry of bureaucracy, telegrams and phone calls between the Home Office, MI5 and political intelligence departments trying to find where he was. These several government departments, even though they deemed him 'so particularly suitable for our requirements', hadn't checked what name or passport he would be travelling under. Instead of being brought directly to London and then sent on to Woburn, he had been detained and questioned. Once the mistake was realised, Adam was 'escorted to London by midnight train' by a Lieutenant McMillan.

Two more future recruits to Delmer's operation had also worked alongside Ernst Adam on the Freedom Stations in Madrid and Paris. Alexander and Margit Maass were helped to escape by British agents too. Alexander Maass had been one of the Weimar Republic's earliest broadcasters, a radio pioneer who started working for West Deutsche Rundfunk in Cologne in 1927, the year after he had joined the Communist Party.[43] He moved to Moscow in 1931 to work on the development of Soviet radio stations. After the Nazi takeover, Maass travelled widely, with spells in Bermuda, Canada and England before arriving in Spain during the civil war. That's where he had his first experience of a 'freedom station', working as a presenter for the German Freedom Station in Madrid and also for Republican radio. The German Freedom Station was an antifascist station and the voice of exiled German communists, and which also broadcast talks by other German exiles and foreign opponents of the Nazi regime, including Albert Einstein, Ernest Hemingway, Bertholt Brecht and both Heinrich and Thomas Mann. The station broadcast on a frequency deliberately close to that of the Deutschlandsender, for German audiences still in the country. Like Adam, Maass joined the French propaganda station in Paris after leaving Spain. His wife, Margit, was an actress with a versatile voice, who would become one of Delmer's talents. The couple had both, separately, been arrested and imprisoned in France, but had managed to escape from Marseille and reach Oran in Algeria. They had been travelling onwards to Mexico when they were intercepted by the British in a 'cloak and dagger' operation in Bermuda.[44] From there, they were taken to New York, then Canada, and finally via transatlantic convoy, to England.[45] Not all of those who worked on black propaganda had such a fraught arrival as Ernst Adam and the Maasses, but many had escaped danger to reach safety in Britain.

Arriving at Woburn for the first time gave these new recruits a sense of being initiated into a sort of conspiracy. Peter Ritchie Calder, a journalist, had been recruited that summer through a hushed conversation in the unlikely surroundings of a Lyons tearoom. He walked through the quiet corridors of the ducal palace, beneath massive and forbidding portraits, only for a door to open and to be greeted with laughter and the familiar voice of Dick Crossman saying, 'So they've kidnapped you, too, Ritchie.' For Ritchie Calder, it was like 'a surprise party which my friends had arranged for my benefit'. Here at Woburn, he found the 'Missing Men', a convivial gathering of likeminded friends who had been unaccountably absent for the last couple of years.[46]

Delmer's entry into the British propaganda effort was innovative and risky. He brought fresh ideas and the energy to put them into practice. Accordingly, the research units began to sound completely different. This was the work that Ritchie Calder described as 'propaganda in battledress', a type of political warfare able to convert propaganda into a striking force and translate ideas and emotions into action. Delmer's race ahead left the politicians stumbling to catch up.[47]

7

The Unquiet Cemetery

While the propagandists in Woburn and London were left frustrated by Churchill's reluctance to exploit Rudolf Hess's landing for their purposes, the prime minister was happy with the results. In particular, he was pleased with the work that his loyal aide, Brendan Bracken, had done in handling the press. It was soon clear that Churchill wanted Bracken as his new minister of information, replacing Duff Cooper. Bracken, however, wasn't so happy about his impending promotion, even though it would mean he reached the Cabinet. The Ministry of Information was widely seen as a political graveyard – in Bracken's opinion it was an 'unquiet cemetery' which had 'swallowed up alive the reputations of the unfortunate trio of incumbents who had already held the office'.[1] There had been three ministers in fewer than two years. Bracken wrote to one ministerial colleague that the prime minister had told him the job was 'worse than manning a bomb-disposal post'.[2]

It was clear by June 1941 that neither the Ministry of Information, nor the system for control of propaganda divided between several ministers, was working effectively. Sir John Anderson, the lord president of the council, a man whose role was to help solve disputes, wrote to Churchill in June 1941 to tell him that he couldn't get Dalton and Duff Cooper to reconcile their differences. Anthony Eden, the foreign secretary, had also now joined the discussion. Anderson realised that they needed a 'machinery of control' to resolve the situation.[3] The issue was becoming more urgent as Parliament was planning to debate propaganda in the coming weeks. Anderson proposed creating a standing ministerial committee on propaganda policy which would consist of Eden, Duff Cooper and Dalton. The introduction of a third, more senior, minister into the mix was designed to make it easier to overrule one or other of the two ministers. Duff Cooper, who had been ill and hadn't had a chance to respond to the proposals, was unhappy, and rather in the manner of a child being told off, blamed Dalton for starting the fight. 'On each occasion,' he wrote to Anderson, 'the trouble has been started and the appeal made by the Minister of Economic Warfare'.

Behind the scenes, Max Beaverbrook, who had recently resigned as minister of aircraft production and been moved to be the minister of supply, also got involved in pushing his own possible candidates to run propaganda. He tried to entice and flatter Robert Bruce Lockhart with the promise of a more important job. On 30 May, Beaverbrook phoned Bruce Lockhart at Woburn Abbey and told him that his name was being mentioned in connection with a job that was very much to his advantage. Bruce Lockhart had the Woburn chauffeur race to Downing Street in just over an hour; on his arrival, he then chased around offices in Whitehall trying to find Beaverbrook.[4]

When the two men found one another, Beaverbrook gave Bruce Lockhart the hard sell, telling him that Eden wanted to make him an extra Foreign Office under-secretary in charge of co-ordinating policy and propaganda. Beaverbrook also held out the prospect of further promotions, saying that he'd told the foreign secretary, in Churchill's presence, that Bruce Lockhart was 'of [the] calibre to be Minister of Information'. Bruce Lockhart was interested but wary; he knew how deep the rifts between Dalton at the Ministry of Economic Warfare and Duff Cooper at the Ministry of Information ran.

Two weeks later, Eden met Bruce Lockhart and explained what the proposed job would be. Under the so-called 'Anderson award' – the compromise that had been negotiated over propaganda and agreed on 14 June – two committees would be created. One was the committee of three ministers with joint propaganda control; the second was an operational committee which would do the 'actual work'. Eden wanted Bruce Lockhart to chair the latter. Bruce Lockhart thought the Cabinet's agreement on the new system was 'a thoroughly bad compromise' and was unhappy about the offer.[5] He rightly suspected that he was being produced, 'like a rabbit out of a conjurer's hat', to solve a 'silly ministerial squabble'. He asked for a few days to consider, not least because he was reluctant to leave his role working with the Czech government-in-exile. It was down to Beaverbrook to cajole him further.

Bruce Lockhart was invited to a late dinner in a 'big fine room' at 12 Downing Street, where Beaverbrook was based. Brendan Bracken dropped in for 'futile talks on propaganda' where Bracken was 'very anti-Dalton'.[6] Dalton, too, had tried to work on Bruce Lockhart, finding him 'irritatingly reluctant' to accept the job offer.[7] Bruce Lockhart stayed up all night with Beaverbrook, going with him to the BBC for a broadcast to the USA at 3am, after which the two men drove to Beaverbrook's Surrey estate, Cherkley Court.

Bruce Lockhart hadn't got to bed until quarter to five, but he was woken after a few hours' sleep by another summons from his host. He found Beaverbrook in his bedroom, 'stark-naked with his hairy little brown body covered with moles or blotches', shaving with an electric razor. The naked mogul advised Bruce Lockhart to take the job he had been offered, saying it was only a beginning. 'He would make me his confi-dant,' Bruce Lockhart observed. 'His ambition was to make me Minister of Information.' Persuaded that there might ultimately be more in it for him, Bruce Lockhart told Eden the next day, 19 June, that he would accept the job.

The following weekend, on the day that Germany invaded Russia, Beaverbrook insisted that Bruce Lockhart come back to Cherkley from Woburn, to discuss ways to reform the Ministry of Information. This time, the persuasion having achieved its object, Bruce Lockhart found himself being teased over dinner. Beaverbrook told the whole table that 'but for women, Bruce would have been Prime Minister and certainly Foreign Secretary by now'.[8] In his more considered version of events, Bruce Lockhart didn't mention that quip, but said that they had watched a film that evening in Beaver-brook's private cinema, called *Dust is my Destiny*. 'I felt that it was mine also,' he wrote, in his typically deadpan manner.[9]

Bruce Lockhart sustained a lifestyle, even in wartime, that was far beyond his means and he found it hard to refuse Beaverbrook's requests, since he owed him both money and favours. Beaverbrook had bailed him out financially in earlier years, paying off his debts as well as employing him as a journalist. In 1930, Beaverbrook's office estimated Bruce Lockhart's debts at £10,366, equivalent to over half a million pounds at current prices.[10] On 2 July, Bruce Lockhart noted that he had signed the document for another loan, though he did not say from whom. That same day, his social life was in full swing. First, he headed to the Savoy for drinks with Noël Coward and the designer Gladys Calthrop, before the first night at the Piccadilly Theatre of *Blithe Spirit*, where he sat in a box with Coward. The premiere was a full house and Duff Cooper, the Vansittarts and the Mountbattens were also in attendance. Coward, however, was nervous and 'very critical of Margaret Rutherford', who was playing Madame Arcati.

After the show, the party continued at the flat of the author Clemence Dane, where Coward entertained the guests with a rendition of 'London Pride', the song he had composed in response to one of the spring's air raids. He also sang a 'new song about the Home Guard', presumably 'Could You Please Oblige Us with a Bren Gun?' Bruce Lockhart's love life was a complicated juggle: divorced from his first wife, Jean, he was still involved in a long-lasting affair with the Countess of Rosslyn, Vera, known as 'Tommy', which had been going on for over a decade. Tommy had been widowed in 1939. Bruce Lockhart was also in regular contact with his lover from his Russia days, Moura Budberg.

The following day, Bruce Lockhart's appointment to his new job – as a deputy under-secretary within the Foreign Office, with responsibility for foreign propaganda – was first spoken of in the House of Commons, by Sir John Anderson. As his name was mentioned, the Communist MP for West Fife, Willie Gallacher, exclaimed that Bruce Lockhart was 'a notorious anti-Soviet man'.[11] Anderson's debate on the role of the Ministry of Information revealed intense criticisms from MPs of the government's propaganda effort. Anderson tried to head off this criticism by explaining his new procedures, but that didn't allay MPs' unhappiness. He acknowledged the main line of criticism about foreign propaganda, that 'a number of different agencies are at work, without apparently any single control'. However, he resisted the suggestion that the Ministry of Information should be in overall charge, saying 'foreign propaganda must be in line with foreign policy', and therefore should come under the control of the foreign secretary.

Russia's entry into the war had 'made political warfare ten times more important', the Liberal MP, Rob Bernays, argued. He was not impressed with the way the Ministry of Information was working, calling it a 'clumsy monster stretching right across Whitehall'. The ministry, he continued, 'reminds me of the brontosaurus, which was, I believe, 60 feet long and weighed some 60 tons, but it had a very small brain and a very slender spinal cord'. He wanted the minister, in a rather double-edged comment, to be that brain and spinal cord. Bernays pointed out how the debate had been delayed for the government to decide on its policy; he had heard of 'a great battle going on in Bloomsbury', where the ministry was based. Bernays, whose opposition to Nazi Germany had been cemented by his own visits there in the 1930s, and who had some Jewish ancestry, said that Britain needed a far more definite policy behind its propaganda to foreign countries, with more attention paid to both Germany and Russia in that regard.[12] He believed that 'such a policy could bind our listeners into the most powerful secret society of revolution ever known in the world'.

Many MPs offered their suggestions as to how propaganda could be made more effective, including Captain Leonard Plugge, a Conservative who had set up the commercial International Broadcasting Company, which operated until the start of the war, and therefore knew about radio. Plugge made the case that British radio propaganda could have a far greater reach, and avoid jamming, if it used newer technology, such as 'frequency modulation' (later to become more familiar to listeners as FM), which the Germans were already exploiting.

The Labour MP Philip Noel-Baker made what he called a 'vigorous attack' on the current system. He was incensed about the 'slum conditions' that the BBC had to work in at what he referred to as 'the black hole of Tooting Bec'. By this he meant the glass-roofed former ice rink of Maida Vale, where the BBC's foreign services had worked. He described it as being in Tooting Bec, on the opposite side of London and across the Thames, so as not to publicise the true former whereabouts of the BBC to Goering's Luftwaffe. The BBC staff, he said, had worked in unsafe conditions for five months under almost continuous bombing. Even in their new premises, Noel-Baker added, they were overcrowded, so much so that one man who went into a room occupied by forty people in order to make a telephone call came out 'gasping for breath'. More serious still was Noel-Baker's critique of the messages Britain was putting out. There was, he said, 'too much appeasement, too little democracy, and no clear, constructive message of hope and reconstruction'. He concluded his speech laying the blame for all of these failings at the door of the Ministry of Information, urging drastic reform. 'The Government ought to make a real Ministry of Information, with real authority and real power, and close the doors of the unhappy institution that we have to-day.'

As Duff Cooper rose to wind up the debate, faced with criticism from all sides of the House, he must have realised that his days in charge at Senate House, the ministry's head-quarters, were coming to an end. Well before the public announcement, it was widespread knowledge in Westminster that he would be replaced by Brendan Bracken. But as with any coalition government, reshuffles were tricky to arrange.

Robert Bruce Lockhart reported back to the foreign secre-tary, Anthony Eden, each week on his progress in the new role. On 14 July, he commented on some of the reactions to his appointment among his friends. They didn't seem hopeful of his prospects. One of those friends, George Malcolm Thomson, who had been working 'eighteen hours a day' in the Ministry of Supply alongside Lord Beaverbrook, and who Bruce Lockhart described as being a brother Scot who saw alike with him on most questions, observed: 'You and I had better have a wake before our funerals. There is only one difference between us: I am being murdered: you have com-mitted suicide.' He added in his note to Eden, 'metaphori-cally true; literally a future possibility'.[13] Bruce Lockhart and Thomson had their doubtless boozy wake.

By 16 July, Dalton had learned from the Labour leader, Clement Attlee, that Bracken would be appointed minister of information. Attlee tried to reassure Dalton that Bracken was well-qualified, as he knew the press, the press lords and the City. Dalton, who believed Bracken to be 'reactionary and anti-Labour', was still unhappy. Dalton reminded Attlee of his previous run-in with Bracken – alluding to the Carlton Grill incident – saying that if Bracken tried to use his influence with Churchill to get the better of him, he would 'make a row'. Attlee recalled that Bracken had been ticked off for his previous behaviour and said he didn't think he would do it again. The Labour leader proposed to resolve the tension by inviting both Bracken and Dalton to a 'little dinner party', at which the two men would 'fall on each others' necks', presumably in a friendly manner.[14] Dalton still believed that he could 'raise much greater hell in the Labour party' than Bracken could with the Tories.[15]

On Sunday the 20th, Bruce Lockhart too had the news of the reshuffle confirmed from Beaverbrook, whose advice was to 'Back Brendan 100 per cent'. That evening, the details of the reshuffle were announced by Downing Street. *The Times* the next morning described Bracken's appointment as 'an expected choice' and the paper took the view that his experience of working in daily touch with Churchill, as well as his 'first hand knowledge of newspapers and their work' would stand him in good stead and help Bracken 'bring a fresh mind to the difficult problems of the Ministry'.[16]

This was a huge promotion for Bracken, and despite his professed qualms about it, he was making a sudden entry to the Cabinet. For all that he was well-known in political and society circles, this was the first time that he would have a significant public role. In many ways, he was extremely well-suited to propaganda. Put bluntly, Brendan Bracken was an outrageous liar.

Bracken was so close to Churchill that one of the many rumours which followed him for years was that he was his illegitimate son. He wasn't, but Randolph Churchill, the prime minister's real son, half-jokingly referred to Bracken as 'my brother, the bastard'. Randolph, perhaps not surprisingly,

Brendan Bracken at 10 Downing Street on 21 July 1941, the day he was appointed minister of information

disliked Bracken. He once told Bruce Lockhart that Bracken was 'God's greatest liar because he does not mind being found out'.[17] The myth of his paternity was one of many untrue stories that Bracken did nothing to stop – and probably even encouraged himself.

Bracken lied about his origins, his family and his education. He was anxious to conceal the truth about his birthplace. In reality, he had been born in Templemore, in Tipperary in Ireland, in February 1901. Bracken often denied that he was Irish. When he first stood for Parliament for North Paddington in 1929, he let it be known to the local paper, the *Paddington Mercury*, that he was of 'Anglo-Irish stock' and had been born in Bedfordshire. Bracken's election agent responded to questions about his background by printing a leaflet which insisted in large letters that 'Bracken is British' and stated: 'Mr Bracken is British by birth and comes of a long succession of generations of British stock without any intermixture of foreign blood.'[18] Bracken had a troubled time at school, ran away from the boarding school he was later sent to, briefly worked as a trainee journalist on a local newspaper and then left Ireland for Australia.

His first great act of reinventing himself was to become an English public schoolboy. Returning from Australia, he presented himself at the private Sedbergh School in Cumbria. Bracken, claiming to be fifteen, enrolled himself at the school and paid his own fees. The trouble was that, in September 1920, Brendan Bracken was nineteen years old. Although he left after a term, it was enough for him trade on a connection with the school for the rest of his life. At the 1929 election, the *Paddington Mercury* also wrote that he had attended Oxford University, although Bracken had never been to any university.

Bracken also claimed, prematurely, to be an orphan. One of his biographers, Andrew Boyle, wrote that Bracken told the children of the headmaster at Sedbergh a vivid tale of how his parents had been 'burnt to a crisp' in an Australian bushfire.[19] While his father, Joseph, really was dead – he had died in Ireland when Bracken was only three – his mother, Hannah, was alive, well, remarried and still in her home country. Bracken wrote home to her regularly until her death in 1928, and she even visited him in London at his Westminster home in Lord North Street. His other biographer, Charles Lysaght, suggested that those London visits 'were doubtless conducted with some discretion' in case Bracken and his mother happened to bump into one of the people who believed him to be an Australian orphan. Later, he also claimed that his mother had left him a palazzo in Venice. No-one seems to have been recorded asking him directly how his Australian farming mother had come by her luxurious Italian property.

Although Bracken did have real siblings and half-siblings, the relative he most frequently mentioned was his imaginary brother. This brother isn't given a name in the anecdotes about him, but he had remarkable powers of survival. He had walked all the way across Africa, had bought Bracken a complete set of Hansard, and regularly contemplated buying houses or paintings.[20] He had a heroic and miraculous war record. Ronald Tree, fellow MP and the owner of Churchill's frequent retreat at Ditchley Park, had known Bracken for many years. Tree wrote that 'whenever a major battle or action took place, Brendan movingly announced the entirely fictitious death of his allegedly combatant brother. One evening at Ditchley, he reduced my son, on leave from the Army, to tears by describing in great detail the brother's gallant death at Narvik. The whole thing was an invention.' What was so strange was that these inventions seem to have gone unchallenged by those who heard them, like Tree's genuine serving soldier son, no matter how many times the imaginary brother died. No-one even seemed to ask the brother's name, let alone whether they could attend his memorial. On another occasion, Bracken told an MP that his wealthy brother was a lieutenant commander in the Royal Navy. Ronald Tree wrote mildly that these stories were 'somewhat reprehensible', before explaining that 'the many dramatic deaths of Brendan's brother occasionally caused comment, but he continued to repeat them with undiminished zest'.[21]

Brendan Bracken managed to create himself as the person he wanted to be through these frequent lies: a member of the English establishment, with a public-school education, a man of property. By association with his fake brother, he became closely connected to a hero, albeit a fictional one. It didn't appear to have been the done thing to question – at least in the public domain – whether his accounts were true. Bracken relied on the assumption that 'no true gentleman would ever cast doubt on the credentials of an obvious stranger, especially one already accepted at face value by that gentleman's friends'.[22]

Although there were widespread rumours about him, they didn't seem to extend to many serious attempts to check Bracken's casual attitude to the facts. At the same time, he was building a career as a newspaper proprietor which gave him more access to society, more influence and more control over stories in the news. Bracken had spent a few months as a teacher before moving into publishing. Helped by his ability to make powerful friends, he progressed quickly. He began by rebranding the *Illustrated Review*, owned by Eyre and Spottiswoode, as *English Life*. He shifted into financial news, creating *The Banker* magazine and reaching the boardroom of the publisher. The company bought not only the *Financial News* and the *Investors Chronicle*, but also a 50 per cent share of the *Economist*.

By the end of the decade, Bracken was genuinely wealthy, well-established and well-connected in both journalism and politics. He had also cultivated a friendship with Max Beaverbrook, the owner of the *Daily Express*, since at least 1925. The two men wrote to each other regularly and exchanged gifts; in July 1938, Beaverbrook even gave Bracken a dog – a 'very small terrier'.[23]

While some of his colleagues, like Tom Delmer, told their own stories that were laced with untruths and omissions, Bracken lied habitually. Lying came easily to him, but he made no attempt to be consistent. He appeared to lie mostly in order to bolster his own position in society and to protect and conceal his private life. In death, he made it harder for anyone to pin down the truth by ordering that all of his personal papers be destroyed within twenty-four hours, although some of his letters survive in official archives and the collections of his correspondents. Bracken has an unmistakable, acerbic and often sarcastic tone, and the awkward, careful handwriting of someone who hadn't attended school for very long. His public rows and the stories that were told about him often survive, because he was frequently the cause of drama and the source of gossip. But his private thoughts and feelings remain elusive. One of Bracken's biographers called the work of writing his life story primarily 'a work of detection'.[24]

It's hard to imagine a twenty-first-century politician getting away with quite so much. This is probably because so much less of public life before the war was actually accessible to the public. Westminster gossip was just as prevalent, if not more so, but it largely remained within the closed circles of clubs and private dinners. Bracken's lies could continue – and vary constantly – because even if they did reach the newspapers, there would have been less ability and less willingness to fact-check them. A modern journalist would have been encouraged to find out the supposed name, rank and serial number of Bracken's imaginary brother, for instance, and to check whether he existed or not. It didn't hurt that Bracken owned media organisations himself and was close friends with one of the country's most powerful proprietors, who was also in the government. Investigative or tabloid journalism, freedom of information and social media might not necessarily have destroyed Bracken's political career – others have survived lies and scandal in recent times, and he was protected by his powerful friends – but they would have made his telling of tales more obvious to those outside his political world.

Privately, though, many of Bracken's colleagues and friends did try to find out more about him. Beaverbrook, with a journalist's instinct, had sent his crime reporter to check Bracken's birth certificate in Ireland. Some political rivals had made similar inquiries. Bruce Lockhart knew more about Bracken through a coincidental personal connection; his brother became headmaster of Sedbergh School in 1937. When Bruce Lockhart went to holiday with his brother at the school in October 1941, he met a housemaster who gave him some inside information about Bracken's brief time as a pupil there. Bracken, he was told, had given his date of birth as 1904, lying about his age to make himself three years younger. The housemaster, Sumner, had been impressed by Bracken's photographic memory and ability in history and economics, and believed the student had done a deal with the then headmaster – Weech, described as 'more of a businessman than a headmaster' – to ignore his real age and allow him to be admitted. Another teacher revealed that Bracken had paid his term's fees from 'a wad of notes in his pocket'.[25] Bruce Lockhart noted this down in his diary, but it's not clear whether or how he used this information about the man who was by then his new boss. A few years later, towards the end of the war, Bruce Lockhart accompanied Bracken on a visit to the school, where they strode across the fells together and shared pints in a nearby pub. Again, Bruce Lockhart didn't mention having questioned Bracken about his past, and Bracken remained proud of his connection to the school, rather than shying away from the place.

Something that Bracken might not have felt the need to be so evasive about in the modern world was his sexuality. His biographers wrote about his unsuccessful attempts to marry, which were rejected by the society women he pursued. Bracken certainly had many close friendships with men who were gay, such as Evan Morgan, Viscount Tredegar. Morgan helped the young Bracken get his first job in publishing, at Eyre and Spottiswoode.[26] Gavin Henderson, Lord Faringdon, another gay man, was friends with both men and a neighbour of Bracken's in Lord North Street, describing how Bracken fell on him 'like a long-lost brother' when they first met. Morgan and Bracken, in Henderson's view, were 'birds of a feather – and so extremely well-matched'.[27] His biographers, writing in the 1970s, only a few years after male homosexuality was decriminalised in England, raised the rumours about Bracken's sexuality that had circulated widely, but were inclined not to believe them.

So perhaps we should take Bracken's show of reluctance over his promotion with a generous helping of salt. On his appointment, he wrote to a friend that 'in a very short time I shall be joining the happy band of ex-Ministers of Information'.[28] Beaverbrook, despite having suggested to Bruce Lockhart that he could be in line for the job, was quick to offer his effusive congratulations to the new minister. On Bracken's first day at Senate House, Beaverbrook wrote: 'My dear Brendan, In the ordinary way, it would be looked on as a sarcastic or even an unfriendly act to offer a man congratulations on becoming Minister of Information. In your case, this is not so. You are going to make a great success in this office. Your gifts of imagination and energy will be given a scope they have never enjoyed before. And the glory you will win will be all the brighter because it shines in a dark and dismal sky.'[29]

A week later, Bracken wrote back from his new office on Malet Street, saying that Beaverbrook's letter was a great encouragement to him. 'I have no illusions about this job,' he wrote, 'and I would not have taken it without your backing. You know all that needs to be known about how to run this Ministry. And as I shall be wanting your help, you will curse the day that you pressed me to come here! For you are already overworked, and have little time for the affairs of other Departments. Bless you.'

This chatty style was typical of Bracken's surviving personal letters, a manner which also helped to endear him to the journalists who came to the Ministry of Information for briefings. He held weekly press conferences, where reporters could expect to hear 'hard-hitting arguments and tit-bits from late-night chats with the Prime Minister', as well as the occasional unplanned indiscretion from the minister, even if the censor often then had to withdraw some of Bracken's comments and say that they weren't for publication.[30] For the journalists, this was a refreshing change from the previous briefings and allowed them to feel that they were getting the inside gossip.

For the civil servants at the ministry, however, the atmosphere wasn't as congenial. Bracken came into Senate House determined to shake things up. Harold Nicolson, who had himself been fired as a junior minister at the Ministry of Information in the reshuffle and who was in despond at what he believed was the end of his political career, spoke to Bracken soon after his appointment and observed that 'he seems to be sacking everybody at the Ministry'.[31] Bracken set about this almost as soon as he arrived in the building, having first found his way about the corridors and learned the names of the staff. He didn't trouble with the niceties for those who were dismissed. One young aide said his introductions would go: 'Ah yes, you're Mr so-and-so. Well, you're out. The letter terminating your employment is on its way.' He made his way through the complex, the aide said, as though it was suffering 'a series of direct hits by anti-personnel bombs'.[32] Nor did Bracken let personal ties restrict him; one of those fired was his own (real) half-sister, Cora Dunlop, who was told she had to resign at once. Her half-brother informed her that 'I have to sack half the people in this joint and I cannot have it said in parliament that I am giving jobs to members of my own family.'[33] Those who survived the bombardment, however, were impressed by Bracken's speed of action and reform.

In his weekly update to Eden, Bruce Lockhart reflected on Bracken's first day in the job. 'I have known Mr Brendan Bracken very intimately for fifteen years. Our personal relations are good, but I do not assume that on this account he will be easy to work with. He has drive, ambition and some ruthlessness. He will certainly urge speed of action. In my opinion he is more likely to succeed in his difficult task than any previous Minister of Information.'[34] At Bruce Lockhart's first meeting with Bracken, two days later, it was already clear that for some this would not be an easy time. Bracken 'made little attempt to conceal his desire to get rid of Dalton'.[35]

One of Bracken's first tasks was to work on creating the more effective system for control of propaganda that was being so widely demanded. At the end of July, he already seemed exasperated by what he had found, writing: 'Since assuming my present functions, I find that at least eight government departments are engaged in, or interfering with, foreign propaganda. This multiplicity of control has created confusion and inter-departmental bickering. Energy which should have been directed against the enemy has been dissipated.'[36]

He proposed the creation of 'what would virtually amount to a secret department of Political Warfare for conducting propaganda by all means at our disposal in the war-zone area'. What this would mean in practice is that control of foreign propaganda, which had been known as SO1, would be formally separated from its undercover subversive counterpart in SO2. Until now, both had been the responsibility of the Ministry of Economic Warfare and therefore of Dalton. Dalton did not realise at first that the territory he had been so reluctant to concede to Duff Cooper was now lost. When Bracken and Dalton had lunch together on 28 July, the latter appeared to be lulled into a false sense of security, writing in his diary that Bracken seemed 'very friendly and co-operative' and claimed not to be all that interested in foreign propaganda. Bracken also seemed convinced that creating a Department of Political Warfare would be good domestic propaganda in itself. Bracken, Dalton wrote, 'thinks that this would make a great impression in Parliament and in the press, where "political warfare" is a much beloved phrase, and that this would settle for good the question of secrecy'.[37] Dalton should perhaps have realised that Bracken was not one to let their previous rivalry go lightly.

8

A Nuisance to the Government

Brendan Bracken, confidently installed in his minister-ial job, enjoyed spreading gossip about his rival, Hugh Dalton, more than ever. He circulated stories about how Churchill was unhappy with Dalton's running of SO2, the sabotage operation, as well as the management of SO1. It was probably even more pleasing to Bracken that he got to do so in ever more elegant surroundings. As they waited in the Ambassadors' Room at the Foreign Office ahead of a meeting with Eden and Dalton in early August 1941, Bracken glee-fully related to Robert Bruce Lockhart a story from a dinner with Gladwyn Jebb, Dalton's Economic Warfare colleague. Bracken had made some disparaging comments about Dalton to Jebb, who promptly told his boss, much as had happened in the Carlton Grill incident in February. Dalton, this time, complained to Churchill. When the prime minister sent for Bracken to explain, he asked: 'Is it true that at dinner the other night you attacked SO2 and Dalton's work?' Bracken said he'd responded: 'What I said was that Dalton was the biggest bloodiest shit I've ever met!' Churchill, Bracken claimed, had laughed.[1]

Dalton clearly didn't overhear this conversation before his meeting, but noticed during it that Eden was sipping milk because he was suffering from duodenal ulcers. Dalton, in his diary, was far from sympathetic to the foreign secretary's ailments, blaming them on 'excessive worry' and calling Eden a 'nervy fusser'. Dalton left London that afternoon for few days away at his house in Wiltshire, where he read Gissing, Gibbon and *I, Claudius*, cut the grass and made hay.

As Dalton went away on holiday, the outlines of a new organisation that would be in charge of political warfare had essentially been set out. Bracken's idea of a separate, secret department, overseen by all three ministers – the foreign secretary (Eden), the minister of information (himself) and the minister for economic warfare (Dalton) – was going ahead. In discussions, it was referred to as the Department of Political Warfare, but its eventual name would be the Political Warfare Executive. It was commonly referred to by its acronym, PWE – though some, such as Dalton, sounded that out as 'Peewee', and called its civil servants, disparagingly, the Peawits.

Bruce Lockhart described the negotiations between Bracken and Dalton in his report to Eden on 11 August. Bracken had been 'forceful, sometimes pugnacious, sometimes impulsive, yet adroitly skilful in tactics, always good-humoured and always tractable'.[2] 'Above all,' Bruce Lockhart continued, 'by quick-fire speech he has proved himself at least the equal of Dr Dalton in argument . . . The scientific definition of daltonism is inability to distinguish between green and red, and I doubt very much if [Dalton] has ever seen any danger signal to himself. He relies on his charter from the Prime Minister, and this may have to be amended.'[3]

Eden also seemed satisfied, noting in the margin that this was 'good progress' and that Bruce Lockhart was to be congratulated on having got into his stride. This satisfaction didn't last. Back from holiday, once Dalton saw Rex Leeper's plan for political warfare, which was to be presented at a meeting of the three ministers on the 21st, he was horrified. He wrote to Eden and Bracken ahead of their meeting that he 'could not possibly agree to the complete disappearance of one half of the Special Operations Executive' which, he argued, was his by charter of the prime minister.[4] As Bruce Lockhart had predicted, Dalton would always appeal to a higher authority.

Dalton felt the ministerial meeting was rushed, with his two counterparts sparing only twenty minutes for a discussion. He detected that he was being bounced into Bracken's proposals with little time for discussion. This was probably deliberate on their part. Dalton didn't want to surrender all of his SO1 staff to Bracken's control, and there were also arguments to be had about the role of the BBC and how much of the operation would remain at Woburn.

When Bruce Lockhart replied to a letter from Eden asking him to proceed with the creation of the new executive, his response, on 22 August, was so frank that it was archived in a folder titled 'Mr Lockhart's reply raising embarrassing questions'.[5] This was not going to be easy, Bruce Lockhart cautioned his boss. He wanted to call the foreign secretary's attention to what he called the 'deplorable situation' of our propaganda. He wrote: 'It is the plain truth which will be denied by no honest person inside our various propaganda organisations that most of the energy which should have been directed against the enemy has been dissipated in inter-departmental strife and jealousies.'[6]

That weekend, Dalton headed for Woburn, determined to maintain his influence there. But, as was often the case, he succeeded in irritating his colleagues, telling them he would rather have been at his own country cottage. Rex Leeper confided in Bruce Lockhart that Dalton had 'decided with reluctance to agree to complete fusion in a new department'.[7] When Dalton departed, he left Rex Leeper – whom a few weeks earlier, he'd compared to 'a very immobile old sheep' – with the snide parting shot that Leeper needed a break and looked 'not at all well'.

Back in London on Wednesday the 27th, Dalton found the trio of Bruce Lockhart, Leeper and Dallas Brooks arriving together for a meeting. Bracken had been pushing them for the last week to sort things out; he told his officials that they had the powers to deal with any ministry as they thought fit, under the authority which the prime minister had given the PWE. Bruce Lockhart told him they wanted to be able to hire and fire their own staff without reference to ministers. Bracken, the propagandists told Dalton, had given them control over the BBC, as well as authority over personnel in both the BBC and the Ministry of Information. Bracken wanted to know whether Dalton had agreed to similar powers regarding staff in SO1. The three officials wanted to make clear that they would be running the PWE, hoping for less interference by the trio of ministers in charge.

This combined push forced Dalton to accept the idea of creating the PWE, even though in a long letter to Bracken he expressed many conditions for doing so. He wrote that he had understood at the beginning of August that there would be a division of overt and covert propaganda; Bracken in charge of the former, himself in charge of the latter. Dalton said he was willing to agree to the new structure and to give it a trial, 'even though it appears to involve the complete liquidation of SO1, which I certainly did not contemplate when these discussions began, provided that certain points are made unmistakably clear'.[8] He wanted more involvement from the Ministry of Economic Warfare written into the plan, as well as an assurance that if the PWE was engaged in any activity outside British territory, it should only do so through what was then known as SO2 – the active operations part of SOE.

Dalton also insisted that 'Ministerial control and Ministerial stimulus must remain a reality'. By this, he meant that he wanted 'the fullest information' about the PWE to be available to all three ministers. He also asserted the right of any minister to visit any of the PWE establishments, in London or in the country, 'to acquaint himself with what is going on'.

This last proviso was particularly irritating to the other ministers, as well as to Bruce Lockhart, Leeper and Brooks, who had put up with Dalton's regular energetic visits to Woburn, interspersed with his complaints. In an aide memoire to Bracken, they observed that Dalton seemed to have more time at his disposal than either Bracken or Eden did, so it would be an 'intolerable situation' if Dalton persisted in 'sending for and questioning subordinates of the Executive Committee' and 'paying constant visits to Woburn Abbey and to the BBC'.

The same day, Saturday 6 September, that Dalton wrote to Bracken about his objections, he also wrote a 'Secret and Personal' letter to 'My dear Brendan'. In this, he effectively accused the new minister of information of leaking secrets about the creation of the PWE to friendly newspapers ahead of the planned announcement to Parliament. Dalton referred to the morning and evening papers on Thursday, which had carried 'a good deal about our new arrangements for Political Warfare'. Dalton was annoyed that the *Evening Standard* had reported that 'parliamentary curiosity about the department will not be encouraged. The Minister answerable for its activities will probably be Mr. Brendan Bracken.' Dalton complained that there should have been consultation with him 'before any such hint was given to the Press'. He was also angry about reports in the *Daily Telegraph* saying that the 'Department for Political Warfare will assume responsibility for all non-military activities in Europe directed to hastening the defeat of Germany'. 'I was very much surprised at this,' Dalton wrote, 'and I do not know who used such language to the Press.' Dalton wanted assurances that the activities referred to were only the activities of SO1 and not SO2, which still came under the Ministry of Economic Warfare's control.[9]

Dalton clearly implied that it was Bracken himself who had been leaking to the press, rather than any other official spokesman. It was not only the leaks that would have put Dalton out. It was also that Bracken was overstepping what had so far been agreed and putting his own version of how things would work in the media first. The leaks were saying that Bracken would be the minister responsible to Parliament and would have control over subversive activities, both things that Dalton thought were still in question.

Bracken's reply was a picture of injured innocence. He wrote back to say he shared Dalton's regret that the press had got hold of the story of the PWE, adding that 'the fact that it got it wrong adds to one's annoyance'. He added: 'I don't understand your reference to an official spokesman in this Ministry. No-one in this Ministry gave any information to the Press.' It was probably a rather disingenuous denial.

Eden, who had plans in hand for announcing the PWE in an answer to an 'inspired' Parliamentary Question the following week, put further pressure on Dalton in the last ministerial meeting ahead of the announcement.[10] At a meeting that Dalton described as 'a bit sticky', Eden told him that he had been thinking a great deal about the question and had concluded that 'if we were starting afresh, much the best solution would be to have one minister, rather than three, and one principal official'.[11] That minister, he thought, should be Bracken. But since the plans were already in place, Eden didn't think it worthwhile to change them and take them back to the prime minister again. Faced with the threat of ripping up the negotiated plans and having everything handed over to Bracken, Dalton retreated. He told himself that once the system was announced in Parliament, he would have the benefit of having the Labour Party on his side as the only Labour minister of the three.

The official news of the creation of the Political Warfare Executive came on 11 September. The MP who had been 'inspired', presumably by a helpful minister or whip, to ask the prime minister a question about it was Commander Stephen King-Hall, an independent MP who had been a naval officer and a regular broadcaster on the BBC since the 1920s, including on *Children's Hour*. He asked Churchill whether any steps had recently been taken to improve the co-ordination of the several organisations responsible for political warfare and, if so, what the nature of the reorganisation was. Churchill obliged: the foreign secretary, the minister of information and the minister of economic warfare had recommended 'a small special executive for the conduct of Political Warfare should be established, in lieu of the various agencies concerned at present, which have done very excellent work, to conduct such propaganda in all its forms. This executive has already begun its work, but it would be contrary to the national interest to make any public statement regarding its personnel or the nature of its activities.'[12] This was the form of words that Eden had set out a month earlier in his plans. Asked to whom questions should be put about its work, Churchill told King-Hall there could be no questions on secret matters, but on all other matters they should be put to the minister of information – just as Bracken or other sources had briefed the *Evening Standard*.

Other MPs tried to elicit more information about the PWE from the prime minister, but without much greater success. Philip Noel-Baker and Leonard Plugge both took the opportunity to ask Churchill about the issues they had raised in the summer's debate on propaganda – the facilities available to the BBC and the use of newer technology. George Garro-Jones wanted to know more about what a secret question was and how it was decided what counted as a secret; this was not as abstract a query as it sounded, as it meant defining the limits of which aspects of the war MPs could ask about in public debate.

Sir Rupert de la Bère, a Conservative MP, pressed a similar question on the PM. 'What is the difference between a secret Question and an awkward Question?' he asked.[13] Churchill responded with a quip: 'One is a danger to the country, and the other is a nuisance to the Government.'

Dalton was quite happy with how the day had gone, though he made sure to mention to various MPs he encountered that he was jointly responsible for all enemy and enemy-occupied propaganda, including BBC broadcasts. He also invited Attlee to dinner to press his case about political warfare. Dalton said he felt that 'a game was being played which I do not care about', insisting to Attlee that since he had now been named as in joint charge of political warfare, he would be expected by the Labour Party to take a keen interest in such matters. Attlee reassured Dalton that if he had any trouble, he himself would take it up again with the prime minister.[14]

It would take less than a month, however, for Bracken and Dalton to run into conflict again. Bruce Lockhart had already realised that Dalton did not fundamentally accept the new status quo. After a dinner at one of the Woburn houses, Dalton summoned many of the SO1 heads and gave them a long speech, praising his own machine, offering a 'sarcastic sneer of contempt' for the Ministry of Information and the BBC, and telling the regional heads to ignore the paper plans and to run things their own way. Bruce Lockhart feared 'the situation was hopeless' and that nothing had changed. He predicted that, as chair of the new body with 'all responsibility and no power', he would face the most criticism, confiding in his diary that 'I shall have to resign very soon – before it is too late.'[15] It was a dinner designed to bring Bracken and Dalton closer together which drove them further apart.

Charles Hambro, the banker turned SOE official, hosted the dinner on 9 October. The other guests were Gladwyn Jebb and David Bowes-Lyon, both of whom were colleagues of Dalton at the Ministry of Economic Warfare. Dalton didn't record what precisely triggered the argument between himself and Bracken, but said his rival minister had been 'rude, assertive, ignorant, inconsequent, stupid, angular and unreceptive'.[16] So much so, in fact, that the host, Hambro, had to take the 'insufferable oaf' away. It's likely, of course, that Dalton gave as good as he got.

The hostility was apparent to others in the PWE's now-regular Tuesday meetings. The arguments continued with occasional lulls. On 21 October, Dalton said he had a most infuriating afternoon, where 'Bracken is worse than ever. He brings no papers, has studied nothing, is arrogant, rude, inconsequent, critical, purely destructive.' The mutual distrust between the ministers was clear to the others in the room. Bruce Lockhart, who was also there, said that 'the fur began to fly', with Bracken on the attack. An argument about confusion over propaganda in South America left Dalton 'white to the top of his bald head with rage'.[17] Bracken then exclaimed that this was 'Alice in Blunderland', calling the mistakes a gross waste of taxpayers' money. Sir Alec Cadogan of the Foreign Office, who had joined the meeting just before the argument, called it a 'dogfight between Dalton and Brendan', and said to Bruce Lockhart that he found himself 'moving in a very sinister jungle'.[18] Although the next week's meeting was far calmer, with Dalton finding 'everything going swimmingly' and Bracken even 'amiable', things blew up again at the end of the month.

Writing from his sickbed in the village of Great Bedwyn in Wiltshire, where he was laid up with a cold, Bracken accused Dalton of having delayed passing on important information from President Roosevelt about an offer of radio transmitters. 'I do not understand your way of transacting public business,' he complained. Dalton, in his view, had not raised these important issues at the meeting on the 21st and his assertions about what was going on had 'no foundations in fact' – he was effectively accusing Dalton of lying. Bracken summed up with a line that was bound to infuriate Dalton by demeaning his importance, saying: 'Surely you should give up the role of postman. Who can welcome a postman who does not deliver messages, but sends an assistant to interpret them?'[19]

Dalton responded with a letter that was on the surface an attempt to calm things down, wishing Bracken better – and hoping, with a slightly snide undertone, that he would be back for Eden's important ministerial meeting. He wasn't going to apologise for anything, though, explaining that 'this wicked animal, when set upon, must sometimes counter-attack!' Dalton offered the apparent hope that their respective ministry staff could co-operate, writing: 'I would much rather get on with the war, than get on with such debates.' That didn't seem likely to happen.[20]

Bracken 'exploded with a complaint' about some leaflets and Dalton described him as a 'vexatious little blighter' who was too prone to appeal to the prime minister for backing. Almost every week brought a similar list of complaints: Bracken had 'a long string of grievances, which he put with his customary rudeness' and exhibited 'brainless bad manners'.

Although Dalton continued to protest that he wanted to avoid squabbling and get on with their work, his actions didn't match those words. On 8 November, he wrote to Bracken to discuss a complaint about leaflets in Thailand, concluding that 'it would give me much more satisfaction, if we could make an end of this silly bickering, to join with you in knocking the real enemy on the head!'[21] A subsequent letter from Bracken to Eden – though ostensibly about an American idea of dis-tributing propaganda posters in neutral countries, something Bracken thought unwise – revealed what he was really driving at. His conclusion was about 'the folly of maintaining two Government propagandist machines'. 'We shall never have a sound policy,' Bracken wrote, 'until all propaganda, overt and covert, is given over to this Ministry.' He continued, asserting that 'there is no justification for allowing another Ministry to discharge some of its most important functions'.[22]

Since none of Bracken's personal papers survive, it is harder to know his reactions to Dalton, although his official letters reveal that he often goaded and needled his fellow minister, intent on getting a rise out of him. Andrew Boyle, his biographer, says that Bracken relied on 'time, luck and sheer pressure' to gradually wear Dalton down. By the middle of November, that seemed to be working. Dalton was depressed and contemplated resigning, musing on the 'embarrassed, transient, jealous, embittered phantoms' that politicians were. 'We win our battles today and lose them tomorrow; we come in and go out, generally at quite short intervals. To me, sometimes, the idea of going out has great attractions.'[23]

Dalton's letter to Bracken, the day after he'd sounded so defeated to his diary, was filed under the heading 'The Dalton-Bracken Vendetta continues'. Copied to the foreign secretary, again Dalton appealed to Eden to help 'put an end to these tiresome squabbles which waste so much of our time'. After rattling through some of their disputes centred on Asia and the Americas, Dalton came to the crux of his view. There was no foundation in Bracken's allegation that SOE was 'duplicating propagandist organisations'. He argued that, since SOE was in charge of subversion, 'in carrying out this work it must to some extent engage in propaganda'. SOE also had a direct role in spreading rumours indirectly and through direct action, where 'PWE leaflets are smuggled over the frontiers'.[24] Dalton was making the point that it wasn't possible to have an entirely clear demarcation between subversion and propaganda, something to which Eden seemed broadly sympathetic.

As an official noted by hand on the letter, 'this looks like more trouble', adding 'the more Dalton explains, the more fraught the whole story becomes'. Eden responded that 'the letter might have been _less_ moderate!' Dalton, despite being upset that Bracken would regularly take his own disagreements over Eden's head to Churchill, was doing the same, discussing his unhappiness with Bracken over dinner with Clement Attlee. Attlee seemed persuaded that Bracken was up to no good, telling Dalton that 'this man is not fit to be a minister in the middle of a war'.[25]

Even though Dalton wrote in his diary that 'writing letters is no good', neither man backed down. Bracken, on 24 November, accused Dalton and the Ministry of Economic Warfare of moves which could get Britain in serious trouble with the United States, by setting up news agencies as a cover for intelligence and propaganda work. The agencies risked deceiving an ally. Bracken concluded that 'no-one with the slightest knowledge of how to conduct propaganda would start news agencies as a cover for subversive activities'.[26]

On 2 December, Bracken sent a further missive that Dalton found 'so offensive' that he couldn't bring himself to answer it.[27] Instead, he sent the 'remarkable effusion' straight on to Eden. Bracken called Dalton's officials 'furtive representatives', who were 'melodramatic agents' carrying 'grimy papers' in order to carry out 'absurd propagandist activities'. Bracken saw Dalton as carrying out a landgrab in countries which were about to come into the war. He did not want Dalton's ministry to work in new territories like Asia, where they hoped to co-operate with the Americans on broadcasts to Japan. If SOE began to function in Latin America, Bracken believed there would be a 'repetition of the muddle, waste and boastings' that he thought SOE had already made in the Balkans. He wanted this to be settled by the prime minister.[28]

It was little wonder then that, towards the end of the year, Bruce Lockhart noticed that he, 'like most people in Whitehall these days', was drinking far too much, as were his ministers. It perhaps goes some way towards explaining the ferocity of the ministerial arguments. According to Bruce Lockhart, 'Dalton has a strong head, drinks hard and has a particular liking for brandy; Brendan is rarely completely sober after 11pm, and even Eden takes a man's full share in the evening.'[29] For even Bruce Lockhart to think that the quantities involved were too much, they must have been extremely generous. He attributed this heavy drinking to war's effect on the nerves.

Neither Eden nor Churchill wanted to be constantly involved in this ongoing feud. Eden was about to set out for Russia, to meet Stalin, on a potentially dangerous journey via the Arctic. Five days after Bracken's 'offensive' letter, Japan attacked Pearl Harbor. The two ministers were both attempting to intervene in issues over propaganda in Asia and in Latin America because they knew that the scope of the war was likely to increase. Each wanted to assert their own sphere of influence during the wider war that was to come.

9

Admirable in Efficiency and in Conduct

The Political Warfare Executive was a growing operation and many of the staff and their families now lived and worked in the country. In August 1941, when the PWE was created, the number of staff was more than double that of the first Freedom Stations when they were set up a year earlier. The organisation now employed 438 people, or 213 excluding its support staff.[1]

Robert Bruce Lockhart and his committee of officials wrote to Anthony Eden in September 1941 to insist that it was necessary to maintain the Woburn establishment, at least in part, because of the need for secrecy. 'For geographical and security reasons, (eg proximity of the freedom stations to the secret transmitters and control of the foreigners who deliver these freedom broadcasts demand the maintenance of a secret unit in the country) "complete fusion" is not physically possible,' they submitted.[2] Sir Leonard Browett, a civil servant who had been commissioned to look at the structure of the PWE with the aim of reducing the overlap with existing propaganda efforts that Bracken and Dalton rowed about so fiercely, accepted that black propaganda was a special case. For reasons of security, 'the work connected with the black side of propaganda should be conducted away from London, especially as it involves the employment of aliens whose connection with this work must not be disclosed'.[3]

Although it was decided in November 1941 that more staff should be moved to Bush House in London 'in order to avoid loss of time and to ensure speedy and effective control' – with the regional directors based in the capital and travelling to the Country HQ as required, rather than being based in Woburn – this was only the case for those in certain positions in the operation. Many others would stay in the hush-hush villages.[4] Foreign staff and, later, prisoners of war were mostly required to stay in their village houses and were extremely restricted in their movements. It would be harder to keep that control – or to prevent the public knowing that 'black' radio stations were being broadcast from Britain – if the foreign staff were able to move freely around London.

Many of the staff who stayed working in Woburn were women. At the beginning of the war, recruiting women to political warfare was an innovative, tentative suggestion. One official at Woburn wrote to Valentine Williams in August 1940 with the suggestion that 'some of the new staff to be engaged might, I submit, be women. There must be a great many women available who would be most suitable for intelligence work. Also, judging from the experience of the Administration, it seems easier to accommodate women than men.'[5] By the end of the war, the staff of the PWE were largely women, although most of them were not in senior roles. Bruce Lockhart was full of praise for the work of his female colleagues. 'We relied for staff mainly on women who were vastly in the majority,' he wrote.[6] 'Taken by and large, they were admirable in efficiency and in conduct. Two were expert propagandists who ran their own section with men under them.' It wasn't until December 1941 that women in Britain – starting with single women aged between twenty and thirty – began to be called up for war work. But in propaganda, there were already many female recruits.

In Woburn and the hush-hush villages, the women were, in many cases, expected to have a dual role, both professional and domestic. It was assumed that the wives of the senior men in the organisation, like Zita Crossman at Dawn Edge, would be happy to carry out the role of 'housemistress', overseeing the domestic arrangements and the catering of the secret houses – although they did have staff such as cooks and housekeepers to help them.

Tom Delmer's artist wife, Isabel, was not particularly happy with the role she was at first allotted. When Delmer joined the organisation, he had initially left her behind in the couple's Suffolk farmhouse. It was a beautiful but draughty Elizabethan building, with electricity only running from a generator. Isabel was summoned first to London, then onwards to a secret destination, being told that she would probably not be able to return home for several weeks.

When she arrived at Larchfield in Aspley Guise, where her husband was also living while he was in Woburn, Isabel was dismayed to discover that her secret work was to be running a household. That prospect was 'hardly attractive'. At first, her housemates included three Germans. When they moved

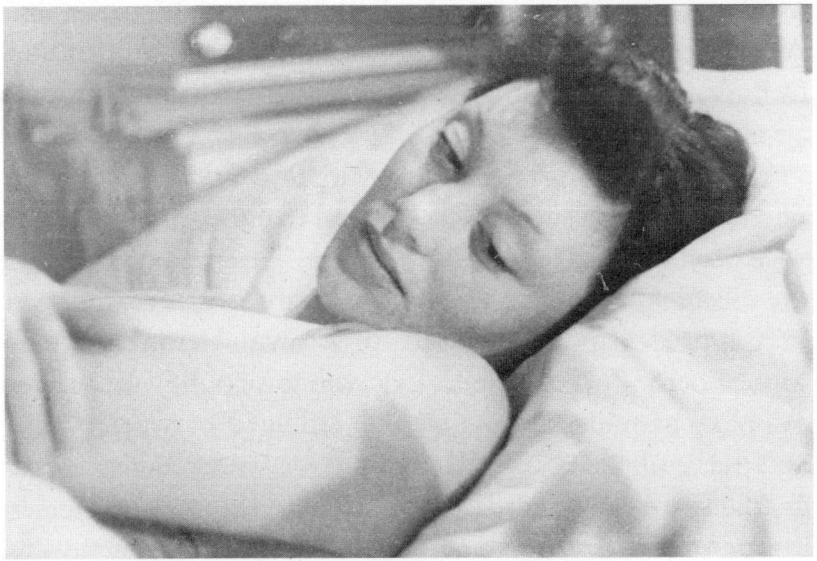

Isabel Delmer, 1936, photograph taken by her husband

to The Rookery, her home for the next three years, the household grew to include around twelve to fourteen people, comprised of the typical mixture of émigrés, refugees and later, prisoners of war, including Ernst Adam and Alexander and Margit Maass.[7]

The atmosphere at The Rookery was convivial; one visitor described it as a closely-knit family party, with a relaxed atmosphere, where Delmer could be found 'engaged in a cherry-stone spitting contest' with whoever was at the opposite end of the large dining table.[8] Isabel wrote that they played games of croquet and target practice in the summer and games of chess in the winter. She described herself as being no good at housekeeping and said that she left the food up to the cook, but her husband and other male guests believed that she had taught the cook, Freda Maddy, what she had picked up in Paris about French food.

The residents of the hush-hush houses supplemented their rations with venison culled from the notorious Woburn deer – other non-rationed game, such as hare or rabbit, could also be obtained. They kept chickens in the houses' gardens, which also provided eggs. There was a vegetable garden and the residents also foraged for mushrooms in the countryside. Delmer managed, through a wine merchant friend, to provide a well-stocked wine cellar.[9]

After the war, the *Sunday Express* printed details about the 'alien propaganda corps', whose life at Woburn they would not have been allowed to report on before. This report expressed the villagers' surprise that well-dressed foreigners, living in large houses, had been able to enjoy 'mushrooms cooked in wine', beer and whisky delivered from local pubs, and to have 434 pints of milk delivered a week.[10]

This tendency to believe that parts of the country establishment were extravagant and unnecessary was shared in London. Of course, the Country HQ's very existence was supposed to be secret, but as we have seen, it was a widespread topic for gossip. Bruce Lockhart related a story that he had been told about the early days of the organisation's work at 2 Fitzmaurice Place in Mayfair. A US Air Force colonel told Bruce Lockhart how he ran into an old naval friend outside the office. The naval friend had looked around at the cars waiting outside and confided in him. 'D'ye see these big cars in front? They belong to a show called PID Foreign Office. You wait about for a bit and you'll see a sight. The cars will fill up with two men and two girls. Then they shove a case or two of champagne on behind and then they drive off to their safe retreat in the country. It's the biggest, bloodiest ramp in the war.'[11] Even if the talk of girls and champagne was somewhat exaggerated, it was clear that life in Woburn was the cause of significant envy in Blitz-struck London.

This perception might have been even worse if they had heard, as Delmer wrote later, about the parties that he organised to celebrate each year of successful black broadcasting. He claimed that romances blossomed at these gatherings among the prisoners of war, the secretaries and others, and where Father Eisenberger could be spotted dancing by an American who, Delmer reported, exclaimed, 'never, never, never did I expect to see a priest in a Conga line!'[12]

Isabel, even though she was able to pursue her own art to a certain extent, was isolated and rather bored. She wasn't yet able to do the war work that she might have been suited for, but the authorities eventually realised that she could be employed to produce art for propaganda leaflets. As a 'tame artist' who had security clearance, Isabel could be an asset.

In her own work, she liked to paint natural forms, often of objects in states of decay, and was particularly suited to working on what were known as the 'malingering leaflets' – tiny booklets designed to be small enough to pick up and hide inside a cigarette packet. These gave German soldiers detailed and graphic descriptions of how to feign illness or injury in a convincing manner.[13] They drew on the expertise

of Dr John MacCurdy, a Cambridge lecturer in psychopath-
ology who Tom Delmer called a 'wise old one-eyed Canadian'.
Dr MacCurdy, according to Isabel, conducted experiments to
show how plants could be used to create rashes or swellings,
by persuading The Rookery's inhabitants to make gashes in
their arms or legs and then binding plants to the wound.[14]
Isabel's task was to draw the plant with detailed accuracy. This
was made more difficult by the need to reduce the drawings
down so that the leaflet could be kept small enough. The size
and weight of the leaflets had to be carefully controlled, down
to the amount of printers' ink required, and the leaflets also
had to be eye-catching, so that people would pick them up, as
well as being easily legible. Some of her later work was even
more lurid.

The Old Rectory in Tingrith, a village to the east of
Woburn, was another of the secret houses, full of seventeenth-
century furniture and with an oak-panelled dining room.
Ralph Murray, who was in charge of the central and eastern
European radio stations and houses, was based there with his
family. One housemate, though, wrote that Murray was rarely
present; 'we saw little of him, probably because he had little
interest in food or sleep.'[15] His Austrian-born wife, Mauricette, whom Murray had married in Vienna before the war, had
two children and was presumably also expected to run the
secret household. But some of her husband's colleagues suggested that they could make use of her talent for languages.
In January 1942, Edward Halliday suggested to David Bowes-
Lyon that Mauricette Murray should also be hired to work for
the organisation. Halliday, who was in charge of radio operations, saw a job for her as a censor-monitor – these were staff
with linguistic expertise whose responsibility was to check
that no uncensored and unscripted remarks were going out
over the air. Mauricette Murray was eminently well-qualified
for this. As Halliday wrote, 'I suggest that Mrs Murray, who
speaks French, Italian, German, Danish, Norwegian, Swedish,

(with slight knowledge of Dutch and Flemish) should be engaged as stand-by to relieve either of the full time people for leave, or illness.'[16]

Like the Murrays, many of the families living and working around Woburn had children, but there is little discussion in the records of how the children were looked after. It would have been difficult for small children to keep the secrets of life in the hush-hush houses, particularly if they were sent to local schools. Richard Crossman's stepchildren, Zita's children from her first marriage, Venice and Gilbert, were not there as they were evacuated to the United States during the war.[17] Some men, like Edward Halliday, complained about not being allowed to have their families join them. Halliday pointed out that others had their wives accompany them.[18] A Mr Neate of the Balkan section also asked to have his family with him, which suggests he might have brought children too. Security and the lack of accommodation in the increasingly crowded houses were given as reasons not to allow more families.

Younger and single women were not expected to have an extra domestic role, but they weren't given as much space of their own. When Elisabeth Barker first joined the PWE, she spent two nights a week at Woburn, sharing a room in Woburn Abbey with Joanna Scott-Moncrieff. Scott-Moncrieff, who was just nineteen at the start of the war and had been studying French, would go on to become the editor of *Woman's Hour* at the BBC. Later, as Barker progressed in the organisation, becoming one of the two heads of sections that Bruce Lockhart referred to – she was in charge of the Balkans – she would spend her weekends at one of the secret houses with her Yugoslav colleagues. The rest of the week would be spent in London, first at Fitzmaurice Place, then later back at Bush House when the PWE moved there.

The émigré women who worked on the Freedom Stations found it even harder to have their work properly valued than the British women did. The first Italian RU, Radio Italia, based at The Grange in the village of Newton Longville, came to rely heavily on the work of the women married to the Italian employees. Friedl Bamberger was the wife of the Sicilian journalist and poet, Ruggero Orlando. Orlando had been the London correspondent of Italian radio before the war, while Friedl was a German Jewish refugee, originally from Frankfurt, who had managed to bring a splendid collection of German Expressionist paintings to Britain with her.[19] Bamberger was able to turn her hand to almost everything. She not only did all the secretarial work of the unit, was 'intelligent and hard-working', but also wrote talks for others, particularly ones aimed at women and ones about the United States. One of her bosses wrote that she was also 'a regular contributor in her own name to the daily programmes and her assistance is, generally speaking, invaluable to the unit'.

Anita Fano, the wife of another Italian staff member, Pier Paolo Fano, was 'our best voice' on the station, with her editor Ivor Thomas calling her broadcasting style 'clear as a bell, simple and sincere . . . beautifully suited for her talks to her women compatriots'.[20] But the quality of their work didn't mean the women were paid adequately for what they did. Anita Fano, who was living in Oxford with her children and commuting to Woburn, was only paid ten shillings a week for part-time work. George Martelli, another of the station's bosses, wrote to David Bowes-Lyon in February 1942 saying that Friedl and Anita deserved a pay rise. The latter was one of the principal voices on Radio Italia and, since she had to travel from Oxford, 'her present allowance hardly covers expenses'. Martelli proposed tripling her salary to thirty shillings a week, but he was knocked back. Bowes-Lyon was unsympathetic to the exiles' requests for better pay, writing to Rex Leeper that 'they are all well paid, work moderately and if they were not there would be most uncomfortable in the Isle of Man'.[21] He was suggesting that if the foreign broadcasters were unhappy, they could be sent back to internment.

He relented a little: Anita would be paid a pound a week, doubling her previous allowance. Friedl had her pay increased from £3 to £4 a week.

However, augmenting the women's salaries was still largely seen as a way of making up the pay of their husbands without giving the men a direct increase. (Martelli suggested that he could 'get round the difficulties of increasing the salaries of the men by giving small increases to the women'.) Magda Ungar, an Austrian Jew who was a language teacher by training and who was married to Lorenzo Minio-Paluello, an academic turned broadcaster, had not been paid at all for her role as the housekeeper at Newton Longville, even though she was a 'very good manager' and got on well with the servants. It was proposed that she should also be paid a pound a week. The women's husbands were being paid four hundred pounds a year – much more than their spouses, even on a pro rata basis. The families were also expected to contribute towards the cost of their lodgings.

By comparison, their male colleagues who were managing the organisation were very well-paid – although, for the profligate Robert Bruce Lockhart, his salary was never enough. In October 1941, less than a month after the PWE was set up, he wrote: 'I have to find my own rent, have no car, no entertainment allowance, and have as salary £2,000 a year.'[22] He was paying approximately half of this income in tax, but even so, this meant a pre-tax salary of around £85,000 per year in today's money. Bruce Lockhart felt hard done by in comparison with his diplomat colleague, Rex Leeper, who was being paid nearly double at £3,750 a year (£159,000) and also received a 'free house, free car, free petrol and entertainment allowance', probably because he had a longer history of government service. Bruce Lockhart was still desperate for money and constantly in debt, living an extravagant life even during wartime. He wrote that he had to find between £200 and £250 before the end of that month (between £8,500 and £10,600 in 2024 prices), although he did not say what he needed the money for or where he expected to find it.

On the German stations, the émigré women took similar roles to the Italian-speakers. Margit Maass, the wife of Alexander, was one of Tom Delmer's most versatile on-air voices, with her experience as an actress in pre-war Germany. Many of the women exiles, like the men, had been active in the anti-Nazi resistance before the war and had written public condemnations of the situation in Germany. Evelyn Anderson, who was born Lore Seligmann, had written a book in 1938 entitled *The Underground Struggle in Germany* under the pseudonym of Evelyn Lend. She worked for the PWE alongside her husband, Paul Anderson. There was a group of actresses and singers, whose number included Agnes Bernauer, known as Agnes Bernelle, who had left Germany as a child in 1936 and who performed music and sketches on the Soldatensender Calais, one of Delmer's later radio stations.

Hilde Meisel was an extremely brave woman, only twenty-five at the outbreak of war, who also went by the names of Hilde Monte and, after her marriage of convenience to a gay German-Scottish author and cartoonist, John Olday, Hilde Olday.[23] Hilde had been born in Austria and studied in Berlin and was a militant socialist who had been involved in plots to assassinate Hitler in the late 1930s. Escaping to Britain before the war started, Hilde continued to return to mainland Europe on resistance missions. Together with Fritz Eberhard, she broadcast for Crossman's early RU, the Sender der Europäische Revolution. Later, she gave talks on the BBC. She was also a prolific journalist and author, who became a regular contributor to *Tribune* magazine. She wrote pamphlets, including *Help Germany to Revolt*, a message urging Labour supporters in Britain to help their German counterparts. She even wrote a novel, *Where Freedom Perished*.

But Hilde's heart and her dedication lay in direct action. She was sent to Lisbon and other locations on undercover missions and was killed crossing the border from Austria into Liechtenstein, only a few weeks before the end of the war in Europe in April 1945.[24] Delmer often referred to the 'girl sec-retaries' at Woburn and the radio studios but, as with his own wife Isabel, women of different nationalities showed what they were able to do.

British women, as with their male counterparts, were eligible to be promoted into more senior roles in a way that their foreign-born colleagues were not. Bruce Lockhart listed his staff as having been drawn from almost every walk of life. They included 'journalists, business men, advertising experts, schoolmasters, authors, literary agents, farmers, barristers, stockbrokers, psychologists, university dons, and a landscape gardener'.[25] Among these, he believed that 'the journalists were undoubtedly the best exponents of propaganda'. He put this down to their way with both the spoken and written word, and to their 'requisite sense of urgency', something the other professions lacked.

Both the women who went on to run their own depart-ments had been journalists: Elisabeth Barker, as we have already seen, had come from the BBC, while Dilys Powell, who ran the Greek section, had been made the film critic of the *Sunday Times* in 1939, a role she would hold for several decades after the war. Powell had been married to Humfry Payne, an archaeologist who had been the director of the British School of Archaeology in Athens, and she spent many archae-ological seasons in the country before her husband's early death in 1936. Writing in 1957 about her return to post-war Greece, she referred to her wartime role only briefly, saying that she began working at the PWE 'in 1941, soon after the fall of Crete had clenched the German hold on the Balkans', and that she remained there until the end of the war, but little more.[26]

The men who worked with Dilys Powell recalled her very clearly. When she joined the PWE in September 1941, Noel

Newsome, the BBC editor, introduced her to the head of the Greek section, George Angeloglou. Newsome said that the new political adviser was 'intelligent, charming, very good looking and Oxford educated'. That, he thought, would suit his Greek colleague. 'And with a First in history and languages, and the looks of a film star.'[27] Newsome reassured Angeloglou that the PWE would not be able to challenge the authority of the BBC's European Service, even though by and large the PWE's directives were accepted.

When she was introduced to the rest of the Greek section, Dilys Powell had to face more sceptical and sexist comments from other members of staff, as well as their lecherous gazes. She was greeted with 'disapproving murmurs, one loud cough and one despairing voice', that of a man complaining that he would have a woman guiding the team through the labyrinth of Greek politics. The men, in Angeloglou's account, were however captivated by Powell when she arrived in the office 'beautifully coiffured and wearing a striking two-piece black suit with a white blouse'. After that first meeting with the team, Dilys Powell was able to move onto more serious matters, discussing the members of the team with Angeloglou and then moving on to the complexities of Greek politics and how she would be able to work with the Greek government-in-exile, headed by the prime minister Emmanouil Tsouderos and King George II. The Greek government had just arrived in London, leaving Greece following the German invasion first for Cairo, then South Africa, arriving in Britain in September 1941.

The Greek government, like many of the other exiled administrations, often frustrated British officials, both while they were based in London and after their return to Cairo in 1943, with one observer writing that 'the basic attitude in British official circles was that that government was an irritating and irrelevant nuisance but one that had perforce to be tolerated'.[28] Britain wanted to promote the prestige of the king through its propaganda; many of those working for the Greek service were less keen on the idea and were prepared to resist the PWE's attempts to do so, whatever Dilys Powell's charms.

Powell, for her part, was also 'living a double life', wrote her Greek Service colleague. For her, though, this meant continuing secretly with her former day job as the film critic of the *Sunday Times*. 'Every so often,' Angeloglou wrote, 'she would slip out of Bush House and go and see a film.'[29] Then she would return to work, most of her colleagues none the wiser. One day, a Greek Service announcer spotted her walking down the Strand and entering the Tivoli cinema. He followed her and discovered she was at a screening of a John Wayne film for critics. When he told Angeloglou, his boss claimed this was all part of Powell's propaganda work, but the Greek announcer was mostly outraged that, even if she were paid for watching the film as part of her work, it wasn't a worthy work about Greece but rather American trash, which he considered to be 'kids' stuff, not political intelligence!' Reviewing films, Angeloglou thought, was for Powell 'a tremendous relaxation from the constant fireworks of Greek politics'.[30]

Alison Outhwaite, a journalist and foreign policy expert who had been the assistant editor of *World Review* magazine, first joined the BBC's propaganda research section and later moved to the PWE. She played 'a notable part in Intelligence work'.[31] Many of her younger female colleagues in research had been recruited straight from university. Of the women in the propaganda research area, 'a fair number of excellent quality came more or less fresh from Oxford or Cambridge'.[32]

Bruce Lockhart also praised the women who 'excelled in administrative work' and 'showed a spirit of co-operation and loyalty'. He believed that women, unlike some of their male counterparts, were usually good at keeping secrets. 'I think the belief is widely held in Whitehall,' he wrote, 'that women keep official secrets far better than men including most ministers.'[33]

This is perhaps partly why so few of the women of the PWE, even those who wrote histories or memoirs, wrote about their own wartime roles, even many years later. Their stories are often hidden or subsumed into the stories of others.

One exception to this rule was the future novelist Muriel Spark. Although she didn't join the organisation until later in the war, Spark was inspired by her experiences to write the strange and uncanny novel *The Hothouse by the East River*, whose characters had worked in a mysterious wartime agency. Arriving in London from Southern Rhodesia, Spark had gone to the employment bureau in Ladbroke Grove not expecting anything beyond a secretarial job. Since she had brought a book by Ivy Compton-Burnett with her to read while she waited, though, the woman recruiting administrator engaged her in a literary discussion, before then asking if Spark would be interested in secret work with the Foreign Office that would involve 'long irregular hours. In the country.'[34]

She was, and this led to an interview with Tom Delmer at Bush House, where she managed to avoid being tripped up by his question about her sea journey to Britain – a question Spark knew she was not supposed to answer for security reasons. As a duty secretary, she spent her long shifts taking in information from the RAF and the Foreign Office that made its way into Delmer's black bulletins. Spark took calls from the air force on a green scrambler line, informing her about British sorties flown and targets hit. These details were then translated by Delmer and the rest of the team into stories about damage that had been inflicted on German cities. Spark lived in one of the Old Rectories – possibly Walton Rectory – alongside five other women.[35] The women in the house scarcely saw each other due to their different shift patterns, but Spark, who worked from 4pm until midnight, struck up a strange, if awkward, friendship with one of them, Marcelle Quennell. Since Spark and Quennell were on the late shift, they missed the 'dreary normal breakfast of rationed tea, toast and margarine' which would already have been cleared away by the time the two women came down to the kitchen 'in our dressing-gowns, to the housekeeper's horror'. Instead, Quennell made coffee, which was off the ration.[36]

Quennell was a tragic character who herself would not have been out of place in a novel. She was older than Spark, though only by a few years, and argued with her about the room allocation in the Rectory, complaining that women under thirty – Spark was twenty-six at the time – should have to share rooms rather than have a room of their own. Quennell worked as a switch censor because she spoke several languages following a childhood where she travelled widely. The switch censors – whose job only came into being once live broadcasts began – were described by one of their male colleagues as 'well vetted British women with a good under-standing of German'.[37] Several of them were former citizens of other countries who had become British by marriage.

Quennell had led a traumatic and troubled life; she was the daughter of a Belgian diplomat and had previously been married to Peter Quennell, the biographer and critic, in the 1930s. Marcelle, thinly disguised as 'Isabelle' in his memoirs, had left him for a man he referred to as 'l'Ami' and described as the 'crown prince of an English financial dynasty'. This rela-tionship didn't work out and although she had hoped to marry the wealthy heir, he broke off their engagement, perhaps due to her heavy drinking. She made two attempts at suicide but survived them and was living in Paris at the outbreak of war. There, she had become involved with a young French jour-nalist. She made her way southwards through France, where she was robbed by a French family she thought would help her and found herself eventually in Marseille, pregnant with twins. According to her former husband, after she gave birth, 'it was a cold winter; food was severely rationed; the hospital, managed by a few nuns, was entirely unheated; both the children soon died. Although she remembered the pain and misery she had suffered, she could not remember if she had ever seen their faces.'[38] Marcelle Quennell somehow managed to return to Britain by 1942, though it's not clear when she was recruited to the PWE.

Isabel Delmer also recalled Quennell, though remembered her as working as a disc jockey on the black stations as well as a censor. She was clearly attractive; Spark wrote that Quennell had become involved in a relationship with a 'tall, good-looking, reckless' German prisoner of war who had been broadcasting pseudonymously on one of the black stations. However, when the POW then broadcast in his own right on a 'white' station as a prisoner sending greetings home from captivity, this was a huge breach of security. His voice could have been recognised as appearing on both the fake station and the real one. He was sent back to the prisoner of war camp, to Quennell's upset.[39] She also came close to losing her own job due to her drinking when her landlady found a bottle of gin in her bedroom. Her language skills, however, were too valuable to lose. Both Muriel Spark and Isabel Delmer were sad to learn of Quennell's death by suicide, two years after the war ended.

The very week that Robert Bruce Lockhart accepted his new job as head of the PWE, he had one of his regular encounters with a woman who played a hugely significant part in his life, but who was deemed to be far too much of a security risk to work alongside him. Their meetings usually consisted of long, gossipy and alcoholic lunches or dinners. She, too, had a facility with languages and a huge network of contacts, but there were many questions about her. Moura Budberg and Bruce Lockhart had first met in revolution-ary Moscow. Despite both being married to other people, they embarked on an intense affair. A British report later described Budberg at the time as having been 'a woman of great beauty and . . . no great morality'. Born Maria Zakrev-skaya in Russia in 1892, Budberg had been married twice; her first husband was killed during the Russian Revolution. When Bruce Lockhart was imprisoned in the Kremlin by the revolutionaries, Budberg was pregnant with his child, but she lost the baby.[40]

The first suspicions about Budberg were aroused back in Russia, where it was likely that she co-operated with the Cheka, the early Soviet secret police, in order to help get Bruce Lockhart released from his captivity in exchange for Maxim Litvinov. She also had long relationships with Maxim Gorky and H.G. Wells, coming to Britain in 1929. During the war, the British security services were still deeply suspicious about Budberg's allegiances. She was blocked from working for the BBC and a 'red refusal stamp' put on her file which barred her from most kinds of war work. She found a job working on the journal *La France Libre* instead. Because Budberg was so well-connected, close to Duff Cooper in addition to Wells and Bruce Lockhart, her contacts were questioned at very high levels of government.

In May 1941, she had written to Duff Cooper to enquire whether she could have the restrictions on her work lifted. The civil servant dealing with the request described her as 'a friend of my Minister'. Although a few limitations on her were removed, she was still effectively blocked from many areas of work. Later in the year, Special Branch received a report that Budberg was 'secretly working for the Russians'. They took this report seriously enough that, at the end of October 1941, the security services obtained a warrant to tap her phone calls and intercept her post, on the grounds that Budberg was 'suspected of espionage on behalf of a foreign power'.[41]

She was also followed around London by a Special Branch officer, though the surveillance was rather inept. The officer assigned to her often lost his target in traffic and didn't recognise the people she was meeting. Nor did the police officer realise that many of the people she was associating with also probably worked for secret British organisations.

On 4 November, the police officer followed her to lunch at Claridge's, where, as well as her two lunch companions, Budberg met a British army officer in his fifties, with greying hair and a small grey moustache, who was dressed in a brigadier's uniform and a British Warm overcoat and carrying a briefcase. The army officer then left the hotel with another man in his fifties, of medium to heavy build, who was wearing a light-grey suit and a black Homburg hat. He apparently bore a resemblance to the famous Austrian tenor Richard Tauber. The two middle-aged men left in a car that turned out to be registered to the Political Intelligence Department – the PWE's cover name. It seems highly likely that the two men the observer saw were Dallas Brooks – then a brigadier, albeit in his forties, and who in a 1944 portrait has a small grey moustache and greying temples – and Bruce Lockhart, who often ate together. Bruce Lockhart's published diaries don't mention a lunch on that date, though the previous day he mentions that Dallas Brooks had just returned from leave and Bruce Lockhart gave him lunch at St James's.

By 24 November, Moura Budberg seemed to realise that something was up. The officer trailing her reported that she was 'very suspicious of being followed' while on a shopping expedition around South Kensington and Knightsbridge and so the observation was lifted. It's possible, of course, that she was better at losing someone trailing her than the police were at following her scent. The report summed up nearly a month of surveillance by saying that 'she has been seen to lunch in first class establishments and mix with leaders of Society. She has not, however, been seen to publicly contact members of the Soviet Embassy or other Soviet organisations here.'

There were conflicting views within the British government about whether Budberg was a spy or not. Desmond Morton, Churchill's personal assistant, was concerned enough to write to Sir David Petrie, the director-general of MI5, about her in April 1942. He called her an 'appalling female' who was 'a perfect terror at intrigue in Free French affairs' and a violent enemy of de Gaulle. In Petrie's reply, he confirmed that there was a 'recent serious suggestion' that she was a foreign agent, possibly working for the Russians, but maintained that they were not able to find any substance to the reports. She was, according to Petrie, 'a woman who delights in political intrigue', but he believed this not to be anything but helpful to the Allied cause.

Special Branch, however, in April 1944, remained insistent. 'There is not the slightest doubt,' their latest report concluded, 'that this clever woman is working in an underground capacity for the Russians.' MI 5 still weren't convinced. Roger Hollis of MI 5 wrote to Special Branch saying that there was 'nothing to confirm the allegations that she is a Russian agent', repeating his assertion when the Americans raised questions about her towards the end of the war. What we know now, thanks to the Venona decrypts of Soviet cypher traffic, is that two of Budberg's colleagues at *La France Libre*, the French exile journal that was often critical of de Gaulle, were Soviet agents. André Labarthe and Martha Lecoutre were paid for information under the codenames Jerome and Martha.[42] Budberg herself was mentioned in Soviet files of the 1930s as having been in contact with the NKVD, the USSR's secret police.[43] It therefore seems more likely, with hindsight, that she had been some sort of informant later on.

No recorded attempt seems to have been made to warn Bruce Lockhart away from seeing her. Nor do we know what information Budberg might have gained from their conversations, though she had a multiplicity of sources and would probably have known much of what was going on in politics and propaganda. Bruce Lockhart had defended her against allegations of disloyalty before the war; in his diaries, he seems more concerned with the fact that Budberg was not a cheap date. She was 'expensive to feed or, rather, to water'. In 1944, as Paris was liberated, she drank 'an aperitif of three double gins at eight shillings apiece and with her coffee a double brandy at twelve shillings', as well as beer with her lunch.

One of the arguments for keeping the Woburn operation running had always been the need for secrecy. The prevalence of gossip and leaks in London were harder to control, with even government ministers guilty of passing on supposedly secret information. Foreign governments were keen to pick up any information they could about Britain's plans for the war. Moving the PWE's operations from Fitzmaurice Place in Mayfair to Bush House was supposed to make it easier to have closer links with the BBC, in the same building, and to allow the PWE to instruct the BBC on 'white' propaganda. But there were plenty in London who were still prepared to leak some of the organisation's secrets.

10

He Often Appears to Talk
Complete Nonsense

While Richard Crossman appeared to be comfortably installed as the new director of the German Section of the Political Warfare Executive, his propensity for making enemies still caused him problems. Even the enemies he thought he had defeated in the past had not completely gone away. The PWE had scarcely been established when criticisms of Crossman's role began to make their way into the public domain.

The first hint of these problems came as soon as the new organisation was set up. The September 1941 issue of the *National Review*, a right-wing magazine edited by Lady Violet Milner, divulged the secrets of British black propaganda to its readership. In the magazine's regular 'Episodes of the Month' feature, it had two articles, one on propaganda, and one on 'The "Hess" radio station'.[1] The piece on propaganda was critical of both white and black propaganda; 'We, in England, also have a propaganda service, or rather we have several. The British public is not allowed to hear about it, but anyone with a radio set can tune in to some part of this, and if he knows German, listen to what we say to the German people and the German Army.' Listeners, the magazine thought, would be surprised at what they heard. 'He will hear the rasping, hate-filled, arrogant voices of tame Germans – many of them obviously Jews – who are employed by the BBC.' The news bulletins, the piece went on, were 'sustained polemics' and 'besides hate and arrogance the broadcasts ingeminate vulgarity'. Its further criticism was that the 'facts' in the German bulletins were of 'very doubtful authenticity'. Being 'vulgar and silly', for the writer, was bad enough, but it was worse to be untruthful, 'for when the time comes to talk about peace, it is important that our word should be believed'.

The next article went further still: the 'mild vulgarities and tendencious [sic] news of the BBC' paled before the black stations. The magazine repeated a mention in *The Times* of the 'Hess-sender', which said that GS1, broadcasting seven minutes before the hour, made the 'most revolting revelations', emphasising a section where the newspaper had described the broadcasts, saying 'the coarseness of the language eclipses everything which can be called "Billingsgate"' – meaning that it was worse than you might hear in London's fish market. Then, the *National Review* posed a question: 'Where is this garbage – for garbage it is – put together?' It is known, they said, that the BBC had nothing to do with it, but the corporation 'must be totally exonerated from such a nasty affair'.

The suggestion, even disguised, that Tom Delmer's black station originated in Britain was a worrying breach of security. *The Times* article of 21 July had been from a 'special correspondent' on the German frontier. It took a more favourable view of the station, saying that 'incalculable damage is being inflicted on Nazi prestige' by the station's exposure of German immorality, corruption and embezzlement. Although calling it the 'Hess-sender' might suggest, between the lines, that the station came from outside Germany, crucially, *The Times* article did not say that it was a British project.[2]

To allow publication of stories about GS1 being a British initiative would be to undermine the entire purpose of its existence as a supposed German opposition station. Even if the Germans may have had their suspicions about the provenance of GS1, it would do no good to confirm them.

The government reacted strongly, contacting the proprietor of the *National Review*. Violet Milner was a well-connected figure, nearly seventy years old, who had taken over the magazine's editorship from her brother in 1929 and pursued a pro-empire, anti-German and anti-appeasement line in its pages. David Bowes-Lyon, an even better-connected man, as he was the Queen's brother, was deputed to speak to Lady Milner and warn her against repeating these claims. A quiet word, even from the best circles, however, was not enough.

Crossman was often the implied target of these criticisms, not just because he was in charge of German broadcasts but because his political positions were well known. The insidious language about 'tame Germans' and voices that 'sounded Jewish' was a frequent, unfounded criticism from the political right. Brendan Bracken had already expressed some objections to Crossman's presence – probably because he was seen as Dalton's Labour protege – and had to be persuaded by Robert Bruce Lockhart and Rex Leeper to allow Crossman to stay. When Leeper had written to Bruce Lockhart – 'Dear Bertie' – in his most secret and personal letter of August, he confided that Crossman was a 'difficult selection' but 'much superior' to others in the BBC, such as Hugh Carleton Greene. The problem was getting Bracken to tolerate his appointment. Leeper wrote: 'Brendan will, however, only accept Crossman if we stop most of his Socialist stuff on the BBC and that we must do. Crossman has now got to be controlled as he never was by the Ministry of Information. If he doesn't accept control, he must go.'[3]

Crossman appeared to have accepted the constraints on his new role. But by the new year of 1942, there were rumblings of further trouble. He had seen Bracken on 19 January and told Dalton of their conversation. Bracken had, according to Dalton, 'pretended to be very friendly' towards Crossman and said that he was not going to let him down 'in reply to a Parliamentary Question by some Tory which picks a phrase out of its context and suggests that our broadcasts are pro-German'.[4] Dalton, however, seemed disenchanted with Crossman, saying that the younger man wasn't a great favourite of his at that moment and talked 'nonsense' about matters to do with broadcasts to Germany.

Dalton was still pursuing his vendetta against Bracken, to less and less effect. Despite occasional interludes of what he called 'Precarious Peace' in the new year, by early February he was back to calling Bracken's behaviour 'reckless rudeness' and the man himself 'simply a guttersnipe'. David Bowes-Lyon tried to console Dalton with the thought that Bracken was just a very small man who hated Dalton personally, and to pass on gossip that Bracken wasn't happy either; he had been snubbed by the prime minister and told not to interfere in others' business. Nor had Bracken even been to visit his new charges at the Country HQ in his six months in office. Despite this, as Dalton retired to bed on 6 February, a defeatist thought crossed his mind. 'I think that we just don't deserve to win the war. We are all fighting each other instead of the enemy, and with such zest.'

Crossman, meanwhile, was starting to become suspicious about the growing number of leaks of hostile information about the PWE in the press. On 9 February, he wrote a memo to the PWE executive, setting out a matter which had been causing him concern for some weeks. A recent article by Quinton Varley in the *Daily Mail* and a front-page splash by the diplomatic correspondent of the *Sunday Dispatch* had brought things to a head.

It's not hard to see why the *Sunday Dispatch* front page made Crossman so irate. The banner headline read 'The "Free German" trick: exposure of influential groups working here to save the enemy'. The story led off by announcing that 'the *Sunday Dispatch* considers it a duty to reveal a dangerous movement which, if not checked, may negative all that the Allies can gain by military success and enable Germany to wage another war against us in a few years'. The paper said that there was a scheme to try to obtain official recognition for a Free German movement in Britain, backed by political elements among German emigrants and 'some influential Britons'. Although the piece acknowledged that there was little likelihood of such recognition for a prospective German government-in-exile, saying that this had already been ruled out by Eden, it was still aiming to create fears among its readership of a 'pro-German' movement. The correspondent said that although the purported movement was 'admittedly anti-Nazi', it wanted 'to save Germany from retribution after the war – from occupation, disarmament, control or any severe consequences'.[5]

The article continued with a long list of German emigrants whom it claimed were involved with the Free German movement. This list included former members of the German Bundestag, such as Dr August Weber of the Democratic Party and Arthur Arzt of the Socialist Party. Also on the list were Max and Heinz Braun, two brothers from the Saarland who joined Tom Delmer's black propaganda operation in Britain. The pair were socialists who had fled their home after Germany's annexation of the Saarland in 1935. Delmer described Max as a 'dumpy, pot-bellied figure', who was an early recruit to GS1, although Delmer said he wasn't good at maintaining his secret cover. According to Delmer, Max Braun's cover name of Albert Simon was blown on his first day in Aspley Guise when he came down to breakfast in a silk dressing gown with the initials M.B. embroidered on the breast pocket.[6] Nonetheless, the Brauns' identities should not have reached the front page of a Sunday newspaper.

The *Sunday Dispatch* cited the groups as well as the individuals which it claimed were 'working for the preservation of Germany's unity and strength after the war', ranging from the social democrats to the trades unions to the communists and a small group it called 'Neu Beginnen', the last of which the paper said was influential over British broadcasting, despite only having seven members.

Most infuriating for Crossman would have been that he himself was mentioned – though his name was misprinted as 'Mr. S. H. S. Crossman', described as being responsible for broadcasts which appealed to the 'other Germany' as distinct from the Nazis, and naming him as working with the Political Warfare Department of the Foreign Office. Worse still, the piece recalled his BBC broadcast after the Night of the Long Knives in 1934 and said that Crossman 'found the Germans as a whole in agreement with these events'. He was doubly misrepresented in this description of his BBC talk; not only had his talk been a piece of reporting rather than expressing his own agreement, but it also said he had 'told Britain over the German wireless' about the events. This wasn't true. Crossman had been reporting on the BBC from a German radio studio; he had not been broadcasting on a German radio station, which was the implication.

The *Daily Mail* story of three days earlier was less detailed in its criticism, but more outraged in its tone. Under the headline 'They're telling the Germans we <u>respect</u> them!', Quinton Varley insisted 'it is time that the scandal of our propaganda to Germany were stopped'. (The next headline for the *Mail*'s readers on the same page asked 'Why can't we make our own syrup?') Varley said, however, that it was not the BBC who should be blamed, but that 'the responsibility rests with P.W.E.'. He observed that 'our German broadcasts show no understanding of the German situation and of the German mind'. Varley criticised the broadcasts, which he said had talked about respecting German soldiers. He took particular exception to a talk about Lord Vansittart, which posed a series of questions and answers about the peer and suggested that Vansittart's *Black Record* talks had 'aroused a great deal of contradiction'. Varley defended Vansittart as 'a great public servant' and 'a peer, a public figure and a patriot'. 'Have we nothing better to do in our propaganda,' he asked, 'than to belittle a distinguished fellow countryman?' Varley was opposed to 'the theory of the two Germanys' that he believed underlay British propaganda; he was also against the use of cheery, uplifting music, which he felt comforted the enemy. His solution, which would have angered Crossman, was that there should be 'a thorough inquiry into the conduct of Political Warfare in general and of propaganda to the enemy in particular'. The broadcasts should be 'truthful, simple, and dignified', rather than prey to the misguided notion that the Germans 'are really very nice people, and that when the war is over they and everyone else will be happy in the happiest of worlds'.[7] Although Varley did concede that the broadcasts — and, throughout the article, he was only overtly referring to 'white' propaganda — went some way towards helping to discredit German official lies, he thought they could do this more effectively. He also rehearsed the familiar criticism that propaganda to enemy countries was costing the nation too much money and employing too many people.

It was no wonder, then, that Crossman detected the hand of Freddy Voigt, who had resigned the year before in protest against Crossman's methods, in briefing hostile stories against him. In his memo to the PWE executive, Crossman said it was 'common knowledge' that the *Mail*'s story was 'inspired by Mr. Voigt'. He suspected him of talking to the *National Review* as well. Crossman wrote: 'Mr Voigt has not been averse from using knowledge gained during his tenure of office in a secret department. On leaving the Department, he circulated widely a libellous memorandum disclosing all its secrets and the "National Review" suggested that the secret station "Gustav Siegfried Eins" was of British origin.'[8]

'Quinton Varley' was a pseudonym. The *National Review*, in a later article which upset the government still further, revealed that it was the 'pen-name of a very distinguished writer who lived 11 years in Germany as the correspondent of a well-known newspaper'. Varley wrote 'both with knowledge and deep mistrust of the way in which these broadcasts are given'. It was most probably Freddy Voigt himself, who had spent around twelve years in Germany as the *Manchester Guardian* correspondent and, of course, had worked on political warfare until his resignation.

As well as Voigt, Crossman blamed another man, Walter Loeb, for briefing the *Sunday Dispatch* story, saying that both he and Voigt had the ear of Lord Vansittart. Crossman called Loeb 'a German banker of shady reputation' who had a group of other émigrés in his pay. In his view, 'these two gentlemen have for some months been carrying on a campaign in the Press and, even more, in the clubs and lobbies, against PWE, more particularly its German section'. Loeb and the other émigrés Crossman mentioned, Curt Geyer and Bernhard Menne, were also broadly of the left, but disagreed fundamentally with some of their fellow émigrés about Germany's post-war future. They were broadly sympathetic to Vansittart's view that Germany's history had led to the present regime, and believed there was little meaningful internal opposition; Germany, they thought, would need re-education rather than revolution. Other officials in the PWE agreed with Crossman's assessment of Loeb, saying later in the year that he had a 'personal grudge' against the German section for refusing him employment.[9]

Crossman wrote, furiously, that 'this campaign would, in Balkan countries, be called "Political Blackmail"'. He protested that, because he and his colleagues were bound by secrecy, they were unable to reply in public to these kinds of allegations. Nor did he feel that enough was being done to defend the work of the PWE, so that 'the field is left open for vilification and fantastic rumours; and the secrecy of the Department does not protect it from gross misrepresentation of its policy in the Press and in Parliament'. He added that there were clearly 'gross security breaches' in allowing this kind of information into the public domain. In his opinion, the PWE would not be able to work effectively unless leaks like these were prevented in the first place – or rebutted firmly if they had happened. 'If Political Warfare is to be conducted effectively in the coming months – and the chances for Political Warfare in these months are very great indeed – then its executants should surely be shielded from such attacks.'

Crossman knew from both Bracken and Dalton that MPs were again asking questions in Parliament which touched on political warfare in general and Crossman's role in particular. On 17 February 1942, the Conservative MP representing Cambridge University, Kenneth Pickthorn, used a debate on overseas broadcasting to lay into the role of propaganda and those who created it. Pickthorn, a Tudor historian who had advised the War Office on conditions in Germany in 1918, drew on his background to assert that, at the end of the First World War, 'our propaganda had no effect at all except when it came immediately after victory'. In Pickthorn's view, the landing of Rudolf Hess had been particularly badly handled, giving out contradictory information. 'All sorts of things were said about it on the British wireless,' he inveighed, 'nine-tenths of which could not have been true because no two of them agreed with each other.' He disliked what he called the 'pinkish, leftist intelligentsia' whom he claimed had a disproportionate influence on British broadcasting, saying the talks by the likes of Crossman, Vernon Bartlett, J.B. Priestley, E.M. Forster and others were the 'kind of opinion which has a far larger share of what is said over the ether for Britain than it can ever have had in this country'.[10]

British propaganda, he believed, should build up the country's reputation for truth and dignity. Pickthorn's complaints were primarily about white propaganda over the BBC; Priestley's role in particular had been a cause of dispute. His series of Sunday-night talks, titled *Postscript*, had first run in 1940, when the author spoke about Dunkirk and the fall of France.

These talks for British listeners were seen as down-to-earth and appealing to a wide audience. Some, though, claimed he was too left-wing: Priestley himself addressed this in his *Postscript* of October 1940. He said he was not bringing party politics into his talks but talking about democracy, social justice and decency, telling his critics that they were 'at liberty to call me a Socialist, a Communist or an Anarchist, though I would implore you to stop merely pasting on labels and instead to think a little'.[11] Priestley was subsequently 'rested' from the domestic airwaves due to the political controversy, but continued to give talks under the title *Britain Speaks* on international services in English.

Pickthorn echoed the Vansittart view that the current war against Germany was just an episode in an ongoing war that had continued for decades. Many of the failings, though, he laid at the door of 'one of our most frequent and influential broadcasters'. He then raised again the question of Crossman's 1934 BBC broadcast, quoting selections from it that had appeared in the next day's newspaper. Other MPs immediately rose to ask Pickthorn who the broadcaster he referred to was – though many of them must have known precisely who he meant. Pickthorn was initially reluctant to answer but, pushed by other MPs, he responded: 'Very well. I do not mind. His name is R.H.S. Crossman.'[12] Pickthorn's main argument was that he wanted the content of British broadcasting aimed at overseas listeners to be more easily available, so that MPs could scrutinise it. Without that ability to know what was being broadcast, Pickthorn believed the area would become 'a sort of little secret business for a lot of little secret experts, who are not experts at all, and it is high time that the winds of criticism blew roughly through the whole thing'.

Another Tory MP, Henry Strauss, agreed with Pickthorn. Strauss was highly critical both of Crossman's broadcasts and his background. He deplored what he saw as the tendency of British propaganda to 'encourage a sham revolution in

Germany'. He maintained that Crossman had broadcast more, and had more influence over British broadcasting to Germany, than most other people. 'I do not doubt for a moment that he has certain abilities,' said Strauss. 'I do not doubt that he believes that what he is doing or proposing is useful, but he often appears to talk complete nonsense, and repeats what has already been demonstrated in Germany to be nonsense.' His complaint was not so much with what Crossman had said in the past, but with his more recent comments on Hitler's policies. He described Crossman pointing out Hitler's mistakes as proof that the German leader was not infallible; Strauss said Hitler had responded by saying that he had made many more mistakes than the BBC broadcast had suggested. Strauss believed this point about infallibility wasn't a useful line of attack – although, as another MP pointed out, it seemed contradictory to claim that Crossman's propaganda was useless while at the same time saying that Hitler himself had gone out of his way to respond to his broadcasts.

The Labour MP Sydney Silverman detected a co-ordinated plan to undermine Crossman, calling Strauss 'patronising and supercilious'. It was a 'remarkable coincidence', he observed, that so many on the Conservative side had fastened on a particular broadcaster and distributed among themselves quotations from his speeches. This, Silverman thought, was evidence of a 'planned, deliberate and concerted attack'.

Brendan Bracken, responding to the debate, was dismissive of Pickthorn. Bracken said he wished 'some Tories would learn how to broadcast as well as these "pinkish-leftists"'. If they did, he believed, the BBC would give them ample opportunities. Bracken also leapt to Crossman's defence, saying he did not like at all the part of Pickthorn's speech that referred to him. Pickthorn, he said, had 'dug up something which Mr Crossman had said years ago'. 'What would happen to us,' Bracken continued, 'if our speeches of eight or ten years ago were dug up?' He called this a 'most unfair type of political attack' and said it bewildered him that the representative of a liberal university had adopted such tactics.

The same day that MPs debated overseas broadcasting, the prime minister answered questions on a military debacle in the Channel. The mood of the House, *The Times* reported, was 'worried and unhappy, as it ought to be on the morrow of a great disaster'.[13] The restive mood among Conservative MPs was partly explained by a more general sense of prevailing political crisis at the start of 1942. As the *National Review* summed it up, 'February was a month of disaster by land and by sea'.

It was only a few weeks since Churchill had called a vote of confidence in his own government. Although he won it by 464 votes to one, the fact that he had to use this tactic at all was a sign of political uncertainty. A succession of military disasters followed which tarnished the optimism resulting from the Russian and American entries into the war. On 11 February, three German ships, the battle-cruisers *Scharnhorst* and *Gneisenau*, and the cruiser *Prinz Eugen*, managed to leave port at Brest in Brittany and make their way through the minefields of the Channel. Despite the efforts of the British Navy and the RAF to stop them, the ships were able to return to Kiel, a port city on Germany's Baltic coast. Public and press opinion were horrified that the three ships could sail past Dover in daylight.

On 15 February, Singapore had fallen to Japan, an event which Churchill would later call 'the worst disaster and largest capitulation in British history'.[14] His response to the defeat in Parliament, first trying to avoid any debate and later responding in an ill-judged and bad-tempered manner, was seen as a sign of weakness. It was no surprise then that questions about propaganda reflected the general sense of unease about the government's grip on the war.

Robert Bruce Lockhart observed that, 'as usually happens when the Government are in trouble, the critics seize on any available stick with which to beat them'.[15] Political warfare, he believed, would take its share of hard knocks in the Commons as a result.

For Brendan Bracken, however, the crisis provided him with an opportunity. Bruce Lockhart admired Bracken's willingness to stand up for his staff – such as Crossman – and defend them in Parliament, but he also saw an element of theatre and pretence in his demeanour. 'Mr Bracken,' he wrote, 'has a temperament which is as fiery as his aureole of flaming Celtic hair.' But, Bruce Lockhart believed, he was not as emotional as he appeared on first acquaintance. 'The illusion of emotional lack of control is dangerous, for underneath he possesses a self-restraint which his opponents often fail to appreciate.' This ability to control his temper gave Bracken an advantage 'when he seems to be hitting hardest', Bruce Lockhart observed. 'At such times his anger is feigned. He is, in fact, playing a part which is sometimes carefully rehearsed, but more often than not is extemporised to suit the impulse of the moment.'[16] Bruce Lockhart also said that Bracken had told him, a few days before the parliamentary debate, that he would resign in order to allow Sir Stafford Cripps control of propaganda. This seems likely to have been another Bracken pretence.

Churchill carried out a reshuffle in order to show that the government was grasping the situation. Bracken stayed in his job at the Ministry of Information, but the reshuffle gave key roles to some senior Labour figures in the War Cabinet, moving Clement Attlee to deputy prime minister and bringing Ernest Bevin, the minister of labour, into the group to replace Kingsley Wood, the chancellor of the exchequer.

Having been advised by Attlee that he wouldn't be affected by the reshuffle, Dalton set off for his Bishop Auckland constituency in the north-east of England for a rare weekend visit. On a snowy February day, Dalton was in Shildon, taking the salute at a military procession before making a speech, where he gave his audience the grim exhortation that they needed both to work harder and to consume less in order to allow more resources to be put into the war.[17] In the usual unforgiving manner of reshuffles, Dalton learned that he would be moving ministerial jobs in awkward circumstances. He was interrupted at the parade by a message that he needed to call the prime minister. Putting the call through from an air-raid shelter, Dalton was eventually connected to Churchill, who told him that he wanted him to move to the Board of Trade. Dalton said the proposed switch was a bit of a surprise and asked for time to consider it; Churchill would not give him until the next day to think it over, asking for his response within an hour. 'I suppose the Board of Trade is a very full-time job,' Dalton said. The prime minister agreed that it was. Told that he would have to give up all his other duties, Dalton nonetheless accepted, assured that Churchill had confidence in him.[18] He was still in charge of an important government department, but as he made his way back to London by train, catching a little sleep in his (now former) department building in the early hours, he was unsettled, writing that 'handing over SOE twangs at my heart strings'. He didn't seem to take this as a promotion, although it was. He was replaced at the Ministry of Economic Warfare by the Earl of Selborne, a Conservative. Bracken had effectively won his ongoing battle against his Labour rival for the control of propaganda.

Even Dalton's removal from the arena, though, didn't seem to stop the leaks and briefings against the PWE. Many still suspected British propaganda of having pro-German sympathies. The leaking was taken so seriously this time that both Delmer and Crossman threatened to resign if their positions continued to be undermined. The culprit, once again, was the *National Review*. In its March 1942 issue, the article 'Our Broadcasts to Germany' said that 'there is a permanent fog screen over our propaganda to Germany'. When the fog lifted, the magazine complained, the 'disreputable' wireless stations could be found putting out stuff that was 'horrible and most damaging to our good name'. This article laid the blame at the Political Warfare Executive's door, and also named Crossman, although they spelled his name 'Crossmann', in a German style – possibly accidentally, but probably on purpose. Crossman had, they believed, 'an undue admiration for Germans and little knowledge of them'.[19] Again, he was accused of respecting the German people's qualities and of disparaging Lord Vansittart. 'What is the purpose of all this sucking-up to a ruthless and savage enemy?' the magazine demanded.

Delmer was furious. On 15 March, he wrote to Rex Leeper, angry that 'the *National Review* has for a second time – after a warning in September – revealed that GS1 is a British-controlled station'. He demanded that something be done about it: 'unless action is taken under the Official Secrets Act against this fresh infringement of the security regulations, our own efforts to preserve secrecy have no meaning.' This issue was so serious to Delmer that he threatened to resign, in the conclusion of his brief note to Leeper: 'I feel that I must tell you that I would prefer to give up my connection with the Unit if its activities are to be continually endangered by the toleration of gross breaches of security.'[20] Thomas Barman raised the issue with Bruce Lockhart on the same day, writing to draw his attention to the 'glaring indiscretion' of the *National Review*. This reference to GS1's work, he believed, was 'very damaging', emphasising that it was 'important to take action vigorous enough to prevent any repetition'. Delmer had also told Barman just how unhappy he was: 'Sefton Delmer informed me to-day that he feels he cannot carry on if this sort of thing is allowed to continue. He adds that, if the "National Review" is allowed to discuss our secrets in this way, there is nothing to prevent the Press generally from doing so, and that, in this case, his station will lose all the power it now has and might as well close down.'

Barman suggested that MI5 should be involved in taking 'the strongest possible action'.

In early May, Richard Crossman complained that nothing had yet been done about this security breach. He had been assured that 'drastic action' would be taken against the *National Review*'s piece, but this hadn't happened. Worse still, the reference to Gustav Siegfried Eins now seemed to have been picked up in Germany by the weekly newspaper *Das Reich*. Its piece, on 26 April, was headlined 'Gustav is silent' and mocked the radio station, which it described as coming from Scotland, 'quite a long way from the Potsdamer Platz' in the centre of Berlin. The writer of the piece knew that GS1's broadcasts regularly started with the phrase 'The Chief is speaking!' and claimed that the voice was that of a 'Scottish comedian'. The article characterised the methods the station used as having 'delectable piles of indecent literature, plenty of which can still be obtained in England in spite of paper shortage' on one side of his desk and 'a bunch of cuttings from German newspapers' on the other.

It's quite likely that the German regime and Goebbels's propaganda operation did realise that GS1 and some of the other RUs originated from Britain; it was possible to locate the source of the stations and the fact that jamming was aimed against them suggests that the Germans saw it as a good idea to block them. It was another thing for this to reach the wider population in Germany. For Crossman, it was a 'cardinal matter of principle affecting the very existence of the work on which we are engaged'. He did not see how they could continue the work unless security was rigorously enforced. Crossman wanted this matter raised at the next ministerial meeting.

This seems to have prompted Bracken to belatedly send off his stiff letter to Lady Milner, drafted for him by Rex Leeper. Leeper added a note to the minister that he knew Lady Milner well and believed she had been misled; there seems to have been a reluctance to offend her. Bracken wrote to her that the matter was causing 'serious anxiety'. The freedom broadcasts, he said, were a 'carefully kept secret', which should be treated in the same way as any military secret. He accused Lady Milner of playing into the enemy's hands. 'It does not serve the national interest,' Bracken wrote, 'that the *National Review* should reveal our secrets for the benefit of Dr Goebbels, who is delighted to find any excuse for denouncing our propaganda, which is being widely listened to in Germany and which is a thorn in his side.' He made clear this was a second offence and if it were repeated, there would be consequences: 'we are prepared to take the necessary steps if this warning is neglected.' Bracken reiterated his reference to Goebbels, saying the magazine had 'unwittingly helped Goebbels in a way which is most welcome to him'.[21] Accusing his critics of playing into the hands of the Germans' chief propagandist was a frequent tactic of Bracken's when he found himself on the back foot regarding propaganda.

At the end of March, a group of MPs who were still unhappy with propaganda policy took the issues they'd raised in the Commons to a meeting with Anthony Eden. Bruce Lockhart, who was present, described Kenneth Pickthorn, who was among the group from the Parliamentary Committee on Propaganda, as his 'old but tiresome friend'. As he sat around the conference table in Eden's room on a Wednesday evening with ten or eleven disgruntled MPs, Bruce Lockhart reflected that his was the same table where he'd observed many previous disputes; 'so many disastrous sittings of the ministerial committee and so many fantastically rude duels between Brendan and Dalton'.[22]

Among the group was a newly elected Labour MP, Ivor Thomas, who had only taken his seat on the day of the propaganda debate. When Thomas was elected unopposed at a by-election in Keighley, Hugh Dalton had congratulated himself on the selection as 'my first real success in getting into

the House of Commons one of my proteges of the next gen-
eration'.[23] Thomas, he believed, would cause a 'nasty jolt' for
Rex Leeper and Dallas Brooks – although Dalton was reshuffled away from his propaganda job too soon to see any benefit
from his acolyte's presence. But Thomas still seemed willing
to cause that jolt. Bruce Lockhart noted that the new MP had
resigned from his job at Woburn, where he had run the Italian
Freedom Stations during their first year.[24] Bruce Lockhart
indicated to Eden that Thomas had been got rid of, rather than
left of his own accord. At the meeting with the foreign secretary, Thomas had an 'outburst', according to Bruce Lockhart,
launching into a 'savage attack' on the Country HQ, declaring that 'the extravagance was appalling, that the staff should
be brought back to London in order to save petrol, that the
whole place was a hotbed of reaction'.[25]

Thomas also believed that the names of the regional
directors of the PWE should be in the public domain. This
accusation of being reactionary apparently annoyed both
Eden and the tiresome Pickthorn, because Pickthorn argued
rather that the Country Headquarters was a den of socialists.
Eden 'offered to bet Thomas a hatful of guineas' that if a
census of 'country' headquarters were made, there would be
more socialists than Tories.

Crossman was accused during the meeting of being both
'too socialist' and a fascist. Pickthorn repeated his accusation
that Crossman's broadcast after the Night of the Long Knives
'made it, or should have made it, impossible for him ever to
broadcast to Germany during a war'. He believed the 1934
broadcast had shown Crossman was sympathetic to the Nazis.

Ivor Thomas kept complaining to the foreign secretary
until Eden finally asked Thomas what authority he had for his
accusations. 'Were they not merely his opinions?' Eden asked.
When Thomas said 'yes', Eden responded that 'perhaps other
people do not think very highly of your opinions'. This was
a stinging putdown for Thomas. Eden looked 'flushed with

success'; the foreign secretary wanted to have more such meetings. Bruce Lockhart thought Eden had handled the job of challenging the disgruntled MPs really well, writing that 'he understands this kind of thing, and now *I* understand how his charm works'. It seemed that having Eden take a closer interest in the workings of political warfare would be helpful, particularly in managing the domestic politics of the work.

It was only at the end of March that Brendan Bracken – perhaps prompted by these arguments about extravagance and waste – finally found the time to visit the Country HQ at Woburn, after eight months in the job. On a wet and depressing morning, Bruce Lockhart climbed into Bracken's Bentley for the minister's maiden journey to the estate and its surrounding secret houses. Ronald Tree, the owner of Ditchley Park, and Freddie Birkenhead, Churchill's godson, were also along for the ride. The journey was 'enlivened by the sparkle of the conversation'. The conversation seems to have been rather one-sided, with Bracken doing most of the talking. He regaled his passengers with many of the subjects on which he had made himself an expert, from architecture to the history of the Russell family, that of the Duke of Bedford. Bracken had, apparently, once owned and redecorated a 'charming' Queen Anne house in the Dunstable area, and he made a detour into a little side road to show it to Bruce Lockhart, who was underwhelmed.[26] He had the habitual scepticism of those who dealt with Bracken regularly, confiding to his diary that the minister had a 'very lively and active imagination which transports him on occasions to realms of pure invention'.

Once they arrived at Woburn, Rex Leeper was keen to impress the minister of information on his inaugural visit. Bracken, however, appeared easily distracted from what he was supposed to be looking at. As Leeper showed him through the abbey's rooms, where the Country section was working amid Victorian furniture jumbled with filing cabinets and typewriters, he would attempt to interest Bracken in the work of the French section or other departments. Bracken, however, would catch sight of a piece of art on the walls or an interesting quirk of architecture and exclaim to his fellow visitors, 'Look at that Canaletto – absolutely first-class. Just about the best in England.'

Bracken was less distracted once in the less inspiring modern surroundings of the other parts of the Woburn establishment. At Marylands, he visited the production unit, responsible for creating leaflets, and discussed the PWE's poor relationship with the Air Ministry, who were often reluctant to take on the dropping of leaflets over Europe. At Simpson, where he was given a tour of the recording studios, Bracken became really interested, praising the 'virile and effective' voices of the announcers on the black propaganda radio stations, which he thought were better than those of the BBC.[27]

He was persuaded by Bruce Lockhart that he should try his voice at making a recording. This was something of a Woburn tradition – important visitors being invited to record some comments in the studio. Although Bracken often gave gossipy briefings to journalists as minister of information, he rarely broadcast himself and there are few surviving recordings of his voice. Bruce Lockhart called the audio visitors' book – organised by Richard Gambier-Parry, the SIS officer with a background in radio who was in charge of Woburn's technical side – the 'Rogues' Record'. Bracken obliged them, saying 'This is the first time I have seen anything of your work. I am very glad that the house of the quisling Duke of Bedford is being put to the best possible use in the war.'[28] While his father had reluctantly tolerated having propagandists on the premises, the twelfth duke, a fascist sympathiser, was banned from Woburn during the war because he was a security risk.

Rex Leeper seemed relieved after Bracken's visit that all appeared to have gone well. Leeper knew that Bracken was keen on dismantling the Woburn operation and returning most of the staff to London and had been anxious to give the best account of his work. He told Bruce Lockhart privately that Bracken had asked no difficult questions. For a moment, Bruce Lockhart was worried that he had overstated the risks to Leeper and had been misleading his old friend. However, Bruce Lockhart's instincts about Bracken turned out to be correct; not even the Canalettos and the Inigo Jones elements of the abbey had been enough to change the minister's mind.

On the return journey, despite a lunch at the Old Rectory that had involved a lot of white wine and two large whiskies, Bracken became serious. He told Bruce Lockhart that there were two main problems with Woburn: it was too far from London and the constant commuting of staff between the two used too much petrol at a time of rationing. His proposed solution was that most of the personnel – except those involved in the most secretive work – should be brought to London. Petrol consumption needed to be halved and Bruce Lockhart was instructed to organise an enquiry into the transport situation. Bracken suggested someone to run the investigation, promising that he would have the necessary accommodation in London organised for officials. Bruce Lockhart was impressed by this decisive approach.

In London, the PWE had moved into a new headquarters at Bush House, on a floor above the BBC's overseas services. This meant that all of the PWE's London operations were in the same place, which was supposed to make their work more efficient. For Bruce Lockhart, the move from his previous base at the Foreign Office – where he worked in a set of temporary cubicles put up inside the building that were alternately stuffy or draughty – was 'like a journey from an old-world English home into a brand-new skyscraper in a Middle West American township'.[29] He did not necessarily think this was a good thing. He found his world convenient for work, with the

Foreign Office on Whitehall and the Ministry of Information on Malet Street in Bloomsbury each only a few minutes away, but he was further from his favourite clubs and restaurants.

While the move to Bush House allowed the PWE to oversee white propaganda more easily – with a flurry of weekly directives from the executive to the BBC, setting out what the main developments in the war were and what the themes of propaganda should be – they were still at some distance from the black propaganda operations. The qualms about the work Delmer and his colleagues were doing would reach beyond the readers of the *National Review* and other sceptical papers – and those misgivings were about to be raised at Cabinet level.

11

A Rare Artist and a Good Fellow

On 12 June 1942, Sir Stafford Cripps sat at his ministerial desk in his office in Gwydyr House on Whitehall to write a personal and private note. The letter was to Anthony Eden, the foreign secretary. Cripps, the lord privy seal, had good reason for writing to his fellow Cabinet member by hand. Eden would soon see, Cripps began, why he could not dictate such a sensitive letter to his young lady typist. This was not just for reasons of wartime secrecy, but because of the nature of his complaint to Eden. Cripps was extremely distressed about a broadcast which had gone out on GS1.

One of the lines being put out over the station, Cripps protested, was 'the worst foul and filthy pornography'. This was being put out and paid for by the British government, and since Cripps said he was sure that Eden couldn't be aware of such a thing, he set it out in great detail. He had heard rumours of the nature of this broadcast and asked someone who understood German to listen to it for him.

The broadcast, Cripps was told, gave 'detailed description of a named German admiral who takes home 4 or 5 sailors with his own mistress. He makes the sailors drunk and excites himself by instigating the sailors to rape his mistress in turn.' The story, Cripps said, was told in a running commentary which described 'in the minutest detail' the difficulties of the sailors owing to their drunkenness. He was particularly disgusted by one part, which he quoted to Eden in its original

German, discussing how the sailors had used butter to lubricate their victim. The narrator of the orgy scene followed this with the 'indignant comment' that butter was not available to the ordinary Germans. This line would doubtless have been Tom Delmer's idea of a joke, a typical use of humour in black propaganda to sneak in a political point. 'The climax of the orgy,' Cripps fumed, 'is an even more detailed description of how the old Admiral finally works himself up into a state in which he, too, can copulate with the woman.'[1]

'What good this is supposed to do I cannot imagine,' Cripps continued. He believed it would only 'play up to the most foul and filthy Nazis who we shall never catch – I hope'. Cripps thought that other groups – such as the 'decent minded' liberals, socialists, Catholics and Protestants within Germany – would be as revolted as he had been.

Even though this was deniable propaganda, Cripps, who had returned from a visit to Moscow a few months earlier, believed that the Russians were likely to know that GS1 originated from Britain. In any case, deniable or not, Cripps objected 'most strongly to such filth being allowed to go out of this country'.

Robert Bruce Lockhart invited Cripps to dinner in response to this letter, hoping to convince him that the PWE was 'not as black as he had painted us'.[2] The dinner, on 23 June, was the first time the two men had met. Bruce Lockhart was impressed by Cripps, despite their differences. Cripps arrived in a dark grey suit with carefully pressed trousers, and his characteristic rimless half-glasses. He was tall, with a straight-backed posture which he owed to the Alexander Technique. Bruce Lockhart thought the glasses rather spoilt his looks, but that, despite a sallow complexion, Cripps looked otherwise fit.

Sir Stafford Cripps was known to be a rigorously ascetic man. Vernon Bartlett called him 'one of the most austere men I have ever met'.[3] Cripps was a teetotaller and a vegetarian – both were for the good of his health, as he had suffered from terrible digestive problems as a young man. He worked sixteen-hour days, starting early in the morning, and took cold baths. He was also devoutly religious. His only vice was to continue smoking cigarettes, cigars and pipes, all three of which he indulged in during the course of the evening's dinner.

Bruce Lockhart saw him as 'very rigid with his mind quite clear on everything. Has the highest moral principles and lives up to them.'[4] It would be hard to imagine a man more different from Delmer or Bruce Lockhart in his habits. Cripps and his wife lived in a two-room apartment on a budget of five pounds a week and when he wasn't eating at home and doing his own washing-up, he was dining cheaply in a Lyons restaurant.

Cripps was a pivotal figure in Churchill's reshuffled government. He had been made a member of the War Cabinet and taken on his role as lord privy seal – effectively a minister without portfolio – and leader of the House of Commons in February. Churchill had initially offered him the job of minister of supply, but without membership of the War Cabinet, something Cripps had turned down. Although he had previously been a Labour MP, he had been thrown out of the party before the start of the war over his petition to start a Popular Front of the Left. He had been made ambassador to Russia and his popularity surged when Russia entered the war, because public opinion had given him much credit for his role in dealing with Moscow. Germany, however, felt Cripps's appointment was something they could exploit in propaganda: Goebbels called him 'Stalin's emissary in London', because of his left-wing views and his stay in the Soviet Union.[5] Cripps was, for a while, so popular that he was sometimes considered a possible alternative prime minister. That popularity had faded after his unsuccessful visit to India in March 1942, where he had tried to forge a deal over future independence, but he was still a very influential man. If Cripps was concerned about the nature of British propaganda, Bruce Lockhart and his colleagues needed to try to win him round to their way of thinking.

Cripps seemed at ease, with a smile that was 'pleasant and dangerously disarming'.[6] He was very calm and didn't lose his temper, speaking to Bruce Lockhart clearly and concisely, never at a loss for words. But his irritation at Delmer's use of pornography was equally clear. Bruce Lockhart saw Cripps as an aristocratic missionary, 'more set on making converts than on being converted'.

He was no doubt genuinely offended by the pornographic radio broadcast. Despite his quiet manner, though, Bruce Lockhart thought his offence was exaggerated. Cripps told him that he had heard of one household where people had listened to the broadcast about the orgy and that 'two young women had been there and had been physically sick!' He didn't explain – or at least Bruce Lockhart didn't record – where this house had been or how Cripps had come to hear of this story. Aside from the people working on the stations, they were only supposed to be heard in Germany and occupied Europe. Bruce Lockhart dismissed this observation of the listeners' disgust, writing in his diary: 'This is typical of Cripps's extravagance of views; he is very near to being a religious maniac.'

Cripps went further, telling Bruce Lockhart that even if GS1 was good propaganda, he would rather lose the war than win by such methods; he was sure, though, that it was bad propaganda. In Delmer's retelling of the story, he gave Cripps the snappier line: 'If this is the kind of thing we have to do to win the war . . . w-w-why I would rather lose it!' As ever, Delmer added his own invented flourishes to the tale in the interests of a good story. He described Cripps, whom he called 'that fine old Socialist Puritan', racing round to the Foreign Office, 'pale with indignation', to tell Eden of his outrage face-to-face, rather than sitting down to write him a letter.[7]

Behind the scenes, before Bruce Lockhart's dinner with Cripps, he and his colleagues had been keen to get their side of the story to Anthony Eden first, before Sir Stafford could attempt to persuade the foreign secretary that this kind of propaganda should be stopped. Rex Leeper wrote a memo in defence of black propaganda operations, accompanied with a personal minute to Bruce Lockhart. In Leeper's view, the conduct of propaganda was 'war with the gloves off', and that when he had been asked to deal with black propaganda, he had not restrained his staff because 'if you are told to fight you must fight all out'. Leeper made an analogy with the work of the Secret Service, who were likewise able to use unorthodox methods. If the Secret Service were to be too squeamish, he wrote, it could not operate – even if that meant that 'women were used by them for purposes which we would not like our women to be used'. Leeper said that he personally was bored rather than disgusted by pornography, and thought Cripps's outrage was unjustified. 'I dislike the baser sides of human life as much as Sir S. Cripps does, but in this case moral indignation does not seem to be called for.'[8]

Bruce Lockhart and Leeper mounted a defence against Cripps on several grounds. The first was that the use of pornography was justified because it appealed to their target audience. Bruce Lockhart wrote to Eden that the broadcast had been made as a result of a request from the Admiralty, who wanted to create disaffection among German U-boat crews. Leeper said that the pornography had just served as the introduction to an 'operational item' which aimed to undermine the confidence of German sailors in the materials used in their submarines. The 'depraved Admiral' was quoted as the man responsible for the failure to supply proper materials, with the use of pornography a way to whip up further indignation against him. The story, Leeper insisted, had 'a foundation of truth'. The pornographic element was just there to attract listeners, 'not for the sake of pornography in itself', and to suggest to them that the admiral was up to no good. Bruce Lockhart maintained that their hoped-for audience of German sailors was particularly keen on the sort of thing that Cripps so detested. Having spent more than a quarter of a century of his life in central and eastern Europe, he argued that he had 'no hesitation in saying that there is no European man so lecherous or so coarse in his lechery as the German'. Leeper echoed this view, saying that 'there is a sadism in the German nature quite alien to the British nature'. The Germans, he said, were far from being revolted by the sadistic content. He defended Delmer's 'intimate understanding' of German psychology and his introduction of 'coarse realism'.

Bruce Lockhart also suggested that Cripps was being manipulated by those who continued to have an axe to grind against the British propaganda operation towards Germany. He was suspicious as to who might have helped Cripps hear this material and blamed 'a cabal working in London against the country' – meaning the Country HQ at Woburn. Cripps's letter had been written in June, Bruce Lockhart observed, but the broadcast which Cripps had got someone to listen to was made six months before, in December 1941. 'The deduction that someone has been "getting" at Sir Stafford seems fair,' Bruce Lockhart told the foreign secretary. He said that the Woburn establishment had 'two very bitter opponents' – Freddy Voigt on the right wing and Ivor Thomas on the left – and that both of them had been edged out of the abbey and 'harboured bitter resentment' against Leeper.[9] In other words, he detected a continuation of the campaigns against Crossman and others by a new means.

Delmer put the blame elsewhere: he was convinced that Cripps had been set up by the 'European Revolutionaries', the disaffected German émigré left-wingers who had worked with Crossman on the earliest propaganda stations. He accused them of sending Cripps an exaggerated translation of the

GS1 script in what he called 'an outrageous breach of all the department's rules of security'.

Although Bruce Lockhart acknowledged that perhaps, in this instance, Delmer had gone too far, he believed it would nonetheless be a mistake to impose any further restrictions on what black propaganda was allowed to do. He wanted to establish the principle that, of necessity, black propaganda operated by different methods and to different standards than white propaganda. Leeper wrote that the aim of the station was to turn Germans against Germans, rather than to bring them round to the British point of view. This, he thought, required methods that might otherwise be unpalatable. He insisted that 'no secret, subversive organisation can operate successfully if its operations are to be limited to what the moral standards of our country would require for work undertaken openly'.

Leeper was forthright in his defence of Delmer, writing to Bruce Lockhart that he was 'a rare artist and a good fellow'. Leeper hoped that Cripps's protest would not mean that the organisation lost Delmer. Like Bruce Lockhart, he was prepared to admit that Delmer might have gone a bit over the top on this occasion, but he maintained that, in any case, since the broadcast was six months old, things had already changed and there was less use of outright pornography.

Both Bruce Lockhart and Leeper were dismissive of Cripps's further point that the Russians probably already knew that the Freedom Stations were being broadcast from Britain. Both men knew Russia well – Leeper added a postscript to his handwritten minute, saying 'Have you ever met an Englishman who could shock a Russian?' In his more formal memo, Leeper conceded that the German authorities were aware that GS1 originated from Britain, but the more important thing was that the German listeners did not. He cited prisoners of war who claimed to know that the broadcasts were coming from Hamburg. Leeper wasn't so concerned that the

German authorities knew the truth, since they had mainly decided to respond by attempting to block the station rather than by drawing attention to it. He wrote that 'provided that in this country secrecy is observed, there is little risk that the truth will be revealed'.

After their dinner together, Cripps and Bruce Lockhart parted on good terms. In Delmer's twist on the tale, he said that Cripps left their encounter 'mollified and smiling'. Bruce Lockhart confided in his diary that he himself believed that secret stations and forgeries were 'in the nature more of stunts than of serious propaganda', though this was not the view that he defended in his correspondence with Anthony Eden. One area where Cripps and Bruce Lockhart agreed was that it was inefficient for propaganda to be divided between Woburn and London. In Bruce Lockhart's view, the increasing tempo of the war made it 'more hopeless than ever' to run propaganda 'from a place fifty miles distant from London'. He pleaded with Cripps to use his influence with the authorities to help the PWE get more accommodation for its staff in London.

The two men's positions on the use of Freedom Stations also weren't as far apart as might have been expected. Cripps was keen on creating RU stations much as they had been in the early part of the war – with Catholic, socialist or liberal stations appealing to different opposition tendencies within Germany. This position might also have been influenced by Voigt and others who were against the development of full black propaganda rather than the early 'grey' stations; it didn't recognise the confusion that had so often resulted from different propaganda stations taking entirely different points of view on what exactly they were fighting for. Bruce Lockhart said that Cripps – unlike Vansittart – obviously believed in the existence of a considerable number of 'good Germans'.

Bruce Lockhart tried to impress on the minister that the PWE was constrained in what it could offer to anti-Nazi elements within Germany. As he put it, they needed to be allowed to hold out some hope of a better future to those who opposed the regime, but they were 'severely restricted' in that respect.[10] He put this limitation down to common sense being 'swamped by popular emotion' in wartime.

Eden delayed his reply to Cripps's letter until after his long-planned visit to Woburn. This was the first time the foreign secretary had seen the hush-hush village and its facilities for himself. Eden and Bracken had not been frequent guests, unlike Hugh Dalton who had often turned up for weekends. Bruce Lockhart accompanied Eden in his chauffeur-driven car, with a detective sitting in the front seat.

At Woburn, the staff had been making detailed plans for how to welcome the foreign secretary for over a month, as he had first been expected to visit in mid-May. Ralph Murray wrote to Rex Leeper that 'the important thing in our view is the work and not the frills and semi-technical attractions of it'.[11] Murray would have preferred Eden to discuss and listen to the output at Woburn Abbey itself, but if the foreign secretary did visit the radio studios at Simpson in Wavendon Tower, Murray thought it was important that the studio trip should be 'on the most business-like basis possible and not the tour of a new toy'.

Eden arrived with Bruce Lockhart on the evening of Thursday 25 June and was escorted to the radio studios. Murray had also been concerned that not everyone should turn up to greet the distinguished visitor. Although he did want Crossman and Delmer to be present, he didn't want there to be a 'full parade' of regional directors. He was perhaps worried about the government's perception that there were too many staff in Woburn working on too diverse a set of programmes. Murray also made sure that there was a selection of recordings of the various stations for Eden to listen to, asking the departments to prepare a selection of discs for him to hear, in order of importance. Most of the time should be spent on the French stations, Murray specified, the rest on Germany, with broadcasts in other languages available if Eden requested them. Eden did not require translations as he spoke fluent French and German, in addition to the classical Arabic and Persian he had studied at university.

Eden, however, was less impressed by the French broadcast, thinking it 'too theatrical'. He was more interested in the German broadcasts, telling Bruce Lockhart that Delmer, despite being fairly coarse, was an artist.[12] This echoed exactly what he and Rex Leeper wanted him to think, so the visit seemed to have scored a success.

Eden excused his belated reply to Cripps by saying that, since he had already planned a visit to Woburn, he waited until he had made a personal inquiry into the matter. He reassured Cripps that pornography had not been used in recent broadcasts, but emphasised that he had said items of such a nature were to be avoided. However, Eden wasn't prepared to impose too narrow restrictions on a station which was intended to be 'tough'. 'Its special purpose,' he reminded Cripps, 'is not to win Germans to our side, but to turn Germans against Germans and thereby weaken the German war machine.'[13]

As Eden had stood in the cubicle of the recording studio at Simpson, watching a record being made, he asked Ralph Murray whether it would be possible for the Freedom Stations to reach a bigger audience, beyond the listeners who could only pick up the stations on short-wave radio. This was also helpful to the PWE's cause, as plans were already underway to allow them to use a new radio transmitter that was being bought and constructed.

Eden also agreed to contribute to the Woburn 'Rogues' Record', the audio visitors' book that Brendan Bracken had made a recording for a few months earlier. Sadly, none of the recordings made by the ministerial visitors appear to have survived.

Black propaganda's future, once it had survived Cripps's protests, seemed more assured. Over the year since GS1 had first gone on the air, Delmer had been working on more sophisticated ways of sourcing information and rumours which it could exploit as black propaganda. Crossman had asked Delmer to make it clearer which themes he was developing and show how those themes were related to the course of events in the war. At the beginning of 1942, Delmer was working on another story designed to undermine the morale of sailors, though this time with less pornographic content: he created a story about the corruption of a U-boat officer called Hesemann who had been robbing his ship of the crew's supplies in order to traffic them on the black market. This, Delmer said, was a true story.[14] Among the overarching themes that he was pursuing was showing that the SS were 'having a good time behind the front while the real soldiers died in snow and desert sand'. He wanted to sow dissent and dissatisfaction among troops who had returned from the eastern front to recuperate before being sent back to Russia to fight. He aimed to encourage desertion and to undermine the morale of the air force and of factory workers.

Delmer often returned to encouraging the fear of disease among German troops: in 1942, he fomented worries about typhus. He didn't do this straight on, but at an angle. Der Chef demanded that special rations of fat, soap and coal should be released in order to combat what he said was an epidemic of typhus.[15] He spread rumours that the blood transfusions given to German casualties on the eastern front came from Russian and Polish donors and that the donors had not been screened for syphilis, so that there were outbreaks of venereal disease within field hospitals.[16]

In December 1941, black propaganda encouraged the German population to distrust all meat and sausages by spreading the 'revelation' that infected meat from French colonies had been put on the market. By the summer of 1942, Delmer put out a line saying 'we have now got to the point that they are making shit into butter'. He seemed to take some delight in drawing Leeper's attention to this script and telling him that the story about excrement and butter 'would undoubtedly have ranked among the pornographic variety to which exception was taken' by Cripps. He wanted the German civilian population, as well as the soldiers at the front, to believe that their ruling elite was better fed than they were. In one case, the black propaganda section drew on intercepted letters from the American-born wife of a German industrialist, based in Cologne, where she had written about her wartime social life. The stories had some basis in truth, but were exaggerated by Delmer's team. According to the version put on air, the mayor of Cologne had thrown a party where the guests were served a huge cake in the shape of the city's cathedral, which had required kilos of sugar to make. At the same time, Der Chef complained that the sugar ration had just been cut dramatically for the rest of the people.[17]

Some GS1 stories achieved their aim of being spread so widely within Germany that many people believed them. The rumour that the head of the German Labour Front, Robert Ley, had special 'diplomat rations' for his household, which allowed him more food than the rest of the country, originated from GS1 and gained such currency that Dr Ley tried to deny it in a regime newspaper. 'The normal rations are enough,' Ley wrote. 'I myself am a normal consumer and live on them.'[18] This reaction, as many politicians have come to realise since, had precisely the opposite effect from the one he wanted: by denying the rumours, he gave them even broader circulation. As Ley was well known to be a heavy drinker, the rumours escalated further and Der Chef was able to exploit this, in turn asking whether Ley was a 'normal consumer' as far as either bread or alcohol were concerned.

As black propaganda became more elaborate, Delmer started to build up a larger staff who could provide him with the research that he needed to make sure his rumours were grounded in truth. For his stories to be believed, they depended on the most accurate information it was possible to get out of Germany and elsewhere in Europe. Some of this information came from the questioning of prisoners of war, who had more up-to-date knowledge of conditions at home than anyone who had left Germany before the war began.

The more Delmer and his team could analyse this information on what life was really like in wartime Germany, where Allied bombs had fallen and how people lived, the more they could focus on undermining the morale of the troops ahead of the coming battles, in the air, at sea and on land.

You Have No Chance!

S ir Arthur Harris, the head of the RAF's Bomber
Command, was normally sceptical, to say the least, of
the idea of using his planes to drop propaganda leaflets
over Europe. He was unconvinced about the value of propaganda at all, believing as he did in the supremacy of air power
and relentless, widespread bombing. Indeed, he was reported
to have expressed the personal view that the main function of
wartime propaganda leaflets was to have kept the continent
plentifully supplied with lavatory paper.[1] When Robert Bruce
Lockhart first met Harris in the spring of 1942, the PWE
chief described him as 'heavily built with blue eyes, fair complexion, firm jaw and broad shoulders'. The air marshal was
both 'burly in appearance and tough in mind'.[2] He told Bruce
Lockhart of his objections to dropping what he called 'pieces
of bumph'. While he recognised that the leaflets could have
some value, he was worried that the logistics of dropping them
put his air crew at risk. The leaflets had to be dropped manually
and, for that to happen, a rear gunner had to leave his gun for
five to ten minutes. Over areas like Holland, he argued, and in
the presence of night-fighters, a gunner could not afford to
leave his weapon for that long without endangering the plane
and its crew. Harris would have preferred a mechanical device
to do that work, but such a thing had not yet been created.[3]

'Bomber' Harris would become one of the war's best-
known commanders. His role in the area bombing of Europe
was controversial, with some seeing the extensive air raids

as causing unnecessary civilian casualties, even verging on war crimes. What Bruce Lockhart saw as tough-mindedness, others described as boorishness or bluntness. He was 'a man of startling directness'.[4] However, his high profile, 'boundless energy' and bombast were assets that Bomber Command thought they could turn to their advantage at a time when they had been getting a bad press. Bomber Command were being criticised for the failure to spot and destroy the German cruisers that made it through the Channel, and there was a widespread belief among the public that British bombing raids were inefficient and ineffective.[5]

Harris knew that he needed to influence public opinion in his favour, and he was willing to give interviews in newspapers and occasionally on film. Some of his messages to his air crew, such as to those manning the raids over Cologne in May, were bold and stirring. He urged on the airmen to attack Germany, saying of the enemy: 'Let him have it – right on the chin.'[6]

Sir Arthur 'Bomber' Harris, 1941

Unfortunately, Harris, 'an inflexible man, chronically resistant to negotiation and compromise', was tricky to handle.[7] He was potentially a great asset to propaganda, but needed to be treated carefully – and on this occasion he wasn't. At an operational propaganda committee meeting at Bush House on 4 June 1942, David Garnett of the PWE, acting as secretary to the committee, suggested that a 'military man rather than a politician' should front a broadcast campaign that would encourage people in occupied Europe to sabotage transport and other infrastructure, such as fuel and power. Oliver Lawrence of the Ministry of Economic Warfare suggested Bomber Harris's name and the rest of the committee agreed that Ivone Kirkpatrick should approach him about the proposed talk.[8] Two weeks later, Harris had agreed to the broadcast. Having the commander broadcast on the BBC must have seemed like a natural progression from his newspaper interviews. It was decided that Harris's talk in English to Europe should be introduced by Colonel Britton – Douglas Ritchie's pseudonymous character who had been the voice of the V Campaign – whereas the translations of his speech into other languages would be without introductions. This suggestion seems to also have gone through the PWE for their approval, as Bruce Lockhart wrote that the invitation to the air marshal had been approved by the PWE, the Foreign Office and the chiefs of staff after 7 July. A week later, his script had been signed off – as part of what was euphemistically called the 'Campaign to Increase the Enemy's Transport Difficulties' – and was ready for the air marshal to record.

The recently knighted Sir Arthur Harris recorded this talk in his own voice. 'My job is transport,' he began, rather innocuously, before rapidly raising the stakes. 'The transport of bombs in the right quantities at the right time to the right place. A bomb on a Boche or on a dozen Boches is the best bomb of all. It is certainly the most satisfying.' There were certainly threats to the Germans in the script; for instance, when he said that the German transport network would be hit a lot harder than it was currently being so that 'the sole means of transport left to the Boche is his boots, if he is lucky enough, by then, to have boots'. But the main thrust of the broadcast was to tell Germans about the problems and delays facing their country in transporting its men and materiel around Europe. 'It is Bomber Command's job to paralyse and cripple the Hun,' Harris said. Although the Allies would provide deliverance from Germany, they needed the population's help, he continued. Harris ended with an incitement to the German people and others in Europe to commit sabotage on the transport network. 'If everyone of you did just a little to cause delays, that would amount in total to such a vast amount that not a wheel would roll for Germany.' He suggested that grains of sand or carborundum – an abrasive form of silicon – finding their way into oil pipes or grease boxes on the transport network could help this process. 'I look after the big bombs,' he concluded. 'You look after the grains of sand.'[9]

But at the same time as this broadcast was being arranged, the PWE was also approaching the Air Ministry about another campaign. The German section, under Crossman, asked whether Harris would be willing to contribute a message to the German people to be included in a 'magazine leaflet' – a small, illustrated leaflet to be dropped over the country. This was where the confusion began.

The second message, which in its early draft form was titled, 'Why We Bomb You', was a much more aggressive and political text. The English draft was written by the Air Ministry and sent to Dallas Brooks at the PWE for approval on 23 July. 'Never before has the man who is directing the bombing of a country sent a message to the people of that country,' it began. It talked of Britain's experience under the Blitz and told Germans that Britain had 'hardly started' its own bombing campaign. 'We are going to bomb you more and more heavily; city by city and town by town,' the message read, although it insisted 'it is not revenge'. It warned that this would only escalate with the United States' entry into the war and with the greater American strength. In the Air Ministry's initial version, Harris did veer into politics. He – or his officials – wrote that 'your Nazis were crazy to attack Russia and America when they were already fighting us. But then your Nazis <u>are</u> crazy.'[10] The German people were to be told that they could end the war and the bombing if they were to overthrow the Nazis and make peace. The Allies would make it impossible for Germany to start a war again.

When Crossman saw the suggested text, on Friday 24 July, he told the Air Ministry that it was too long for the proposed leaflet and would need editing. He also thought that the piece 'was so good that he wished to have it broadcast as well as dropped from the air'. That would mean making it shorter still. Crossman rewrote it and sent the revised script back to the Air Ministry by teleprinter on Sunday morning.

The ministry's own original draft contained some vivid and striking phrases. 'Soon we shall be coming every night and every day, rain, blow or snow,' Harris's message told the German people. 'You have no chance,' the message said, against the Allied forces. The original wording about overthrowing the Nazis in order to make peace remained, though it was now the conclusion to a shorter and snappier piece. In fact, it was probably Crossman's sharp editing and ear for a good line that helped make Harris's message so troublesome. The teleprinted pages were gone over again by Wing Commander Rose of the Air Ministry, who added in his own alterations in red pencil. But he didn't raise any objections to what he had read.

The Air Ministry seems to have been naive about what contributing to the propaganda effort would involve. At the very least, the officials who were dealing with different arms of the PWE and the BBC didn't really seem to understand how the process worked, and attempts to explain it seem to have confused them even more. There was a flurry of phone calls on the evening of Tuesday the 28th to let the Air Ministry know that Harris's words would be going out a day early on the air. First the BBC rang, then David Stephens of the PWE called Rose to make sure he was clear that what was being broadcast was not Harris's talk about transport sabotage, but rather the one about bombs. The Air Ministry seemed to have some qualms about the publicity the talks might receive, but when questioned further, Rose wasn't sure which of the two broadcasts he believed might cause problems. As Stephens noted in his account of his phone calls, it was clear to him at least that the bomb talk would be the bigger story. 'This broadcast was extremely likely to be picked up in the British press, much more like[ly] than the transport script, as it was a better story, and there was no way of stopping this.'

The Air Ministry at first seemed positively excited that Air Marshal Harris's words were going to appear on the BBC. An unnamed person from Bomber Command called the BBC on Tuesday evening to say that Harris wanted to know when his message was going out and on what wavelength. When the official was told that it would not only go out on the German service but also in English at 10.15 in the evening, he replied, 'Oh, yes, that's a good service. Will it be on that?' The official then said he'd tell the air marshal right away. Thompson of the BBC then told his colleague in the English section, 'for God's sake put it in'. Since there would be a distinguished listener, he wanted to make sure the report was broadcast as promised.

At the same time, the authorised leaflet had been printed and sent to Bomber Command for their planes to drop the message over Germany. Millions of copies of Harris's message to the German people fluttered down from the sky.

The radio message, although it was in Harris's name, wasn't in his own voice. It wasn't until the script was sent to the British papers that the problems really began. The next morning, *The Times* ran all of Harris's words on page 2 under the headline, 'You Have No Chance'. As *The Times* wrote it up, Harris had said that 'we and the Americans were going to scourge the Third Reich from end to end unless the people of Germany overthrew the Nazis and made peace'.[11] This was a fair summary of what Harris had written, but it caused immediate consternation over the breakfast tables of politicians and military officers in London.

That day, according to Bruce Lockhart, 'several hells gaped simultaneously'.[12] Having been away in Scotland during the lead-up to the broadcast, he was summoned by Anthony Eden as soon as he got back to his desk. The foreign secretary wanted to see both Bracken and Bruce Lockhart before Cabinet met that morning. Arriving before Bracken, Bruce Lockhart 'received part of the blast which had already blown over Mr Eden'. That blast had come not only from the air minister, Sir Archibald Sinclair, but also from the prime minister. Sinclair had managed to dash off a letter that had already reached Eden. Churchill too had called the foreign secretary to express his anger. The prime minister was not so much upset about the content of the broadcast, but more annoyed that a service chief would venture into making a political statement without the approval of a minister. Churchill was keen to make a statement that Bruce Lockhart felt would clear Sir Arthur Harris of controversy, but at the same time discredit the PWE's propaganda effort. Bruce Lockhart wanted to avoid any more public controversy in the House of Commons, and to save Crossman's skin in particular.

Bruce Lockhart, feeling under huge pressure, tried to play for time as Eden demanded answers he could not yet give. He was granted that time by chance, because Eden was told that Bracken couldn't make the meeting before Cabinet – he had been summoned instead to an audience with the king at Buckingham Palace, which inevitably took priority. Eden left for

Cabinet without having seen Bracken. 'God Save The King,' Bruce Lockhart thought to himself.

After his meeting at the Palace, Bracken met Sinclair over lunch. The air minister continued to press his protest. According to Sinclair, it had come as a 'sad shock' to Harris that the broadcast had been published within Britain. Sinclair followed up his lunch with a letter to Bracken setting out his concerns for the record. Air Marshal Harris had maintained to his political bosses that his words had been provided solely as a leaflet to be dropped over Germany and not for domestic consumption. This, he said, was what had been agreed with senior officials on both sides. Although Sinclair acknowledged that the words might have been valuable for propaganda intended only for Germans, they were 'quite unsuitable for publication in this country'. The other service chiefs of staff, Sinclair wrote, had already protested to the chief of the air staff. One of Harris's worries was that he had promised something in the script that he could not deliver. Bombing come rain, blow or snow was more than he could guarantee. Sinclair wrote that 'it is unfair to the Commander-in-Chief as it will be quoted against him whenever his aircraft are grounded by bad weather'. Sinclair himself did not want to have to go to the House of Commons – where he was honour-bound not to mislead – and have to accept responsibility for a statement that Bomber Command could bomb Germany every day and every night in the next winter. Nor did Sinclair think it was desirable for 'a serving officer to make declarations of Government policy' in this way.[13]

Labour's leader in the House of Lords, Lord Addison, asked a question in the Lords the same day, which hinted at the rumble of discontent in Parliament. He wanted to know whether the broadcast had been approved by the government and, if so, whether other individual officers of the services would also be allowed to broadcast statements on 'war aims and on strategic policy'.[14] Replying, Lord Selborne said that the government had approved it but that it would choose which person was suitable for any particular broadcast in future.

By the time Bracken spoke to Bruce Lockhart in the afternoon, both Bruce Lockhart and Crossman had effectively been given a stay of execution. Bracken, angry but helpful, said that he would speak to Churchill about the affair. By the next morning, the 30th, Eden told Bruce Lockhart that there was good news. The prime minister had liked Harris's message, been persuaded not to put out an immediate statement in response and Bruce Lockhart would be allowed to conduct an investigation and make a report on it. He accordingly sent a series of letters to all of his senior team who had been involved, asking for their answers.

Crossman was quick to get his defence in, replying to Bruce Lockhart that what he had received from the Air Ministry was a 'verbose draft' that needed 'drastic editing'. Nor did he accept that he had put politics into the text; on the contrary, he had taken some of it out. There was 'no question of PWE tampering with the text or inserting politics. PWE excised, among other doubtful matter, a good deal of politics. The text was agreed by the Air Ministry in precisely the same way as any other leaflet.' It was true that the PWE had taken some of the political matter out of the text. For instance, Crossman had removed a disparaging reference to Italian forces. He had also taken out some potentially sensitive details about the precise strength of American air power. What he wasn't so quick to mention was that he had certainly cut corners. Crossman had dealt directly with a relatively junior official at the Air Ministry, Wing Commander Rose, instead of going through the proper channels to organise turning the leaflet into a broadcast, so the Air Ministry could reasonably complain that the correct procedure hadn't been followed. They were protesting rather much, though, given that their own official had said he was happy with the text of the message. Sir Archibald Sinclair issued a ruling that in future, no serving officer was to broadcast without it being authorised by him personally.

Noel Newsome, the independent-minded editor at the BBC, also came in for criticism, since he was the person who had decided to send the text of Harris's broadcast message to the news agencies, which meant it appeared in the next morning's newspapers, uncensored. It was, as others had spotted, undeniably a good story, with its vivid phrases from the Air Marshal. If the message hadn't appeared so prominently in the British press, or if they had been given the rather duller talk about transport sabotage instead, the crisis would not have blown up.

After what he called 'forty-eight hours of almost incessant pre-occupation with the problems', Bruce Lockhart wrote to Bracken to update him on what his investigations had so far uncovered. He admitted to Crossman and Newsome's mistakes, but also put some of the blame on the Air Ministry. Harris, he wrote, was 'committed up to the hilt' on the matter of war aims and there was no question of Crossman having put words into Harris's mouth. The controversial words were Harris's own.

Bruce Lockhart also maintained that there was 'very considerable evidence to show that the broadcast was excellent propaganda' for both enemy countries and Allies. He would have liked Lord Selborne to say more to the House of Lords about the value of 'tough fighting words' in boosting Allied morale. The PWE's own research had looked at the German response to the broadcast and concluded that the German Propaganda Ministry feared that the message would have a serious impact within Germany and beyond. The research, however, based this conclusion on an absence; they believed the fact that German propaganda had hardly mentioned the broadcast or leaflet, or Harris's name, was a sign that they were worried. According to the research, Goebbels's propaganda usually mentioned broadcasts where German civilians were told they would suffer, but this broadcast was far more specific about the targets and what would happen, so they avoided it. The conclusions, though, were exactly what Bruce Lockhart wanted to hear.

Bruce Lockhart also argued that pushing things further to the point of an inquest would only 'embitter relations' between the PWE and the Air Ministry, because the PWE had plenty of evidence that blamed the Air Ministry's own officials. He suggested that Bracken himself, with his powerful network, was well placed to help sort out the problem and mollify the parties. This was a clever bit of flattery: 'As you yourself were solely instrumental in convincing Air Marshal Harris of the value of leaflets, you can restore peace after this tea-cup storm by giving another luncheon.' Bracken, Bruce Lockhart thought, should invite Harris and Sinclair to lunch and smooth things over.

Perhaps knowing that Bracken was inclined to dislike Crossman, someone he linked with his former nemesis Hugh Dalton, Bruce Lockhart also went out of his way to defend Crossman and even to suggest he should be promoted rather than fired. Crossman came out of his investigation rather well, he wrote. It would be enough disciplinary action to 'reprove him severely for his excess of zeal'. Bruce Lockhart had something else in mind for Crossman. He wanted to give him a new job, moving him from the German section to a 'central function' where he would work under his own 'immediate supervision'. Bruce Lockhart praised Crossman, saying he was 'outstanding in ability' and that his work was highly commended by many he worked with in the Foreign Office.

Bracken sent a brief note to Harris himself on 4 August, saying that he very much regretted 'the annoyance and inconvenience that was caused' last week by the 'muddle' over the message. This was not much of an apology, since Bracken, in the classic politician's style, only regretted the annoyance and the muddle rather than the broadcast of the message itself.

He said the matter had been dealt with in 'a slipshod manner on a low plane'. He was also very keen to distance himself from what had gone on, saying that neither he nor Eden was given any information about it.

Bracken also wrote back to Sir Archibald Sinclair telling him that Harris's statement was a 'valuable contribution to our political warfare' that had 'done more good than harm'. In this, he had followed Bruce Lockhart's suggested line. But Bracken didn't seem entirely convinced that everything was so easily resolved.

Bruce Lockhart wasn't yet out of trouble. He told his diary that, at the regular ministerial meeting on 6 August, more than a week after the broadcast had gone out, Bracken and Eden were 'back on' the Harris broadcast incident. They were still insisting on disciplinary action, reproof and censure for those involved. Bracken was in favour of an outside inquiry, despite Bruce Lockhart's telling him that doing so would attribute more blame to the Air Ministry.[15]

Churchill had left the country, en route for Moscow via Cairo, for his first face-to-face meeting with Stalin, so the pressure from that quarter had lessened, but other ministers were still not satisfied. Discontent continued to rumble on in Parliament, and Bruce Lockhart had detected a hardening of opinion against Crossman. Lord Addison had organised a debate on the affair on 4 August in which he compared Harris's broadcast to both Mussolini and Goebbels. Addison said this kind of 'deplorable bombast' was not the British way of doing things; 'it has not been the British habit to brag or boast in advance'. Much as Sinclair had said to Bracken, he announced it was wrong of Harris to have promised to bomb come rain, blow or snow, when bad weather and other problems would often overcome Bomber Command's ability to fly. To promise this, the peer said, 'sounds like Goebbels's statement that no bombs shall fall on the Reich' and was just about as sensible. Talking about the kind of peace that might be on offer to Germany was also, as others had said, not something that was within the remit of an RAF officer and should have been left to ministers. Some of the statement sounded, Addison believed, 'so bombastic that you might have thought that Mussolini made it'.[16] Addison did not blame Harris personally, rather the 'amateur' unnamed officials behind the scenes. Harris may have had bombastic tendencies of his own, but being compared to the Italian dictator or the German propaganda chief was beyond the pale.

In submitting his final report on the incident to Eden and Bracken, Bruce Lockhart was at pains to tell them how much important work his department did and how rarely, in his view, they made serious mistakes. His covering letter has the rather self-pitying tone that he often used, particularly when he was feeling low. By the summer of 1942, he was already beginning to suffer with health problems brought on by stress.

His letter to Eden began by telling him that the PWE's main sin was a 'sin of commission' – they had done things they should not have done. He tried to persuade them that, particularly in wartime, this was better than not having done what they should have, as he thought often happened in other parts of the civil service. The PWE was not an ordinary department, he said; 'in leaflets and in broadcasting millions of words go out yearly and thousands of words daily'. The need to liaise with several other departments and to make rapid decisions entailed risks. If Bruce Lockhart did not delegate, he told the ministers, he became a bottle-neck. 'Our work is therefore done at high pressure combined with very long hours,' he continued. 'The surprise is not that mistakes occur but that they occur so seldom.'[17]

The next part of Bruce Lockhart's *mea culpa* was so contrite that it almost reads now as though he were asking the ministers to fire him, before setting out why it would be difficult to find anyone else to take on the job. The PWE 'has many defects', he admitted; 'it is not an easy organisation to run'. The organisation was composed of what he called 'a clam-jamfry of what were formerly warring elements'.[18] Despite this, he argued that it was now running smoothly and harmoniously. His organisation possessed 'a wealth of talent' and its knowledge of political warfare and propaganda was ahead of any other department, either in Britain or the United States. Having just been introduced to General Eisenhower, Bruce Lockhart realised that the ability to work closely with the United States was about to become extremely important, so he emphasised this.

He rather plaintively observed that the PWE didn't receive any recognition for its work. That credit went to the BBC for good work and, by implication, the PWE took the blame for the bad. 'Since PWE came into existence, our broadcasts to Europe have improved out of all knowledge,' he wrote. Of course, not getting public recognition was to be expected in an organisation whose work was supposed to be largely secret.

Bruce Lockhart concluded by telling Eden that 'all work and no praise is not good for any organisation'. To punish the organisation now, he believed, would be disastrous. The complaints against his colleagues Dallas Brooks and Ivone Kirkpatrick were trivial, being merely mistakes in correct procedure; those against Crossman and the BBC's Newsome were more serious, but all the same, Newsome, despite his obstinacy, had 'great qualities of leadership and decision'. Bruce Lockhart again went out of his way to defend Crossman. Though requiring control, he was the 'most stimulating personality in the whole organisation'.

In the full report, Bruce Lockhart was also happy to shift the blame onto the hapless Wing Commander Rose at the Air Ministry who, like Crossman, had gone ahead without consulting his bosses. 'The conduct of Wing Commander Rose,' he wrote, 'is open to grave suspicion.' But in the end, it was not worth the PWE's while to pursue a vendetta against the

Air Ministry. He warned against any further inquest, as this would mean blaming Rose as much as Crossman.

Just before he submitted his final report into the situation, Bruce Lockhart also made efforts to smooth over the situation in person. He went to see Sir Archie Sinclair himself on the pretext of asking the air minister if he would put his own name to the ill-fated talk on transport sabotage which Harris had recorded but which had still not yet been broadcast. Sinclair was happy to allow that to happen, but didn't want the talk to go out in English. The conversation was made easier for Bruce Lockhart since Sinclair, a fellow Scot, was 'an old friend, and the interview was most satisfactory'.

As far as Sinclair was concerned, it all seemed to be water under the bridge, despite the furious rows of the previous two weeks. He told Bruce Lockhart that 'he had been momentarily annoyed, but now felt that more good than harm had been done by the broadcast'. His staff were prepared to forgive the PWE and said they were usually 'most friendly and efficient'. Sir Arthur Harris, too, was in forgiving mood, having told Sinclair that he 'bore no grudge'; 'all were agreed that the incident should be closed and forgotten'.

At the following week's ministerial meeting on Thursday 13 August, the whole affair was finally settled, though Bruce Lockhart felt the ministers were 'chipping' – teasing – him about his despatch on the treatment of the PWE.[19] Having squared all the responsible ministers, he wrote to his colleagues the week after to tell them of his findings and the ministers' responses.

He told Crossman that the ministers had largely found him to blame. Bruce Lockhart wrote that he considered Crossman's work 'of the greatest value to PWE', observing that 'otherwise, I would not have wasted weeks of precious time in order to defend it'. But he warned his junior that his habit of ignoring the rules to his own ends was going to cause him problems. It wasn't just about what Crossman thought would be the best propaganda, but about getting things done in the right way. 'I think it is a pity that you should sometimes jeopardise your own good work and the prestige of the department by excess of zeal and by a tendency to disregard the irksome but necessary rules of procedure which govern all forms of administrative life.' Bruce Lockhart warned him that they were reaching a stage in the war where any further mistakes would have more serious consequences.

Crossman was grateful for Bruce Lockhart's help in saving his job, writing back that 'no-one has the right to expect his boss to waste a week defending him from execution. But you did; and the least I can do in return is to take your advice, subsume zeal under discretion and prove to you that I was worth the wasted week.'

An incident which might have meant the end of Crossman's career instead took him into new areas. He was sent to the United States for discussions on how the two countries' political warfare teams could work together more effectively. That didn't mean, though, that his bosses trusted him entirely. In the absence of Bruce Lockhart, Dallas Brooks sat Crossman down for a long discussion, two days before his departure. Crossman asked what he should do if he was presented with a completed American plan for propaganda towards Germany with no opportunity to alter it. Brooks pointed out that no plan could be complete until they knew what the situation would be on the ground by the coming winter. He advised Crossman just to work on a draft plan. Reporting back to Bruce Lockhart, who was away, Brooks said he had also told Crossman to put everything he planned in writing to his boss 'to make sure that he does not go off the rails'.[20]

When Brooks called Bracken that evening, Bracken demanded to know why he hadn't been told about Crossman's American trip. Bracken's main fear was that Crossman would get in the hands of the American press, which he thought would result in even more questions in the House of

Commons if he stepped out of line. Bracken told Brooks that he would sleep on the problem, and when Brooks called the next morning, Bracken was 'perfectly reasonable' and agreed that Crossman should go, on condition that he was given written instructions.

Dallas Brooks sent Crossman those instructions the day before he was due to leave for New York.[21] First on the list was a warning: 'In no circumstances are you to give an interview to the Press.'[22] In fact, he should try to avoid all contact with the press. Nor did Brooks want him to get involved in politics; he told Crossman sternly that he was not in a position to commit the government to any line of action. Brooks must have known, however, as Bracken would also have done, that politics and journalism were Crossman's lifeblood and getting him to stay entirely out of either would have been impossible. But even Bracken seemed to accept that Crossman's presence in the States might be a help to good relations with the Americans.

The PWE had accepted much of the criticism over Air Marshal Harris's controversial broadcast because they needed to keep good relations with the Air Ministry – they needed Bomber Command and their planes as a means to drop leaflets far more than the Air Ministry needed them. Across 1942 as a whole, 125 million leaflets would be dropped by aircraft over Germany, 152 million over France.[23] As Crossman flew across the Atlantic, he might have appreciated all the more the risks that their pilots and crews ran.

The main preoccupation of the late summer and early autumn of 1942 was the preparations for the planned Operation Torch – the Allied landings in North Africa. As those gathered pace, keeping in the Air Ministry's good books, as well as those of the Americans, would become even more important. The landings would be accompanied by a propaganda offensive on a scale and level of organisation that had not yet been seen during the war.

PART 3

We Come as Your Friends

13

The End of the Beginning

On the early August Bank Holiday of 1942, Robert Bruce Lockhart had lunch in a private room at Claridge's to meet General Dwight Eisenhower. This was the beginning of the real political warfare planning for Operation Torch, the intended invasion of North Africa later in the year. Bruce Lockhart studied Eisenhower, 'blond, with clear, blue eyes, bullet-shaped head and firm jaw', and thought him 'amiable, frank and direct'.[1] He was impressed by his performance and saw him as a man who knew exactly what he wanted to do. Eisenhower was clear that he wanted an integrated Allied team and that the need to work together overrode other considerations; he was not impressed by the plethora of acronyms governing political warfare on either side. It had taken long negotiations between the United States and Britain to agree on an invasion of French territories in North Africa as their military strategy – initially the Americans had pushed for an early landing in northern Europe, which Britain wasn't prepared for – and Eisenhower didn't want this agreement to be jeopardised by any further differences. The military operation also aimed to take the pressure off the Soviet forces on the eastern front, and to make sure Germany couldn't regain any territory in North Africa, after the fierce fighting in the desert over previous years.

Eisenhower emphasised his view in his telegrams: political warfare should always take second place to military considerations. A couple of weeks earlier, he had written to the chief of staff, General George Marshall, that 'subversive activities, propaganda and political warfare are not only inappropriate, but a positive menace unless carefully and completely co-ordinated with all military plans'. All such matters needed to be 'subjected immediately to the most rigid control'. Otherwise, Eisenhower wrote, it risked catastrophe. In his view, in Operation Torch, 'disaster will inevitably follow mistaken and uncoordinated efforts of agencies not fully informed as to the scope and timing of contemplated operations'.[2]

Torch was an enormous operation: the first Allied amphibious landings in Morocco and Algeria meant moving huge numbers of ships and men across the Atlantic and down from Britain towards Gibraltar. Although there were also deception operations going on to divert the enemy, it was crucial that none of the secret planning leaked out. Therefore, very few people were allowed to know the plans for Torch. Bruce Lockhart wrote that only a select handful held a special ticket allowing them to discuss the operations with others who could show the same card, creating the conspiratorial atmosphere of 'special secrecy inside a secret department'. These cardboard tickets, three inches wide, carried the name of the operation and the person authorised to discuss it. Some weren't as careful with their talk as others, however. At a meeting later in August, Brendan Bracken was in the chair and, despite several people in the meeting not having the right clearance, a horrified Bruce Lockhart watched as 'Brendan then proceeded to give away all the secrets in a series of amazing indiscretions'.[3] One colleague of Dallas Brooks's reported another indiscretion, saying that a 'senior civilian member' of the PWE had disobeyed every security order and had elected to take 'a top-secret file out of the office, leave it on the bar in a Fleet Street pub and fail to report the loss'.[4] The file turned up ten days later at Scotland Yard's Lost Property Office. The official was let off with a reprimand.

At the beginning of the planning operation, there was a great deal of mutual mistrust between the Americans and the British. From the American side, that was not surprising given the briefing they'd had earlier in the summer on what to watch out for in British propaganda. Percy Winner, who worked for the US Office of War Information, their propaganda body, in London, wrote a long note bringing William Donovan, the head of US intelligence, up to speed on what he called 'personalities and problems in London'.[5] It's fair to say the Americans were generally not as impressed by their British colleagues as the British were by Eisenhower and others. Winner explained the conflicts that were rife between different organisations in London and the flaws of those he had met. Brendan Bracken, in Winner's view, was 'able, but more ambitious than able'; he was a man who despite knowing a lot about British politics was 'totally ignorant' about Europe and Asia and held 'very odd and unsound notions about the United States' – although Winner didn't specify what those notions were. He explained the background of the Bracken–Dalton feud over SOE and the PWE, which he said had been so intense that Ministry of Information and SOE officials had not been allowed to talk to one another. Winner detected huge opposition to the Americans at the Ministry of Information, particularly in the person of its director-general, Cyril Radcliffe, who he thought was trying to 'push PWE to the wall', as well as being sincerely anti-American and 'openly sabotaging Anglo-American relations in the field of propaganda'.

The struggle for power between the PWE and the Ministry of Information, Winner observed, was not so much between the ministers, Eden and Bracken, as between their respective directors, Bruce Lockhart and Radcliffe. In that fight, the American did not much fancy Bruce Lockhart's chances. Winner was scathing about Bruce Lockhart, calling him an 'outside operator' with 'no real sense of executive or organisational work or loyalties'. In his most withering comment,

Winner said Bruce Lockhart 'once was an extremely aggressive person but for various reasons including his "personal
habits" is a shell of the man he formerly was'[6] – presumably a
reference to Bruce Lockhart's drinking. Winner recommended
that his colleagues should go over the head of this 'essentially
weak man' and deal with ministers directly. His view of Bruce
Lockhart's friend and close colleague Dallas Brooks was just
as dismissive; he was a 'formal, rather stuffy, not overly bright
individual who is intensely vain and susceptible to flattery'.

Earlier British authors writing about the PWE – some of
whom had worked in the organisation – were appalled by this
American document when it was released. Ellic Howe called
it a preposterous and extraordinary document, containing 'ill-
informed and often malicious chatter'.[7] He declined to repeat
many of the claims made about his former colleagues, even
though they had not been averse to malicious chatter themselves. The view of the American outsiders was that of people
arriving new to the situation in London and who hadn't gone
through the strains of the early years of the war. Winner, who
had been a journalist before the war, was frank and didn't couch
his impressions in the bureaucratic euphemisms that the British
civil service sometimes used. But there seems to have been
little wrong with Winner's analysis. He was clear on how the
tensions between ministers in the past had often hamstrung
the PWE's efforts and how the frequent arguments between the
different institutions caused complications. By October 1942,
Bruce Lockhart was confiding in his diary that he was regularly drinking too much and feared that he would 'ruin both
his health and his finances' unless he tried to sort himself out.[8]

Working together with the Americans required a greater
degree of clarity about what the aims of propaganda and
political warfare – which the Americans more often called
psychological warfare – should be. Peter Ritchie Calder, newly
made director of plans, set out these aims in clear language
in a document which described the methods and techniques

of political warfare. He stated that 'in this war of machines, the human element is, in the long run, more important than the machines themselves'. The war aims of propaganda were to make the enemy think, and act on, certain ideas. The four key things Ritchie Calder wanted them to think were: get the Nazis off my neck; give me tomorrow's breakfast; give me the work or the outlet for my work which will make sure of next week's breakfast; and 'May I go round the corner, now, please, and talk to my friends?'[9]

The planning of the propaganda operation around Operation Torch required a far higher level of organisation and co-ordination than anything the PWE had yet achieved. The British propagandists reluctantly accepted that they were now the junior partners in the operation and were essentially doing what they were asked to. In October, Bruce Lockhart wrote to David Bowes-Lyon, who had been brought into the select circle of those in the know as the new head of the Political Warfare Mission in Washington, that the military and political aspects of the organisation were predominantly American. The PWE's role was 'to lend its experience and its resources' rather than to make policy decisions. The PWE had printed the proclamations and leaflets that were to be dropped over North Africa, but had little say in their contents. All the plans also had to be cleared with Washington, which made the scheduling trickier. Bruce Lockhart wasn't happy with this more subservient role – perhaps realising that he was being kept away from the centre of things. As he wrote to Bowes-Lyon, for his personal and most secret information, 'we have misgivings about the quality of the work and the efficiency of the executive organisation'.[10]

Bruce Lockhart told his ministers a few days later that 'the role of PWE in relation to TORCH has been that of a handmaid'. The PWE had provided thirty-six members of military staff at very short notice to form the majority of psychological warfare teams in the field. He also stressed the sheer quantity of work they had already done – producing posters, booklets and leaflets. Five and a quarter million leaflets had already been printed in both French and Arabic.

Encouraging the French population in North Africa to trust the Americans was a key theme of the leaflets. Some leaflets were particularly aimed at the troops. '*Souvenez-Vous*' – remember – was the headline on one colour leaflet, with an image of the monument to the 1.2 million American troops who took part in the battle of the Argonne in the First World War. Inside, photos reminded the French how their generals had co-operated with the United States in the last war. President Franklin D. Roosevelt's personal message to the population, both in leaflets and his radio broadcast, recalled how he had been in France in 1918 with the French Army and Navy. He appealed to the people's realism, their own interest and French national ideals in asking for their support to rid France of its occupiers.[11] A message from Eisenhower would give French forces more detailed instructions on how to behave when the Allies arrived – for instance, to keep all aircraft on the ground and not to scuttle or move ships.

But that trust in the Americans was somewhat lacking on the British part. In Bruce Lockhart's report, which he noted that he had read aloud to his ministers rather than sent in written form, he repeated his 'grave misgivings' about the Americans' work and mentioned that the United States Office of War Information's relations with the American military were not nearly as happy as the PWE's were with the British armed forces.

It was going to be a huge task. As well as the writing and printing of leaflets, there were plans to be made for broadcasts at the time of the landings and directives on how the operation should be represented in broadcasting to other countries, in particular to France and Italy. There was also the question of how black propaganda should be used in broadcasting to Germany. Message discipline had become more important than ever now that Allied troops were going into operations. Of equal importance was strict control over the timing of any announcements and broadcasts.

The British secret weapon in this operation was the Aspidistra radio transmitter. The radio mast had been given its codename after the Gracie Fields song, 'The Biggest Aspidistra in the World', on the fairly easily decipherable basis that, like the overgrown houseplant in the 1938 hit, it nearly reached the sky. Fields had recorded a new version of her song as a piece of propaganda while she toured entertaining the troops during the war, so it was a song that was still widely popular. Aspidistra would allow radio broadcasts from Britain to reach further into Europe. It was more powerful than anything available before and it used medium wave rather than short wave, so the signals could be picked up further away. The Aspidistra transmitter could also shift frequencies easily, to outmanoeuvre German jamming.

Getting Aspidistra into operation, though, was a process fraught with problems and delays, and it was a matter of great urgency that it was ready to use before Operation Torch launched. The original idea for building the transmitter had been put forward by Hugh Dalton in May 1941. He had set out a proposal on its construction and potential uses to which Churchill immediately responded, 'Proceed as you propose'. Dalton had worked out the costs of the project, but Churchill's adviser Desmond Morton told him not to worry about the money. He had the prime minister's approval and, in any case, the cost in dollars was 'such a fragmentary proportion of one day's war' that it would matter little if things went wrong.[12] Putting the transmitter together was not so straightforward, however.

Even in 1941, it was known that the technology to build such a transmitter existed. RCA had made one in the United States with a strength of 500kW, at the time the most powerful in the world, but the American authorities had decided it was too big to put into operation. It was therefore sitting unused in storage in New Jersey. Harold Robin, the man in charge of the PWE's technical operations, was sent to New York in the summer of 1941 to negotiate its purchase, with the help of William Stephenson, the head of British intelligence in the States.

The process of getting the transmitter shipped across the Atlantic and finding a suitable site for it took over a year. At 600kW, the final version of the transmitter would be stronger still than the original. The pieces had to be exported across the Atlantic on naval ships. One ship carrying the mast was torpedoed and sunk, so a new mast had to be made. The original plan had been to put Aspidistra up near Woburn, but this site was unsuitable and the team had to pore over maps, with the assistance of the RAF, in order to find somewhere that was remote, near to the coast, but wouldn't cause problems for flights.[13] They eventually agreed on Ashdown Forest in Sussex. Robin recruited some Canadian road builders waiting to be deployed in Europe – who had access to a digger and explosives, and whom he paid largely in beer – to dig the fifty-foot-deep, bomb-proof bunker that was needed to hide all the apparatus surrounding the transmitter.

By the beginning of September 1942, Churchill was getting impatient that the project wasn't finished. He requested an eight-line report from Bruce Lockhart saying what Aspidistra's advantages would be, to be followed up with a progress report every three days on when it would be ready for use. Bruce Lockhart's concise list of advantages told the prime minister that Aspidistra was more powerful than any station the enemy was known to possess, that its range could be as much as 1,100 miles during the hours of darkness, and that it could overcome enemy jamming in north and western France.[14] This range would allow broadcasts from the south coast of England to reach as far as southern Italy and the coast of Algeria. The transmitter could also potentially be used to 'create confusion in enemy broadcasts', by intruding on their frequencies, but the risks of the enemy retaliating were currently too high to make that worthwhile.

In his first updates to the prime minister, Bruce Lockhart explained that everything was ready to go except for one missing valve – the original part ordered had been sunk en route and the transmitter would otherwise have been ready in July. A new valve would have to be flown over from the States.

Churchill took a far more keen and close interest in Aspidistra than he did in most matters to do with propaganda. Sometimes his telegrams on the subject were plastered with the red 'Action This Day' labels that he favoured for urgent matters. He clearly felt that the ability to broadcast messages from the Allied leaders at the time of the landings would influence the prospects of Torch. But the PWE often felt that the prime minister didn't really understand what he was talking about. Dallas Brooks, keeping Bruce Lockhart informed while his boss was away on leave, wrote on 16 September that there was much confusion in Downing Street about Aspidistra. Churchill was, he reported, 'extremely vague about what Aspidistra is', although he had been heard telling President Roosevelt that he would have 'a very loud W/T [wireless telegraphy] instrument which will be available on Zero day'. Brooks blamed Bracken for the PM's misunderstanding, claiming that over the past six weeks, he had 'completely misinformed the Prime Minister as to the nature of the instrument, its controlling authority and its possible uses'.[15]

Bruce Lockhart's twice-weekly updates continued through September, along with Churchill's insistent requests to know 'when will it be able to work?' The arrival of the missing valve, followed by the shipping of the last of the three masts, meant that, by 26 September, Bruce Lockhart was able to tell the prime minister that 'provided no technical hitches occur, the instrument will be ready to operate full blast by October 15th'.[16]

But as Anthony Eden explained to Churchill, even at full blast, Aspidistra's ability to operate was severely restricted for technical and security reasons. The transmitter might have been a powerful weapon in broadcasting British propaganda into Europe, but it was also, unfortunately, beaming a huge potential signal to the enemy. Eden warned the prime minister that it could operate at its most effective only from one hour after sunset until one hour before dawn. (This was because radio waves on long wavelengths can travel much further at night.)[17] This wasn't so much a problem, as night-time operation coincided with the times that the PWE most wanted to broadcast to their potential audiences – in the evening. A bigger issue was that the Air Ministry said that, in order to avoid the transmitter serving as a beacon to Germany, it was only allowed to operate for ten minutes at a time. It might be possible to increase that figure slightly during the military operation itself – hence the need for a clear plan of exactly what, during Torch, could be broadcast, to whom, on what frequency and when.

Aspidistra also needed spare parts, which was another area where Churchill's enthusiastic intervention wasn't always helpful. Eden asked him to put in a good word with Roosevelt since they needed six spare valves, or tubes as the Americans called them. Churchill seems to have become confused after an exchange of telegrams with Roosevelt's envoy Harry Hopkins and demanded, 'Have we really built this gigantic machine dependent on valves which are obsolete, obsolescent or passing out of manufacture, with no provision for replacement?' Hopkins had contributed to the confusion by telling the prime minister that the valves he wanted could only be made on special order and would take a long time to arrange, but saying that he could suggest some alternatives.[18] The answer that came back to the PM from the PWE, provided by Bruce Lockhart, was that this was incorrect. It wasn't that the valves were obsolete, rather that GEC, who made the parts, were giving priority to the US Navy. Hopkins had sorted out the problem and would provide a total of nine valves, some new and others second-hand. 'The only difficulty,' Churchill was told, 'is to get our requirements in competition with those of the American services.'[19]

There was another unexpected problem with Aspidistra: it was almost too powerful. Although the seventy-acre site in the middle of a Sussex forest had been chosen for its distance from highly populated areas, there were still people living relatively nearby, with the town of Crowborough only about ten miles away. Every time Aspidistra was switched on, the superpowerful transmitter would be so strong that it would knock out the signals of every other radio transmitter in the area. As a PWE memo said, 'the population within a radius of ten miles at Crowborough will hear nothing but Aspidistra when it is operating'. If the inhabitants of the town tuned in to their radios just when Aspidistra was broadcasting, their BBC programmes would be interrupted by broadcasts aimed at people in occupied Europe.

The implications of this were significant: if it became known in public that a particular area of East Sussex was regularly hearing Allied propaganda broadcasts, it would be easy for the enemy to work out where the transmitter was and for it to become a target for bombing. Worse perhaps, if Aspidistra was used for black propaganda, unsuspecting Sussex listeners would find themselves hearing Tom Delmer's shouting fake German officers or broadcasts in other European languages. The PWE observed that 'this will cause talk, comments in the Press, questions in the House of Commons'.[20] It might also have caused a certain amount of public panic. Any public comment would also finally give away the fact that black propaganda originated from within Britain. The Ministry of

Information and the Home Office were told to make sure that nothing about this got into the public domain. Closer to the date of the landings, it was noted that 'steps have also been taken to prevent questions on the subject being asked in Parliament'.[21] Presumably this meant notifying the local MPs that such questions would be unwelcome.

Aspidistra would allow people in North Africa to hear directly from Allied leaders about the landings. Getting messages to them from Roosevelt, Eisenhower and Churchill was crucial. Both the president and the prime minister were to make records that would be broadcast immediately when the landings were confirmed, which would be played out via the new transmitter. Even the finest technical details of these recordings were discussed directly by personal telegram between the leaders – with Churchill using his codename of 'Former Naval Person' – explaining how the records needed to be made. They should be in French, less than ten minutes long, recorded at 33⅓ rpm, 'not, repeat not, 78', and recorded from the centre of the disc outwards onto discs which should be made of aluminium, to avoid the danger of the president's recording breaking as it would be sent to Britain by air. Roosevelt replied to Churchill saying that he was making his radio disc immediately, teasing the PM that 'incidentally, while your French Grammar is better than mine my accent is most alluring'.[22]

Roosevelt's message played heavily on his 'deep friendship with the French people' and his 'hundreds of French friends', as well as his experience serving with the American forces in France during the First World War. He believed in liberty, equality and fraternity. The United States' aim, he told them, was to 'drive out the cruel invaders', reassuring them that 'we wish you no harm'. The president urged the people not to hinder 'this great undertaking' and to co-operate with the Allies.

For this message and those from Eisenhower and Churchill to have any effect, though, people had to be able to listen to them. Aspidistra would do the job of getting the broadcasts the distance they needed to go, but the question was how listeners would hear them.

After discussing whether the Allies should try to broadcast near the French frequencies that the Vichy government regularly used – on the grounds that Vichy-favouring listeners were 'in greatest need of conversion' – it was decided that, instead, Allied propaganda was most effective coming via BBC broadcasts at the times that the BBC usually broadcast news to France. Thomas Barman of the PWE said that the leaders' broadcasts should be trailed frequently. With listeners being told that they would be able to hear Churchill's speech several times during the day, many thousands of people would 'rush to their wireless sets' in order to hear it. This, Barman thought, would 'create its own audience without any tricks or stunts'.[23]

The PWE put forward a convincing argument that, for the leaders' messages to be heard as authentic, they had to come from an authentic source. A broadcast adjacent to a Vichy channel was essentially a trick. It was argued that 'such tricks are unworthy of the Prime Minister, who speaks with the voice of Britain'.[24] To broadcast on an unofficial channel might, it followed, lead to the enemy saying that the Churchill broadcast was a fake. Also, on a less high-minded note, it would destroy the effectiveness of Aspidistra on an unusual frequency as a medium when Britain *did* want to produce counterfeit news. It would give the game away in advance. The memo noted that 'we shall have disclosed to the enemy that we have a transmitter capable of playing tricks'.

The conclusion was that Aspidistra would be used to boost the BBC's signal so that, overnight at least, it could be heard in North Africa as well as on the French mainland. In the early hours of the morning, they would also be able to broadcast on the Rabat frequency, which would reach Morocco directly.

This time, all broadcasting on Aspidistra was explicitly cleared with the chiefs of staff. They would accept any potential interference with their own radio systems for the first forty-eight hours of the operation.

Because the Allies wanted to be sure that they were both believed and trusted at the beginning of the operation, it was decided that there would be no black propaganda sent out via Aspidistra for the first, crucial, forty-eight hours. This would allow the messages from Roosevelt, Churchill and Eisenhower to be spread as widely as possible, with their speeches appealing for co-operation and trust. Other, more insidious, messages could come later.

After the first two days of operations, black propaganda would be allowed to use the powerful transmitter. Black broadcasts to France would only begin if there were a signal from Eisenhower in the field that Vichy was to be considered hostile. That decision would hang on the sensitive negotiations on the ground between the American commanders and their French counterparts. Broadcasts to Germany could begin after the first forty-eight hours had elapsed.

The PWE had plans to create counterfeit broadcasts. These would be as close as possible to the German broadcasts that they were imitating, on a nearby frequency and even mimicking the original programme before making out that it had fallen off air, interrupting it and then repeating the fake British version. This was designed to 'deceive the inexpert listener' into thinking that they were hearing genuine programmes. The aims of the black propaganda plan were to 'create maximum confusion' among German listeners and to 'sow doubt and suspicion' in German minds about events in unoccupied France and North Africa.

For those listening to what they thought were German broadcasts in Vichy France, the aim was to make the French listeners believe the Germans had lost faith in Vichy policy and thereby increase friction between occupied France and

Germany. The same went for Italy, the aim being to create
tension between Rome and Berlin.[25] It was suggested that
some of the fake stories could include reports that Marshal
Pétain had left Vichy for an unknown destination with some
of his intimate collaborators. The PWE argued, however, that
to mimic German stations successfully, they would need to be
on the air via Aspidistra for longer than the ten minutes at a
time that the Air Ministry allowed them. A fake station would
not be believable if it came and went within a few minutes
as they would not be able to copy and replicate the original
station in such a short time.

On Saturday 7 November, the landings of Operation Torch
began. The PWE had to wait for a signal from Gibraltar that
the operation was underway before their broadcasts went out.
If the PWE were told that the operation was delayed, they
were then responsible for getting coded messages out over
short-wave radio to SOE agents behind enemy lines to tell
them to postpone their activities. There was a tense wait until,
at 6pm, around half an hour later than expected, the PWE
got the signal that Torch was on. At 8.30pm, the PWE team
was told that they could go ahead with their broadcasts as
soon as Eisenhower's message had been put out by American
radio stations, at about 1am London time. One message from
Roosevelt would go out and be repeated, followed by the
recording from Eisenhower. Two sets of leaflets were dropped:
one over unoccupied France and the other, the leaflet with the
message from Roosevelt, over metropolitan France.

The French people were told by the president of that
intention 'to drive out the cruel invaders' and that the Americans wished them no harm. Eisenhower's message told French
forces that the Allies 'come as your friends and not as your

enemies'. No offensive action would be taken unless the Allies faced definite hostile action first. The leaflet to the general French population told them that this was the first indispensable step towards liberation, that it was the actions of Hitler and the French prime minister Pierre Laval which had failed, and reassured the people that the Allies did not have territorial designs on France. This was an explicit attempt to counter German and Vichy propaganda.

In the meantime, Bruce Lockhart treated those of his colleagues who had been in on the secret to dinner at the Savoy, on the condition that they didn't talk in public about what they had been working on. They returned to Bush House after their meal to oversee the broadcasts in the early hours. These were again slightly delayed, but they were generally happy with the outcome.

Although Bruce Lockhart reported seeing the streets full of happy faces in London the next morning as news of the landings spread, it was a time of little sleep and frayed tempers. Not everyone was happy with how the operation had been planned. At the BBC, Noel Newsome found his French staff 'almost on the verge of mutiny'.[26] The French service, generally in sympathy with de Gaulle, were almost as angry as the general himself that he had been excluded from the invasion plans and that Eisenhower planned to deal instead with the Vichy commanders General Giraud and Admiral Darlan on the ground. Some of the BBC staff, according to Newsome, were refusing to broadcast in their fury.

The next day, Bruce Lockhart found himself in the unusual position – for the director of a secret department – of having to take part in a press conference. Bracken had summoned him to the briefing as no-one had been willing to wake the US general Walter Bedell Smith, who had been overseeing operations in London. Bracken was vague on the details of what was going on the ground, but the journalists seemed to let him get away with the relative lack of news.

Everyone concerned remembers that a furious row erupted between Bracken and the BBC that evening, but their recollections of what prompted it conflict. Noel Newsome said that he had gone forty-eight hours without sleep and he blamed Bracken's bad temper that evening on a long lunch with Churchill and de Gaulle at which there was 'much cognac' offered in an attempt to assuage de Gaulle's temper. Bracken, however, had also managed to get through the mid-afternoon press conference, with most accounts of the Downing Street lunch where Churchill, de Gaulle and Eden were present suggesting that it hadn't been nearly as bad-tempered as the British ministers had expected. Although de Gaulle had been furious in the morning, exclaiming that he hoped Vichy forces would throw the Americans back into the sea, by lunchtime he had calmed down and left the meal almost euphoric.[27]

Perhaps it was Newsome's sleeplessness that left him confused, but he also remembered the origin of the row differently. He recalled Bracken phoning the BBC to ask about the contents of a Hitler speech that Newsome was monitoring. In Bruce Lockhart's diary, though, he recorded the argument being about a broadcast by General Giraud. It's possible that Bracken was on the warpath about both, but Bruce Lockhart recorded the dispute in his diary at the time. Whatever prompted Bracken's anger, there was a flurry of furious phone calls between Downing Street, the BBC and the PWE.

Bruce Lockhart had been trying to catch up on his sleep at nine on Sunday evening when he was disturbed by 'a violent assault' from his telephone.[28] Bracken had called him on a private line from Downing Street where he was with Churchill. The prime minister and the minister of information had heard about a broadcast supposedly made by General Giraud from Algiers. Bracken said Churchill demanded to know whether the Giraud broadcast was genuine or 'phoney'. Churchill suspected it couldn't have been real, since he knew that Giraud, codenamed Kingpin, was still in Gibraltar, not yet in Algiers.

Newsome was eating supper from a tray in his office at around ten o'clock when Bracken called him back, asking why the BBC editor hadn't responded to his earlier call. Newsome protested that he had been trying to get through to Bracken without success. Bracken said to Bruce Lockhart that the BBC staff member – whose name he wasn't sure of – had told him it wasn't his job to find out such things. Bracken retorted that he wasn't accustomed to being spoken to in such a manner and Newsome slammed the phone down on him. Newsome picked up his supper tray and threw it at the ceiling, showering himself and his colleague Peter Ritchie Calder with grated cheese, lettuce and the rest of the meal.[29]

Bracken called Bruce Lockhart to complain that, although he wasn't sure exactly who he'd spoken to at the BBC, he didn't like the man's manners or his voice, and even if he had never seen his face, he wanted Bruce Lockhart to make sure it wasn't there the next day. Bracken continued to ring an increasingly tired and fractious Bruce Lockhart up with further questions until the early hours of the morning. Who had made the broadcast in Giraud's name? It appeared that this was Giraud's colleague, General Mast, who *was* in Algiers and who had read out Giraud's script while his boss was still talking terms with the Americans. Had Algiers really fallen, as a broadcast from Vichy had said? And should Britain put out this news even if they weren't absolutely sure about it? Yes, it had, and there would have been no harm in spreading the rumour of the capitulation in Algiers even if it weren't yet true. Bruce Lockhart was left relieved when his phone line also capitulated under Bracken's barrage of calls and needed to be repaired.

In the morning, Bruce Lockhart, still not having slept, returned to Bush House to meet an equally exhausted Newsome, who was bedraggled and with bloodshot eyes.

Newsome maintained he was still angry, even though Bruce Lockhart saw him as contrite. Bruce Lockhart called Bracken to try to smooth things over; the minister, as often happened, forgave Newsome and told Bruce Lockhart that the BBC editor had done a good job.

Ministers were quick to praise the PWE for their work in the planning and execution of propaganda for Operation Torch. Bruce Lockhart wrote to Anthony Eden even before the operation had actually launched to praise the work of his own team and to stress how much effort they had put in. 'We are now operating a twenty-four hours service,' he wrote, 'and the strain on the small number of officials who have been entrusted with the secret has been severe.' Bruce Lockhart singled out some of the women on his team for particular praise, saying that 'two lady secretaries' were worthy of special commendation because they had 'typed and re-typed the numerous documents' about the plans while working incredibly long hours over several weeks.[30]

Writing to Crossman, who was back in London, Bruce Lockhart conveyed praise even from Bracken. The minister of information thanked the PWE for 'the really fine work accomplished during the last strenuous days' and concluded his letter by saying that 'PWE's work was far ahead of anything achieved by any other Government Publicity Institution in the world'. The praise cascaded down from ministers and military chiefs alike to the PWE, in a way they were hardly used to. General Bedell Smith, Eisenhower's chief of staff, wrote to Eden to thank the PWE for their 'very good work' at the planning stage of the operation and saying that he was conscious of how much the Americans would owe the PWE when the operation was successfully completed. General Bedell Smith's letter was shown to the prime minister, who added the government's official thanks and congratulations. Eden, too, sent his personal congratulations. The foreign secretary also, on Bruce Lockhart's advice, made a special point of thanking Sir Archibald Sinclair, the air minister, for his service's work in delivering twenty-two-and-a-half million leaflets, with a total weight of around forty-five tons. The PWE, for once, was praised in the House of Commons. Aspidistra had worked, too, with the PWE's official history concluding that it was able to overcome the jamming of BBC services at a crucial moment for influencing French opinion.[31]

This may all have sounded like mutual backslapping but, to the PWE, the recognition really mattered. They had come through a period where their every operation had been criticised from a variety of sides, so to be acknowledged as successful once an invasion began was a huge improvement. In part this can be put down to the necessity of military discipline and control: there was less opportunity for internal conflict and freelancing by different sections of the PWE when they were all bound by the highest secrecy of an impending invasion. It probably also helped that only a few members of staff were cleared to know what was really happening. The PWE's internal organisation was also becoming more systematic and rigorous, with greater emphasis on planning and co-ordination rather than the feuds and personality clashes that had characterised the early years of the war. Aspidistra had worked as it had been designed to do and this meant that future propaganda operations would be able to reach further into Europe and beyond.

That didn't mean that everything was perfect, however. The first members of the PWE to set foot in the conflict zone found that when propaganda plans came into contact with the confusion and constant change of war, things were inevitably not as straightforward as the plans and memos set out. Lieutenant Colonel Ken Johnstone, sent into Algiers with the invading troops as the head of the PWE's Field Unit, sent back long letters to Dallas Brooks describing the chaos of the first landings, with seasick troops struggling to get ashore. The politics on the ground, in particular the relationship between the Americans and the French, were also hugely complex. Johnstone, a diplomat who had joined the Welsh Guards at the start of the war, wrote back that he had 'never known any scheme turn out so utterly unlike its intention'.[32] He had not expected to be involved so directly in operations but found himself summoning his best German to arrest the German consul-general at his magnificent Algiers villa. The consul-general, 'pale, tightlipped and correct', surrendered quietly, as long as he was allowed to finish his lunch before being taken into protective custody. Johnstone also found himself in charge of censorship and propaganda in Algeria as well as overseeing radio stations, though supplies were still hard to get. By the end of the year, he was asking for more paper and film, as well as a trained journalist to help with propaganda operations and a more abundant supply of news, articles, photographs and posters that he could use to spread the British point of view.

In London, though, the operation was treated as a triumph. Combined with Field Marshal Montgomery's military success at El Alamein, there was a sense that the direction of the war was turning in the Allies' favour. At midday on 10 November, Bruce Lockhart, having passed on the official tributes to his team, went down from Bush House into the Strand to watch Churchill drive past on his way to the lord mayor's luncheon. The streets were lined with cheering crowds; the prime minister and his wife Clementine made a 'triumphal progress' in an open car with loudspeakers announcing his arrival.[33] As Churchill drove past the BBC, Bruce Lockhart said that the PM's face, 'still marvellously cherubic, was one big smile'. He watched as Churchill made the V sign, thinking that 'opposite the European Service of the BBC, which had started the V campaign, was the right place to make it'.[34] But as Churchill would famously say when he arrived at Mansion House and made his speech, 'it is not even the beginning of the end. But it is, perhaps, the end of the beginning.'

14

Caught at Last!

Early in 1943, Tom Delmer and the black propaganda operation moved into new, purpose-built studios in the village of Milton Bryan, just outside the bounds of the Woburn estate. The building itself was not grand. Rather, it was a 'neat and functional' building of two storeys, in red brick, which Tom Delmer thought looked like any other new wartime factory or workshop. The studio building sat incongruously down a track, slightly hidden from the road behind a row of cottages. It was surrounded with a large grass lawn and, away from the village, gave onto fields beyond towards the Woburn parkland.

During the war, the main indication that something secret was going on in the premises would have been the twelve-foot-high wire fence topped with barbed wire, along with the special constables patrolling the bounds with Alsatian dogs. Within the barbed wire, everything was 'the last word in up-to-dateness and efficiency'.[1] There were several telephone operators and a secure 'scrambler' phone for confidential communications. One member of staff described the new set-up as resembling a combination of a smaller-scale BBC, 'a secret intelligence centre and a press agency'.

Work had begun at Milton Bryan before the building was even completely finished, in the autumn of 1942. Robert Bruce Lockhart had inspected the new premises in October and was impressed by the 'very fine' studios and the police presence, with senior police officers accompanying him on the visit.[2] 'We have obviously spared no money,' he wrote. Another recruit who started work there in October described his work monitoring German radio broadcasts from a small individual office equipped with a radio receiver, a typewriter, a telephone and a padlocked box for waste paper to be disposed of securely.[3] This was a change from the previous improvised working arrangements at the 'secret houses' that were both homes and offices.

This new building would allow Delmer and his growing team to produce a more modern, lively-sounding type of propaganda radio. As he had long insisted, 'radio news to be news, and sound like news . . . must be broadcast live'.[4] At the old Simpson studio, which had required long, occasionally hazardous drives through blackout and fog to deliver pre-recorded discs to the broadcast studio, this hadn't been possible. Delmer wanted to make his stations sound less stuffy and ever less like the BBC. His empire was expanding and, with new stations, black propaganda could be on the air for longer and provide more regular listening for its intended audiences.

The first of these new stations was the Wehrmachtsender Nord – the northern army station – a station aimed at German troops in northern Europe, which pretended to be broadcast from Norway. The station went on air in May 1942. It was still pre-recorded, but was trying to move towards the new style that Delmer wanted.

Peter Weichmann was not quite twenty-one when he began working on Wehrmachtsender Nord. Arriving in Aspley Guise, he stayed at first in the Crossman household at Dawn Edge, where Zita Crossman was the host, later moving to the Tingrith Old Rectory. The young recruit was thrown into the deep end about a month after he first arrived in Woburn. Told that they were one voice short for the Wehrmachtsender station, he was taken to Simpson to record his first broadcast, which seems to have gone well since he became a regular freelance announcer in addition to his main work. Peter, sometimes known as Tom, had been born in Berlin but had come to England for his education. Like Delmer, he had been at St Paul's School – Peter wondered if this had helped in his recruitment – and had later studied at London University, though he had been interned in Wales for more than a year after war broke out. At his interview, he had been asked a series of detailed questions about little-known German politicians and tested for his fluency in German and his radio voice. Before he began broadcasting himself, he was responsible for listening to what German radio stations sounded like more than what they actually said – noting the structure and the duration of the shows. Peter was thrown together with a variety of German or German-speaking colleagues. The many German émigrés included a novelist, a lawyer and a young business executive. Their British counterparts included the Oxford classicist and friend of J.R.R Tolkien, C.E. Stevens, and the historian Clifton Child. Stevens – who also, confusingly, went by the nickname 'Tom' – was a man with a photographic memory who 'could remember everything that he read, which was a great deal'.[5] Child had a knack for forming logical and correct conclusions from obscure evidence.

His colleagues began to introduce more variety into their programmes, with different voices and sketches. René Halkett was able to create characters with a variety of German regional accents. Delmer valued his versatility: Halkett created the character of 'Heiner mit den Sehrohr', a submariner with his periscope passing comment on events. Halkett was a multi-talented man who had studied theatre design with the Bauhaus and worked as an actor, stage designer, writer and painter before leaving Germany for Britain in 1936.[6] He had been born Albrecht von Fritsch into an aristocratic family and fought in the First World War, but rejected his background for a bohemian life. Weichmann said that one of Halkett's abilities was putting humorous or ironic subversion across with a straight face. He was enough of a musician that he even wrote and sang the theme tune to one of Delmer's other new stations, the Atlantiksender.

Black propaganda was becoming more professional. Beneath the lighter touch, jokes and music lay much hard work and intense research, working on Delmer's principle that the lies should only be deliberate, never accidental. They gained their intelligence through a variety of means, sometimes from monitoring German radio stations. Delmer had also acquired a Hellschreiber machine, a wireless teleprinter that sent German news copy. He claimed to have got hold of the machine via Reuters, who in turn had taken it from the German news agency's offices in London when they were closed down at the start of the war. This information, however it had been come by, allowed Delmer to access the raw material of German news before it reached the newspapers or airwaves.

In some cases, Delmer was able to say that he had predicted what the German government would do before it actually happened. In October 1942, he noted what he called 'pleasing coincidences' that showed Der Chef was on the right lines: in July, Der Chef had announced that a new regulation would come into force in October which would require families to share their homes with others and single people to give up their flats and move into barracks. The object of Delmer's story was to undermine morale among troops at the front about the conditions their families were living in at home. It was also intended to make women at home reluctant to send their children away and to go to work in factories. The story had also gone out on Wehrmachtsender Nord. Delmer was delighted to discover that, a month later than he had suggested, a similar decree was in fact issued. The black propaganda team had come up with their rumour on the basis of their estimate of the housing situation in Berlin and intelligence photographs of nameplates on Berlin office buildings.[7]

Delmer was seemingly dissatisfied with Wehrmachtsender Nord. He claimed that it had only operated for a few weeks, whereas in fact it was running until February 1943. It was halfway towards the kind of production he aimed to create, but wasn't yet able to make full use of the new live studios and the more specialised team. At times, black propaganda seemed to be sticking with its old habits of sending out broadcasts aimed in splintered directions, in the hope that audiences of the right sort would eventually hear them. In some cases, the programmes never even made it to air.

For three weeks in the spring of 1942, a station that had been given the working title Astrologie und Okkultismus – Astrology and the Occult – recorded eighteen programmes that weren't broadcast. Margit Maass, the actress and wife of Alex Maass, took on the role of a spiritualist medium who channelled the spirits of the German war dead to speak to their relatives, sending them messages from the beyond. She even gave the names and home addresses of the casualties. Although this must have relied on the kind of detailed information Delmer prized about German fatalities, it was clearly not a success. Maass herself said that one of the problems was that she couldn't manage to read the scripts without bursting out laughing and spoiling the recordings.[8] If the people supposed to be putting over propaganda from the afterlife couldn't take it seriously, the potential audience couldn't be expected to either. Instead, as 'Red Johanna', she worked on another station, a German Workers' programme which operated from 1942 to 1943, which seemed to be aimed primarily at Polish agents, providing news for them to use in clandestine newspapers.

A religious station, Christus der König – Christ the King – lasted longer, from September 1942 almost until the end of the war, though it took a very different tone from the ribald style of the programmes for soldiers and sailors. 'Father Andreas' was a genuine Austrian Catholic priest – his real name was Elmar Eisenberger – who had come to Britain before the war and lived at a priory in Faversham, in Kent. He gave religious services which were followed with short talks, and although he didn't strictly make black propaganda, he spoke about the moral horrors of the Nazi regime, telling the Germans things that were true but which they would not otherwise hear.

The departure of Richard Crossman, first to the United States in the autumn of 1942 and later to North Africa in 1943, gave Delmer more of a free hand to expand black propaganda without Crossman raising his habitual objections. In January 1943, with Rex Leeper resigning from the PWE, as he felt there was little left for him to do in 'the country', to rejoin the Foreign Office, another constraint on Delmer had gone. Leeper and Delmer exchanged surprisingly warm notes on his departure for Cairo to take up the job of ambassador to the Greek government, with Leeper saying that he had enjoyed working with Delmer as much as Delmer had enjoyed the work, and urging Delmer to 'continue to work with the same enthusiasm' in his absence.[9] For his part, Delmer said he would be sure they would continue working on black propaganda under the new conditions, because that was their war, but he was worried about what the future held and that 'the loss of our boss was a vote of no confidence in us and our work'.[10]

Delmer had the influential support of some of his old friends in the Naval Intelligence Division (NID), where Ian Fleming now worked, to create a station that would be picked up by German U-boat crews in the Atlantic.[11] Delmer credited Donald McLachlan, another former journalist in Berlin, who now worked in Section 17z of the NID, with the new idea. They discussed it, Delmer claimed, over a champagne-fuelled lunch at Frascati's restaurant on Oxford Street, a place of plush chairs and 'gilded Edwardian cherubs', where Delmer could indulge his 'almost necrolatrous passion for old champagne'.[12] McLachlan and Delmer certainly did work together well, as shown by one surviving, jokey letter between the two men, where McLachlan addressed Delmer as 'my dear Monster', called him 'your Hitlerian majesty' and referred to him making 'phallic sandcastles' while away on leave.[13] With McLachlan's help, the new station came into being.

The Atlantiksender – the Atlantic station – was going to put Delmer's ideas about what propaganda radio should really sound like into full effect. He wanted his team to write in easier, catchier German so that their broadcasts sounded less formal and more immediate. It would, finally, be able to go out live. For the first couple of months of the new year in 1943, they were rehearsing the sound and the format of the new station. Still on short wave for now – denied access to Aspidistra – this would be what Delmer and his colleagues thought U-boat crews beneath the Atlantic would want to hear. By March 1943, when the Kurzwellensender Atlantik (its formal name) launched, they would broadcast fifteen different transmissions of thirty minutes each, containing both news and music.[14]

Frank Lynder, who had previously been the voice of Der Chef's assistant, now made himself an expert on all aspects of life on board a German submarine. In this he was helped by former prisoners on war who could give the most up-to-date information possible on what it was like to serve. Prisoners of war who gave helpful information during their interrogation in POW camps were sometimes sent to work with the PWE on black propaganda. Although he had by now become more of a producer behind the scenes than a broadcaster, Lynder himself made a vivid, improvised report on the sinking of the *Scharnhorst* in the Arctic Circle, playing the part of a sailor who had been rescued from the freezing sea, even though he had been in Woburn, nowhere near the incident.[15]

Music was another innovative element of the new station. This, too, was designed to capture and hold the attention of bored, fearful submariners beneath the Atlantic. From the evidence of the few surviving recordings of black propaganda stations, the mixture of records was eclectic. American dance and big band music and jazz were used often on the station. The music that was familiar to American troops and to British audiences was officially banned in Germany; Duke Ellington, Count Basie, Artie Shaw, Benny Goodman, or Glenn Miller had the allure of the forbidden as well as being catchy.[16] The records were American imports on the new sixteen-inch vinyl discs. They also played music that would have been familiar to the German soldiers and sailors, such as the songs of Kirsten Heiberg, a Norwegian-German star who appeared in many films during the Nazi era and sang to entertain the troops.

The radio station even managed to run a music request programme for German troops. It was presented by Agnes Bernelle, an aspiring actress who was just twenty and had left Germany with her Jewish father around the same time as René Halkett. Agnes played 'Vicky', the presenter who began her broadcast saying 'This is Vicky with three kisses for you', smacking her lips into the microphone and introducing jazz tunes. Her elaborate shows came to involve concerts, songs and sketches that she performed with her Austrian and Czech émigré women colleagues, Lisl, Trudi and Hilde. They had a subversive element, of course: Vicky was able to incite panic-buying by mentioning shortages of food, while purporting to criticise 'unprincipled hoarders'. They drew their information from intercepted letters and POWs; some listeners unwittingly provided their own intelligence as Vicky even received genuine letters that had been sent somehow from Germany. Bernelle claimed that one German submarine commander off the coast of Scotland had been encouraged to surrender when he heard a broadcast congratulating him personally on the birth of his new son, even though he hadn't been home in two years.[17]

The use of banned music was a technique that was also used on white propaganda broadcasts to Germany. The

BBC's German service had a programme called *Aus der Freien Welt* – From the Free World – which played the jazz and swing records German listeners weren't allowed to hear, and developed characters such as 'Kurt and Willi', who broadcast in Berlin dialect.[18] Delmer had often criticised the BBC for its stilted formality, but they too were learning how to speak more directly and vividly to their foreign listeners.

For more details to flesh out Delmer's black news operations, prisoners of war were given detailed questionnaires about the situation within Germany. One intelligence document gives an exhaustive list of questions which potential sources, whether prisoners or refugees, could be asked. They ranged from the type of radio stations the sources listened to, to queries about the local economy or transport situation. The interrogators wanted to know who the smart set were in any important town, and who the important people in smaller towns were. Rumours, stories of food shortages or details about clothes could all have more significance than might have been thought. The interrogators were reminded not to ignore 'long rambling accounts of family and domestic affairs' as these could give rise to interesting information. 'It may seem unimportant to him that a French housewife, for example, has had a bitter quarrel with her milkman; but it may give us a very good explanation of why she accuses the milkman of being a German agent.'[19]

From the point of view of the intelligence services, black propaganda created a virtuous circle in those who had heard black stations and subsequently been captured. According to Donald McLachlan, who worked with Ian Fleming in the Naval Intelligence Division, Germans who had listened to Kurzwellensender Atlantik were astonished by the level of detailed knowledge that the programmes displayed. They might have heard about troubles with research scientists over radar or the situation facing blockade runners in the Gironde River. If they suspected, or were told, that the programmes came from a British source, they became more inclined to break with their training and to tell the interrogators what they knew, as they assumed that British intelligence had this knowledge anyway. McLachlan wrote that the prisoners told themselves, 'Why say "I don't know" if the British showed an amused and ribald interest in the whereabouts of the red-haired waitress at the Cafe de Rennes in Lorient? Why deny that Lieutenant Commander Z had the reputation of being scared stiff of mines, whereas his own commander, now captured, was a dare-devil? Why not accept the probability that comrades had talked?'[20]

This was precisely the kind of rumour that the Atlantiksender loved to spread. Ellic Howe reported that one script told the story of how 'a beautiful girl, a blonde called Rita Doris, has been shot as a spy. She came from Saarbrücken. She was previously a bar girl. She was known to scores of U-boatmen and had frequently been on U-boats.'[21] The submariners were left to imagine the beautiful Rita and her sad fate, while wondering if they might have passed on information to her.

The new station was not only used to undermine morale by talking about the problems that German seafarers were facing, but also to send specific pieces of misinformation supplied by naval intelligence. In one case, Delmer's team were given details of supposed mining operations at sea, with locations where mines had been placed. Of these, around 25–40 per cent were true, 20 per cent were half-true, and the remainder were completely false. Such misinformation was intended to confuse the submariners and divert them.

The most obscure and unexpected sources of information could sometimes be put to use for black propaganda. One prisoner of war had, in peacetime, spent so long travelling across the German railway network as a train enthusiast that he knew the timetables almost by heart. He was able to use this knowledge to allow the PWE to send messages to resistance workers to change the labelling on the trains and send them to the wrong places.

Prisoners of war who were chosen to work in the Country were in a precarious situation, though. If they infringed the strict rules about their behaviour or were suspected of compromising security in any way, they could find themselves sent back to prisoner of war camps. In one case, a prisoner known as Neumann, a communist submariner, was returned to detention because he was suspected of communicating with other communist sympathisers in London. Most other foreign residents of Aspley Guise and its neighbouring villages remained under close supervision.

Ernst Adam, whom Delmer had helped to escape from Lisbon earlier in the war, was not a prisoner, but all the same found himself under Special Branch surveillance. On one of his permitted visits to London, Adam – who was known as Albrecht on air – met a woman. By 4 July 1942, news of his relationship had reached MI5, who were 'not very happy about this association'. Adam was seeing a good deal of the lady and 'may even contemplate marrying her'. The reason for the official unhappiness soon became clear: Margaret Foster, a slim, 'not unattractive' woman of twenty-five with dark brown hair – and who went by several other aliases, including Marjorie, Joan, Forster, Forrester and Clarke – was a prostitute. She lived in an expensively furnished apartment with a grand piano, near Paddington. More worrying still, in official eyes, was that she was Irish and had held an Irish passport, though she claimed it had been lost in a fire. MI5 and Special Branch suspected that Adam might have been passing on secrets to Foster. An informer who also knew Foster told the police that she had given him plenty of information about Adam, even reading out his letters to her, including stories of his escape from Paris and that he was engaged in 'very secret work' in the countryside. She had shown the informer, who was Austrian, entries in a notebook that included the names

of the German towns Kassel and Ehrenhausen. Since Foster
was Irish and thus a citizen of a neutral country, the authorities were afraid that she might be passing secrets on to the
enemy. Both Adam and Foster's post was intercepted and
opened, on the grounds that 'some of the letters may confirm
our suspicions that ADAM has been passing on confidential
information to unauthorised persons'.

Adam's letters to Foster, copied and preserved in his MI5
file, are innocuous – he writes about wanting to be able to
visit her and looking forward to their life together. All the
same, Delmer had to be told about the suspicions and the
relationship. MI5 suggested that he use the information in
the Special Branch report they supplied to him to warn Adam
against his proposed marriage. According to their informant,
Adam knew that Foster was a prostitute because she said he
had picked her up while she was soliciting. When Delmer con-
fronted him about the relationship in August, however, Adam
reportedly told his friend and boss that he was 'considerably
taken aback by the revelation that his fiancée was a prostitute'.
He refused to break off the engagement and offered his resignation instead. Delmer wouldn't accept it; he told his MI5
contact that he thought highly of Adam and was 'not at all
anxious to dispense with his services'. Adam could stay at the
PWE, although the security services would continue to keep
an eye on the couple. In the days between Delmer being told
to raise the issue with Adam and the decision to allow him
to stay, Adam wrote tense and worried letters to Foster. He
wasn't sleeping well but he insisted that he hadn't changed
his mind and still wanted to marry her, even if that meant
that he lost his job. He might need to wait eight days, though,
before his 'friend' could be able to resolve things.

Four days later, his letters still monitored, Adam wrote
to Foster with the good news that he was not going to be
sacked, although he had to convey it somewhat crypti-
cally. His affair would be finally settled, he wrote. When his

'friend' – presumably Delmer – had told him the news, Adam told his fiancée that 'If he were a girl, I should kiss him for his help'. The friend had laughed. The couple planned to marry as soon as possible by special licence. Adam seems to have been allowed to travel to London more regularly than most German PWE staff, perhaps working at Bush House as well as in Aspley Guise. He and Foster were married in Paddington within a few weeks.

Foster moved to a new flat in Bloomsbury and by September was writing to her new husband with an odd mixture of domesticity and extravagance, one moment talking about darning his socks and in the same letter planning to drink champagne and eat caviar and chocolates. She now signed herself 'your loving and obedient wife, Peg'. Adam stayed with the PWE until the end of the war, when he went to work with the British occupation in Germany. There was no recorded trace of either him or Foster passing on any secret information, though while Adam was out of the country, she seems to have returned to prostitution and the marriage did not long outlast the war.[22]

While Delmer was prepared to go out of his way to help the friends and colleagues he believed to be valuable, he was also a demanding boss, often rewriting scripts and insisting that work be performed better. Like many of his colleagues, he kept late hours, poring over the details, always concerned about how the broadcasts would sound. Peter Weichmann said Delmer was 'a master not only at conceiving a subversive line but also at achieving the optimum phrasing'. However, Weichmann also noted, he could be a difficult person to work for. This became more marked later in the war, which Weichmann thought was because of 'domestic reasons'. Although he didn't spell this out, it is likely that the domestic reasons were to do with Delmer and his wife Isabel's failing relationship.

At some point in late 1942, Isabel had begun an affair with John Rayner. Rayner was working at the PWE alongside her husband; the two men had both worked at the *Daily Express*, where Rayner had been features editor. Rayner too was married, but his wife Joan – who had been a friend of Isabel's since her Paris days – was leaving the country to work as a cypher clerk. Joan, in turn, had also had frequent affairs. Isabel and Rayner took to walking together in the countryside around Woburn, once walking more than thirty miles to Dunstable and back. It was clear they both wanted to find some escape together from the claustrophobic and secretive atmosphere in Aspley Guise.[23] As more of the PWE's work moved to London and Delmer divided his time between the two locations, the affair would have been easier to pursue.

Isabel's work on black propaganda was becoming darker during the course of the war. Had Sir Stafford Cripps realised what was being dropped over Germany in the form of leaflets as well as broadcast over the airwaves, he would have been even more shocked. While Delmer had reluctantly agreed to tone down the pornography in radio propaganda, the production of graphic leaflets continued. The so-called 'greetings cards' were colour leaflets which Isabel described as being of a 'highly sexual nature'. She found these great fun to produce and, as she exclaimed in her memoir, 'fancy being employed by the government to create pornography!' One of her leaflet illustrations showed what she called a 'painstakingly realistic' image of a foreign worker making love to a blonde German girl. Some of these leaflets must have reached their intended targets, as the writer Patrick Leigh Fermor later told Isabel that he had seen the leaflet in Greece and was surprised to discover that she was the artist. Another design, which was never put into production, was a fake menu card for a supposed banquet thrown by Hermann Goering, the head of the Luftwaffe. Goering was renowned for his excesses, so the black propaganda department decided to invent a party for him. Delmer chose the menu and his wife designed the menu card. What looked at first like an innocuous frieze surrounding the card was, on closer inspection, composed of images of a chain of men, women and boys in sexual positions.

Isabel realised, though, that these leaflets were fringe efforts, mainly produced while the war was going badly. She felt that they were a way of creating something to do in the absence of military progress. Once there was news of action on the ground, the creative talents at The Rookery were diverted to more serious matters.

One of those creative talents was Ellic Howe, a man who also went by a variety of names. Born Ellic Fourman, the child of Russian immigrants, he was sometimes known as Armin Hull. Having spent a 'disgracefully idle' time at Oxford and leaving without taking a degree, he then – much like his fellow Oxford students and PWE colleagues Delmer, Richard Crossman and Elisabeth Barker – spent several years in the early 1930s travelling through Europe, to Paris, Berlin, Rome and Vienna. Howe picked up some European languages but, on returning to England, most usefully for his future career, he trained as a printer. While serving in the Anti-Aircraft Command in August 1941, Howe decided to write a paper on what printing – and more specifically, forgery – could contribute to the war effort. He believed that 'mankind has an almost superstitious belief in the power of the written word' and that documents which looked official would be readily trusted. Howe argued that 'in time of war, the printing press allied with the typewriter and the technique of calligraphic forgery or deception is a powerful weapon. Documents can reach places and persons which are outside the reach of our armoured divisions or agents.'[24] Howe suggested a long list of the kind of documents that could be faked: from identity cards and passports to currency and share certificates, ration books or military operational orders. He knew about the technicalities of printing and exactly what would be needed to produce authentic-looking documents. Even better, he knew where to find a press in Britain that owned a set of German type which had actually been used to produce genuine German documents for the Reichsbank before the war.

Howe sent his proposal through his superiors to Military Intelligence, who invited Howe to discuss his ideas with a brigadier in St James's. Soon afterwards, he was summoned to another meeting with John Rayner of the PWE. The meeting was clearly a success, as Rayner was keen to hire Howe as soon as possible. Rayner wrote in early October that he had half a dozen jobs waiting that needed expert calligraphic and typographic knowledge.[25] Things moved unusually quickly and, within a month, Ellic Howe had started in his new position. He sourced small, secret printing presses and the correct types of paper.

By the spring of 1942, when Howe first met Delmer, the demand for his services was increasing; by the summer, Howe found himself run off his feet. Delmer was less interested in forged documents – credible copies of the real thing – than in creating believable fakes. The forged items, though, could be used to lend credibility to the fake documents. SOE were able to distribute leaflets by post within Germany, for example, rather than have them dropped by air, because Howe's unit had created plausible forged stamps. Delmer was more interested in creating documents that would complement his radio broadcasts, such as a purported 'SS brochure' that was supposed to be a manual for candidates wanting to join the organisation, setting out invented privileges for SS officers – for instance, that they would be given free rein to abuse women.[26] What interested Delmer in forgeries was their use in stirring up political trouble for the German regime.

Delmer could be persuaded to take on ever more unorthodox colleagues to help create his fake news. Louis de Wohl was probably the strangest of all. Delmer described him as a famous Berlin-born astrologer, who lived in his basement flat off Piccadilly, in Athenaeum Court, like 'a vast spectacled jellyfish of a man dressed in the uniform of a British army captain',[27] puffing on an oversized cigar. Delmer used de Wohl to help produce a magazine of horoscopes called Zenith, aimed at German troops, providing horoscopes for their leaders and forecasts for U-boats and aircraft. Howe created realistic adverts for the magazine copied from genuine German publications. Delmer would help the magazine become more accurate by backdating the issues so that they seemed to foretell events that had already happened – an issue dated June 1942 claimed to predict German defeats at Stalingrad and El Alamein, but it had been printed in March 1943.

Delmer's story of how he used de Wohl was true as far as it went, but as so often with his version of events, it was a heightened yet partial version of the whole story. De Wohl was put to work for the PWE as a way of solving a problem for the other secret services. De Wohl, who was born in Germany but had claimed Hungarian nationality, had arrived in Britain in around 1935.[28] The British authorities were unable at the time to pin down his name or origins, but what de Wohl told them was, with hindsight, true: he was born Lajos Wohl in Berlin.[29] Lajos is the Hungarian form of Louis or Ludwig, and he used those first names interchangeably. He was described by intelligence sources as having written twenty to thirty novels of 'extremely dubious value', as well as having been a bank clerk, a film scenario writer, a commercial traveller and a shoe salesman. De Wohl had even published an autobiography in English, *I Follow My Stars*, in 1937, in which, although some of his tales seem extravagant and unlikely, the basic facts of his life are set out. In London, de Wohl made a living charging up to thirty guineas for personal horoscopes. The first volume of his MI5 file was lost in an air raid, so his early dealings with the security services remain obscure. However, he was taken on by Charles Hambro of SO2, who thought highly of de Wohl and hired him to produce horoscopes of the German leaders. Hambro, in May 1941, was reportedly 'convinced that de Wohl is a perfectly splendid chap' and would not hear a word against him. Hambro's thinking seems to have been that since Hitler and some of those around him were reported to believe in astrology, casting their horoscopes could provide insights into what they might believe would happen. De Wohl was sent to the United States to spread his predictions among other astrologers.

De Wohl returned to London in February 1942 to find the furniture removed from his previous apartment, his job gone and his department moved away from its former offices in Fitzmaurice Place. SO2 no longer required his services, but no-one had told him. Nor had the stars, apparently, revealed this. Since the department was secret, no-one would put de Wohl directly in touch with Charles Hambro or tell him where to find him, so he traipsed around London looking for his boss or any of his former colleagues, all of whom seemed to have disappeared. When an unnamed MI5 officer did contact him, de Wohl poured his heart out. With no money and no papers, he was at a loss. He claimed the right to wear an army captain's uniform, since he said that Hambro had appointed him a captain in a special ceremony at Horse Guards.

Although there was a view among some in the intelligence services that de Wohl was a dangerous charlatan and a 'confidence-trick merchant', others in MI5 viewed him slightly more kindly. W.T. Caulfield of MI5 wrote to his SIS counterpart that de Wohl was 'extraordinarily clever and astute with a faculty for assessing other people's psychology and character'. He was, however, 'extremely vain' and 'likely to be governed by nothing but self-interest'. These qualities, combined with his 'remarkable knowledge of Continental mentality' would apparently make him 'extremely suitable for propaganda work'. The security services wanted to keep tabs on him and although de Wohl, in his new lodgings off Piccadilly, no longer had a phone, they would intercept his letters.

The PWE, with the agreement of both Delmer and Bruce Lockhart, were happy to take him on, albeit on a 'special list' of staff rather than the official list. This would allow de Wohl to keep his army uniform and – a particular source of anxiety for him – allow him to have ration cards. Solving the ration card problem had given MI5 a headache, as they did not want de Wohl to be taken to court for not having the correct papers, thereby telling his story to an 'astonished Magistrate and gaping reporters'.

By the end of 1942, Charles Hambro had washed his hands of the man he called his 'tame astrologer'. De Wohl, back in contact, had sent him an assessment of the success of his astrological predictions for 1941 and 1942, together with his forecasts for the year to come. Hambro had clearly not bothered to look at them, writing to Rex Leeper that 'I have no doubt if I checked up his successes I would see that he had more than an equal number of failures, but I have not the inclination nor the time to do so'. Hambro suggested that the 1943 horoscope might be useful for the PWE to 'embody in some of your more lurid efforts'. While Delmer was already using de Wohl's services, Hambro suggested that he could be used for other output as well, with the astrologer keen to earn more money. De Wohl continued to be employed in his semi-official capacity, even though the security services did raise occasional objections, such as when he told a meeting of the White Hawk circle of spiritualists in Kensington that he was doing secret work. MI5 officers believed he was an 'indiscreet talker and a bumptious seeker after notoriety'.[30] (Though of course, perhaps the spiritualists already knew all of this.)

There were, however, some limits on what Delmer thought black propaganda could realistically achieve, even if he didn't turn his nose up at confected horoscopes. When it was suggested that he might set up a station aimed at Romany listeners in Europe, Delmer was scathing in his response. Quite apart from the difficulty of finding enough native speakers whose Roma language could be well understood in every community, he wasn't convinced that there would be enough potential listeners with access to radios to make this idea worthwhile, calling the possible audience 'an admittedly infinitesimal number of radio-listening gypsies'. 'If there are only a couple of thousand gypsies rich enough to own a radio,' he wrote, 'it is very unlikely indeed that among a couple of thousand we shall be lucky enough to hit on a twiddler who strikes the Gypsy RU. It might be years before we collected as much as a single listener.'[31]

There was one significant casualty of the shift to new, livelier and more ambitious stations. It was the original voice of black propaganda, Der Chef, and his station GS1. Der Chef came to a dramatic end in November 1943 when his secret broadcasting station was supposedly 'discovered' by the German authorities. He exclaimed 'Caught at last!' as he was interrupted and then shot. This was, of course, all acting, and all pre-recorded. The problem was that the radio death of Der Chef was accidentally played out again – so Der Chef died twice. Delmer was cavalier about the mistake. 'Fortunately I heard it. I have never met anyone else who did.' It was a worrying admission, though, even several years later. Did this mean that few of its intended audience had ever really heard what Der Chef had to say, or was it rather that, as Delmer and his supporters would claim, it didn't matter so much that a propaganda station's cover was blown once it was no longer on the air?

GS1 was to be replaced by an expanded version of the Atlantiksender, which would have a greater reach into Germany and western Europe. Concentrating black propaganda's efforts on soldiers, it would use newer techniques to reach its audience, building on production advancements, such as live broadcasting and playing music that the Milton Bryan studios allowed. In the next phase of the war, the black propaganda stations across Europe would have the potential to play a bigger role.

15

Greeks in This American Empire

Richard Crossman looked back on Algiers in the summer of 1943 as a paradise, though one he admitted he saw through rose-tinted spectacles.[1] He described the five months he spent there, though briefer than he had expected, as the most exhilarating period of his life. The rose-tinted glasses allowed Crossman to ignore what others saw as the difficulties setting up political and diplomatic operations in the Algerian capital. When Harold Macmillan arrived as the British minister resident – in charge of political liaison – at the beginning of the year, he was glad to have purloined two typewriters from the Colonial Office, as otherwise he would have had no office supplies at all. No paper, pens, pencils or filing cabinets. Nor did he have a fire or any heating in his hotel. Finding food and the means to cook it was a problem too. Macmillan said, 'There is not a saucepan, teapot, kettle, kitchen knife or anything like it in North Africa.'[2]

Food could only be found on the black market and the Allies felt they shouldn't be competing with the locals for it. Macmillan's staff helped themselves to household goods, like towels and blankets, from the contents rescued from a sunk P&O liner and began to furnish a villa. Macmillan's private secretary, the twenty-two-year-old John Wyndham, was in charge of finding resources wherever he could. Wyndham wrote home that he'd been told there were white houses, sunshine and the deep blue Mediterranean fifty yards beyond his window, but since the window was boarded up after an air-raid, 'it might be midnight in Manchester so far as I am concerned'.[3]

But the 'jungle of palm and cypress-covered hills, green as jade',[4] the sea, and – probably most importantly for Dick Crossman – the chance to play a significant role in international politics, outweighed the discomforts. Within a month, Wyndham was organising evening entertainments, where the Americans, French and British dined together, and drank 'quarts of Algerian wine'. He even hosted the prime minister.

Although he had been given his new posting in February 1943, Crossman didn't arrive in Algiers until late May, around the time that de Gaulle also arrived to make the city his headquarters.[5] In the meantime, Macmillan had only narrowly survived a plane crash on take-off at Algiers airport. He escaped from the burning aircraft through the pilot's window, with his face and moustache badly burned, wounds in his legs, and his eyesight only saved because he had been wearing glasses. Even so, he managed a quip at the expense of the French Admiral Missoffe, who had lost his cap in the crash and complained, '*J'ai perdu ma casquette!*' Macmillan, from his stretcher, retorted: 'I don't care a damn about your *casquette. J'ai perdu* my bloody face.' Taken to a military hospital, Macmillan was in such severe shock that he had flashbacks and believed he was back in the last field hospital he had experienced, after being wounded on the Somme thirty years before.[6]

'We propagandists were stationed in a squalid building called the Maison d'Agriculture,' Crossman wrote. The heat of the Algerian summer was already a huge contrast with London. His intelligence colleague, Robert Walmsley, described the working conditions in the Algiers office, writing on paper left behind by the Italians in Tunisia, headed Intendenza Italiana Tunisia. 'If the windows are closed you suffocate,' Walmsley wrote, 'if they are opened you can't hear yourself think.'[7] Crossman's job was to form a joint team of

propagandists with the Americans, where he would take direct
charge of radio and leaflets; he had 'full executive control of
radio and policy control of leaflets'.[8] On 1 June 1943, Macmillan wrote back to London that Crossman and his American
counterpart C.D. Jackson were 'doing excellently after a difficult start for both of them'. He didn't specify what had
been difficult in their first weeks. Working in the field was a
matter of learning to improvise with, at first, fewer resources
and staff. The positive side of being away from close political control in London was that the Algiers team was able to
make up its own mind to a far greater extent about what they
wanted to do.

Macmillan was by that time set up in relative comfort, in a
spacious villa on the hills, behind the Hotel St George where
Eisenhower had his headquarters. The hotel sat in gardens
full of palms, orange and lemon trees. In Crossman's retelling of his first meeting with Macmillan, the minister gave
the newcomer some advice on how to handle his new colleagues. When Crossman went into the Hotel St George,
Macmillan said, 'you will regularly enter a room and see an
American Colonel, his cigar in his mouth and his feet on the
table. In front of him will be an empty in-tray and an empty
out-tray. When your eyes get used to the darkness, you will
see in a corner an English captain, his feet down, his shoulders hunched, writing like mad, with a full in-tray and a full
out-tray, and no cigar.' The Americans might have been better
paid and had higher status, but the British still wanted to feel
like they were the real power.

'We, my dear Crossman,' continued Macmillan, 'are Greeks
in this American empire. You will find the Americans much
as the Greeks found the Romans – great big, vulgar, bustling
people, more vigorous than we are and also more idle, with
more unspoiled virtues but also more corrupt.'[9] Crossman's
task, Macmillan thought, was to make the Americans think
they were running the show but in fact to be the one who

was in charge. This may have been wishful thinking on Macmillan's part – and the story itself has the air of a Crossman gloss, more than twenty years after the fact – but it illustrates how the British saw their changing role.[10]

Algiers was a new centre of political power in the war. After it had been taken over during Operation Torch by the Allied forces, Eisenhower had established his base there, in his suite at the St George. The Americans had recognised Admiral Darlan as the leader of the French administration in Algeria, to the anger of both the British and the Free French, as Darlan had been a collaborator with the Germans. Darlan's assassination in Algiers at Christmas 1942, by a young French royalist and resistance member, was remarkably convenient for all, as it removed a political problem that caused friction between the Allies.

The scene for the next stage of the war had been set to the west of Algiers, at the Casablanca conference in January 1943, where Roosevelt and Churchill agreed that they intended to bring about the unconditional surrender of the Axis powers. The leaders also decided that they would pursue an invasion of Sicily as the next offensive in the war. Stalin stayed at home, preoccupied with the closing stages of the battle for Stalingrad. Churchill travelled through Algiers on his way back to London from North Africa and the Middle East, coming down with pneumonia soon after returning to Britain; he would make several further visits. Once Tunis fell to the Allied forces in May, with German troops surrendering, the three-year battle for North Africa was over and the Allies could concentrate on the plans for retaking Europe.

Algiers was also key to the political future of France. When de Gaulle arrived there at the end of May, although he was greeted with official ceremony and the 'Marseillaise', he was not given the publicity he had hoped for. The general was relieved that impromptu crowds cheered and sang when he laid a Cross of Lorraine at a war memorial in the city.[11] He set up his initial base at the Villa des Glycines, a place Macmillan described as being 'like the court of a visiting monarch'.[12]

The Conservative Harold Macmillan and Labour's Dick Crossman got on remarkably well. Crossman saw his favourite political boss of the war as a 'supremely intelligent man' who 'understood at once how to use psychological warfare without falling into grotesque exaggeration of its uses'.[13] Macmillan found his younger colleague a congenial man with whom he could have 'pleasant talk about books and Greek philosophy'. He also liked Crossman's American colleague, C.D. Jackson, calling the pair 'two admirable men – intelligent, humorous and loyal'.[14]

As with the preparations for Operation Torch in London, co-ordination between the Americans and the British in terms of propaganda was now key to their plans for the next stage of the war. Their main focus would be on how they should approach propaganda towards Italy as the planned invasion of Sicily, Operation Husky, approached. This was what Crossman later characterised as the second stage of political warfare, the offensive stage 'where we had sufficient military power for our words to be listened to with some respect'.[15]

Political warfare was integral to the planning of the operation. Long before any forces were deployed, there were discussions at the very top of the Allied governments and military as to what the Italian people should be told about the invasion: what should they expect and how could the Allies influence the Italian public reaction? The debate about whether black propaganda was a help or a hindrance was a central and contested part of these discussions.

Eisenhower was more convinced of the importance of propaganda ahead of the Sicilian operation than he had been before the North African landings. He wasn't yet persuaded that the propaganda plans were going about things the right way. The main objective of the existing PWE plan for propaganda to Italy was 'to convince the Italians that defeat is inevitable: by prolonging the war, the Italians will merely bring devastation on their country'.[16] Propaganda would tell the Italians that it was both in their power and in their interests to get out of the war, and that they could do so with honour. Between the fall of Tunisia and the landings in Italy, the time was ripe to exploit the fears of the Italians about invasion and aerial bombardment, exacerbating the sense of apprehension and panic that were expected to prevail in the country. Fear should predominate. The commanders-in-chief had their own ideas: Italians should be told that 'the longer Italian resistance the greater will be the destruction'.

Eisenhower looked at the plan and thought it took the wrong approach. The general sent a telegram to the British chiefs of staff, telling them that the 'cost to us of the operation may depend very largely on the extent to which we can undermine their morale beforehand'.[17] But the plan as it stood, in his view, was not sufficient and would not succeed in making any substantial contribution to the operation. Threats to the Italians, without the offer of a way out of the war, Eisenhower thought, might just make them rally round their leaders. Instead, he wanted propaganda to change tack straight away and start urging the Italians to cease hostilities, telling them this could lead to a peace with honour. Leaving this shift from 'hard' to 'soft' propaganda until later risked not giving it time to work. 'If we postpone it until the eve of the operation,' said Eisenhower, 'it will be entirely lost in the heat of the battle.'

Although the chiefs of staff agreed with the American general, the War Cabinet did not. This debate was conducted by telegrams buzzing across the Atlantic, since Churchill was in Washington at the time for discussions with President Roosevelt. The meeting of the two leaders also made a decision on propaganda policy more pressing: a joint statement about a new approach to Italy would be more powerful than separate ones. Eden was doubtful and felt that changing tack now would give the Allies nothing more to promise the Italians nearer the invasion. [18]

After two successive discussions at the War Cabinet, it was decided to tell the prime minister that the consensus lay with Eden. Eden relayed their opinions via another telegram – that 'any pronouncement now would be "shot to pieces" by enemy propaganda, and could be interpreted as a sign of weakness'. If the statement were issued too soon, 'instead of "soaking in" it will evaporate'. The War Cabinet considered that, combined with further bombing ahead of an assault, propaganda should change course at a moment 'calculated to cause confusion'.[19]

At a jovial joint press conference with Roosevelt in Washington on 25 May, Churchill did soften the line towards Italy somewhat. Asked by journalists whether he cared to say anything about Italy, Churchill suggested that the situation could be aided at any time by 'a change of heart' or a weakening of morale on the part of enemy countries. He said no-one was proposing to take Italy's 'native soil' away from the Italian people. 'They will have their life in the new Europe,'[20] he promised.

The fall of Tunis gave the PWE a victory that it was able to exploit. They could point to a vast Axis surrender. The Allies took over 240,000 prisoners, around half of whom were German. This defeat, following on from Stalingrad earlier in the year, led to the PWE coining the name 'Tunisgrad' for the surrender. It was quickly used in leaflets dropped over Germany, telling readers in the Ruhr that these two catastrophic defeats were unprecedented. In the space of a week, 2.84 million leaflets fell from the sky over Dusseldorf and other cities.[21] Tom Delmer's Atlantiksender also put the phrase into circulation. The PWE detected mentions of the phrase 'Tunisgrad' in European newspapers, including reports that it was scrawled on the walls of houses in German towns. Con O'Neill, Crossman's former assistant, now based near the

Tunisia/Algeria border, was given a captured German diary whose author described jokes about 'Tunisgrad'.[22] German troops in Tunis at the time of its fall were reported to be listening to Atlantiksender broadcasts.[23]

Within days of the capitulation in Tunisia, the first bombs fell on Pantelleria. This was the beginning of Operation Corkscrew. Pantelleria is a rocky volcanic island lying between Tunisia and Sicily, around a hundred kilometres off the Sicilian coast. Strategically, Pantelleria and its neighbours, Lampedusa and Linosa, were both stepping stones from North Africa to the Italian mainland and allowed whoever held them to survey and control sea traffic between the east and west of the Mediterranean. The island held radio stations, observation posts and an airfield, as well as 12,000 Italian troops, who outnumbered the usual inhabitants (there were around 9,000 in peacetime, although many would have been evacuated).

The small island was a tricky prospect for an invasion, though. There was only one beach that was at all suitable for a landing. Eisenhower wanted to make the task of the troops and the navy easier by beginning with a heavy bombardment. In his view, it was a test of how effective this strategy might be for future landings. The aim was to break the resistance of both the garrison and the civilian population. For more than a month, Pantelleria was hit by waves of bombing, first from the air, later from the sea.[24] Alongside the bombs fell leaflets. The early ones had described the strength of the Allied forces, warned civilians to stay away from military targets, and told those living and serving on the island about what had happened during the Tunisian campaign in 'terse and clear-cut fashion'.[25] As the planned day for the assault neared, three pilots swooped in to drop very specifically targeted calls to surrender: over the airport, over the main town square and over the governor's residence. These set out the terms on which a surrender would be accepted. Then thousands more general leaflets were dropped, encouraging the population to support the call for a surrender. At first, there was no indication of surrender, so after a pause in the bombardment, the Allies made another appeal.

When British infantry went ashore on 11 June, they occupied the island within twenty minutes. White flags of surrender were hoisted above a town that was shrouded in 'the infernal dust-laden fog of heavy bombing'.[26] The governor offered his surrender to the occupiers on the grounds that the population did not have enough water or food.

How much did the propaganda assault contribute to this surrender? The propagandists claimed that their leaflets, alongside the bombs, made a big difference. In 1946, Robert Bruce Lockhart claimed the fall of Pantelleria as a 'considerable success' that he and his colleagues had achieved. In fact, he said, they won it. Speaking to experts at Chatham House, he said that 'the island of Pantelleria, as you all know, capitulated to a propaganda attack'.[27] The director of the PWE's Italian section, he continued, had been publicly congratulated by General Eisenhower for the part that he had played.

Bruce Lockhart's American counterparts were likewise keen to take credit for their propaganda operations. Giving evidence to Congress in the autumn of 1943, Robert Sherwood, the playwright turned head of the overseas section of the Office of War Information, pointed out that Eisenhower had praised the work of the psychological warfare team, who had made a 'definite contribution as an integral part of the armed forces'. Eisenhower had paid tribute to the political warriors in a cable to the Combined Chiefs of Staff, singling out their work in Tunisia and Pantelleria. Sherwood, asking for more money to be allocated to propaganda by Congress, set out quite how much work his team had done. Over six months, he said, they had brought over 900 tons of paper, 7.7 million publications, 7,500 reels of motion pictures and more than 300 tons of radio parts to North Africa alone.

Others were more sceptical about what propaganda alone had achieved. A cascade of paper alone would not have brought about Pantelleria's surrender without bombing, but there were disagreements about how much difference the leaflets really made. Even thirty years afterwards, once the participants felt able to speak in public about their work, they took part in a heated exchange of views through *The Times* letters page, prompted by an article written by Richard Crossman. Peter Ritchie Calder, who had been head of plans and operations in the PWE, thought that the executive's role in Pantelleria had been that of 'writ-servers' – just delivering a message.[28]

George Martelli, the head of the PWE's Italian section, had been sent to Algeria ahead of the operations. Although he was a colleague of Crossman's, he was clearly one of those who disliked him. Martelli felt that Crossman was laying down the law on Italy, a country about which he knew little. Martelli thought his work had some effect, but it had been minor.

On the day that Pantelleria surrendered, Martelli went ashore with the British troops. He wandered into the interior of the island, where he found the Italian admiral, who commanded the garrison, standing with his staff in the courtyard of a small farm. Martelli asked the admiral whether he had seen any of the Allied leaflets. Yes, the admiral had – and he pulled a leaflet from his pocket to show the British man. The leaflet praised the heroic resistance of the valiant Italian soldiers and gave the admiral the option of honourable capitulation or undergoing further bombardment. 'It was on receiving this,' the admiral replied, 'that I asked permission from Rome to surrender.'[29] So, in one significant case at least, the leaflets did play a part in changing hearts and minds.

The invasion of Sicily was planned for the July moon. This would be a much bigger and more complex operation. Churchill insisted this time that – unlike in Operation Torch, where the British had been mere 'handmaidens' to an American-led operation – this would be an invasion of equals. As the two leaders discussed the statement that they would make to the Italian people once the invasion had begun, Churchill stressed to Roosevelt that Operation Husky should be a 'joint enterprise on terms of perfect equality'.[30]

The PWE wanted to know when exactly the long-planned shift from 'hard' to 'soft' propaganda towards Italy should be made. The scale of the logistics for the new propaganda operation was huge, far bigger than anything they had attempted up until that point. The PWE calculated how many leaflets they would need to print to reach as many Italians as possible. They assumed that one leaflet was picked up for every ten dropped; and each leaflet picked up could reach four people. In order to target the whole population of Italy – 45 million – they needed between 10 and 12 million to be read. So, in total, the PWE would need to drop 100 million leaflets over Italy. Most of these – 80 million of them – would be dropped over the north of the country, the remainder over Sicily, Sardinia and the south.[31] That meant organising the paper to print the leaflets and the aircraft to drop them.

In a similar way to the leaflets dropped over North Africa to appeal to the French, the leaflets aimed at Italy urged soldiers not to fight. 'Why die for Hitler?' asked one. The message was that Italy's leaders were not acting in the interest of their own country, but rather that of Germany.

By the beginning of June, Dallas Brooks needed answers about how exactly they should plan to make official announcements. His boss, Bruce Lockhart, had spent two months off sick earlier in the year, suffering with psoriasis, and Brooks was one of those called on to stand in for him when his health problems recurred.

Brooks wrote to Anthony Eden to ask whether Churchill and Roosevelt were going to put out a joint declaration to Italy before the invasion began. The PWE wanted at least six days before the invasion date to make the switch to the new, softer propaganda line – enough time for them to get the message out to as many Italians as possible, yet not giving too much time for Germany and Italy to react with their own propaganda.

At the PWE's meeting on 10 June, Eden said that there would not be a joint declaration from Churchill and Roosevelt before the invasion. Brooks pointed out, a couple of days later, that the president's most recent press conference on Italy had jumped the gun and effectively already changed position. Roosevelt had offered Italy the opportunity to return to being a 'respected member of the European family of nations, with emphasis on the word respected'.[32] Brooks urged Eden to get a member of the War Cabinet to echo this line and endorse what the president had said. He pointed out that the PWE had, on instruction, been playing down the similar words that Churchill had used in Washington about Italy's future role in Europe.

There was an even more tricky and secret decision to be taken about how the Allies should use black propaganda ahead of the invasion. It went to the core of the arguments about black propaganda that raged throughout the war. Eisenhower sent a telegram to the chiefs of staff on 29 June: 'I am considering possibility of using BLACK radio just prior to D day to spread false rumour that Italy has asked for and been granted armistice.'[33] He thought that the fake news of an armistice might cause 'confusion and discouragement' among the Italians at a critical moment. Eisenhower was aware that there was a potential downside, though: the fake news might be picked up and inadvertently spread by Allied radio monitoring, which could have the unwanted result that 'we may deceive our own people with possible far-reaching repercussions', particularly if the operation in Sicily didn't go according to plan.

In the first couple of days of July, the leaders of the Allied governments discussed the morality of – and the possible justification for – announcing a fake armistice. The decision came down to the fundamental point about the use of black propaganda: was it right to use lies tactically, in the hope of shortening the war, or was there a risk of jeopardising the Allies' reputation for being truthful to their own people as well as their enemies?

On 1 July, General Hastings Ismay, Churchill's liaison with the chiefs of staff, set out the military's support for Eisenhower's plan. They felt a black rumour would help the invasion. They wanted it to go out on short-wave black radio from the UK, backed up with black leaflets sent over from North Africa. They were aware of the risks of the broadcast being picked up by monitoring services elsewhere, but believed those risks could be managed, as long as Aspidistra wasn't used to send the black reports out on medium wave. Eden was ambivalent, saying he doubted the plan's value, but that he wouldn't oppose it. That is, he wouldn't 'press his instinctive opposition' if the chiefs wanted to go ahead.

Delmer had worked out a sophisticated plan for making the 'special rumour', as he called it, as believable as possible. The PWE had drawn up a bogus declaration from King Victor Emmanuel, which told the Italian people that 'for Italy, as from midnight tonight, the war is over'. The fake king would say he had dismissed Mussolini, that Italy had been abandoned by her German allies and that he had been assured that Italy would not be broken up but would be on an equal footing with the other peoples of Europe.[34]

Delmer argued that this declaration shouldn't go out on the regular black stations, such as in the voice of Der Chef, on the Atlantiksender, or on Radio Risorgi to Italy. What he wanted to do was to create counterfeit German and Italian stations, breaking into legitimate German frequencies and broadcasting the fake news on a station that German or Italian listeners would believe to be their own usual programme. He would also use the Hellschreiber – the German news agency machine – to spread the information. If the German and Italian authorities tried to respond after the message had gone out over what seemed to be their own stations, Delmer thought the audiences would find the official denials a 'ridiculous lie' invented by the Germans to cover up a German–Italian crisis.[35]

At first, Churchill was receptive to the black armistice idea. At a meeting with the chiefs of staff, he said he thought it would not matter if it became known that the armistice terms were fake. This would just be a '*ruse de guerre*'. Although at the meeting on the afternoon of Friday 2 July, Brendan Bracken seemed prepared to go along with the idea if the generals wanted to, later the same day, he wrote to Churchill in much more strongly negative terms. Bracken had discussed the matter with Bruce Lockhart, who agreed with him that the idea was 'deplorable'. Bracken – a man not averse to a lie where it would help him personally – realised the dangers of Britain being caught out in such a deception. His sardonic letter to the prime minister said he assumed the generals who had come up with 'this bright idea of faking the news of an armistice' had considered what would happen if Operation Husky didn't work out. If the Allied operation in Sicily failed, Bracken said, then the generals 'will be the laughing stock of the world and many a day will pass before British propaganda will be taken seriously'. Bracken was worried about jeopardising Britain's reputation for reliable news. But, as he had said at the meeting, if the generals wanted the black operation, he would do what the generals desired 'against our better judgment'.

Some of Churchill's closest advisers in Downing Street agreed with Bracken and Bruce Lockhart. Anthony Bevir, Churchill's private secretary, wrote to General Leslie Hollis, the War Cabinet secretary, expressing his misgivings. The black operation, Bevir thought, was 'frightfully dangerous'. Decent Italians would characterise it as a German trick, while forging the Italian king's name would bring Britain, in Italian eyes, 'even lower than the Germans'. It would never be forgotten. There was a risk of the whole plan backfiring, said Bevir. 'I see no objection to a good bouncing lie, but not one which might bounce in our own direction.'[36]

This argument about the rebounding dangers of a good bouncing lie convinced Churchill. A handwritten note was added on the top of Bevir's letter that the PM had seen it and 'entirely agreed'. Churchill dictated a series of telegrams to the generals. While he was still wavering, he wrote to Field Marshal Dill, his envoy in Washington, that 'we should consider whether the price to be paid does not exceed the advantage likely to be gained'.[37] The next day, he had come down more firmly on one side. To Eisenhower, he wrote that the black operation 'would do far more harm than good'. To General Alexander, commanding the Sicilian campaign, the message said that the government could not approve the proposal and that, if necessary, Churchill would discuss the matter directly with President Roosevelt. He hoped, though, that it would be 'squelched' locally. The PM explained his reasoning. 'It would not materially influence the battle, but would rob victory of its fame.'

But, first, they had to win the battle. On 9 July, Operation Husky was launched. The joint declaration from the PM and the president came once the operation was in full swing. Six days after the invasion of Sicily had begun, Roosevelt and Churchill told the people of Italy that the 'sole hope for Italy's survival lies in honourable capitulation'. They concluded their message thus: 'The time has come for you to decide whether Italians shall die for Mussolini and Hitler – or live for Italy, and for civilisation.'[38]

Getting any message directly to the Italian people by radio, whether white or black, was not straightforward. The Italian people didn't have as many radios as the Germans, and few were able to pick up short-wave broadcasts. Black propaganda to Italy had been a shambles in the earlier part of the war.

To put Eisenhower's directives into practice, both black and white propaganda to Italy needed to be more effective.

In fact, there had been no functioning RU broadcasting to Italy for the nine months until February 1943. The first black station, Radio Italia, had been taken off air in May 1942 amid great acrimony. Two of its main presenters, Pier Paolo Fano and Ruggero Orlando, resigned, protesting that their RU was about to be 'dismembered and reduced'. The view of those in charge at the PWE was that Radio Italia had no coherent viewpoint and that the impression on the listener was one of 'inconsistency if not of confusion'. It wasn't clear what propaganda to Italy was trying to do.[39]

The view of the former head of the Italian section, Ivor Thomas, who had become an MP in early 1942, was that the guiding principle in British propaganda towards Italy should be that 'Italy is our enemy; she can be made our friend.'[40] He argued that British policy should hold out some positive hope for the future to Italy, as long as the people threw off fascism. Thomas, as we have already seen, took his criticisms of the Woburn operation to Westminster. His former colleagues suggested that he had left the PWE under a cloud, although they didn't specify exactly why. Before his departure, he had written in glowing terms of the work of his Italian staff, looking back at the first year of Radio Italia's operations.

What others saw as chaos, Thomas thought was 'a felicitous example of unity in diversity'. The staff were largely young Italian lawyers, journalists and academics who were opposed to fascism and had left the country. Like the other RUs, Radio Italia started in an improvised way. Other staff were more eccentric and less valuable. Harold Robin, the sound engineer, told a story of a Sicilian sea captain who liked to ad lib his broadcasts with a bottle of whisky in hand, refused to take political direction and one day stormed out of the studio, content to return to internment on the Isle of Man.[41] The Italian propaganda RU did not seem to be a happy ship.

Radio Italia was replaced, as the planning for Operation Husky began, by a new station, Radio Risorgi. Risorgi was meant to sound like the voice of a group of well-connected anti-fascists with diplomatic links, who supported the Italian monarchy. It provided a mixture of real news and fake – about 20 per cent 'fiction' – but without a clear and detailed system like that operated by Delmer on the German stations.

As the invasion of Sicily continued, the Allies were already making their plans for the landings on the Italian mainland at Calabria and Salerno. By 25 July, Mussolini had been removed from office by the king and replaced with Marshal Badoglio. Mussolini was imprisoned in an art deco hotel on the Gran Sasso, at more than 2,000 metres altitude, in the Apennine mountains. The battle for Italy, though, was far from over.

With George Martelli on the ground in North Africa and the Italian islands, Delmer was given more authority over Italian black propaganda. A new station, Radio Livorno, began transmission on 25 July, the day that Mussolini was arrested. Like the Atlantiksender broadcasting to German troops, this was a station that was aimed at serving sailors. The station took its name from the Tuscan port which housed the Italian Naval Academy. Radio Livorno claimed to be broadcasting from the radio cabin of an Italian warship, just off the coast, with the voices supposedly those of an Italian naval officer and his wireless operator. Here, too, there were staffing problems: the original speaker quit after his first broadcast and had to be replaced; his replacement was reportedly almost as tricky to work with.[42] The main broadcaster was, according to Delmer, a Maltese officer of the British Army. In his Italian character, he warned his naval comrades to be on guard against the Germans. Livorno was working even more closely with British naval intelligence than Atlantiksender was; Delmer said that, day by day, the Admiralty told him the rough gist of the messages they would like Livorno to put out. Through August and into September, as the Allied forces prepared to launch their assaults on the Italian mainland, black propaganda was sending regular messages to the Italian fleet at sea. Radio Risorgi went off air at this point.

Delmer took credit for preparing the Italian fleet to surrender on 10 September. He claimed that the regular messages from Radio Livorno had accustomed the naval officers to following its instructions, so much so that when they were given details via Livorno of how to surrender, they sailed to the rendezvous at Malta and handed themselves and their ships over to Britain's Admiral Cunningham.

After the surrender, Peter Ritchie Calder sent Bruce Lockhart a message received from the Admiralty. The message related that the Italian Admiral Da Zara said that he and his men had been 'much influenced' by Admiral Cunningham's appeal issued immediately after the Armistice. The Italian sailors, their commander said, had been taught for the past four years that 'green was red' and it would take time to convince them that 'green really was green' – presumably the admiral meant by this that until that point, the Italian Navy had been heavily convinced by its own government's propaganda. Ritchie Calder called this 'gratifying evidence of the success of our propaganda'. Bruce Lockhart, however, feared British ministers would not be convinced without more information.[43]

Robert Sherwood from the Office of War Information told Congress that the broadcasts to the Italian Navy had been extremely effective and gave details of a technical trick that allowed black radio to reach its desired listeners. Even though Italian ships weren't supposed to listen to any foreign radio stations, an OWI engineer had worked out how to shift a transmitter in Algiers onto the international distress frequency, which meant all broadcasts would be picked up by any vessels in the region. The Allies' message to the Italian fleet, urging their sailors to come over to their side rather than scuttle their ships or go over to the Germans, was broadcast every fifteen minutes on the emergency frequency for several hours. The message got through. According to Sherwood's testimony, Admiral Cunningham told General McClure, the head of the largely American Psychological Warfare Branch (PWB), that he had 'accomplished in 1 day with propaganda what I've been trying to do for 3 years with the Navy'.[44] Cunningham, in his memoirs published in 1951, does not mention the role of propaganda, although he skips over many of the details of the operation as he said they had been told elsewhere; at that time, he was still bound to avoid mentioning other secrets, such as the role of codebreaking.[45]

George Martelli was not as convinced of Delmer's version regarding the navy as he was of propaganda's importance regarding Pantelleria. He said that he had been one of the first British officers to go on board the Italian flagship in Malta. When he asked the Italian admiral what he thought of the Allied propaganda, he was told he had not heard of anything except the BBC. Martelli attributed the fleet's surrender instead to the Italian Navy's loyalty to the king. Once the king was back in charge after Mussolini's removal, the navy were prepared to accept his armistice and surrender.[46]

Although perhaps Admiral Da Zara, in the aftermath of his surrender, told slightly different things to different people, it appears that he and his sailors might have been influenced to some extent by British propaganda. It was more effective because it had worked closely with the Admiralty, meaning the propaganda was tied into military strategy with a specific objective in mind, rather than a plan only conceived of within the PWE with a general ambition.

Sherwood maintained that Italy's collapse and surrender were proof of the efficacy of Allied propaganda. This was borne out, in his view, by the fact that more than 80 per cent of the German and Italian prisoners of war captured in

Sicily confessed that they had been 'influenced and impelled' towards surrender by propaganda leaflets and broadcasts. Even allowing for the propagandist talking up his own work, particularly where continued government funds were at stake, Sherwood would have had to be honest with the Congressional hearing; it would have been a crime for him to give false evidence. Propaganda was clearly part of the reason Italians were encouraged to surrender. Although military considerations were most important, propaganda gave sailors and soldiers the message that the future in defeat might not be as bad as they feared. This was why getting a clear and largely truthful line from the Allies was so important.

Of course, the situation in Italy was not going to be as simple as might have been hoped at the time of the first Allied landings on the Italian mainland. It would affect the Balkans and the course of the war there, too. Italy's armistice and surrender were a moment of hope that did not last. Once Mussolini was sprung from captivity and the breakaway northern Italian republic of Salò declared in September 1943, the situation got trickier.

Crossman reported back to a convalescent Robert Bruce Lockhart soon after the Sicilian invasion had begun (he added at the end of his letter that Syracuse had just fallen) on how things were going in Algiers. He was full of suggestions for how the joint British and American operation could work better.

Algiers was getting good intelligence from London, Crossman felt, with good 'creative liaison' between those working on the propaganda output and those working in intelligence, but the channels of information weren't working well in the other direction. The useful knowledge they sent from Algiers – such as intelligence gleaned from prisoners of war – was not being picked up in London. Crossman wanted clearer lines in the directives on propaganda that emanated from London, but also greater insight into the thinking behind British strategy.

The PWB team had built up an entire radio station from scratch, which they were now calling 'United Nations Radio'.[47] It had two powerful transmitters, in Tunis and Algiers, that could broadcast into southern Europe, and a third, twice as powerful, on the way. The station had a staff of fifty, though Crossman was concerned that only three of them were British, which meant that it sounded overwhelmingly American. He appealed to Bruce Lockhart for more staff, particularly those with editing experience on British radio. Some of Delmer's black propaganda team, though, were working on intelligence, with direct access to German prisoners of war and enemy documents. Although originally German, they were being 'treated out here precisely as Englishmen' – a sign of great trust in their reliability and their work.

Crossman was already thinking ahead to his own future as the war progressed. It was clear that he was enjoying being on the ground in the middle of operations and wanted to move where the battle went next. He appealed to his boss to 'let me stay out here as long as possible during this campaign', but was keen to play a part once the second front was opened up. 'Do call me back,' he requested, 'when the serious preparations for the western front begin.' Crossman wanted to be back working on propaganda to Germany, his first interest; he acknowledged he was no Italy expert. As well as what he'd learned alongside his colleagues about setting up a radio station on 'nothing but chewing gum and shoe strings', he felt he knew much about propaganda in a hot war zone – specifically, 'what an enlargement of political warfare front line and occupation propaganda provide' – as long as it was fully integrated with the military command.[48]

Typically, Crossman would claim that he had played a vital role in the timing of the Italian armistice, signed in secret five days before it was announced in early September. He told Hugh Dalton that 'he had a great thrill in actually negotiating the timing of the Italian Armistice and the publicity connected with it'. In the Crossman version, he and his American counterpart, C.D. Jackson, had been left alone with the Italian generals in a Sicilian olive yard to discuss the ceasefire, while the British and American generals who were supposed to join the rendezvous had temporarily been somewhere else. Again, there were discussions about whether they could make a fake broadcast, purportedly by Marshal Badoglio, Italy's new prime minister, while they tried to get the real Badoglio to agree to send his own message. The message was broadcast, though not in a fake voice, and within an hour, the new prime minister had been bounced into going on air himself. Timing was everything, Crossman said. 'It was rather complicated trying to make sure that nothing came out too soon to compromise operations, or too late to have the hoped-for propaganda effects.'[49]

Whether this was strictly true or not, Crossman had delighted in the autonomy he found working with Macmillan in North Africa. He was effectively running his own propaganda operation together with his American colleagues. Crossman claimed that Macmillan even went as far as to ignore an order from Churchill, throwing the telegram from London into the fire.[50] He loved the confidence that Macmillan inspired in his underlings; 'he encouraged us to speak up and he really enjoyed any success that we achieved.' This, Crossman thought, was a very American quality and he contrasted it with the years of 'Whitehall jealousy and peevishness' that he had experienced earlier. Crossman had helped to set up a radio station in Tunis, with five language desks and its own policies. His loyalty was now to what he saw as 'a new breed of man – the Anglo-American', embodied in Harold and Ike.[51]

But inevitably, this hubris came at a political cost. Eisenhower was rebuked by Churchill for excessive interference in politics when he put his name to a declaration telling the Italians there would be a pause in bombing for them to make up their minds to join the Allies. There was a certain parallel here with Crossman's earlier misstep over Bomber Harris, except that this time he was telling the Italians that they would not be bombed, rather than telling the Germans that they would be. Crossman was recalled home in early October to be told that he was overreaching and that he was seen as so far embedded in the Anglo-American staff that he was no longer representing British policy. Crossman later acknowledged this, saying that he felt a 'fanatical Anglo-American team spirit' which assumed that any directions from the governments at home were usually insane and not to be followed.

Once again, Crossman's political boss came to his rescue. Macmillan had stalked into the Foreign Office and said: 'Crossman is our man, and I am responsible for everything he did.'[52] He was allowed to return to Algiers 'in triumph'. But here, too, the glory did not last more than a few days. This time it was not a political blunder that brought disaster for Crossman, but something far less predictable and more dangerous.

16

Ignore the Civil War

The Italian surrender of September 1943 meant that the Allies looked across the Adriatic Sea towards Yugoslavia with fresher eyes. Italy's surrender, Elisabeth Barker said, 'had for the moment badly shaken the German occupation forces in the Balkans. It had shown that sooner or later the Germans would have to get out.' Russian troops, however, were also likely to head for the Balkans, even if the Allies, landing in Italy, had less far to go to reach them. She characterised the Allied response in this period as taking a 'very definite if rather nervous and muddled interest in the Balkans'.[1]

British policy towards the Balkans was certainly muddled. It was characterised by confusion and a lack of reliable information and understanding about what was happening on the ground. While Britain had been backing resistance in Yugoslavia – in contrast to elsewhere in Europe, where British propaganda was keen not to encourage premature revolt before any help could come – there was uncertainty about who to support. After Britain's withdrawal from Crete in May 1941, Yugoslavia was the only place where guerrilla fighting was still going on.

When German troops invaded Yugoslavia in April 1941, with forces from Bulgaria and Hungary alongside them, the Yugoslav government went into exile. Italian troops also moved into Slovenia. The seventeen-year-old King Peter II arrived in London with his ministers in June, where they were 'received as heroes'.[2] A week after his arrival, he made a broadcast celebrating the Serbian national day, saying that he came to Britain 'not as a stranger in exile but as a friend and even as a kinsman'.[3] His eighteenth birthday in September was marked with a coming-of-age ceremony at St Paul's Cathedral, the first service held in the cathedral since it had been damaged in the Blitz, with the British king, queen and prime minister in attendance, along with other exiled European royalty.[4] While the teenage king and his government might have been treated with all due protocol and deference, the reality was that the country they had left behind had ceased to exist.

Yugoslavia had capitulated and was effectively broken up into several parts, with a Nazi puppet state established in Croatia, which included present-day Bosnia. The Ustaše regime persecuted Serbs, Jews and Roma, murdering hundreds of thousands of people during the course of the war. The Balkan sections of the BBC and the PWE were therefore dealing with broadcasting to several countries where there had formerly, since the end of the First World War, been one. Rex Leeper had to explain to the Ministry of Information in May 1941 that this was the case; the Ministry had not wanted to encourage separatism by having separate broadcasts to Croatians. 'As Croatia has been separated from Serbia,' Leeper wrote wryly, 'I think that argument loses some of its strength.'[5] The war years in Yugoslavia have been described as 'a nightmare of inter-ethnic bloodletting, fighting and wars within wars'.[6] Resistance and guerrilla fighting against the occupiers continued alongside Yugoslav groups fighting each other.

The initial preference of the Foreign Office was to support the government-in-exile, and beyond that, to back the Serb general Draža Mihailović, a royalist and nationalist who led the Četniks. Mihailović tried to get control of remnants of the Yugoslav Army and based himself in Serbia. When he managed to make contact with the exiled government in

September 1941, he announced that he would continue to fight the Axis. The Četniks, too, carried out massacres of those who opposed them, particularly non-Serbs.

At the same time, the Partisans, led by Josip Broz, known as Tito, were also fighting the Axis occupation. Tito was the leader of the Yugoslav communists who had left Belgrade to set up a resistance force. Britain was soon aware, by late in 1941, that the Četniks weren't the only resistance force in the area and that Mihailović had a rival. Their assumption, however, was that Mihailović would be able to unite Yugoslav patriots behind him. This didn't turn out to be true.[7]

The tangled politics of the Balkans was reflected in the plethora of black radio stations which were broadcasting to the listeners there. In a recording played for the king and queen's visit to Woburn in November 1941, Ralph Murray, the regional director for south-east Europe, told them that on his stations, 'we don't play tricks, we're strictly political, national-istic and very passionate'.[8] As Murray explained, there were three stations speaking separately to Slovenes, Croats and Serbs. He told his royal listeners how complex their task was. 'They have to make the Yugoslavs sink their differences by speaking to each nationality separately, to the separate inter-ests of each, to make and keep them bitterly hostile to the Germans and Italians, to keep some in the hills with rifles in their hands, to stop others from boiling over too soon, and to put the fear of revenge into collaborators.'

He detailed how these tasks played out on the separate radio stations. On the Croat station, Y1, Radio Zrinjski, Murray said, 'we are frankly murderous'. Its callsign was an old popular tune from the Italian occupation of Dalmatia, whose words were 'Out with them, out with them', the tune whistled or played on a concertina. The station wanted to 'rouse Croats to action'. It threatened Ante Pavelić, the prime minister of the puppet state of Croatia and leader of the Ustaše, for his attitude to the 'Italian paymasters' in the country. In a more sober written document, the aim of the station was described as 'to destroy the authority and influence of the Quisling Government in Croatia'.[9] Its intended audience was the 'town bourgeoisie', largely because they had more access to radios and were potentially more easily persuaded to oppose the Ustaše regime. The RU used 'stories, rumours, satirical jokes, appeals, threats to the "ungodly" and reasoned argument' to appeal to its Zagreb listeners. The station had run an early 'scandal and ridicule' campaign against the Ustaše, which the PWE believed had been successful. Its political programme was described as an 'effort to fill the gap in white propaganda to Croats left by the political failure of the émigré Jugoslav government', which had been agreed with 'responsible Croat politicians' in Britain. This was a hint at one of the main problems in broadcasting to Yugoslavia: the government-in-exile did not want to countenance any mention of the separate and opposing forces within the country, let alone allow any expression of support for them. The PWE was constantly arguing that it was necessary to reflect the facts on the ground, regardless of what the exiled government would like them to say.

This was more of a true black station than the Serbian station Y2, Radio Šumadija, which was supportive of General Mihailović and was aimed at an audience of young and progressive Serbs. It had first gone on air in August 1941 and initially had warned its listeners that they should be restrained in how they responded to the Germans, because premature action would bring reprisals. According to Murray, it was aimed at listeners in the 'forested hills', where Serb irregulars were still fighting. Following reports that the Serbian guerrilla forces had adopted the slogan 'Our home is the forest', the radio station echoed this, telling them that they should remain in the forest and await further instructions before rising up.[10] It called for the 'unity of Četniks and communists' – something that would prove impossible to achieve.

Broadcasts to the Slovenes also initially stressed the importance, for the listeners, of 'obedience, patience, organisation and above all, waiting', as Murray explained in late 1941. The initial station aimed at Slovenia was Y3, Radio Triglav, also set up in August 1941, which Murray described as 'attacking collaborators'. The station was soon considered not to be very effective in these aims and, by January 1943, it was replaced by a new RU. This station, codenamed Y4, was called Za Staro Pravdo or Radio Ancient Justice and was meant as 'a weapon of political warfare against Italy', which aimed to increase 'alarm and despondency among Italians', particularly seamen in Trieste, and encourage Slovene separatism.[11] It would do this by adopting an attitude of 'uncompromising Slovene nationalism', advocating the uniting of all Slovene lands in a single political entity. The Italians, the PWE hoped, would then hear about the 'realities of Italy's military and naval situation'. They hoped the Italians would come to feel that Slovenes in the Italian forces were not reliable and would move them away from the front lines to elsewhere in Italy.

Another Serb station, Radio Karageorge, operated from Jerusalem. The PWE did not directly control this station, which put out Četnik material and called itself 'the voice of truth, the voice of Draža Mihailović'. Neither the PWE nor the Foreign Office liked what they sometimes heard on this station; in one case, it accused the Partisans of being paid by the Gestapo.[12] Radio Karageorge was closed down not long after this report in December 1942.

The 'long struggle' to persuade the British government to switch its support from Mihailović to Tito went on from late 1941 to 1943, Elisabeth Barker wrote. She witnessed it at close quarters and was arguing strongly for the shift, so much so that she was seen as 'an unrepentant Titoist'. As a historian, she later became one of the experts on this convoluted period. She wrote that, from 1942 to 1943, propaganda to Yugoslavia became important in the absence of any military progress; it 'was seen as the only available weapon for aiding, and influencing, the resisting elements there.'[13]

Although she had not yet been given the formal title, by the beginning of 1943, Barker was effectively in charge of the Balkan section of black propaganda. She was working on both the bigger strategic decisions and the day-to-day problems of managing the staff. Her nominal boss and close colleague, Ralph Murray, had been sent to Cairo as the PWE's representative to the Greek government-in-exile there. She was thirty-three and one of the most senior women working on policy. Barker later described her role in charge of the Balkan section as spending most of her time trying to argue with the Foreign Office on the one hand and the SOE on the other, and to reconcile those both with the PWE's views of what ought to be going on. As Barker put it, 'my SOE opposite numbers were much more pro Mihailović, and the Foreign Office was in a state of dither because they were having to deal with an exiled government and an exiled King'.[14] In March 1943, commenting on a note about the confused situation as to whether Britain was supporting the Partisans, she described the PWE being close to the Foreign Office and 'at loggerheads' with SOE and the War Office.[15]

The role of SOE was more important for the PWE with regards to Yugoslavia than it was for many other countries, because much of Britain's intelligence concerning what was happening came from SOE agents who had been dropped in to Yugoslavia and reported back on what they had learned. The trouble was that the evidence they came up with was often partial and contradictory. The SOE organisation itself was divided: it was prone to infighting and there was a lack of central control from London, as there was another SOE operation in Cairo. Those conflicting signals were amplified as telegrams and messages bounced back and forth between

Cairo and London. Nothing, where the Balkans were concerned, was simple.

Beyond Yugoslavia, there were radio stations aimed at
Hungary, Romania and Bulgaria. The Hungarian station
was designed to appeal to 'the peasant, the small farmer, the
worker and the intellectual classes' – although it was acknowledged that, of these, the intellectuals were most likely to have
access to radios.

Finding the staff to work for the Balkan stations, along
with places for these staff to live, was not quite as complex
as negotiating the politics of the region, but at times caused
similar headaches. When the stations were first set up, in July
1941, Ralph Murray wrote to the official in charge of logistics that it was not a question of one Balkan RU, but rather
of six different ones, requiring a staff of at least a dozen and
probably twenty. 'As you know,' Murray observed, 'they cannot
all bed-down together.'[16] While many PWE staff were moved
back to London, the Balkan RUs stayed in the country. Elisabeth Barker was left to wrestle with the persistent problem:
the four Slav RUs, Yugoslav and Bulgarian, could be housed
together, but the Hungarians and the Romanians had to be
separate from both the Slavs and from each other.[17]

Nor was there enough room for everyone. One house,
Larchfield, in Aspley Guise – the former home of the
Delmers – was so overcrowded by March 1943 that Barker
had to warn officials that there was a risk of 'some sort of
breakdown' if the situation continued for even three more
weeks. The small house was already home to four separate
radio teams, as well as other staff who visited regularly. There
was only one room for all of them to work in when they
needed at least three. This was causing domestic difficulties
and making it hard to work. Barker reported 'tension, friction
and lack of concentration'.[18] As she spent her weekends at
the 'secret houses', overseeing operations while working in
London during the week, she was well aware of the stress.

Finding the right voices for the Balkan stations was even trickier than it was for their German or Italian counterparts, as there were far fewer potential candidates to choose from. SOE had initially helped to get some Yugoslavs out of occupied Europe via Lisbon at the beginning of the war. Some potential broadcasters were released from prisoner of war camps, like a Sergeant Kožlin, a thirty-one-year-old described to Barker as 'modest and keen', who spoke Slovene, Italian, Serbo-Croat and German, and who was politically suitable. He was described as the 'best type of Slovene' who opposed the Italians and wanted to unite Slovenia within Yugoslavia. Other potential recruits were not nearly as promising, but the Balkan section found themselves taking them on anyway, in the absence of alternatives.

Major Nicol, who was hired for the Bulgarian station, was a questionable prospect. Elisabeth Barker wrote to Thomas Barman explaining the problems she'd had trying to find a Bulgarian expert. Having failed to find anyone else who knew Bulgaria and its language, they were left with Nicol, who had lived in the country for many years but said he knew the peasants and the simple people better than the politicians. He was in his 'advanced 60s' and although 'energetic and sprightly', he was a 'simple minded man' and 'certainly not brilliant'. He was also rumoured to have a drink problem. Despite Nicol being 'obviously not a first class person', Barker felt she had no option but to take him on.[19] Within a month, though, Nicol was complaining of being allocated a top-floor room in the overcrowded Larchfield house and wanted to move elsewhere. One Bulgarian family, a Madame Karastoyanova and her daughter, was thrown out of Larchfield in 1942 because Murray felt that 'the old lady had allowed her Bulgarian temperament to get rather above her', making the living situation intolerable, though he did not explain how she had been temperamental.

Since Bulgarians were in such short supply, Barker also had to contend with SOE trying to poach her staff for their operational work; she was annoyed that SOE wanted to recruit a Mr Nikolov, her only male Bulgarian radio voice, who was just beginning, 'after a good deal of training, to do useful work'. The traffic in scarce experts also went the other way: in October, Barker was pleading with MI6 – having learnt by 'devious routes' that there was a Hungarian expert who was working for them but not using his languages – to allow him to work for her, as the PWE had to release their 'one and only Hungarian expert for an important job abroad and we are therefore in the soup'.

By March 1943, the stations were putting out more than eleven and a half hours of programming a day, plus a further three hours of repeats. Barker was leading a team in London that was mainly made up of women. Of the fifteen Balkan section staff then working at Bush House, only four were men, while the team working on Balkan intelligence were all women bar one.[20] This was possibly because the scarcity of Balkan experts made it more likely that women were promoted to the available jobs. In June, there was a discussion about whether Barker, too, should be sent to work in Cairo, but it was decided that she should remain in London and Woburn.

After a slightly bumpy start, Barker seems to have had a good working relationship with Tom Delmer. In February 1943, he appears to have attempted his own land grab on the Balkan region, trying to take over more control of operations. This was perhaps because he felt that, in the absence of Ralph Murray in Cairo, he could expand his own area of influence. Barker seems to have spotted this quickly, objecting to a plan of Delmer's for black propaganda to Italy which she saw as encroaching too far onto the territory of the Balkan region. Barker implied in her response that she had so far had little contact with Delmer, writing that the Balkan section could 'profit considerably' from a 'more regular exchange of ideas' with him and from closer collaboration. But she resisted the idea that Delmer should have more control over work on the Balkans: both policy control and technique should remain in the hands of the region, since they had the detailed know-ledge of the countries concerned.

By May, though, they were united against a threat to the black Balkan stations from the Foreign Office. Barker and Delmer joined forces once the very purpose of black propaganda to the satellite countries was called into question. In May 1943, the Foreign Office was wavering over the idea of continuing the broadcasts at all. Sir Orme Sargent, Sir Alec Cadogan's deputy, called a meeting at the Foreign Office with Barker, Delmer and others, starting it by saying that the justification for the Balkan RUs was not clear. The PWE team argued back forcefully, setting out the purpose of what they were doing. The stations, they stated, were 'an essential weapon of Political Warfare against the satellites, particularly during a phase of the war when the satellites' loyalty to Germany is already shaky, and when it is not yet possible to use military weapons against them'.[21] Their aim was to 'increase alarm and despondency' among the countries' listeners. In a memo that was read out to the meeting, clandestine radio was called 'purely destructive' – but that was meant as a good quality. The PWE's aim was to make those countries 'as great a drain on the German war effort as possible' and to turn the listeners there into 'unconscious allies of the united nations' out of self-interest. Black radio allowed Britain and her allies to put across news that was not necessarily in pursuit of British policy, or as honest and straightforward as the BBC broadcasts had to be, but which was 'sufficiently plausible to be believed'. The PWE explained that since these countries were no longer enemies but potential allies, 'since we are addressing our friends, we must never put anything forward to them for which we can be reproached after the war'. The PWE did not want to broadcast anything that would in future weigh on their consciences. The tendency in the future would have to be for the broadcasts to be 'less black' – to be closer to the truth and more similar to official white radio. They argued that the RUs to friendly countries were 'far from being outworn or redundant'.

These arguments, accompanied by evidence that people within the Balkans were listening to the station, seemed to be accepted by the Foreign Office. The PWE emphasised that they didn't need huge audiences for rumours to be spread effectively by word of mouth. The stations could continue their work. By May, Barker and Delmer were working together on a plan to launch a radio station broadcasting to German-speakers in Hungary and Romania. The Volksdeutsche station would have a dual purpose: it would both send black propaganda to the native German-speakers themselves, aimed at demoralising them, while at the same time encouraging even more resentment of those people among other Hungarians and Romanians who understood German. In the aftermath of the invasion of Sicily, there was a specific request from Cairo to Delmer to broadcast items 'genuine or invented' to show that Italians in the Balkans were making for the coast and were being prevented and disarmed by Germans. It was suggested that it might be reported that fighting had broken out between the two groups.[22]

Delmer, as ever, romanticised the situation, describing how the Italian and Balkan teams were working together at the new Milton Bryan studios alongside those broadcasting to Germany. In Delmer's telling of it, the canteen became a tower of Babel, where 'dark-eyed gypsy beauties from the Balkans flirted with my fair-haired German prisoners over toad-in-the-hole, powdered egg omelette, spam fritters, soya bean sausages, and the other irresistible delicacies from the repertory of war-time cooks'.[23]

The question over who propaganda should be broadcasting to – and whether there was a need for black propaganda at all – reflected the bigger international uncertainty about who

Britain was supporting. Towards the end of 1942, Britain had been receiving reports that Mihailović was at best ineffectual in his resistance to the Germans and Italians, and at worst was actively collaborating with them, being more concerned with fighting against Croats and Partisans rather than foreign forces. The BBC had increasingly been reporting stories about the Partisans' successes. The PWE had for some time been issuing its directives playing down the significance of Mihailović in his military actions, even though the official line was still to support him.[24]

Rumours were circulating in London that such collaboration was going on; Mihailović denied them, but British officers were sent to his headquarters to try to find out more. It was hard to communicate with the men behind the lines. Messages were often held up or lost for a long time, making information out of date.

Where white propaganda tried to gloss over these differences in the interests of diplomacy, the result satisfied no-one. Barker was responsible for the directives that went from the PWE to the BBC, setting out lines to take on the conflict in the Balkans. They contained an element of intelligence, as well as looking ahead to the events expected in the region. There was an argument even about whether the 'Partisans' could be allowed to be mentioned on air at all.[25] When, as Barker told it, the Foreign Office allowed the PWE and the BBC to praise the Yugoslav 'patriots', the diplomats believed that this would cover both Mihailović and Tito's supporters. However, neither of them was happy. 'Mihailovic immediately knew that the patriots really meant the partisans,' wrote Barker, 'and the partisans bitterly resented the fact that the patriots could be taken as covering Mihailovic.'

The policy confusion in London, combined with the divisions between the PWE and the SOE, and the existence of different staff trying to influence decisions both from London and from Cairo, put those trying to make propaganda into paradoxical situations. When the Soviet Union, Britain's ally, decided to back the Partisans and denounced Mihailović, another factor came into play. Ralph Murray protested to Robert Bruce Lockhart that 'the Communist-Mihailovic issue in Jugoslavia is getting us in a mess and has just taken a turn for the worse'. The PWE, he continued, was 'vitally interested' in this. The problem, Murray said, was that on the one hand, British propaganda consisted of appeals by the Yugoslav military cabinet for loyalty to Mihailović, and on the other, of 'abstract and unrealistic appeals for unity against a background of notorious disunity between ourselves and the USSR'.[26]

The Foreign Office, however, explicitly told Murray to ignore precisely the problems that he had raised. In their reply to his questions, although they admitted that it was increasingly difficult for propaganda to remain 'aloof and oblivious' to the issues, that was precisely what they wanted. In propaganda and publicity, the official wrote, 'we must continue to ignore the civil war which is raging between Mihailovic (and/or the Chetniks) and the Partisans'. Likewise, propaganda should 'give no hint' that there was any difference of policy between the British and the Soviet governments. Murray was also told in terms to 'cover up Mihailovic-Partisan differences' by suggesting it was geography rather than ideology which divided the two groups.[27] This demand to ignore or cover up the hard questions was clearly not tenable in the long term.

By the end of December 1942, Eden was tending towards the view that it might be in Britain's short-term interests to support the Partisans, as they were doing more and Mihailović was 'contributing little to the general war effort'. Lord Selborne, who had taken over from Hugh Dalton as the minister for economic warfare and was therefore in charge of SOE, was still holding the line that Britain should continue to support Mihailović, despite some of the reports from his officers in Cairo. Eden, while still wary of Russia's motives in the region and the potential threat of communism, was also worried about Mihailović, seeing him as a man who 'is not fighting our enemies and is being publicly denounced by our Soviet ally'.[28] A speech by Mihailović in February 1943, which suggested that he saw the Germans and Italians as less important enemies than Ustaše, Croats and Partisans within his own country, pushed Britain to making diplomatic protests and seriously considering changing its support.

If Britain was going to shift its policy to support the Partisans, first they needed to know who they were dealing with. Again, this was no simple task. According to Fitzroy Maclean, the Scottish diplomat, soldier and politician who was sent to meet the Partisan leader, while the British government doubted whether Mihailović and his supporters were really resisting the enemy, they knew very little about Tito. Some in the British government weren't even sure whether Tito existed at all, thinking that Josip Broz's *nom de guerre* might just be an acronym for a Partisan organisation. Other theories were that 'Tito' was a name allocated to a variety of leaders or, more wildly, that Tito was in fact a woman. Rex Leeper, now posted to Cairo, met Maclean there and despatched him urgently to London for a job he thought the Scot would suit. Maclean's first briefing was directly from the prime minister, delivered during a weekend at Chequers – a visit which coincided with Mussolini's resignation in July 1943 – although Churchill also spent much of his time watching Mickey Mouse cartoons. Maclean's task was to be dropped into Yugoslavia to find out the truth about Tito.[29] Churchill seemed little concerned about the politics of the Balkans; he told Maclean he should simply 'help find out who was killing the most Germans and suggest means by which we could help them to kill more'.[30] Maclean was to go to Yugoslavia 'without delay'.

Having parachuted into Bosnia, he was taken to meet Tito by his chief of staff, Vladimir Velebit, at his headquarters in a ruined castle in Jajce. Maclean encountered a man with 'tanned regular features and iron-grey hair', who had 'a very firm mouth and alert blue eyes'.[31] Tito told him that there could only be hope of reaching agreement with the Četniks and forming a united front if Mihailović stopped fighting the Partisans and started fighting the Germans instead. He thought that change of heart was no longer within the bounds of possibility. Tito, Maclean thought, clearly possessed 'energy, determination and intelligence' as well as a sense of humour. 'Much,' Maclean reported back to Churchill, would 'depend on Tito, and whether he sees himself in his former role of Comintern agent or as the potential ruler of an independent Jugoslav State.'

By the end of 1943, Mihailović was becoming an outright military obstacle. His forces were obstructing Partisan and British efforts to sabotage German lines of communication. Eden told the War Cabinet in December that there should be all-out support for Tito and an effort to reconcile King Peter with the Partisans.[32] November 1943 also formally saw Elisabeth Barker given the title of head of the PWE's Balkan section, a job she had in fact been doing for almost a year. The change in British policy meant it should have been easier to decide what message Britain was conveying to Yugoslavia in the final phase of the war. Towards the end of the year, some of the broadcasts to the Balkans were able to be made from closer to the region. As the Allies advanced into southern Italy, radio operations were set up in Bari, on the Adriatic coast, just above the heel of the Italian boot. It was thought more effective to broadcast white propaganda on medium wave from Bari into Yugoslavia than black propaganda on short wave all the way from England, as the former would reach more people.[33] Some PWE effort was also moved to Cairo, but this variety of locations made it more difficult to co-ordinate control over the policy and the output. The Croatian black radio station was also taken off the air at the end of the year.

At the beginning of 1944, Fitzroy Maclean decided that he should bring Randolph Churchill, the prime minister's son, to join him on his mission to the Partisans. The PWE and the Foreign Office predicted, correctly, that Randolph's role would cause trouble. It was not just the obvious security risk of dropping the PM's son by parachute into an enemy-occupied guerrilla war zone that was the problem. It was Randolph Churchill himself. Maclean thought that he would be a useful addition to his team and 'just the man'; he had fought alongside Randolph earlier in the war and believed him to be intelligent and thoroughly dependable, 'possessing both endurance and determination'. Maclean clearly realised that others didn't see him the same way, referring cagily to the fact that he wouldn't have chosen him for certain other jobs, such as working alongside 'touchy or sensitive' people. Maclean called Randolph Churchill's attitude to life 'explosive' and that part was certainly true.[34] Others who had to deal with him did not share Maclean's charitable view. Michael Foot, who had been a journalist and political rival of Randolph's, recalled him as a 'friend and enemy worth having', seeing Churchill as a contradictory character who was at the same time 'outrageous and endearing, impossible and unforgettable', but acknowledged that many others had long simply thought Randolph 'bloody awful all round'.[35] Randolph was arrogant, entitled, argumentative, a hard drinker and a womaniser, with a fierce temper. This was not necessarily the man you'd entrust with a sensitive diplomatic mission.

On one of Maclean's missions early in 1944, as he made his parachute jump, he carried with him a personal letter to Tito from Winston Churchill, 'securely buttoned' inside his tunic. Randolph Churchill was beside him as the two men jumped out of the low-flying plane. Tito, who had not been expecting the letter, broke into a 'broad smile of unaffected delight' on seeing the headed paper from 10 Downing Street and the prime minister's signature, a smile which became even broader when the Partisan leader opened a large signed photograph of the older Churchill.[36] There was no doubt that the mission to Tito mattered to Britain; sending the PM's son, as well as the letter and autograph of his father, conveyed the importance that the British government attached to it. There was also the risk of the mission going terribly wrong if Randolph were killed or captured in the process.

The Foreign Office and the PWE were very unhappy about Randolph Churchill claiming to represent them on this mission. A telegram from Ralph Murray in Cairo protested that the British representatives there, who oversaw activities in the Mediterranean, had not been consulted about the posting. Although Randolph Churchill was expected to be given some form of link to the PWE and propaganda work as cover, Murray was insistent. 'The officer should not (repeat not) in any circumstances represent himself as our officer or as sent into Yugoslavia for the purpose of the distribution of propaganda.'[37]

Randolph Churchill himself was clearly excited about his new role and had a strong sense of his own importance. He wanted to be seen to be delivering British propaganda directly to the Partisans on the ground. Being the prime minister's son, he could also appeal directly to the top when he felt that his importance wasn't being correctly recognised. He wrote to Brendan Bracken in the early spring from somewhere inside Yugoslavia, telling him 'we are all having great fun here' and that 'my job is to look after propaganda', both about Britain to the Partisans and vice versa. This wasn't just a kindly note from Tito's headquarters to a family friend to enquire about Bracken's and Winston's health. Randolph wanted Bracken to get him more propaganda materials and speed up the process on his behalf.

Churchill junior had already taken exception to Murray's telegram from Cairo – which he called 'snooty' – about his appointment. He complained that the PWE and the Ministry of Information were being slow to supply him with the long shopping list of materials he had asked to be sent to Yugoslavia. The list included fifty battery radio receivers able to pick up BBC broadcasts to Yugoslavia, fifty copies each of the main London weekly papers (including the *Spectator* and the *New Statesman*), cinema projectors, films, maps and pictures of the Royal Family. He didn't take much account of the difficulties in getting hold of some of this material even in London during wartime – photostatic copies of the magazines, he insisted, were not good enough – or of organising their delivery into Bosnia to reach their destination. He believed that the PWE were being deliberately obstructive, accusing them of having been on 'sit-down strike' for three and a half months and refusing to co-operate with him. From their point of view, it wasn't clear what use dozens of copies of old newspapers would be as British political warfare.

Soon, Randolph Churchill's frustration exploded into anger. When he landed in Bari for a three-day visit in May, he was met by the PWE's Colonel Anderson and someone he called a 'little man', who he assumed was one of Anderson's subordinates. He was dismayed to discover that the little man was Ralph Murray, who was both Anderson's boss and the author of the 'snooty' telegram of January. Murray was the person against whom the younger Churchill had been holding a grudge since his appointment. Even though the telegram came up in conversation, Murray carefully did not mention at this first meeting that he was the person who had sent it. Churchill just thought he was being frank when he raised the issue, writing in explanation that he always thought it better in 'disagreeable matters of this kind' to put his cards on the table, and said that he immediately 'taxed Murray with the matter and went so far as to upbraid him' for being 'shy and disingenuous' by not mentioning that he'd written the telegram.

This was not how Murray saw the meeting. It was difficult to write soberly of what had happened, Murray wrote in a letter for Bruce Lockhart's 'most confidential' information.[38] On the first evening, Churchill only inflicted a 'minor diatribe' on his PWE hosts, but the situation would get worse during his stay in Bari. On Sunday evening, Murray and Anderson invited Churchill to dinner with them in the PWB mess, together with their American colleagues. During the meal, Murray related, Churchill had been rude to his American neighbours and then, after they had eaten, began to 'pick a quarrel' with Murray himself – Murray said he was being conservative in that choice of expression, so the quarrel must quickly have become vicious. Churchill accused both the PWE generally and Murray personally of having lied to him and obstructed him.

The argument flared up so fast that Murray felt he had to leave the mess in embarrassment – to the 'unbounded embarrassment and disgust' of their American colleagues – and continue the row in private. Randolph Churchill didn't let up. On the contrary, he got worse. Murray found it impossible to explain anything to Churchill. Instead, 'for nearly two hours we were treated to a violent and insulting diatribe of such a degrading and shifty and horrible kind' that Murray declined to report all of it in detail to Bruce Lockhart. Churchill insulted Murray personally, in terms so 'foul and deliberate' that Murray wanted 'to hit him on a dozen occasions'. Churchill accused him, over those hours, of being 'a filthy, scheming, obstructive little careerist'. Even though he managed not to punch the prime minister's son, Murray wasn't going to accept this tirade much longer.

Reason and humour weren't working: Murray decided to 'stop the scene'. He shouted Randolph Churchill down with some difficulty and 'ordered him to shut up, telling him that we had listened to his nonsense for two hours and that now he could listen to me for ten minutes', and further telling Churchill 'a proportion' of what Murray thought of him. Churchill didn't accept anything that Murray had to say, including his word of honour, and in the end Murray left for bed, leaving an embarrassed and bewildered Anderson, along with a Yugoslav Major Ivanovic, 'a great friend of England', to deal with Randolph.

After the incident, Murray was left at a loss as to what to do about his unwelcome guest. He observed that Churchill's acquaintances treated this sort of behaviour lightly, but said personally he could not find any remedy – 'damned if I know what other than pistols for two and coffee for one, for he is too big for me to throw him personally down the stairs as his behaviour invited me to do!' Murray was not really likely to challenge the PM's son to a duel as he suggested, but it was a measure of his anger that he put the idea down in an official letter.

This incident was considered serious enough that the Secret Intelligence Service addressed a personal note to Bruce Lockhart to let him know about the conflict before Murray's letter was able to reach London. Murray had passed a message on to the SIS bureau in Cairo who in turn told their boss.[39] Despite the ructions he caused, Randolph would continue his erratic, argumentative and drunken behaviour over the summer.

While Randolph Churchill was causing trouble in Italy, the direction of British propaganda to Yugoslavia, even once it had been decided to support the Partisans, was still being disputed. Fitzroy Maclean, back in London, came to see his old friend Robert Bruce Lockhart at Bush House. Even though they were friends, Bruce Lockhart described Maclean as having more courage and guts in his long frame than brains. Maclean arrived at the PWE's offices in kilt battledress and spent an hour and a half examining their propaganda output, asking many questions and criticising the PWE operation in Cairo.

At the ministerial level, Anthony Eden was becoming concerned that British propaganda to Yugoslavia was too pro-Russian. Bruce Lockhart denied that any 'boosting' of Russia was going on, saying that how Russia was mentioned depended largely on the state of the war: 'when the Russian army advances, it makes propaganda for the Russians'. He assured the foreign secretary that 'the Balkan regions of both PWE London and PWE Cairo are more than eager to project Britain and British propaganda to the Balkans'.[40]

Vladimir Velebit, Tito's chief of staff, had come to London with Fitzroy Maclean. The pair were summoned from Algiers after a confusing phone call where Maclean didn't realise that he was supposed to be speaking in code and wondered why the prime minister kept referring to his son as 'Pippin'. The man Maclean had first encountered in the Bosnian mountains now looked 'more of an intellectual than a soldier'. During his meeting at Bush House with Bruce Lockhart and his colleagues, Velebit looked like the urbane Zagreb lawyer that he was in peacetime, 'dark, clean-shaven, well built but rather sleek with smooth, black glossy hair and with pince-nez'.[41] Although Velebit spoke good English, Eden had decided that he should not be allowed to broadcast on the BBC. The Partisans wanted to be able to produce more of their own propaganda, asking to use printing facilities in Italy to produce their own newspapers and leaflets. Bruce Lockhart realised that this was extremely unlikely ever to happen – Britain would not allow Tito uncontrolled access to produce communist propaganda from outside the country.

Bruce Lockhart drove through the West End with Velebit, escorting him to lunch at Grosvenor House. On the way, the two men were able to talk in confidence. Velebit tried to persuade Bruce Lockhart that, while Tito and his leadership were communist, he stood for Yugoslavia as a whole and did not want to be solely reliant on the Russians. Rather, Velebit said that Tito 'wished to hold the bridge between East and West and in this manner to retain Yugoslav independence'.

Bruce Lockhart found the Yugoslav emissary nervous and sweaty during their talks, even though it wasn't hot for May; he felt that the visitor had been badly handled and not looked after enough by his other hosts. Rather than spending enough time with senior government figures, Bruce Lockhart thought Velebit was given too much access to journalists. Maclean, though, believed the visit had been a success, with Velebit invited to have a personal conversation with both the prime minister and Eisenhower.

Randolph Churchill narrowly escaped being killed twice during his missions to Yugoslavia. In late May, there was a German attack on Tito's headquarters. When Harold Macmillan heard the news, in Bari, he said: 'It appears that the attempt to capture [Tito] and Randolph – which would be the greater prize it would be difficult to say – failed by a hair's breadth.'[42] Randolph vented his frustration on Macmillan when the minister gave orders that Churchill should be taken out of Yugoslavia following this. Macmillan put up with an hour of an indignant Randolph in Sicily, observing that 'he has a certain charm, but his manners are dreadful, and his flow of talk insufferable. He always manages to have a row or make a scene wherever he goes.' Macmillan obviously couldn't have allowed the prime minister's son to remain in imminent danger. He seemed more aware of the risks, writing: 'Of course I did not want him captured and perhaps tortured by the Germans, partly for the PM's sake and partly because he knew too much – including perhaps the date of the Second Front in France.'[43]

When he was allowed to go back to the country in July, he was nearly killed again, this time in a plane crash. Evelyn Waugh, who had just finished writing *Brideshead Revisited*, was travelling with him. The two men had already spent the last few days getting drunk, Waugh waking one morning on Randolph's bathroom floor in Bari. Waugh took an instant dislike to Fitzroy Maclean, calling him 'dour, unprincipled, ambitious, probably very wicked', with a shaved head and 'devil's ears'. Waugh and Churchill took off from Bari on a Sunday evening, in a heavily laden plane. Waugh did not remember the moment of the crash, but came to 'walking in a cornfield by the light of the burning aeroplane', somewhere in Croatia, clearly in shock. He found Randolph Churchill when they were both being treated in a hut, the latter 'in tears because his servant had been killed,' having gone lame in both legs and 'shouting for morphia'.[44] Randolph Churchill was a typically difficult patient, spending his time in a Bari hospital 'drinking, attacking the night nurse, wanting everyone's medicine'. Once recovered and returning to Yugoslavia, he continued to drink and cause arguments for the next several months, more of a liability than an asset to Britain.

No matter the effort that went into the best-laid plans for propaganda as the war's pace accelerated, accident and human frailty still played their part. Even the most brilliant and dedicated of the team could be waylaid by circumstances beyond their control.

PART 4

There Shall Be No Night

17

Near to Death's Door

Not long after returning to Algiers in October 1943, Dick Crossman was stung by a wasp. As occupational hazards went in the Mediterranean war, this might not have seemed the most immediately dangerous. However, the wasp sting caused a severe inflammation in his leg and turned into phlebitis – a swollen vein. Tom Delmer, with his habitual taste for drama, described a 'ferocious wasp sting' and the phlebitis creeping up Crossman's leg and threatening his heart. For once, this wasn't a complete exaggeration. Crossman was at first in an Algiers hospital, his leg elevated to try to reduce the swelling, but he didn't improve, and was evacuated by air to London.

There, Crossman was confined to a nursing home on Bentinck Street, near Harley Street, and for a while his condition grew even worse: he was 'relatively near to death's door for three weeks, with embolism in both lungs'.[1] For seven weeks, he was hoisted up on his hospital bed, immobile, with his infected leg raised in the air and his torso bolt upright because of the clots in his lungs. He described himself as 'suspended in a remarkable position in which my bottom seemed to be the only thing on the bed'.[2]

In the absence of blood-thinning drugs, the main treatment for an inflammation like Crossman's was lying still. Warfarin, which was first developed as a rat poison, wasn't licensed for use in humans until 1954 and Eisenhower was one of the most prominent early patients to be treated with it. Modern patients would be encouraged to move rather than being held immobile.

After three months of enforced stillness, Crossman was finally given the go-ahead to move in the middle of January 1944. Until then, he had not been allowed to shave, to turn over on his side or to move his arms above the elbow. At first, he was only permitted to dangle his legs over the edge of his bed for ten minutes at a time, gradually building up the time spent sitting up until he was eventually allowed to 'fall out of bed into an armchair', at which point, he wrote, he realised that 'my natural equilibrium, after three months, was horizontal, not vertical'.[3]

Although he had been reduced to contemplating both the back of the Welbeck Hotel in Marylebone from his window and his own navel, with a 'mixture of boredom and pleasure',[4] it would have been unlike Crossman, even in extremis, to be mentally idle. He had spent seven to eight hours a day reading, taken French conversation lessons every day for six weeks and 'done' the French Revolution, including studying books on Robespierre. He had only been allowed two visitors a day, for half an hour each. Among the early visitors was Hugh Dalton, who came to see his former protege in the new year and somehow managed to stay at his bedside for two hours, 'during nearly the whole of which,' Dalton wrote, 'he harangued me with great vigour both of voice and mind'. Dalton was as ambivalent as ever about Crossman, observing that he was a dynamic but 'not very lovable' character.[5]

Once Crossman was finally able to send letters – not yet writing them himself, but dictating – the ideas and policy suggestions poured out of him. If, as he said, the doctors were only allowing him to do 'just a very little work every day – provided I don't get the least excited', they must have become as frustrated as those who worked alongside Crossman so often were. He had been kept 'closely informed' about all the latest developments in his absence at both the PWE and the American Office of War Information, while also making a close study both of the BBC Home Service radio and Delmer's black medium wave transmissions, which he seemed to enjoy despite his misgivings about black propaganda, calling them 'the most Rabelaisian entertainment put on in this war, overflowing with high spirits'. When Delmer came to visit, he found Crossman surprisingly enthusiastic about his latest radio efforts (full of 'charm and enthusiasm') and praising the new slick sound of Soldatensender Calais.

Soldatensender Calais was an expansion of Delmer's Atlantiksender. From late October 1943, it had broadcast on both medium wave and short wave, giving it a greater reach into western Europe and Germany itself. Its programmes started with a 'crash of drums and a blare of trumpets', playing a 'jubilantly boisterous German march'. More German soldiers and civilians could now hear Delmer's patent combination of fake news and snappy dance music. He had been allowed to broadcast via the Aspidistra transmitter in the evenings for the first time in November. The 'Calais' part of the name had been carefully chosen as part of British deception tactics ahead of the planned invasion: they wanted the Germans to believe that Calais was the key place to focus their defences.[6]

If the doctors probably didn't approve of all Crossman's activity, Robert Bruce Lockhart certainly didn't either. Bruce Lockhart – himself on sick leave in a nursing home in Edinburgh – had heard that Crossman had been 'behaving very foolishly' while he was unwell. Even before he was given the all-clear to write letters, he had nonetheless managed to dictate an article for his former employer, the *New Statesman*, 'at the most critical moment of his illness'. This kind of behaviour was intolerable, Bruce Lockhart fumed. 'Here is this young man who is very well paid by us, and, in addition, is having his nursing-home expenses paid by us, using the information which he receives in his official capacity to feed the *New Statesman*, a journal which almost weekly criticises the Foreign Office and which openly advocates a peace with "the good Germans".[7] Bruce Lockhart believed with some justification, that Crossman, after his time in Algeria, was 'intriguing' with his American colleagues.

The first article that Crossman had written for the *New Statesman* from his sickbed was not all that controversial – it didn't deal directly with policy or with Germany – but it was critical of the BBC. 'After being concerned for some three years with radio programmes I have been suddenly compelled by a serious illness to become a genuine radio listener,' Crossman had written. In his experience, he found that listeners could be divided into two species: those who were listening intently and those who were just using the radio as background noise. The BBC, Crossman believed, performed the functions of both 'an orchestra in a Lyons' popular cafe, and of a serious transmitter of ideas'. He had wondered, from his bed, why the BBC was devoting about half of its output to the 'background noise' type of programming. The closest he came to mentioning what his wartime work involved was where he referred to the role of propaganda, writing that background music was 'the perfect sugar for the pill of commercial or political propaganda, as the Germans discovered in the Mediterranean when they put on a programme for British and American troops consisting for the most part of light music and with a very few propaganda news items interspersed'.[8] It would have taken a very assiduous reader of the article to realise why Crossman would have known so much about this. In a second article, a week later, he elaborated on his theme, writing of his ten weeks spent listening alone in his bedroom, where he had enjoyed programmes from *Alice in Wonderland* to Betjeman talking about second-hand bookshops, to *Appointment with Fear*. Here, he went further and suggested that foreign audiences were better served than home ones: 'while Europe and the Empire are mentally stimulated by the BBC, such education and enter-tainment are not provided for the home audience.'[9] Foreign broadcasts, he suggested, were also technically more innova-tive than their domestic counterparts.

Bruce Lockhart's frustration, in this case, wasn't because Crossman was causing him more political problems – except perhaps with the BBC – but because of his disregard for the rules. Crossman was certainly, as far as his illness allowed, trying to keep in touch with his colleagues and planning what his involvement in the coming stage of the campaign might be. He was sharing his ideas about how propaganda could be made more effective come the invasion of western Europe and, looking even further ahead, to domestic politics after the end of the war. Although to his colleagues he was physically 'a shadow of the burly Dick we knew', he was itching to get back to work.[10]

Harold Macmillan wrote Crossman a generous letter, saying it was a 'great grief' to him that Crossman would be unlikely to return to the Mediterranean for the rest of the war. He hoped that 'the friendship we have formed may be taken up at a later date' and that they might work together in a peacetime which he expected would be 'more confused and difficult even than the war'.[11]

A letter from Roger Makins, another of the Algiers team, arrived full of political gossip. Crossman already seemed to have his future work lined up, so in this, Bruce Lockhart was right to suggest that Crossman had been 'intriguing' with his American colleagues. Makins wrote that he was 'glad to hear the wellknown [sic] firm of Jackson and Crossman has been booked for the European theatre of operations'[12] – that is to say, that Crossman and C.D. Jackson would be working together again. Crossman planned to work with both Jackson and General McClure, his Algiers partners, in London.

It is clear that Crossman and Jackson got on very well on a personal level. As Crossman wrote to Macmillan, a visit from

Jackson helped revive him when he was suffering a relapse of his illness, breaking through a ring of nurses and doctors to cure him with 'sheer high spirits'. Jackson, Crossman said, 'likes life and he likes people; and he makes you realise how rare men are who like life and people so much'.[13]

Crossman and Jackson were thinking ahead to the imminent invasion of France. This was, of course, the event that would preoccupy everyone involved in military strategy or propaganda. Isolated and immobile in his nursing home bed, anxious to get back to work, Crossman had begun to flesh out his ideas. 'Crossman's Big Idea', as he called it himself in his letter to Jackson, was to find an answer to a key problem of psychological warfare ahead of the Second Front: 'How can you create the Tunis psychosis among the German soldiers in the Atlantic Wall?'[14]

What he meant by the 'Tunis psychosis' was this. Only once in the war up to this point, Crossman argued, had the Germans surrendered en masse when they had ammunition to continue and their morale was otherwise high. That was at Tunis. His answer to the question of why German troops had chosen to surrender was that they had felt that 'honour was satisfied', that they had 'done their bit' and that no soldier now needed to fight on. In a situation where their leaders' plans had failed, the enemy might come to believe that it was no longer the fault of the troops on the ground.

Crossman thought you could not hope to create the conditions for a potential surrender before the beginning of Allied operations in western France. As he wrote to the diplomat Frank Roberts, 'we may not be able to soften up the Germans <u>before</u> the landing, but we may be able to make them crack <u>after</u> the landing'.

However, he believed that a 'sudden surrender psychosis' could be caused once an 'indisputable bridgehead' had been made on the Atlantic coast and the wall of German defences breached. The German forces had to be led to believe at first that the wall was impregnable – but then, once it had been broken through, that further resistance was hopeless.

Crossman elaborated on this idea in a long letter to Frank Roberts at the Foreign Office. Breaking down German morale and resistance could be helped along by a well-timed message from Eisenhower and Montgomery to the serving German soldiers on the front lines. 'A simple talk from soldier to soldier' was the message Crossman thought would have the greatest effect. He thought it would be dangerous to change the commitment to unconditional surrender – what was needed was 'a simple explanation for the simple man' of what it meant. As in Sicily, timing was everything. In Crossman's view, the joint declaration from Roosevelt and Churchill in Italy had come too late to be effective. He proposed that Eisenhower should make a statement four to five weeks before the landings, and Montgomery once he had established a bridgehead and 'when he has Rommel on the run'. Crossman volunteered his services to draft Monty's text.[15]

As soon as he was well enough, Crossman's aim was to get back to the war in Europe. The preparations for D-Day had been gaining pace during the early part of 1944, after the rows between Churchill, Roosevelt and Stalin at Tehran the previous autumn about where and when the main thrust of the invasion should take place. Operation Overlord, the assault on western France, was planned for the early summer. The PWE was under greater pressure than ever before. They had more propaganda to produce and, as usual, political battles to contend with. After more than four years of war, the stress on the propagandists was beginning to tell.

Robert Bruce Lockhart had to weigh up whether his own health had sufficiently improved for the coming operation. 'Strain was getting many people in their weak spot,' Churchill's doctor, Lord Moran, told him. For Bruce Lockhart, that weak spot had long been his skin. In the spring of 1943, he had spent two months in an Edinburgh nursing home with eczema and psoriasis. In October 1943, after the Italian invasion, he was so ill, his legs and arms badly swollen and his face disfigured, that he was prescribed two months' bed rest back in Edinburgh starting straight away. Arriving at the nursing home, he was 'immediately swathed from head to foot in bandages'.

Bruce Lockhart wrote – or more likely dictated – a letter to Max Beaverbrook, who a few months earlier had given him a thousand pounds as an unsolicited gift to contribute towards his medical bills and help his recovery. As well as the bandages, he told Beaverbrook he was in much pain and discomfort, enduring 'being smeared in oily pastes which ruin everything: sheets, pyjamas, pillows and counterpanes. So I am at present not fit for human society and am helpless without a nurse.'[16] He was allowed out twice a week for X-ray treatment. The attempts at a cure included Bruce Lockhart being soaked in silver nitrate and given morphia for the pain.

Like Crossman in his London sickbed, Bruce Lockhart was confined, listening to his own propaganda via the radio with no influence over it. He had little but get-well-soon telegrams from Brendan Bracken and Anthony Eden to console him. Bruce Lockhart, less exuberantly resilient than Crossman, drifted into one of his bouts of depression, feeling that 'the darkness entered into my soul'. His doctor told him not to think or talk of the war, but the doctor was of course 'asking the impossible'.[17] Like Crossman, Bruce Lockhart got worse before he got better.

By December, he had been moved to the Edinburgh Royal Infirmary under the care of specialists, with an even more severe regime. After six weeks being treated with applications of crude tar, his skin had improved enough for him to be allowed to return to London. His doctors warned him that unless he led a more regular life with plenty of fresh air, he risked breaking down again. Bruce Lockhart confided in a friend, over lunch at the Ivy, that his moral dilemma was carrying on at the PWE and run the serious risk of his health collapsing just before D-Day, or quitting for a quieter job and thereby leaving his colleagues in the lurch.[18] He was soon back into his routine of regular lunches and dinners with friends, so it seemed unlikely he was prepared to live a quiet and regular life. Having consulted Lord Moran, Churchill's doctor, a man who knew all too well the precarious state of health of the country's leadership, he was encouraged to stay.

Bruce Lockhart's ministerial bosses were solicitous: Brendan Bracken said he would find Bruce Lockhart a house in the country, paid for by the department, and a car; Eden said he should 'walk and not run'. Hugh Dalton offered him extra ration coupons to help his recovery. Eden and Bracken did consider offering Bruce Lockhart a less strenuous post, perhaps as ambassador to the Czech government-in-exile, but Bruce Lockhart took the gamble of staying on in his current job. He found an 'old-world cottage' near Radlett in Hertford-shire, halfway between Bush House and Woburn.[19]

Bracken himself had been unwell over the last few months and when the two men met, he looked pale and was drinking tea rather than whisky. Bracken had been taking periods of absence from work since the end of 1943 and pleading illness, sometimes sinusitis, spending time at a house in Hampshire. As was typical of Bracken, he explained little and was unlikely to tell anyone the truth about what was really wrong with him, so rumours inevitably spread. In January 1944, Cyril Radcliffe, the most senior civil servant at the Ministry of Information, wrote that Bracken was 'not yet at his cool old best mentally', though he did not know what was really the matter.[20] Some said later in the year that he had a bad heart and was back to drinking too much to cope with stress. He does seem to have had some sort of procedure in the spring of 1944: Randolph Churchill hoped in March that Bracken was fully recovered from his operation.[21] Bracken had sent Bruce Lockhart, a fellow whisky-lover, a jokey telegram during his miserable

Scottish convalescence that the PWE head should just 'open the distillery and stay till July 1st'.[22] Eden, however, appeared to Bruce Lockhart to be thriving and fitter than ever, causing Bruce Lockhart to observe 'good health plus a fair brain will beat the best brain plus bad health'. This appearance, though, was deceptive; Eden too had been instructed by Churchill to take time off for the sake of his health and would spend the month of April on leave.[23]

When Bruce Lockhart returned to work, there was a pile of problems for him to deal with. In March 1944, he declared himself 'beset with difficulties' in trying to make the relationship with the Americans work effectively. The American Psychological Warfare Branch had set up a base in London as well as Algiers in preparation for D-Day. Invited to lunch with Eisenhower's chief of staff General Bedell Smith at the US HQ in Bushy Park, to the west of London, Bruce Lockhart was overwhelmed by the generosity of the American rations. He was treated to an indulgent lunch that began with a Martini with 'real vermouth and a real olive', followed with a pre-war size 'juicy tender beefsteak' and an apple pie with fresh cheese. The more abstemious general just had soup and a sandwich, as he was watching his figure.[24] The problem for the PWE was that once the Americans were established in London on near-equal terms, it was far harder for the British PWE team to have authority over all propaganda. As the military operation that would determine the end of the war approached, it was vital that propaganda was more closely co-ordinated than ever, but the PWE was resistant to giving up the role it had fought to create.

Crossman's behaviour particularly vexed him. According to Bruce Lockhart, Crossman, not long recovered, was already 'power-mad' and 'working on buccaneer lines'. Ever ambitious, he realised where power now lay. He liked the possibility of getting things done more quickly – and his Algiers experience made him aware that accepting the primacy of the military was the best way to do this. Bruce Lockhart was more wedded to the previous way of doing things. He saw Crossman as purely out for his own self-interest – the younger man wanted to grab power and pursued the interests of the American PWB 'because wherever his job is or he is himself becomes automatically the centre of the world'.[25] Despite some good personal relationships, the Americans had never been very keen on Bruce Lockhart, seeing him as a man from a bygone age, and his illness and absence had probably reinforced the sense that he was no longer effectively in control of the organisation. He and General Bedell Smith agreed, however, on a system whereby the PWE would set the policy guidance and the American operation, now rebranded PWD – the Psychological Warfare Division – would follow it. Bedell Smith promised that his door was always open and Bruce Lockhart only had to walk through it if he found any problems. The relationship was set on a more official footing with regular tripartite meetings that Bruce Lockhart would chair. He thought that although it wasn't a perfect system – with some differences of views between the military and the politicos – it generally worked well.

The combination of stress and secrecy had unexpected and sometimes drastic consequences. Peter Ritchie Calder, the director of plans for the PWE, who often deputised for Bruce Lockhart in his absence, was under even more pressure than normal at the beginning of 1944. His wife had just given birth to their fourth child when the family home was destroyed in an air raid in February. They moved out of London to a house in Woburn Sands. Ritchie Calder continued to work intensely on the D-Day preparations, but a week after the landings, he collapsed in Euston Square. Just a couple of weeks short of his thirty-eighth birthday, he had suffered a brain haemorrhage. He was lucky to survive: the first person who had found him on the ground was a doctor who was able to get him taken on a weapon carrier to University College Hospital, very close by, where he was treated successfully by a brain surgeon who happened to be on duty. It took a while for Ritchie Calder's family to be told, as all his papers had been marked 'Top Secret' and it was hard to find out where he had been supposed to be going. In a strange coincidence, one of the first people he met on the hospital ward was a woman 'pouring out a sinister liquid into a medicine glass'. She was Agatha Christie, who was working there as a pharmacist during wartime. They knew each other; as a journalist, Ritchie Calder had reported on Christie's mysterious disappearance in the 1920s. After his recovery, the doctor told Ritchie Calder that the kind of haemorrhage he had suffered was usually down to a physical blow to the head. His response was that he 'had been battering my head against a brick wall in the Foreign Office and something had to give and it *wasn't* the brick wall'.[26]

At Woburn too, the build-up to D-Day was putting the teams producing leaflets and black propaganda under huge strain. They were preparing the biggest and most sophisticated leaflet operation yet ahead of the landings. *Nachrichten für die Truppe* (News for the Troops) was more than a leaflet – it was a full daily newspaper for German soldiers in France. Delmer called it a 'dirty off-white' work of propaganda rather than strictly black. The news in it was largely true, though slanted. In May 1944, for instance, it told its readers that 2,000 aircraft had attacked Berlin and Brandenburg, that Germany lacked fighter planes, that thousands of Germans had been taken prisoner in Italy, and that three U-boats had been sunk and another missing.

Delmer's overriding idea was to emphasise the importance of the eastern front for the German leadership, thereby leading the soldiers in the west to believe they were being neglected and given fewer supplies. The German forces reading the newspaper might well have realised that it was not being produced by their own side, but this mattered less to the propagandists now – what they wanted to do was to give the troops more information about the war than they were able to get from their own leaders.

But getting a daily newspaper written and printed in German to be dropped over France was a challenging operation. The deadlines were tight and the team was small. Preparation for the paper began in March and production started on 25 April 1944, around six weeks ahead of D-Day. A million copies of the paper were printed every day. British and American journalists worked together in a prefabricated hut in the grounds of the Milton Bryan studios. The broadsheet paper was printed in Luton and sent to be loaded onto planes. New American technology, the 'leaflet bomb', allowed more of the copies to reach their intended targets. The leaflets were sealed inside a five-foot-long wax cylinder which was released by means of a fuse and dropped at far lower altitude. The papers would scatter over a smaller area, closer to those who might pick them up and read them.

To get the paper ready in time meant working nights as well as days. People in Woburn, Isabel Delmer said, were putting in fantastically long hours and four hours of sleep was normal. She had been moved to work on the production of the *Nachrichten*, finding herself working overnight and catching around two hours of sleep during the day. She was taught how to do a newspaper layout by an American who she said hadn't had any sleep at all for a week. Many of her colleagues were old Fleet Street or New York newspaper hands who were used to this kind of work, but she was picking it up from scratch. Only once, she said, did she make an obvious mistake, putting a picture in the paper upside down.

The intensity of the work as D-Day approached put the Delmers' marriage under even more pressure. By the time of the landings, they had separated. The couple's versions of exactly what happened, though, were quite different. In Tom's published account, he made out that it was purely the demands of his work that drove them apart. They both agreed that he would be regularly woken in the middle of the night to check over the proofs of the *Nachrichten* before it went to print. Isabel said that he was roused every hour to check some information or other. He gave his description the air of a fantasy, describing the 'blonde angel' of a despatch rider who would appear at his bedside at three in the morning, in high boots and a leather corset, to deliver the proofs for his approval.[27]

This apparition, he claimed, drove Isabel away. 'That was the beginning of the end of my first marriage,' he wrote. Isabel was far clearer that the marriage had been ending for a long time – albeit in an account not for public consumption. Her affair with John Rayner had continued and she was planning to leave Tom. It was a horribly painful process, Isabel confessed. She left The Rookery in Aspley Guise to live at Rayner's flat in Palace Gate, in South Kensington, though Rayner himself was not there. He was working for the PWE in Italy and his wife, Joan, was in Cairo. Isabel knew that when she left Woburn, she had also left her husband. She didn't immediately intend to marry anyone else – John, after all, was still married, and Isabel knew that he had no intention of marrying her. Joan, though, wrote to tell Isabel, her old friend from Paris days, that she should not feel guilty about the affair and insisting that their friendship would continue.

Isabel took a new job. She was still working on propaganda, but now as a picture editor on an Italian magazine called *Il Mondo Libero* (The Free World). She felt 'nearly crushed under a weight of misery,' but her work sustained her. 'I was so desperately unhappy that if it had not been for my gentle work at Bush House I do not know what I would have done'. Isabel felt that she had to leave because she could not face Tom's way of life for the indefinite future. She also believed that the imminent divorce aged her by ten years. When she bumped into him outside Bush House, he was cruel about her appearance, blaming it not on their problems but on her work. 'You look awful, I don't want to be married to an old woman. A magazine isn't worth it.'

Even though the *Nachrichten für die Truppe* could be dropped more accurately than previous leaflets, there were still problems with delivering some of the other propaganda that was being sent out. Despite Delmer's assurances that he wasn't going to continue to produce the kind of pornographic material that had so outraged Sir Stafford Cripps, some similarly offensive leaflets nearly caused another scandal. Crossman told Brendan Bracken's biographer, Andrew Doyle, that the black propaganda team had designed luridly illustrated leaflets to be dropped over the border between France and Spain, where German troops were both far from the action and believed to be susceptible to the porn. The leaflets, unusually for this stage in the war, were to be dropped by balloon. As with all balloon leaflet drops, they were at the mercies of the winds. This time the winds were not co-operating. 'A freak storm blew up unexpectedly,' in Crossman's telling of the story, and some of the balloons headed not to the Pyrenees but back towards England.

One balloon fell to earth on a golf course in Haslemere, where a Surrey golfer was gravely affronted by what he found while hunting for a lost ball in the rough. At least, that's what the golfer apparently said. He complained to authorities and somehow word of this reached both Stafford Cripps and a new MP, J.B. Hynd. Hynd, elected for Sheffield at a by-election in February 1944, intended to 'create a tremendous fuss'.

This time it was Bracken who stepped in to defuse the situation. Although the minister told Crossman that he didn't hold out much hope of changing Hynd's view, he summoned the MP for a meeting. Bracken reportedly told Hynd that 'as a man of the world who claims to understand the German mentality, you shouldn't be surprised at the lengths to which

Goebbels will go. You're playing into Goebbels' hands at this moment.' Bracken blamed the Germans for sending the balloons and the obnoxious leaflets in order to create division among those working on British propaganda. Hynd was prepared to believe this unlikely tale that Bracken had concocted on the spur of the moment, bringing all of his personal skills in manipulating the truth and his listeners to bear. Hynd didn't raise the issue and the matter ended there, apart from a slight repeated warning to the propagandists not to overreach themselves yet again.[28]

18

The Peccant Document

In the weeks before D-Day, the printing presses and the recording studios of the PWE were busier than they had ever been as they planned for the propaganda to accompany the landings. Colonel Britton, the BBC's voice of the V Campaign, last heard on air in 1942, was revived for this phase of the war as the 'master voice' of Allied broadcasting. He was the voice of a new series, *The Voice of SHAEF* – the Supreme Headquarters, Allied Expeditionary Force – to provide a direct link between Eisenhower and the civilian populations of Europe, particularly around the northern and western European coasts. Douglas Ritchie, the BBC editor, was at the microphone again, this time as an anonymous member of Eisenhower's staff, but whose voice might still be familiar.[1] The broadcasts were to be transmitted in five languages, partly so the enemy would not know where to expect the landings: in English, Danish, Dutch, French and Flemish.[2]

Preparing the leaflets with messages from the Allied leaders was crucial and sensitive. Four days ahead of the landings, printing presses were surrounded by security while the leaflets were being printed. Eisenhower's words and those of his fellow leaders were translated into all the languages of western Europe by special teams who were kept isolated in Woburn for a week in advance. The statements from the Allies were backed up with supportive messages from the national leaders in Norway, Belgium and the Netherlands. There were many more specific leaflets aimed at transport workers, troops and other groups in the landing zones. Some were targeted at German soldiers, others at Polish reinforcements in the German Army. German soldiers near the French coast were told that they had been attacked from the front and written off from behind: they were only 'human mines' to their own high command, who were prepared to sacrifice them in the face of the invasion. They were told to note that no new German planes to defend them were replacing the ones that were shot down.[3]

The plans were liable to change at the last minute: the divisional commanders decided they wanted specific leaflets encouraging the Germans to surrender – much as Crossman had suggested earlier in the year. The PWE had been prepared for this and were able to draw up these leaflets at short notice, dropping a million and a half of them in the days following the invasion. In total, 34 million leaflets were dropped over Europe around D-Day.

The leaflet with Eisenhower's message to the French people said – in large block capitals on one side – that the Allied Armies were landing. On the other, he appealed for calm and discipline as the landings took place. Anyone who was already in the Resistance was told to obey the instructions they had been given; anyone who wasn't should not endanger their lives unnecessarily but wait for a further signal. Eisenhower praised the French troops who would fight alongside him, but warned that there could still be losses to come. But he concluded on an uplifting note: 'Together, we will overcome.'[4]

The imminence of the landings, though, did not mean there was political unity around this explosion of propaganda. After Bruce Lockhart returned to work in April 1944, he soon found that Bracken, initially solicitous of his ailments, was in a bad temper again. This might well have been due to political gossip circulating about Churchill's poor health and his prospects at a future election. Over a lunch, Bruce Lockhart had found the conversation dominated by discussion of how

RAF aircraft being loaded with propaganda leaflets, June 1944

Churchill's broadcasts were fading in power, his voice feeble and his appearance tired. One Liberal MP told him that the public would question the prime minister's future as a man approaching seventy who had suffered from pneumonia twice in a year. Bracken, the lunch gossips opined, was 'ruined by his slavish subjection to the PM'. If Churchill's star was fading, Bracken, the man who had hitched himself to it, was likely to fade too. Bracken's tetchiness was directed most often at one of Churchill's possible successors, Anthony Eden.

Eden, in turn, was directing criticism against the PWE for 'boosting' Russia in British propaganda, telling them they should instead be 'projecting Britain'. Bruce Lockhart suspected that Eden was responding to the worries of the Conservative Party ahead of a post-war election and that this was about winning popularity among his fellow Tories, given the questions over Churchill's future.[5]

But in a secret and personal letter to Bracken, Bruce Lockhart said how important it was to the PWE that they stayed close to the Foreign Office. He could not afford to diverge from Foreign Office control. 'We are a secret department,' he wrote. 'We come under the Foreign Office secret vote and we have Foreign Office cover.' In order for the PWE to be able to do its job, Bruce Lockhart believed he needed to be able to see the most secret of political and military intelligence – only closeness to the Foreign Office would allow this. He told Bracken that 'political warfare is the handmaid of foreign policy and military strategy'.[6] He warned that any change at this point in the war would be dangerous. The rumbling rows between Bracken and Eden would continue even as D-Day approached, but they were not the only conflicts within government.

Once more at this key moment in the war, a script with Richard Crossman's fingerprints on it caused trouble and arguments at the top of government. 'Crossman, as usual, is the storm centre,' Bruce Lockhart wrote.[7] The script in question was a message that was addressed to the German population, written on 9 May 1944, billed as the first in a series to be broadcast over British and American radio to Germany by a spokesman for the supreme commander, Eisenhower. The proposed broadcast began with what it called the most difficult and the most urgent question facing its listeners. 'Most of you have begun to wonder what will happen to Germany – and to each one of you and his family – when Germany is defeated.' The tone was familiar and colloquial, playing on the doubts and the fears of Germans at the front or at home. It imagined the German listener saying to themselves 'Defeat – that's the end of Germany and for us Germans'. It then set about trying to change their minds.

Both in style and in content, it was a very Crossman piece of work. It was immediate and chatty, but also conveyed an idea of Germany – and the distinction between the German regime and its people – that Crossman had maintained since before the war. For those who identified Germany with the present system, he argued that 'if you can only see your own personal future as a soldier in a huge German army, or a worker in a vast German Reich', defeat would be the end. But for the 'millions of soldiers who do not give orders but obey them, who do not plan wars but fight them', the little man and his wife and family, things could be different. The voice of the spokesman suggested that the '99 per cent of Germans who obey orders will continue to obey orders – but from a different Leadership'. Occupation was coming and it would be harsh, but it was better than the chaos that the country was already slipping into. The occupying armies would keep order and restore justice.[8]

This was a controversial script for several of the reasons which, by then, must have been familiar to Crossman. Firstly, it made a distinction between the good and the bad Germans, those who gave the orders and those who merely followed them. One Germany could be removed for a new, occupied Germany to take its place. Secondly, this script crossed into the same territory that the Bomber Harris broadcast had encroached on earlier in the war. This was a lesson that Crossman might have been expected to learn, since the previous episode nearly cost him his job. The broadcast would have been a statement from not just a serving soldier but the Allies' most senior commander, and he would have been talking not just about military decisions but about Germany's political future. A final point, made by Anthony Eden when he submitted the script for discussion at the War Cabinet, was that the broadcast was overstepping in what it promised. The nature of the future occupation was yet to be decided among the Allies and was dependent, in particular, on how the Soviet Union would behave. Eden had marked up the draft script with suggested cuts so that it wouldn't prejudge the outcome of the talks the Allies were still having. That was assuming, of course, that they were able to reach any agreement at all with Stalin on how Germany should be occupied.

It wasn't surprising, then, that when Eden put the paper to the War Cabinet, even with his caveats, it was rejected. On 31 May, the Cabinet meeting concluded that 'the War Cabinet were opposed to the proposed broadcast, which, moreover, dealt with matters which were more suitable to be dealt with by Governments'.[9] Eden, however, had suggested that it should be the Foreign Office who vetted other potential broadcasts for similar problems, and this caused Brendan Bracken to fly off the handle.[10]

Bruce Lockhart returned from a week's leave at Sedbergh, where he had been hoping to see off a recurrence of his skin problems, to find Bracken greeting him with a 'violent tirade' against the Foreign Office on the day the Cabinet was meeting. The argument over the broadcast had turned into a skirmish between the Foreign Office and the Ministry of Information. Eden and Bracken, having been hostile to one another during the whole of May, were now bringing their disagreements out into the open. Just as he had during those earlier war years between Bracken and Dalton, Bruce Lockhart shuttled between the two men, hoping to resolve the dispute.

Bracken told Bruce Lockhart that he wanted to raise the issue in Cabinet and to get full control of the PWE, since the Foreign Office seemed incapable of exercising it. In the afternoon, Bruce Lockhart met Eden and told him what had happened with Bracken. Eden, too, was initially furious. Bracken's behaviour, he said, had been 'intolerable for some time past'. Bracken had written Eden a 'very rude' letter that the foreign secretary was angry about. Bruce Lockhart tried to persuade Eden that on this occasion Bracken did have a point: the minister of information hadn't known about the paper on political warfare and broadcasting before the Cabinet meeting and had felt ambushed by the Foreign Office having information which he should have seen. Eden relented and climbed down, saying that he had been too busy.

The foreign secretary was prepared to apologise to Bruce Lockhart, but he still refused to do so to Bracken. With less than a week to go before the D-Day invasion was to be launched, two senior Cabinet ministers were in a standoff, neither willing to back down. Bracken phoned Bruce Lockhart again in the evening, somewhat calmer but likewise refusing to talk directly with Eden.

After the Cabinet meeting, Churchill wrote to Eisenhower saying that he could not agree to the draft script for a broadcast to the German people. The prime minister insisted that 'this is a matter which really must be dealt with by Governments, and cannot be made the subject of fireside talks'. Churchill told Eisenhower that there were 'a large number of reasons why it would be ineffective and look like begging before we have won the battle'. Importantly, Churchill disagreed with what Crossman – and, by extension, Eisenhower – proposed to tell the German people. Again, it was a fundamental question of whether Allied propaganda was being honest with the German public. The broadcast was not meant to be black propaganda – it was in an official voice – but Churchill thought it was misleading. 'I could also show that we are not telling the truth to those people,' he said. He also implied that Crossman's script was giving the Germans too positive a view of what would happen to them after the war. The script referred to what would happen under 'the partition of Germany' and discussions of 'how many millions' of the German male population might be sent to work in rehabilitating Russia, but said that those questions were 'quite unsettled'. Crossman's draft didn't directly mention what might happen to German men after the occupation, except that there would be 'stern, soldierly justice', with 'discipline and purpose', but the Russians were at the time keen on the idea of forcing Germans to work to rebuild the Soviet Union as war reparations. Churchill thought any reference to this would be counterproductive, writing that he had 'never read anything less suitable for the troops'.

Churchill wanted to impress on the American general how important this message was for the conduct of the war. 'This is not like issuing mere leaflets,' he said. 'It is a decision which involves your personal authority.'[11] Eisenhower replied swiftly, telling the prime minister that he had never seen any draft of the proposed radio broadcast script and that this had been done through the British PWE as part of 'comparatively low level planning'. In other words, this seemed to be Crossman freelancing again without superior authority. Eisenhower entirely agreed with Churchill that 'questions such as this are for decision on the highest political levels'.

It took all of Bruce Lockhart's diplomatic efforts to get Bracken and Eden back on speaking terms. Eden was more prepared to compromise, agreeing on 2 June to apologise to Bracken but still reluctant to relinquish control of political warfare. If he did this, he said, he would cease to be the foreign secretary. Bracken was still railing against the Foreign Office, calling it a rotten department and telling Bruce Lockhart that Eden was a nice fellow but a weak man who never knew what he wanted. Ever keen to pass on gossip that would harm a rival, Bracken said he'd heard from the chief whip that the Conservative Party didn't want Eden as a future prime minister at any cost. Even as D-Day approached, the politicians had an eye on the domestic political prize, rather than the war to be won. Eden appealed over Bracken's head to Churchill and made sure to get Bracken's rival discussion paper on political warfare pulled from Cabinet discussion.

On the eve of D-Day, Churchill fired off a minute to both Bracken and Eden which made it clear he was very displeased by the PWE acting on its own initiative. The issue needed to be taken hold of at once and brought under close control as the conflict to come was too important. 'General Eisenhower's attention cannot be distracted from the battle by having to read screeds of this kind,' he wrote, 'with the result that they go out in his name without ever having received scrutiny

by high British or American military or political authority.'
Churchill demanded to know who in the PWE was in charge
and whether they had seen the 'peccant document' – the
sinning draft – before it had been 'safely squelched'.[12] This
was a severe reprimand; Churchill was extremely unhappy
about how the PWE had handled the whole issue.

Even as the D-Day assaults were beginning, on 6 June,
Bracken sent his response to the prime minister. Bracken
reminded him of the history of the PWE and how it had
been created as a joint operation between the Ministry of
Information and the Foreign Office after the 'long struggle'
to merge the rival organisations. Although Bracken didn't say
so, this was a struggle that seemed to be playing itself out
all over again. The draft broadcast, Bracken explained, had
been written by the American team at SHAEF (though at
Crossman's instigation) and seen by the PWE as part of their
co-ordination with the Allies. But the PWE hadn't approved
it – the executive was 'very doubtful' about the draft. Bracken
himself thought that 'far from helping the Allies, it would
only make the Germans fight harder'.[13] He seemed, between
the lines, to be throwing the blame onto the Foreign Office,
since it was Eden who had put the draft script forward for
Cabinet discussion. The PWE, Bracken maintained, were
effectively controlling broadcasts that went out via the BBC.

This time, even though a radio script had gone as far as
a Cabinet meeting and the prime minister's desk, as well as
involving the supreme allied commander, it didn't, surprisingly, result in a call for Crossman to be fired. Probably the
main reason was that the future of one individual seemed so
much less important with the scale of the invasion that was
in the offing. The greater secrecy around Operation Overlord
meant that fewer people were aware of the discussions that
were going on and that this wasn't something that could be discussed by angry MPs in Parliament. The closed circle of those
who knew about the preparations was small and composed of

the main decision-makers: a decision could be reached with a word from the prime minister directly to Eisenhower. No-one seemed entirely happy about the outcome, but it played out as a fight for the role of government departments in the last phases of the war. In the hours before D-Day, everyone was on tenterhooks: both a literal and a political storm were blowing up.

19

The Sound of a Thousand Planes

The arrival of Charles de Gaulle in England from Algiers, wrote Robert Bruce Lockhart, would 'provoke a storm to which the Eden–Bracken squabble was a tea-cup affair'.[1] On 2 June, Churchill had sent a message to the general, asking him to come to Britain urgently and sending his own personal aircraft for the journey. De Gaulle had been invited a week earlier, but had been reluctant to accept, since he was mistrustful of the Americans' intentions for the liberation. The insistence from the prime minister that he should come 'at the earliest possible moment and in the deepest secrecy' prompted a change of heart. After a flight via Casablanca and Gibraltar, de Gaulle landed near London on the morning of 4 June.[2] A real storm was also brewing over the Channel: this was the same day that Eisenhower, on the advice of his meteorologist who had forecast bad weather, decided to postpone the D-Day landings by twenty-four hours.

De Gaulle was escorted to meet Churchill, who was based in a train carriage at Droxford, a dozen or so miles north of Portsmouth, in preparation for D-Day, before they had lunch with other British ministers. The train carriage, although nearer to the action, was an uncomfortable and inconvenient place to work. According to Eden, there was only one bath and one telephone, and 'Mr Churchill seemed to be always in the bath and General Ismay always on the telephone',[3] making it impossible to conduct any business there. Eden walked down the railway line with de Gaulle to meet Churchill, who was waiting on the track, his arms outstretched to greet the French leader. At first, things seemed to be going well and the discussions were friendly – although, as de Gaulle described it, he felt that at lunch Churchill was immediately ready to cross swords. The French leader had arrived at Portsmouth in 'a dudgeon as high as himself', as he was only finding out about the plans at the last minute.[4] The conversation took a turn for the worse when Churchill urged de Gaulle to go and meet President Roosevelt and plead his case for his future authority in France. The issue was that the Americans hadn't recognised de Gaulle's government-in-exile and so weren't planning to mention the Fighting French (the name for the Free French since 1942), the Resistance or de Gaulle himself in any of their communications about the invasion. De Gaulle was outraged, telling Churchill that he didn't have to apply to Roosevelt to hold power in France. 'The French government exists,' he insisted. He did not need permission to establish it from either the British or the Americans.[5]

Churchill retorted that de Gaulle was wrong if he thought that Britain would ever take a position that was distinct from that of the United States. He exclaimed, in words de Gaulle thought were meant more for his British company than his French, that 'if we have to choose between you and the open sea then we will choose the sea every time'. He continued, declaring that 'each time I have to choose between you and Roosevelt, I will always choose Roosevelt'. Eden and Ernest Bevin did not appear to agree with the prime minister, with Bevin telling de Gaulle, in a voice loud enough for everyone to hear, that this was just Churchill's view and not that of the British Cabinet.

De Gaulle then went on to meet Eisenhower, based in a prefab building in the New Forest. Eisenhower showed him the invasion plans, pinned on boards around his temporary HQ, and a typed document – a copy of the message that was due to be issued to western Europe. De Gaulle was not at all happy with this message either. He felt the tone of the message to France was different to that sent to the other occupied countries. Eisenhower addressed himself to the Norwegians, Dutch and others as a soldier, but to the French as a political leader. The French people were being told to follow his orders and that eventually they would get to choose their leadership. The leaflet said that 'when France is freed from her oppressors, you will choose for yourselves your representatives as well as the government under which you want to live'.[6] To de Gaulle, this was unacceptable, as he himself represented the French government. Eisenhower told the French leader that the text was only a draft, although this wasn't strictly true, as leaflets had already been printed bearing the message.

The row continued even after the leaders had returned to London. Churchill continued his rants against de Gaulle at Cabinet on the evening of 5 June, leading Sir Alec Cadogan of the Foreign Office to observe that the leaders were behaving like schoolgirls.

De Gaulle was told that he was due to speak last in a series of radio broadcasts that would include addresses from the king of Norway, the queen of the Netherlands and the Belgian prime minister. De Gaulle was due to broadcast after Eisenhower; he told Charles Peake of the Foreign Office that he wouldn't do it. Following the message from Eisenhower would imply that he accepted the Americans' dominant role in France and this was something he couldn't concede. In the early hours of the morning of D-Day, a succession of envoys was sent to de Gaulle to try to persuade him to change his mind. He ranted at his ambassador, Pierre Viénot, for an hour, telling him that Churchill was a gangster.[7]

Churchill was equally livid. Viénot was screamed at again, this time by the British prime minister.[8] Churchill even threatened to have de Gaulle sent back to Algiers in chains if necessary.[9] He dictated a letter which he wanted Charles Peake to take back to the French, telling de Gaulle that since he had refused to co-operate in 'this great venture to liberate your country', he would be forced to tell the House of Commons. Churchill's plane, which he had sent to fetch de Gaulle on his secret mission to Britain, was 'at your disposal now to take you back'.[10]

Fortunately, the angry letter never reached de Gaulle, though there are differing versions of how it was intercepted. Bruce Lockhart heard that Eden had persuaded Churchill not to send it; other accounts say that Eden even burned the letter.[11] A brief note to Eden the next day told him that the plane the prime minister had ordered put on standby to take de Gaulle back to Algiers had been stood down, though Churchill still wanted to be able to review the option of a plane every twenty-four hours. Eden wrote two exclamation marks in the margin next to this suggestion.[12]

The night of D-Day for the propaganda team was a strange mixture of tension and anticipation. At ten o'clock on the night of 5 June, the regional directors of the PWE at Bush House were finally told exactly what was about to happen. Bruce Lockhart, who had installed himself in a sixth-floor suite at the Savoy, a short walk away on the Strand, for the duration, said the mood at the briefing was one of 'emotional fever'. The propaganda team spent the next couple of days dependent on the whims of their political leaders and all their best-laid plans would hang on the results of those many angry conversations.

The late-night meeting over, Bruce Lockhart went back to the Savoy for a couple of whiskies with Dallas Brooks to wind down. For the first time that night, he intended to go back to his suite and get some sleep before the operation began. Instead, he was sent back to Bush House to attend to some more directives. All seemed to be in order, but Peter Ritchie Calder, who wasn't planning to sleep and was dealing with many phone calls, told him there was an ominous silence from de Gaulle.

The general was supposed to have sent a script for his own broadcast to be released alongside those of the other Allied leaders as the assault began in the morning. No script had arrived. Bruce Lockhart called Eden to check what was going on and was told that de Gaulle was being difficult. While he waited for more news, Bruce Lockhart decided not to go back to bed. Instead, he crossed the Aldwych to Inveresk House, where the American Office for War Information was based, to join his American colleagues, among them Robert Sherwood. Sherwood, both propagandist and playwright, had one of his plays running at the Aldwych Theatre, further along the street where they met, called *There Shall Be No Night*. The pair joked that the title was well suited to these hours of nervous waiting. By half past midnight, Eden had still not called back. Drink and glasses, Bruce Lockhart observed, were on the table and freely offered – and no doubt also freely accepted.

When Bruce Lockhart was eventually called to the phone at three in the morning, Eden demanded to know where on earth he had been. 'We've been trying to get hold of you for ages,' the foreign secretary said. 'Have you been on the binge?' Bruce Lockhart indignantly denied it. The confusion in Eden's office had been caused because when Charles Peake, the British political adviser to Eisenhower, rang the Savoy to ask for Bruce Lockhart, the reception told him no-one by that name was staying there. For security reasons, Bruce Lockhart had been registered at the hotel under the name of Mrs Deacon, a blameless junior administrator in the PWE. When Bracken learned of this the next morning, he taunted Bruce Lockhart over the phone, ringing him up to ask who this Mrs Deacon was that he was sleeping with.

By three in the morning, de Gaulle had finally agreed that he would broadcast, but it wasn't going to be possible to record his message in time for it to go out with the other leaders' speeches. Bruce Lockhart perceived a risk here: what if the BBC announced that de Gaulle was going to address the nation, but the address never came? The risk on the other side was that if they failed to say that de Gaulle would be speaking, the Germans would notice the omission and make propaganda capital out of it. Eden asked Bruce Lockhart's advice on how big the risk was. He returned the question, saying the foreign secretary had more experience of dealing with the general. 'The man is not sane,' Eden said, 'but I suppose we must take risks.'

Bruce Lockhart, calling to speak to Charles Peake at the Foreign Office, was able to eavesdrop on some of these arguments. Once the general had eventually agreed to broadcast, it was a question of timing and of what his message would say. In the meantime, the PWE continued trying to make their plans amid the uncertainty. At quarter to five in the morning, the team at Bush House waited and drank tea as the rain fell outside. It had been, Eden observed to Bruce Lockhart, a crazy night.

As the skies began to clear, they heard 'the sound of a thousand planes' overhead. Dawn was breaking over the Thames. The PWE team inside Bush House pulled down the blackout and looked out towards the river. The wind had dropped and the waters were still. Bruce Lockhart saw the planes make their way towards France, describing how 'the sky was silver sheen and the planes twisted and turned in cohorts'.[13] The operation they had been preparing for so long and so intensely was on.

Sleep, however, was still elusive. Bruce Lockhart stepped out into the early morning, the rain having stopped, and walked back alone to the Savoy. He managed only an hour's sleep before he was woken again, this time by Ritchie Calder.

Back at Bush House, the BBC and the PWE were getting news flashes that German news services had reported Allied landings both in Normandy and near Calais. Noel Newsome, the news editor at the BBC, knew that he was supposed to wait for the official confirmation from SHAEF before he broke the news on British radio. He decided this news was too big to hold back. 'My own overpowering instinct as a news-paperman,' he wrote, 'was to report the news from whatever source as soon as I got it.'[14] At first, the BBC reported the German sources, while saying that they didn't have Allied confirmation. Eventually, Newsome managed to get through to SHAEF for the official version. Ritchie Calder got short shrift from Bruce Lockhart when he asked whether the PWE could do anything to stop the reports before the official state-ments went out, perhaps by issuing emergency directives. No, there was nothing that could be done to stop it, Bruce Lockhart said, testily. He knew he wasn't going to be able to go back to sleep.

At Milton Bryan, Tom Delmer and a couple of close col-leagues were congratulating themselves on being ahead of the news and being able to adjust the angle of their black propa-ganda accordingly. There were fewer people in Aspley Guise who knew what was happening than in London. Only Delmer, Donald McLachlan of the Naval Intelligence Division and Harold Keeble, who printed the daily *Nachrichten*, were in the circle. McLachlan had spent much of the previous day with the Americans at SHAEF headquarters in Bushy Park, waiting for the postponed operation to go ahead. Delmer didn't let the tension keep him and McLachlan from their supper at The Rookery, but they found themselves unable to think about anything else while not being allowed to talk about it in front of others. Delmer had to use subterfuge to get Hans Gutmann, his chief news writer, to come back to the office with him when he knew the operation was getting underway. He pretended to Gutmann that they were just drafting news stories in case the invasion might take place, but Gutmann clearly realised that such a job wouldn't be an urgent, late-night task if the landings weren't in fact imminent. 'Just a mock-up to be kept on ice for the great day,' a sceptical Gutmann said to Delmer, 'and you want us to write it now, at one am.'[15]

As soon as the German news agency flash came through on Delmer's Hellschreiber tape, they had the stories ready to go. The Soldatensender Calais could break the news even before the official German announcement and they interrupted their dance music programme at ten to five in the morning to report that the Atlantic Wall had been breached in several places. As the BBC discussed whether they could break the official embargo, Delmer went ahead without consulting anyone except his Naval Intelligence Division friend and got the story out anyway. He drove from the Milton Bryan studios to the printing operation at Marylands, where the front page of *Nachrichten für die Truppe* would be remade. With the help of advance information from McLachlan, they had good intelligence as to what the invasion would involve, but they added some dark propaganda spin and disinformation to help influence the Germans on the ground. The newspaper told the troops that Allied forces were attacking at the mouth of the Seine and near Calais as well as on the Normandy beaches, where the assault was really happening. They were warned of the 'overwhelming air superiority' of the Allies and read how German torpedo boats were engaged in 'heroic self-sacrifice against the immeasurably superior invasion fleet'.

Later in the morning at Bush House, the news coming in from the front was good. Although this helped to lift spirits and calm sleepless tempers, de Gaulle was yet to speak. By 11.30am, both Eden and Bracken had been working on Churchill to calm him down, though for Eden this was only a brief respite; Churchill began to harangue his foreign secretary again in the evening. Bracken wrote to Eden with some observations about how to solve some of the Americans' concerns

Special D-Day edition of the *Nachrichten für die Truppe*, announcing that the
Atlantic Wall had been breached, 6 June 1944

about France, noting that 'Roosevelt is a great hater and de
Gaulle has certainly given him plenty of provocation'.[16]

Bracken rang Bruce Lockhart to pass on a message from
the prime minister that he should show 'every deference' to
de Gaulle when he arrived. Bruce Lockhart and Ivone Kirkpatrick went down to the grand doors of Bush House on
the Aldwych to greet him. He found that an American dele-
gation of General McClure, C.D. Jackson and William Paley
was already standing there waiting for the French general to

arrive, even though they had not been invited. The ceremony with which de Gaulle was welcomed was far removed from the early days of the war, when Elisabeth Barker, then a junior BBC producer, greeted the French leader on her own.

De Gaulle was early. Five minutes before he was due, 'the giant figure of the General blocked the entrance door'. Despite the success of the landings, he was still in 'his grimmest mood', his face hard set. Although he greeted Bruce Lockhart and the British team in a restrained but friendly way, he was clearly displeased to see the Americans. When he was introduced, 'he stiffened into complete frigidity, made three half-turns as he gave the limpest of hands to each, then, drawing himself to the full stretch of his immense height, strode forward along the stone corridor'.[17]

As Bruce Lockhart accompanied him down to the studio in the bowels of the building, the European Service, 'Gaullist almost to a man', turned out to welcome de Gaulle. He, in turn, was friendly to the French BBC team. The trouble was that no-one had yet seen de Gaulle's script for his broadcast. De Gaulle had been working on his address throughout his interrupted night, scrawling his words at his desk between his bouts of arguing. No-one, not even his ambassador Viénot, had a copy. It was now past 12.30pm and de Gaulle wanted to broadcast live on air at 1pm. If Bruce Lockhart and his colleagues demanded that de Gaulle submit his script for their approval, he was all too likely to storm out again. All the general had were his notes; 'the manuscript was written in almost illegible longhand, with sentences running up & down the margins, holes torn in the paper by a scratchy pen.'[18]

With time running out, Ivone Kirkpatrick, ever the diplomat, had a moment of inspiration. He would flatter de Gaulle enough to get what he needed. Bruce Lockhart called it a flash of genius. Kirkpatrick told de Gaulle that his broadcast today was 'the most momentous that you have ever made, perhaps that you ever will make'. The oppressed countries of the world, he continued emolliently, were waiting for France's lead. 'We have made arrangements to put your talk out in twenty-four languages,' he said, and so they needed a recording in order to make translations. De Gaulle was persuaded and gratified that the world was waiting for his message, so he agreed to record the talk rather than make it live.

Bruce Lockhart watched the recording from the studio cubicle. The team stood in deathly silence around the glass walls, waiting nervously as de Gaulle began to speak from his scribbled notes. 'The supreme battle of France,' de Gaulle declared, 'has begun' after the 'conflict, rage and grief' of the war – not to mention that of the preceding days. He called on the French people to obey their simple and sacred duty to fight the enemy by all means available, promising them that the sun of French greatness would emerge from behind the cloud of their blood and tears.[19]

From behind the glass, tears sprung to Bruce Lockhart's eyes as he heard the general's voice, 'solemn, slow and well-modulated', full of the conviction of sincerity. He was at first embarrassed that he had been so moved, but as Bruce Lockhart looked around the studio, he saw that others were equally emotional. De Gaulle's words had grown in power and in fluency since his earliest broadcasts. Once again, he was able to rise to what the moment demanded.

When Bruce Lockhart took a transcript of the speech to the Foreign Office to show Eden, the foreign secretary had only one objection to point out, which Bruce Lockhart had already spotted. De Gaulle had of course referred to his own government-in-waiting as the French government, not the 'provisional' government, which was the Allies' preferred form of words. Eden, smiling, told Bruce Lockhart that he would have trouble with Churchill over the term, 'but we'll let it go'.

Once de Gaulle's broadcast went out that evening, unchanged, the trickiest diplomatic task for the PWE had been carried off. Bracken and Eden were back on good terms;

Bracken even claimed that he'd engineered the massive row between their two departments to help Bruce Lockhart's position, though that had all the hallmarks of a Bracken untruth. The scale of propaganda operations was as impressive as that of military operations: messages from Europe's leaders had gone out in all the many languages; more than a million leaflets urging troops to hand themselves over as prisoners were dropped on the front lines; and 32 million leaflets in six languages fluttered over the whole of north-western Europe, all aimed at a variety of targets. One of the leaflets directed at German troops told them that they faced a war on four fronts: to the west, east and south, with the fourth front the home front, illustrated with a map dotted with red bombs falling over Germany itself.

War on four fronts: leaflet dropped over Germany on D-Day, 1944

20

A Moment of Winged Thunder

It was around two o'clock on a Friday afternoon at the end of June 1944, lunch hour for many at Bush House and the other office buildings around. Many people had popped out to the bank or the post office. Instead of eating his usual sandwiches at his desk in Bush House, Noel Newsome, the BBC editor, had gone out for lunch at the Waldorf Hotel where he met his sister Helen, an expert on Spanish politics who also worked at the BBC. The siblings had just finished their lunch and Helen had left the hotel to return to Bush House, just across the Aldwych. Newsome stopped briefly to chat to an acquaintance, the two men standing at the top of the stairs that led down to the hotel's grill room.

The next thing Newsome knew, he heard the sound of a 'terrific explosion' and found himself at the bottom of the flight of stairs, blown down by the blast. He picked himself up and rushed back up to the street, desperate to find his sister, relieved that she was not among the first few casualties that he saw lying on the pavement amid the haze of dust and smoke in the street.

The VI rocket that hit the Aldwych on 30 June 1944 was one of the most devastating single attacks on London: forty-eight people died and more than 150 were injured. The bomb flew at high speed out of blue skies and landed on the street just outside the door of the Air Ministry, opposite Bush House. The dead and the wounded were everywhere. William

Sansom, the author turned firefighter, arrived on the scene to see that 'in the canyon of the Aldwych's white masonry they were scattered like the victims of a massacre in some spacious curved arena'.[1] He saw 'the twisted frames of a line of buses' in the street and a 'pathetic snow' of banknotes from the damaged bank falling on the street that was thick with blood. The Aldwych, he said, had been struck by 'a moment of winged thunder'.

Noel Newsome and his sister were among the lucky ones. Helen had reached the entrance of Bush House but a steel rod had gone through her calf – even so, she was less badly hurt than many. Newsome returned to his office to find the steel windows blown into what remained of his desk. Had he been eating his sandwiches there, the windows would have hit him in the back and he would probably have been seriously injured. In the newsroom, 'desks had been upturned and chairs and typewriters flung in all directions'.[2] On all eight floors of Bush House, the situation was similar – windows blown out, glass shattered – but the BBC and the PWE were lucky to escape without any loss of life. There were only three serious casualties within the PWE, who all recovered, with forty members of staff treated for cuts and minor injuries.[3] Since the radio studios were in the basement, BBC broadcasting could continue, with one Czech announcer improvising his bulletin after his script was blown out of his hand.

Robert Bruce Lockhart maintained that morale within the organisation was 'visibly, but not seriously affected' by this close call. Interference with work, he said, was 'negligible'. In his diary, he didn't mention the V1 that had struck his HQ, though he did refer to the ever-present threat of the flying bombs – known as doodlebugs – and how one had been brought down near Eden's country home while he was visiting for the weekend.

For the PWE, the new pilotless Blitz posed bigger problems than just the immediate, practical dangers. Standing further away from the windows when the alert sounded was the main safety change they made in the face of the threat. In terms of propaganda, though, the new Blitz brought new questions of strategy. The Cabinet were expecting the V2 rockets, even more deadly, to begin launches imminently. Where the V1 bombs had been powered by a jet engine, the V2 had rocket engines and could reach supersonic speeds, falling from the edge of space. Since they flew so fast, it was hard to detect or intercept them. The British government was working on new evacuation plans for millions of civilians. How to handle the news coverage within Britain was not the PWE's concern – that was the job of the Ministry of Information. But they did have to work out a plan for how to respond to German propaganda.

For some time, German propaganda had been threatening revenge on Britain with its new V-weapons, the V standing for *Vergeltung*, retribution. The black propaganda team had noticed over the past year that these threats varied in their intensity. The German propaganda campaign would flare up and then die down again. Robert Walmsley, the PWE's specialist in German intelligence, had decided to analyse exactly how the threats arose and subsided, in order to see what predictions he could make from that evidence. Earlier in the war, he had used his research to establish what he saw as a fundamental principle underlying German propaganda: that their home propaganda was 'absolutely determined never to commit Germany's leaders to anything involving an increase of Germany's power unless the event was considered certain to materialise'.[4] In other words, Germany wouldn't promise new initiatives or victories to its domestic audiences unless it was certain they could be delivered. Walmsley deduced that Germany's frequent promises to attack Britain with new weapons of revenge meant that they must be ready to be used. By November 1943, Walmsley had already stated that propaganda alone showed, 'beyond reasonable doubt', that Germany had a new weapon, unlike anything the Allies possessed, which would be devastating to civilians.

Tom Delmer compared the signals Walmsley detected to a distant radio bleep picked up by a submarine. The signal that had faded out when launch dates were postponed was growing louder after D-Day. Delmer agreed with Walmsley's view that 'the Germans were determined to launch their wonder weapon for political reasons, to shore up their own invasion-shattered morale and do what they could to smash ours'.[5] Walmsley had suggested that Germany would launch the V-weapons even if they were not ready to do so on the scale they might have wanted.

Although Delmer would later claim that Walmsley's evidence was conclusive, the predictions weren't as precise as he said they were. In his regular reports on 'German propaganda and a secret weapon', Walmsley could not confidently predict exactly when the new secret weapon would be used. At first, he expected the V-weapons to be used in January, but his initial expectation that they would come at some point between January and April was gradually pushed back. While the analysis of mentions of retaliation gave the PWE and others some idea of German preparations for an attack, it was less useful as a precise prediction. When the V1 bomb did hit the Aldwych, Walmsley was in his office in Ingersoll House, just around the corner, where the blast 'wrecked all the windows and partitions in our rooms'.[6] A month later, in July, Walmsley was reporting that Germany expected to use a further new weapon, which would be 'more effective than the flying bomb', but he wasn't able to draw any conclusions about whether this would be used in the near future or not.

Again, Delmer and Richard Crossman took different approaches to formulating their strategy towards Germany. Crossman argued that playing up the importance of the V1 bombs would result in greater disappointment for the Germans when the new weapons failed to produce the effect they wanted. This, Delmer believed, was fine for white propaganda, but he wanted to pursue another line on the black stations. The voice of the corporal on Soldatensender, and the newspaper, *Nachrichten für die Truppe*, would take a contrasting tack.

Delmer's response, in the corporal's voice, was to question what the doodlebugs – or '*Dödel*' in German – had achieved, what could be expected of them, and whether the new weapon could provide a solution to Germany's military problems. His answers were that the Germans couldn't know enough about the effectiveness of the attacks to make a judgement on whether it was successful, and that the weapon could not ultimately solve Germany's need to defend itself against invasion.

Having planted these themes, Delmer went further, suggesting to his audience that the V-weapons were a 'miserable waste of precious fuel', which could have been better used for supplying German ground troops or the Luftwaffe. Delmer wanted to get the German troops' response to the attacks to be 'There goes our fuel!' He also inserted fake news items into their bulletins suggesting that Albert Speer, the German minister of armaments and war production, was unhappy that factory capacity was being used to build these bombs rather than other materiel like planes or tanks.[7]

Later in July 1944, Delmer first got word of a true story which he declared to be 'the greatest news story of the war'.[8] Hitler's own army officers had tried to blow him up in a bomb plot, planting a suitcase beneath the table where he was meeting in the Wolf's Lair in East Prussia. The British response to the news of the 20 July assassination attempt had many parallels with the reaction to Rudolf Hess's landing in 1941:

initial confusion and disbelief were followed by a reluctance to exploit the news to the fullest propaganda effect on the government's part. As in the case of Hess, the propagandists wanted to go far further in using the story, both on black and white outlets, than senior ministers were willing to let them. Unlike at the time of Hess's landing, though, black propaganda was far more established and Delmer had greater leeway than white propaganda had to make some use of the German internal dissent. In this instance, Churchill and Brendan Bracken's reluctance was born out of their commitment to pursuing unconditional German surrender, rather than allowing new factions within Germany to take over.

Delmer told the story of the night of the attempted revolt with his habitual flair. He and Crossman were at dinner together at Delmer's house, The Rookery in Aspley Guise, when the first reports came through on the Hellschreiber tape machine. According to Delmer, this happened at ten past eight in the evening. He and Crossman were, he said, 'savouring the penultimate bottle of a most perfect Graacher Himmelreich 1934' when Delmer was called to the phone. Their enjoyment of the rare pre-war German Riesling was immediately interrupted. Delmer was briefly sceptical until his colleague Hans Gutmann, on the other end of the phone, played him the official German news reports, which called the attack a 'criminal attempt on the life of the Führer'. Crossman and Delmer abandoned their dinner of venison 'as if we had been stung by another of Crossman's wasps' and raced over to Milton Bryan, where they began to formulate their response.

All that the PWE knew at this point was what they had heard over German radio: an attempt had been made on Hitler's life, which he had survived. In Hitler's own radio broadcast, he announced that a bomb, which had exploded two metres to the right of him, had been planted by Colonel von Stauffenberg, that one person was dead and others had been injured.

Crossman decided to call Bruce Lockhart to tell him what had happened and to ask for ministerial advice. With hindsight, he might well have regretted this. Delmer's initial reaction was to exploit the coup attempt to the full: to suggest that the conspiracy to overthrow Hitler was widespread and that there was confusion within the army. Delmer and Crossman's ability to hear the German radio news reports and to understand them would have meant they were able to make quick judgements.

Bruce Lockhart, in bed with a painful attack of shingles when he received Delmer's call, was reluctant to raise the ministers, but did so at Crossman's urging. When he returned the call, Bruce Lockhart had unwelcome directions from the top. In Delmer's retelling, Bruce Lockhart told Crossman: 'I have a message for you, Dick, from Brendan Bracken who is dining with the PM. Bracken says he is amazed that you should have fallen for this all too obvious Goebbels canard, and will you please never disturb him with such nonsense again. Please tell the BBC to refrain from saying anything that could suggest we accept the story that there had been a revolt by the generals.'⁹

Delmer's version, in this instance, is hard to corroborate, but it sounds a characteristic thing for Bracken to have said. Bracken's first instinct, as with the landing of Hess, was often to attribute an unexpected story to Goebbels's propaganda. Sometimes, he accused others of 'playing into Goebbels' hands', as with both the case of the pornographic leaflets landing on the Surrey golf course and the time he reproached Lady Milner of the *National Review*. Bruce Lockhart's diaries don't refer to the late-night call, which is unusual, but which can perhaps be partly explained by his illness. But Delmer and Crossman weren't, perhaps, as far ahead of their ministerial bosses as they believed themselves to be.

Anthony Eden said he heard the news of the assassination attempt while at Cabinet on 20 July. The War Cabinet had met at 6pm that evening, so this would have been before Delmer heard the German radio reports.[10] Eden was clear that there had been disagreement among the ministers on whether it was a true story and, if so, how to handle it. Ernest Bevin had believed it was a Nazi stunt to popularise Hitler; Bracken, as we know, also argued that it had been Goebbels's work. The foreign secretary himself was more inclined to believe what he had heard: he said it was hard to tell so far, but he didn't think that it was a hoax. When asked about the situation in Germany in the Commons next day, he didn't go into any detail, but Eden wrote in his diary that he was convinced of his original assumptions: 'Quite sure that my diagnosis of H. [Hitler] business was right and that there has been some real trouble in Germany.'[11]

Writing later of the decision to play down the plot in white propaganda, Bruce Lockhart couched the story in euphemisms, saying only that 'the excitement in Britain was intense, and in ministerial circles opinions varied widely, some ministers holding that the whole story was a propaganda trick to increase Hitler's popularity and others insisting that it was the beginning of the German revolution'.[12] Eden had come up with a compromise ruling on propaganda, which Bruce Lockhart agreed with: to ignore the idea that the revelation of the plot was a propaganda stunt, but not to go too far in pushing 'the wild rumours of civil war and open revolt which were then circulating'. They broadcast, Bruce Lockhart said, a 'full and dramatic reconstruction of the attempted assassination' and detected in Hitler's own radio broadcasts that his voice showed he had been shaken.

This wasn't how Delmer saw it. In his view, the political warriors' hopes of 'splitting the Germans and inciting the generals to further rebellion were crushed'. He said that Crossman and Carleton Greene at the BBC were explicitly told to report that the British government was not prepared to absolve the German army of any responsibility for the war. Unconditional surrender on Germany's part remained the order of the day.

Members of the PWE, including their German staff, were arguably better placed to know what had really been going on in Germany than many in government were. Delmer claimed to have got word of a possible plot being organised by Claus von Stauffenberg at least two months ahead of the event. He said – and these comments were echoed by his junior staff member, Muriel Spark – that gossip among prisoners of war, picked up by microphones in their 'country house prison camp', had mentioned Stauffenberg's involvement in a plot against the leader. Although they weren't to know this at the time, another member of the conspiracy, Adam von Trott zu Solz, had been an old acquaintance of Crossman and others in Oxford before the war. (The other German Rhodes Scholar who had arrived in Oxford with von Trott, Adolf Schlepegrell, also worked for Delmer in the PWE, identifying the sites of air raids within Germany.) Crossman and von Trott had fallen out when von Trott decided to return to Germany under the Nazis.

The intelligence that Delmer had doesn't seem to have reached or been acted on within central government, though. When the Foreign Office was asked to provide Downing Street with a briefing on what they knew about Stauffenberg after the bombing, the result was less than a page long and consisted of little more than his name and title, with some mention of his family's ancestry, which reads as though it had been culled from a Foreign Office copy of the *Almanach de Gotha*, the handbook of German nobility.[13]

It was perhaps this lack of background or clear information which made Bracken so sceptical – though he appeared to have nothing except his own hunch to support his belief that this was all a propaganda trick. Bracken's biographer Andrew Boyle called this obstinacy 'his own gravest miscalculation' in office, which was 'wilfully to ignore the positive implications of the plot by the German generals to assassinate Hitler'. Bracken's resistance to Crossman and Bruce Lockhart's attempts to 'introduce subtlety' into white propaganda in order to exploit the divisions in Germany was insurmountable. The message of propaganda since D-Day had been to show German civilians that they had no hope of victory and that surrender might be a better option. Playing on the fact that the German leadership was divided and plotting against Hitler could have helped this aim. According to Boyle, Bracken said 'impenitently' of the Germans: 'It's too late for redemption. They're all tarred with the same diabolical brush.'[14]

The refusal by ministers to allow white propaganda to push the matter further left the field free for Delmer and black propaganda, where the same level of interference didn't seem to apply in this case. The Soldatensender changed tack: from now on it would tell the German soldiers listening that the war needed to end to save Germany. The line that black propaganda directed at the common soldier had always taken was to appear to be on the side of the troops in the field rather than the party leadership, but now they would praise Stauffenberg and his fellow officers. A bigger shift was to begin attacking Hitler directly and personally in a way that the black radio stations hadn't before. While ridiculing the idea which might have spread among German soldiers that this had been a plot sponsored by the Allies, the émigré René Halkett's broadcasts laid into Nazi leaders as lazy profiteers who avoided any danger themselves. He derided Hitler as a man who had 'never learned the soldier's trade'.

One of the plotters against Hitler, who had managed to escape, was even allowed to come and work on black propaganda. Delmer received a call from Bruce Lockhart in November 1944, telling him that one of the 20 July plotters had arrived in Britain. On the afternoon of 22 November, he went to interview Otto John at the Oratory School, which was being used as an interrogation centre.[15] Delmer found, in what was usually a schoolmaster's study, a man with blue eyes, an 'unnecessarily concentrated stare', a 'rather short and stubby nose' and bright peroxide hair. The hair, John explained, was a result of having bleached out some black hair dye which he had used as a disguise.[16]

No-one was quite sure what to do with this new arrival. Otto John, a lawyer who worked for the German airline Lufthansa, had been involved in the anti-Nazi opposition for many years and had been a schoolfriend of Adam von Trott. John told his interrogators in London that he had been an emissary from the opposition. As such, he said he had frequently travelled to Madrid during early 1944 to attempt to get in touch with the Americans to let them know that a plot was underway and to make peace proposals. He escaped from Berlin, four days after the plot's failure, by using his Lufthansa pass to travel as a second pilot on a plane to Madrid. There, he got in touch with British intelligence at the embassy. John had been in regular contact with British intelligence since 1942, having first got in touch with them to pass on information about resistance within Germany and possible plans for attempts on Hitler's life; his Lufthansa job had allowed him to travel regularly to Spain and Portugal and meet his international contacts. Over the summer, John lived in hiding in Madrid before being smuggled out of the country and across the Minho River into Portugal by the British. Despite hiding in Portugal, he was arrested in a roundup and taken to prison before British officials 'obtained his liberation' and got him on a flight to Britain under the alias of John Collinson. Despite the efforts made to help him escape, his arrival in early November still seemed to take the authorities by surprise.

What Otto John's actual involvement in the plot had been was less clear. John's interrogator at the Oratory School, an F. Basett, was not convinced by the details of John's story, finding his account of the days around the Stauffenberg plot in particular 'very confused'. Basett thought that John, a trained barrister, should have been able to give a more consistent account of his movements. Instead, he was 'vague', 'extremely unhelpful' and 'thoroughly muddled'. Basett argued that he was 'not being straightforward and open with us'. He believed that John's interests were 'those of Germany and not of the Allies', arguing that John's main contact in the opposition was a German nationalist. John did not seem, in Basett's view, to be telling the truth about his contacts with the German Abwehr, the military intelligence service. Basett could not recommend that John continued to work for either the intelligence service, SIS, or the Political Intelligence Department – the PWE's cover name – until his story was investigated further, even suggesting that John was a Nazi double agent, raising as a salient point 'the possibility that he was an S.D. agent with a special political mission from Himmler within the Opposition movement'.[17]

SIS didn't want to have anything more to do with their agent. They said that 'our own obligations to him are met already by having brought him over here from Portugal and thus having saved his life'. MI5 protested, saying that he needed to be looked after and not just left in Britain with no plan. Delmer's intervention solved the situation. John, assuming the new identity of Oskar Jürgens, moved into The Rookery at Aspley Guise. Delmer trusted him more than John's interrogators had, describing him as an 'immensely stimulating' presence because he provided proof that the resistance still existed within Germany and gave him new insights into what they were thinking. Delmer was convinced of the 'complete sincerity' of John's fellow members of the opposition.[18]

Otto John found himself something of an outsider at RAG. He was 'an object of suspicion' for the other residents, as he was such a late arrival and he wasn't allowed to give his real name. He was also frustrated that he wasn't permitted to broadcast or to give his own version of the events of July. Delmer told him that there was an official British directive banning him from broadcasting. While he was able to talk to Clifton Child, an academic who worked on Delmer's team, about what he knew about the situation in Germany, he couldn't communicate with the world directly.[19]

John's input did, however, according to Delmer, inspire new campaigns on black radio and in forged documents. For instance, he passed on a story that Himmler had had tentative contacts with the Resistance, which prompted Delmer to instruct Ellic Howe to print stamps with Himmler's head on them instead of Hitler's, suggesting that he aimed to take power. The stamps were created and sent into Germany but to little noticeable effect.

Delmer remained loyal to Otto John even after the war when many were convinced again that he was a double agent, but for a different cause. After his return to Germany, John became the head of West Germany's intelligence service. In a strange series of events, he at first appeared to defect – or be abducted – to the East, on the tenth anniversary of the July plot in 1954, but then returned to the West. Delmer remained an outspoken supporter of his former colleague even after John's trial and conviction for treason in West Germany.

Delmer employed, with apparent reluctance and mistrust, an even more questionable character – a man whom the CIA later described as having an 'extremely dubious background'.[20] Hans Zech-Nenntwich was an SS officer and a man who had joined the Nazi Party before 1933. He escaped to Sweden in 1943 after having been imprisoned: on his account, it was for involvement in anti-Hitler plotting; on others' accounts, it was for rape.[21] Arriving in Britain as Sven Nansen, he was allowed to work with the PWE, although Delmer said he kept him apart from the main operation at Milton Bryan.[22] Zech-Nenntwich lived in Paris House, on the Woburn estate itself, away from the other villages. He had told Delmer that he was 'prepared to collaborate with us to the last inch'.[23]

Delmer proposed Zech-Nenntwich as the voice of a Waffen SS RU, a 'genuine officer of the SS who has escaped to this country' and could provide information about resistance within the SS. The Hagedorn station, Delmer said, broadcast over the last ten months of the war, pretending to be somewhere behind the eastern front. Zech-Nenntwich also contributed to fake 'Scorpion' leaflets which imitated those really produced by Himmler to communicate with the troops. The real Scorpion leaflets were German propaganda aimed at their own side. Zech-Nenntwich was, however, twenty years later, convicted of war crimes for murdering two Jews, and for his part in his regiment's murder of 5,000 Russian and Polish Jews at Pinsk in 1941. Sentenced to four years in prison, he escaped again after his trial in 1964 and was only recaptured to serve his sentence after he was traced in Egypt, ultimately being found back at home in Germany.

While the PWE were frustrated by not being able to make more out of the July plot within Germany, military successes on the ground were helping to make some parts of their job easier. On 14 August, Eisenhower proclaimed that there was 'a fleeting, but definite opportunity for a major Allied victory' that would require the 'utmost zeal, determination and speedy action'. As the Allied forces advanced into France, both from the west and from the south, rumours travelled even more quickly than the troops themselves. De Gaulle returned to France from Algiers, accompanying the American troops as they moved towards the capital. On 23 August, leaving Le Mans and heading towards Chartres, de Gaulle described seeing flags and people shouting 'Vive de Gaulle!', and feeling carried along by a river of joy from his supporters.[24]

The excitement was rising in London too. For Bruce Lockhart, the next two days were 'the most bewildering forty-eight hours in the history of PWE'.[25] At quarter past twelve,

J.B. Clark, the BBC's European Service controller, rang to say he had just received an official communiqué from General Koenig, the commander of the French Forces of the Interior, saying that his forces had liberated Paris. Bruce Lockhart asked Clark whether he'd had any confirmation of this news from SHAEF headquarters. Clark replied that the French communiqués were used automatically. By the time Bruce Lockhart called both Eden and Bracken, both of whom advised him to hold the news, it was already too late to stop it going out. The BBC had put the report out at 12.30, the time they'd been told the information could be released.

Bruce Lockhart told Clark not to go overboard with the news – 'not to make a whoopee programme' – until they had official confirmation from SHAEF that the liberation had definitely happened. That confirmation was slow to come, because Paris had not yet fallen to the Allies. Despite this, the BBC put on a special programme for French listeners. The French BBC staff were convinced that the liberation was happening and they were 'delirious with delight'. Bruce Lockhart met one French broadcaster who 'could hardly speak for tears'. Bruce Lockhart himself, however, felt their delight was premature. He was 'constrained by the agony of uncertainty'.

Eden was happy to go ahead the next day and record a talk that would be broadcast to liberated France, even though the Allied military HQ hadn't confirmed the news. Eden was in effective charge of the government during these days, since both Churchill and Attlee were out of the country – Churchill was in Italy and Attlee had passed through Normandy and Algiers before meeting up with the prime minister in Naples.[26] There was still no word from SHAEF. The BBC's French staff were slow to get to work, a little jaded after having celebrated the liberation all night. De Gaulle, waiting in the Château at Rambouillet to the south-west of Paris, heard the BBC broadcast in the evening. On the morning of the 24th, he received a telegram from the king, offering royal congratulations – a message which was also made public. But, as de Gaulle observed, the news and the despatch were premature.[27]

In the afternoon, Eden managed to record his broadcast at the Foreign Office, but an hour later, Bruce Lockhart received the message from SHAEF. It was not what they wanted to hear: Paris was not free. SHAEF's line was 'alarming in its curtness'. Not only did they say that the city hadn't fallen, but they also suggested that gaining control wasn't the military's priority. Paris, SHAEF said, was not a military objective. By the time this message arrived, Eden had already gone into a Cabinet meeting. The Cabinet heard from General Bedell Smith that the French weren't in control of the situation and that SHAEF would have to divert troops from elsewhere to support Paris. Bruce Lockhart warned the BBC that they might have to postpone the ministerial talk.

As a storm burst from 'the blackest of black skies' over London, a last rain of doodlebugs accompanied the thunder and lightning. Over peals of thunder and the crash of bombs, Bruce Lockhart was juggling calls between the BBC and the Foreign Office. J.B. Clark called from the BBC to tell him that President Roosevelt and his secretary of war, Henry Stimson, had also gone ahead and sent their own radio messages on the liberation of Paris.

Bruce Lockhart called Eden back to tell him that the Americans had gone ahead; he read out Roosevelt's words to the foreign secretary. 'The patch of gloom' that had settled over Paris four years earlier, Roosevelt said, had been dispelled. He rejoiced with the gallant French people at 'this brilliant presage of total victory'.

'This is a bit hot,' Eden replied. 'What do we do now?'

'I think we must let it go,' Bruce Lockhart advised him. 'If you do not, there will be these American messages to the world and nothing from Britain.'[28]

Eden's broadcast in French went ahead at nine-thirty in the evening. Bruce Lockhart thought it was first-class in both delivery and content, and he made sure to tell the foreign secretary so. His message went out before those of the American leaders, which pleased him further.

However, a patch of gloom still hovered over Bruce Lockhart himself. He was enervated and depressed on the Thursday evening. Even the next day, when the liberation remained uncertain, this mood persisted. Bruce Lockhart heard from his senior diplomat friend 'Moley' Sargent, who had been present at the Cabinet meetings, that the situation was grave. Sargent believed that since German troops were still in Paris, the battle might continue for weeks, with street-to-street guerrilla fighting. Over dinner, Bruce Lockhart drank to drown his depression, as was his habit. He had already had a boozy lunch with his lover from Russia days, Moura Budberg, at the Carlton Grill earlier in the day.

At nine on Friday evening, there was better news from Paris that proved Sargent's pessimism wrong. De Gaulle had arrived in the capital and the German commander had surrendered. Making the early announcement of the liberation was, Bruce Lockhart said, the PWE's greatest and perhaps its most successful mistake of the war.

De Gaulle saw design in this, whereas the view from London was much more one of accident. De Gaulle's view was that the first BBC broadcasts and the message from the king had the aim of encouraging the Americans to overcome their misgivings and head for Paris. It didn't seem like that in London. It was more, as had so often happened, a series of miscommunications and jumping to conclusions which led to the premature announcements. De Gaulle detected a reserved, slightly sour tone in the broadcasts on the Voice of America, compared with the warm satisfaction which he heard in the BBC's reporting.

As the end of the war came into sight, the political warriors started to think about what they would do in the peace. Robert Bruce Lockhart celebrated his fifty-seventh birthday at his home near Radlett on 2 September, and despite saying it was 'as happy a birthday as anyone could expect in wartime', he was not, on reflection, looking forward to the future. He was tired, battling with eczema, suffering from nervous exhaustion – which, in his own words, was caused partly by alcohol, 'which keeps most of us going and saps us at the same time' – and conscious of 'failure and frustration'.[29] He doubted whether his work in political warfare had really been valuable, even though so much money had been spent on it.

What did his future hold? He did have prospects of work already, having been offered a job in the Foreign Office, reorganising the post-war foreign publicity service, possibly with a foreign posting to follow. Another plan was to go back to writing books, but this depended on whether his publisher would offer him a sufficient advance and be able to find enough rationed paper. A third possibility was that he would go to the United States as a visiting university lecturer. Bruce Lockhart, as ever, weighed these options up on the basis of which would provide him with the greatest financial security, given that he could never get his spending under control. Still, he worried that these dreams would be difficult to realise, in view of his 'uncertain health'. He concluded his birthday diary entry with the fear that he might end up with 'no prospects except the workhouse', anxious that he hadn't written a word for five years – he clearly didn't include his extensive diary in this – and had defaulted on a film contract to write three synopses. 'Not,' he thought, 'a very cheerful prospect at fifty-seven.' But there were still battles to be fought and the next acts in the propagandists' lives would mostly have to wait.

Their attention had to turn first to the endgame of the war in Europe. Although there might have seemed to be less need for black propaganda as the war entered its closing months – and indeed some of the black stations were wound down as the countries they were broadcasting to were liberated – Delmer was anxious not to stop his projects before the war's end. In fact, he was pushing further to try schemes which he had not been allowed to attempt before. At the end of October 1944, he suggested that 'there are a number of projects for political warfare against Germany which have had to be abandoned in the past either because there were restrictions and conventions forbidding their use or because the time was not thought ripe for an all out effort'.[30]

As well as producing fake stamps and forged banknotes, which he wanted agents to take into Germany, Delmer had ideas that moved into the territory of direct sabotage – not something that the PWE had been permitted to do before. What he called the dissemination of 'simple instruments of sabotage' meant the dropping of small incendiary devices, known as 'Braddocks', over enemy territory. The Braddocks could be used to set fires, but Delmer was more concerned with promoting the fear of fires and the fear of further sabotage than causing the direct damage. Bomber Harris had refused to allow British planes to carry these devices earlier in the war, preferring to drop heavy bombs rather than cargoes of small explosives, but Delmer hoped to have more joy with American bombers. This was agreed, but without the intrusion operations via Aspidistra which Delmer and Crossman wanted. They'd hoped to have fake German stations tell the population to go out and pick up these incendiary devices.

Another suggestion was even more unusual. Delmer proposed using croton oil, which he described as 'the world's most powerful purgative', a toxic substance capable of causing 'diarrhoea verging on dysentery' if it was mixed into the communal cooking vessels of soldiers or civilians. One half-ounce globule of croton oil could put up to three hundred people out of action. As with the incendiaries, the aim was not so much directly to poison as many people as possible, but to create a climate of fear where 'the work of watching

Germany's cooking pots against sabotage would become an unbearable strain'. Croton oil had apparently already been used in small quantities in Delmer's kits for malingerers, which instructed soldiers in how to fake or create illness. There were, however, serious objections to using the oil. Not only would it have to be dropped by air over Germany, but 'we would have to overcome scruples about chemical warfare'.[31] Those scruples prevailed.

Even in January 1944, before the landings in western Europe, Delmer had already been thinking ahead to what would happen once Allied troops reached Germany. He was keen to keep pursuing black propaganda even once Germany was falling to the Allies. In a memo to Peter Ritchie Calder, he proposed that a separate and secret black organisation should run within Germany in what he called the 'Transition stage'. Its aim would be to provide 'news and views likely to cause the German people to act in accordance with British interests' and to combat tendencies in the opposite direction. As 'we should, in fact, be working mainly inside Germany', Delmer thought there was a greater need for secrecy to avoid Germans knowing where this propaganda was coming from. He even believed there was a case for keeping it secret from Britain's allies, in case their interests started to diverge. What he didn't explain was why a black operation, in the event of German defeat, would be believed and acted on where genuine Allied white propaganda wouldn't be. That moment of defeat was now approaching.

21

We Who Live

At the beginning of March 1945, the Allied forces were on the point of crossing the Rhine. Churchill and Roosevelt had met Stalin at Yalta in February to discuss the future of Europe and the last stages of the war. On Sunday the 4th, Churchill was staying with Eisenhower at his headquarters in Reims. The prime minister's chance reading of a newspaper caused one of the war's last fierce rows about propaganda.

As both Richard Crossman and Tom Delmer told the story, Churchill happened to pick up a copy of the American forces' newspaper, the *Stars and Stripes*, over his Sunday breakfast. He spotted an article which reported that both Radio Luxembourg and the BBC were instructing German civilians to stay put as the Allied troops advanced into their country. Delmer, in his dramatic retelling, gave words and gestures to Churchill that he couldn't possibly have known first-hand. In this heightened scenario, Churchill 'growled' at Eisenhower, pointing 'an accusing finger' at the newspaper.

'Pray, General,' the Delmer reconstruction had Churchill snarling, 'what sort of nonsense is this? Surely we should not be telling the German civilians to stay where they are.'[1] Instead, the prime minister told Eisenhower, the Germans should be told to take to the roads and flee. This, Churchill believed, would impede the strategic communications of the German troops, or in the words that Delmer reported Churchill using, 'the Hun armies'. Both Delmer and Crossman said that Churchill recalled the way that the German air force had attacked French civilians who had fled as France fell at the start of the war. Crossman had his leader demanding 'Why be soft to the Germans?' Neither man had been in the room, but they were likely to have heard the story from the Americans, possibly via General Bedell Smith, Eisenhower's chief of staff.

Churchill's stance was contrary to the plans that both the military and the political warfare teams had made over the last several months. The policy until that point had been, firstly, to encourage serving soldiers to surrender to Allied forces and, secondly, to tell civilians that they should obey the regulations of the military government that would be set up once troops arrived on their territory. Crossman thought this a good campaign for several reasons: a key one was that 'we were telling, as is very rarely possible in wartime, the truth, the whole truth, and nothing but the truth'.[2] The instructions given were accurate, the regulations precise. Eisenhower was being built up as a supreme commander who would be recognised by German military and civilians alike.

In this instance, though, it seemed that Eisenhower was prepared to go along with what Churchill wanted, even though the idea of causing disruption on the roads had been discussed, and dismissed, by political and military teams months before. Delmer believed that Eisenhower, 'a politician and a diplomat as well as a soldier', was happy to change tack because this was a small tactical sacrifice to Churchill, many of whose other strategic recommendations he had rejected.

Crossman, who was working with SHAEF, and his American colleagues General McClure and C.D. Jackson, were summoned to Reims – each in a separate Piper Cub plane, according to Delmer – to be told their new instructions. That night, Crossman received the order from General Bedell Smith to reverse his whole propaganda campaign. 'I shall never forget the blackness of our despair,' he wrote.

Even at this crucial strategic point, Crossman was as ready as ever to do what he thought was right, rather than what his superiors told him to do. This time, he would defy direct instructions from the prime minister. Although he and Macmillan had done this before, in Algiers, where Crossman claimed they had destroyed a telegram from Churchill asking for a Vichy supporter to be arrested, in 1945 he was closer to the action and the defiance was more direct.[3] Crossman managed to convince his colleagues in the PWE that what Churchill wanted was dangerous and wrong. The PWE, in turn, used the distinction between white and black propaganda to get away with doing some of what the prime minister wanted, while saving their own principles and, to a certain extent, deceiving him about whether the orders had been obeyed.

In a telegram sent from McClure, the order was set out: the chief of staff had directed a new policy for Germany east of the Rhine. The operational requirement now was to 'embarrass German High Command by inducing maximum movement of German civilians'.[4] This meant killing the new *Voice of SHAEF* broadcast, which was to be aimed at Germans on the east bank of the Rhine, and stopping all leaflets and broadcast advocating the stay-put policy in that area. The telegram further said that they were working on a new psychological warfare plan for propaganda which, in order to avoid 'overt contradiction between new policy and old', would contain specific instructions to civilians in certain areas about what they should do. A new plan for black propaganda was also underway.

But speaking to Crossman unofficially, Eisenhower's chief of staff, General Bedell Smith, seemed to understand that the letter of Churchill's instruction didn't have to be observed. 'Do something,' Bedell Smith told Crossman, 'to satisfy the Old Man – one single thing – and then use your brains to ensure that it doesn't contradict or undermine our main campaign.'[5]

It was a story that Crossman told many times subsequently. Although he didn't specify that the 'Very Important Person' he was disobeying was Churchill himself, it can't have been hard for his listeners or readers to infer who the Old Man was. This was not, however, just Crossman telling a story to boost his own importance. PWE documents show how he and his colleagues managed to get around the instructions to a certain extent. Crossman raised his worries and protests as soon as he could, in a conversation with Donald McLachlan of the Naval Intelligence Division, who noted it down in full.

At eleven-thirty on the morning of Wednesday 7 March 1945, McLachlan took an unscrambled cross-Channel call from Crossman, who said he was speaking on behalf of General McClure. Since Crossman was speaking over an open line, he had to resort to 'double-talk', but his meaning was clear in London. Crossman wanted McLachlan to get the director-general of the PWE, Robert Bruce Lockhart, to tell his ministers the consequences of this U-turn for propaganda and for German policy more generally. This was, Crossman thought, 'a matter of urgency'.

Crossman's objection concerned 'breaking the solemn pledge by the Supreme Commander to the German people that no harm would come to them if they obeyed our orders'. That was the ethical objection; the Allied forces should be shown to be honest and trustworthy. They had told German civilians they would be safe and now they wanted to go back on his promise. As he argued to McLachlan, this change of policy meant that the white propaganda agencies were being asked to 'play a black trick hitherto allotted to our Black media'. This was 'to instruct the German population to take action which will result in loss of life, great suffering and disorganisation'.[6]

Crossman also had a practical objection: that this simply wouldn't work and that urging civilians onto the roads would impede the Allied advance more than the German retreat. A plan along these lines had been considered by the PWE at the end of 1944 and rejected. The idea of causing maximum confusion and a panicked evacuation might also have been open to the criticism that if 'the evacuees are driven off the roads by us, possibly to starve and freeze, there may well be a general outcry on humanitarian grounds'. This, however, had to be weighed against the possibility of shortening the war.[7] The plan of November 1944 was abandoned because, at the time, the United States 12th Army Group was opposed to it, with its chief of staff having taken the view that the creation of German refugees would be 'an embarrassment to the Allies'.[8] Crossman and McLachlan discussed the impact that the change of policy would have on German civilians: Crossman argued that the attempt to disorganise the civilian population and cause them suffering would damage Britain's prospects when it came to the occupation and make their consolidation tasks in northern Germany no easier. In addition, the switch to urging sudden evacuation while battle was still going on would mean that civilians were trying to move under shellfire and bombing behind the front lines. As well as what this might mean for the population, Crossman argued that this was a line German propaganda would counter with the claim that 'the Allies are planning another Dresden'.

Getting the message – about the risks of Churchill's instruction – acted on in London was not easy, however. Bruce Lockhart was ill again. He had been confined to bed with sciatica for more than two weeks by the time of Crossman's call. That day, the new deputy director of the PWE, General Alec Bishop, had been summoned to see Bruce Lockhart, whom he had not yet met. Because of Bruce Lockhart's ailments, Bishop was told 'the middle of the day is the only time when it is possible to see him in view of the treatment he is undergoing'.[9] Given the pharmacopoeia of medication being prescribed, it's astonishing that Bruce Lockhart was able to hold any coherent meetings at all. He was having cocaine injections and had just switched from a regime of codeine, gout pills, sleeping tablets and infra-red electric treatment to a new one that was primarily liquid Omnopon – a sedative combination of morphine and codeine that was often used for emergency treatment on the battlefield.[10]

From his sickbed in Hertfordshire, Bruce Lockhart disagreed with Crossman, telling Bishop, when he visited for lunch a few days later, that he thought it would be 'wicked' to run a policy that was framed for the occupation and not for the battle itself. Bruce Lockhart was outraged that 'Crossman, if you please, wanted me to argue with the PM'.[11] Although he may still have been in contact with his colleagues like Crossman and Delmer, Bruce Lockhart recognised that he himself was no longer effectively in charge of the situation due to his illness.

Alec Bishop sent off minutes to his two ministerial bosses, Eden and Bracken which, while not openly defiant, explained some of the PWE's concerns about the reversal of their previous policy. The minute pointed out the problem of switching from the previous policy and also the fact that foreign workers in Germany were to be told to stay where they were, making for a possibly contradictory approach to these different audiences. However, the note acknowledged that this change had been decided by the highest political and military authorities and hinted that the PWE could find a way around it 'by the exercise of ingenuity and contrivance'. As so often, the two ministers disagreed with each other in their responses. Bracken, not surprisingly, was in accordance with Churchill's instruction. His private secretary, Bernard Sendall, wrote on his copy of the minute that 'the Minister agrees that every effort must be made to implement this decision – which is, in his view, long overdue'. Eden was more circumspect, noting on his copy that he agreed with the PWE, though the point about the policy towards foreign workers would present some difficulties.

Eden was hinting that the workaround that the PWE was planning would allow them to say that they had not completely disobeyed their orders. Deputy director Bishop had met Delmer on 7 March, and Delmer's black propaganda would be key to the new plan: to stick closely to the old policy on white radio while, at the same time, the instruction to cause confusion and get German civilians to take to the roads would be primarily carried on black radio stations. General McClure was to be invited to London for meetings and, in the meantime, while Peter Ritchie Calder was preparing a draft plan for white propaganda, Delmer would draw up a parallel one for black. The BBC was very unhappy about the proposed change in policy. Douglas Ritchie, in charge of European broadcasts, said that the BBC had, up to that point, been doing everything possible to emphasise the instructions to stay put, which had been 'most vigorously broadcast' and which had played on both the Germans' self-interest and an appeal to their 'wider patriotism'. To reverse the policy now, Ritchie said, 'will cost us our reputation', and would also prove ineffective.

Amid a week of urgent meetings and discussions, the PWE tried to work out how they would square this circle. In a part of the draft plan for white propaganda headed 'Political Warfare's Dilemma', they expanded on the problems they faced. The commitment to the stay-put policy had been serious and civilians had been warned frequently and vividly of the 'physical horrors of evacuation, danger from Allied bombing, hardships and forced labour awaiting the nomad at his journey's end'. Leaflets had gone further, telling those who picked them up that 'to order evacuation in the face of a modern Army is murder'. This had been contrasted with the depiction of life under an allied military government, which civilians had been told would be 'secure and comparatively comfortable'.[12]

This line had been taken partly because Germany's own propaganda had been ordering civilians to abandon their homes and head eastwards. The PWE's intelligence was that the party's orders to evacuate had been widely disobeyed and that forced evacuation was very unpopular. Reports from recently captured German towns suggested that people did not want to leave their homes. If the Allies were telling people to do the same thing that German radio was instructing, there would need to be a very strong military imperative for this. But, they observed, if the stakes were high enough, they would do it. 'If Political Warfare can help to end organised resistance in Germany,' the report observed, 'it cannot with propriety develop scruples at this stage of the conflict.' The PWE only wanted to carry the new plan out if they could show that German civilians were being told how to flee to safety and not put in more danger; 'it is not our wish or purpose to cause needless suffering to the German people'. People should be told that they may face danger, but the blame for this should be placed firmly on the Nazi Party and the German Army. The message would be that 'this is what your leaders have brought you to'.

This was a plan designed, in its own concluding words, to 'save face' as much as possible while still being seen to obey orders, but it was clear that there were still deep misgivings about whether any change was wise. Black propaganda, however, was a different matter. It continued to be a way of doing things that white propaganda outlets did not want to be seen to do. Although in some spheres, political warfare was winding down as more countries were liberated, the conflicts over the ethics of black propaganda still raged just as fiercely.

Delmer said that Bruce Lockhart called him to ask him to run a campaign on the Soldatensender that would drive the German civilians on to the roads. Delmer, seeing his team as 'the disavowable scallywags who did the dirty work', was happy to go ahead without formal approval.[13] That may have been the case, but he still had to submit a formal plan to those who were working in Bruce Lockhart's absence.

A big difference in March 1945 was that Delmer was finally allowed to use the Aspidistra transmitter in the way he had long wanted: to take over German frequencies with his own black imitations of German programmes. These 'intruder operations' had long been considered a step too far in black propaganda. Not only were they pretending to be German stations, they would also be pretending to be the real voice of the German regime.

When Delmer, Crossman, McClure and Bishop and others met at Bush House on 15 March, Delmer kicked off the meeting by expressing his opinion that they should paint a 'lurid terror-picture' of conditions in the battle area on the black stations. They would tell civilians, however, that there were certain 'safe areas' that they could leave for.[14] When Crossman, Delmer and McClure continued their discussions in Aspley Guise later in the day, they worked closely on defining the geography of the safe areas more precisely. Crossman said that the main thing was to offer an objective to civilians that was in close reach. If they found the place they were making for to be full, evacuees would not go back but might push on to a new destination.

After their previous experiences of poor communication with the Air Ministry, they were also all aware that both the safe areas and the intruder operations on Aspidistra needed to be closely co-ordinated with the Air Force and Bomber Command. Directing people into the path of bombing or failing to tell the Air Ministry when they were using the Aspidistra transmitter could both have been disastrous.

Delmer had been preparing ways to run intruder operations for a long time: he had his team make precise reports on which German stations broadcast and when. They had also recorded the emergency broadcasts which the authentic stations frequently made so that they were able to copy them more precisely. Delmer said this technique was first used to intervene on the radio frequencies used in Cologne, although most of the discussions recorded in the archives concern operations around Frankfurt.

Being able to run an intruder operation depended on the RAF planning a bombing raid in the relevant area, so Delmer and his team had access to its operational plans. When an air raid was happening over German territory, the local radio station would go off the air so that the transmitter couldn't be used by British aircraft as a locator. Its programme would carry on being broadcast by the Reichsprogramm, but would be sent from a neighbouring transmitter. The team operating Aspidistra, run by the engineer Harold Robin, had worked out how to pick up this programme and how to detect when one transmitter had gone off air and another one taken over. Aspidistra was set up to broadcast on the frequency that had just been switched off, picking up the programme from the second transmitter and relaying the original German programme on the British transmitter.

This allowed them then seamlessly to fade down the substitute programme in Milton Bryan, fade up the studio microphone, and then put Delmer's fake 'emergency announcement' on the air in Germany. Just as the real Cologne radio station had a male and a female presenter, so did he. Margit Maass, the actress who had giggled while attempting to broadcast fake horoscopes, was one announcer, a young German prisoner who had once been a trainee radio broadcaster the other.

Delmer had researched not only the format but also the type of announcements that a German programme would be likely to make, instructing women and children to leave their homes overnight, taking a maximum of fifteen kilos of luggage and bringing anything with wheels to help them carry their possessions.[15]

Technically, 'it worked beautifully,' Harold Robin recalled. Five minutes later, once Delmer's fake announcement finished, they would fade down the studio, fade up the music, and then switch everything off.[16] Delmer was very happy with the results. As he set out in his black propaganda plan, the listeners would not have heard just a conventional-sounding announcement, but he also intended to scare people. Delmer wanted to develop a 'terror motif': that if they did not leave, civilians risked being 'bombed, battered, buried and burned'. They would be told that forests and cellars were no longer safe hiding places, putting those who hid there at the risk of fire or starvation. He contrasted this, on the Soldatensender, with an idealised picture of what life would be like away from the battle – that Bavaria and Austria were 'a land of milk and honey, as the Party have been giving it priority for food supplies'.[17]

Did these messages have the desired effect, though, given what the German authorities were telling people to do anyway? The people who heard them, after all, were hearing a message which they would have believed to be from their own leadership. The German authorities, struggling to keep control over the country in the face of imminent defeat, were certainly confused. The authorities realised what was happening and that fake announcements were being put out in their name. Delmer exploited this as well. After the German announcers insisted on air that 'the enemy is broadcasting counterfeit instructions on our frequencies' and proceeded to declare that their announcements were the only real ones, Delmer copied their words exactly in his next broadcasts. He, too, said that his was the real announcement and that all others were fake.

'Nothing good comes from the enemy,' German Forces Radio insisted to soldiers in western and south-western Germany, telling them that 'the enemy is not so idiotic as to do a good turn to his opponent, he wants to injure you'. The repetition of a message telling the listener not to believe the enemy had the air of a desperate last-ditch attempt to retain control. 'He who believes foreign broadcasters,' the message concluded, 'commits suicide.'[18]

Returning to Germany for the first time since the start of the war, late in March, Delmer did have a slight moral qualm about what he had done. He saw the same sight he had last seen in Spain in the civil war, and in Poland and France in the early days of the German invasions: refugees crowding the roads, 'miserable ragged families, trudging wearily along the Autobahn and through debris-cluttered streets of bomb ruins'. He did not stop to ask them whether they had decided to flee because of the announcements on Radio Cologne or Radio Frankfurt, fearing that their answer might be 'yes'.

A bigger question perhaps was whether the people on the ground believed either what their own government was telling them, by this stage in the war, or the fake black announcements. It must have been clear to the civilians that Germany was losing the war and that their own regime was in jeopardy and not to be trusted. They were probably more likely to take decisions about their own safety on what they could see around them or what they were able to hear locally. Since Delmer did not ask the question, we do not have the answers the refugees might have given, but his only lasting regret was that they had not used Aspidistra earlier to create more confusion.

Crossman's view however was that this had been a political stunt and that, by the spring of 1945, the professional propagandists had discovered that stunts do not pay. He accused Churchill, though not directly by name, of 'infantile Machiavellianism', of treating psychological warfare as a 'war game' rather than what Crossman believed it should be – 'the imposition of the Allied will on the German mind'.[19]

Bruce Lockhart ended his PWE career as much in two minds about Richard Crossman as he had been at the beginning of the conflict. He still suspected Crossman of disloyalty to his original PWE employers in favour of his new ones, the

Americans, and thought it likely that Crossman might, finally, be fired. He was shocked to learn, via Bishop, that General McClure claimed not to have known about Crossman's plan to undermine the Churchill decree. Crossman, however, said that Bedell Smith had given him implicit approval. Bruce Lockhart recollected that he had saved Crossman several times before and would be accused of weakness for not having got rid of him sooner. But his broader assessment was that Crossman 'has oceans of ability, is quick and has guts'. It was 'nonsense' to believe that he was, as some of his political critics thought, a communist or very left-wing. 'Crossman is Crossman and to further his own ambitions he will stick at little.'[20] Bruce Lockhart would not return to work until the end of the war. At the beginning of April, he was sent to Scotland at Bracken's insistence for more medical treatment and convalescence, including a form of 'deep-ray' treatment which couldn't be carried out in London because the rays interfered with radar operations.[21]

One of the fundamental disagreements lying behind the evacuation issue was a theme that had persisted throughout the war: how should the German people ultimately be treated? Crossman was taking a slightly longer-term view and looking ahead to the peace and to the occupation of Germany that would follow. While Delmer agreed to a large extent that political warfare and propaganda should continue even once the fighting was over, they again had different ideas about how Germans should be treated. Delmer felt that the Allies were not trying hard enough to set Germany on a different path for the future, believing that the country's whole culture needed to be forcibly changed. Meanwhile, the ministers and the heads of the PWE were increasingly thinking about their own post-war futures, rather than being set on continuing the war by other means.

Black propaganda operations would, in fact, come to an end shortly before the war in Europe itself did. By April,

Delmer felt that the Soldatensender had become an anachronism. As the German forces collapsed, the radio programme appeared to be 'almost the last unit of the Third Reich functioning with cohesion and coherence'.[22] Delmer said it was his decision to close down and 'go underground', a suggestion that he put to Bishop, his acting boss.

Delmer declared with great exactitude in his memoir that Soldatensender West went off air at 5.59am precisely on 14 April 1945.[23] But, as ever, the more detailed one of Delmer's supposed truths, the more likely it was to contain a falsehood. Harold Robin and his colleagues recorded the last day's broadcast of the Soldatensender, which survives in the Imperial War Museum.[24] The recording is dated 30 April 1945. Listening to its contents, this must be true, because it reports on the huge events which had just happened on that date: it began with the news of Himmler's offer of unconditional surrender and reports that Hitler was dying. 'Mussolini is dead,' the bulletin later declared. The Italian *duce* had died on 28 April.

The last broadcast of the Soldatensender makes for strange listening, its trademark mixture of grim news and cheery dance music sounding incongruous and jarring. It announces itself with jaunty military music and tells the listener that they will continue to bring them the latest news, uninterrupted, before saying 'We start with dance music' and segueing into 'Danube Waves', a Romanian waltz played by Ronnie Munro and his Scottish Variety Orchestra.[25]

The news broadcast painted a grim but only slightly exaggerated picture of what was going on in Berlin. Soldier listeners were told that 'everyone is saving himself who can, in order not to die at five minutes past twelve, after the leadership has dissolved itself'. They heard that only a tenth of the city of Berlin was left standing, that fighting was raging around the führer's bunker and that white flags of surrender were flying while black smoke rose from government bunkers as officials rushed to destroy incriminating documents. Loyal members of the party leadership, they were further told, were convinced that Hitler was already dead and they were hiding in order to save their own lives – if they hadn't already taken the decision to end them.

The eleven-minute bulletin made it clear that Germany was collapsing on all fronts: the Russians advancing in the east, the British crossing the Elbe and only forty kilometres from Hamburg, and the Americans bridging the Danube, with some troops already arriving in Munich. The picture was no better in Italy, where the details of Mussolini's failed escape and killing were given.

And then, having told the listeners the news would be back at twenty minutes before the next hour, the station switched back to music again – this time playing Glenn Miller's 'In the Mood', its swinging American saxophones contrasting with the dark news from the front. The music chosen was a mix of the forbidden and the familiar for a German military audience: American jazz and operetta-like German film music, such as Kristen Heiberg singing 'Komm, Zauber der Nacht', with the occasional French chanson, like Charles Trenet's 'La Vie Qui Va'.

Although this was a black station, the last surviving day of Soldatensender West wasn't really giving black news in the sense that it was untrue or misinformation. It was giving an authentically dismal picture of the catastrophe that was befalling the German regime. Anyone listening to the programme would have been left in no doubt that the war was over and there was no point in attempting to fight on. Submariners, indeed, were given detailed instructions during the programme on what to do in order to show they had surrendered; among other things, they should surface and show a white flag. There was an element of psychological warfare in the way the news was presented, certainly, in that it was discouraging any further resistance, but this was more off-white than black.

Once Soldatensender had disappeared from the airwaves, Delmer wrote, the team celebrated with a fancy-dress party in the printing shop at Marylands, in Woburn, where the black propaganda leaflets had been produced. A second party was held in the Milton Bryan canteen. The party guests included Ian Fleming (then still working in naval intelligence), one of the team's drivers, 'a demure young woman called Peggy Black' and the publisher who had printed the *Nachrichten*, who dressed up as his own newspaper in a suit with the front pages of the propaganda paper printed on calico. We have only Delmer's own word for this, of course.

Delmer began the next day by shaving off the black beard he had worn for the last four years. This was not only a symbolic act but a practical one, as he was due to travel to Germany in uniform and therefore wasn't allowed to wear a beard. He wasn't impressed by the results, writing that the face confronting him in the mirror was 'the pallid, flabby-mouthed face of a crook'.[26] He gathered the team together for a farewell address in Milton Bryan, warning them that though the war may have been close to its end, they should still maintain the security they had observed up to that point. For many of the German staff, their futures in Britain might have seemed unclear at this point. Delmer also said that he didn't want his staff to be tempted to make great claims for what their propaganda had achieved. In his view, the praise that had been heaped on British propaganda after the First World War had helped to fuel the German stab-in-the-back myth and give rise to a perception that it was only propaganda, rather than military force, that had defeated them. 'If we start boasting of the clever things we did,' Delmer said he told his team, 'who knows what the result of that will be. So mum's the word. Propaganda is something one keeps quiet about.'[27]

What we do know for certain is that, as the black propaganda broadcasts wound up, the bosses who oversaw them thanked Delmer for his hard work and likewise regretted that it would have to remain secret for some time to come. On 23 April, the Ministry of Information noted that Brendan Bracken had approved the reorganisation of the PWE and the closing-down of black propaganda. Alec Bishop wrote to Delmer on 30 April to let him know formally that it had been decided that 'the balance of advantage' now lay in 'concentrating our resources and energies' on white propaganda instead.

Bishop praised the work of black propaganda in making a positive difference to the outcome of the war. 'The nature of your work makes it impossible to arrive at a mathematical computation of its exact contribution to the success of the Allied cause. Nevertheless, there is ample evidence from many sources that your labours have been of immense assistance to the Armed Forces of the Allies, and have made a great contribution towards the triumph of the principles for which we stand.'[28]

Although the work would have to remain secret and not acknowledged in public for the foreseeable future, Bishop added that he looked forward 'to the day when it will be possible for some part at least of the veil of secrecy to be lifted from the record of your long and self-sacrificing labours'.

The Naval Intelligence Division, where Delmer had worked in such close co-ordination with Donald McLachlan, particularly in their work aimed at submarines, were also delighted with what black propaganda had done. Commodore Edmund Rushbrooke, NID's director, wrote to Bishop after the end of the war, noting that 'such success as we may have had must be ascribed primarily to Mr Sefton Delmer. We in the Admiralty have the greatest respect for his ability and foresight, and it has all along been his enthusiasm which has been the inspiration of Lieut. Commander McLachlan and the small Section of this Division about whom you have such kind things to say.'[29]

Robert Bruce Lockhart returned from Scotland just in time for the final moments of the war, though he seems in his published version to have made himself out to be closer to the centre of things than his diary says he was. He spent the morning of 7 May writing a message of ministerial thanks to the members of the PWE, with 'a special commendation of the women, who had been splendid'.[30] While he had been expecting to hear the official announcement of the German surrender to the Allies in Reims at 6pm, Bruce Lockhart was instead irritated to hear a long unofficial account of the early-morning surrender on the BBC. As he correctly suspected, Stalin had insisted that the formal announcement had to wait until another signing ceremony in Berlin. On VE Day itself, Bruce Lockhart was in London, celebrating at a lunch at Claridge's with military colleagues, where cocktails were being served with 'lightning rapidity' and he drank more than was good for him.[31] He listened to Churchill's victory announcement at 3pm at Claridge's, on a radio set which the Americans had found. Making his way through the gathering crowds from Mayfair to Bush House, Bruce Lockhart allowed the staff the rest of the afternoon off to celebrate the end of the war in Europe.

On the same day, Richard Crossman flew into Germany for the first time since the late 1930s. Landing briefly at Mannheim, he saw the city almost completely destroyed. When he drove from Frankfurt airport into the city, Frankfurt was unrecognisable until he passed the house where he had lived for almost a year, half of the building destroyed and the door blocked up. Crossman felt a 'queer sensation' of dislocation, finding it hard to be upset by what he saw because the devastated city was no longer, to him, the same place.[32] There was no point of contact, he thought, between the place where he had lived in 1930 and the ruins he was motoring through in 1945. He typed up his diary a week after he first arrived in Germany, under a SHAEF heading; this was not a purely private reflection but a document intended, if not for publication, then at least as a lasting record.

Elsewhere, in the spa town of Bad Nauheim, where Crossman heard the news of the Allied victory, the effects of the war were scarcely to be seen. Apart from the people who had taken to the roads with rucksacks and carts, and the relative lack of young men in the town, things seemed disconcertingly normal to Crossman. Although he and one of his travelling companions, the journalist and fellow PWD employee Hans Habe, planned to celebrate victory when they reached Heidelberg, their celebrations were muted. This seemed to Crossman like just another day in the life of the new post-war occupation. Bill Paley, in charge of PWD, was with them and remembered that, somehow, they had managed to get hold of a bottle of wine, which they ran under cold water from the tap to chill it, and which the men enjoyed 'far more than its temperature or vintage would have merited'.[33]

From the moment he landed in the country, Crossman was thinking about what this all meant for the future of Germany and how it should be treated by the Allies. Its total defeat, he wrote, was only just beginning. There were largely 'no towns left, no communications, no government. And they are going to starve this winter.'[34] But if starvation was prevented, 'Germany, providing we don't divide her up, will again become the most powerful nation in Europe'.

As the pair made their way towards Bavaria, Crossman was continually contrasting the beauty of the landscape and some of the towns with the sudden brutal reminders of the war that had just ended. The effects of the war were haphazard: almost nothing remained of Heilbronn; Stuttgart couldn't be reached. In the Neckar Valley, they approached what appeared at first to be an exquisite walled town, with a castle, but then turned a corner to find 'complete devastation and old ladies shuffling about feebly picking at the ruins'.

It was just after VE Day when Crossman arrived at Dachau. Although his first descriptions of what he saw there are still pervaded with a sense of detachment and distance, it was an experience that affected him and his view of the world deeply. The distancing was perhaps a way to cope – or perhaps Crossman was striving after objectivity. Having been given a special pass which allowed him to enter the site, Crossman had some trouble finding the camp itself, which was 'tucked away', recognising the location at first because of the railway cars which still contained corpses. Reaching the most visible part of the camp from the outside, the 'vast parade ground and solid barrack building of the S.S.', Crossman was struck by the fact that they had been built to last: 'the finely constructed and obviously permanent garrison barracks are the most deadly proof that concentration camps were planned as a permanent institution.'

Near the entrance to the camp, they saw the crematorium, and a long line of carts still bearing the bodies of the dead. One of the first things Crossman noticed was the smell: 'the smell of lime mixed with that of corpses liquifying in the sun was so nauseatingly sweet that it actually distracted your attention from the horror.' Crossman was trying not to be sick from the odour as a Polish priest guided him and his team around.

Crossman was appalled by what was still happening to the survivors, 'the living dead of all ages' in the camp hospital, who were weak with hunger and illness, many close to death. There were no trucks to transport survivors within the camp to the hospital and people were being made to walk to reach help. Even when they were given food, many people were too weak to digest it. Bill Paley 'saw some of these people fall dead in front of me, while on their way to get food in a barracks'. Paley, too, found it difficult to take in what he was seeing. 'In that day we saw more than it was possible to comprehend. I will never understand it and its effect on me will never diminish.'[35]

The dreadful sights that Crossman and Paley saw were also being filmed by army cameramen, with a view to making a documentary to show the world what had happened there. Crossman was commissioned, later in May, to work on a treatment for a film script. The Ministry of Information noted that Crossman, 'having been an eye-witness, his knowledge of German propaganda, German mentality and German language would be invaluable for us'.[36]

The script that Crossman wrote after his trip to Dachau was meant to be for a film that would be directed by Alfred Hitchcock and produced by Sidney Bernstein, who was working for the Ministry of Information. The film went by the provisional title of *German Concentration Camps Factual Survey*. Crossman's words drew on the impressions that he had recorded in his diary. In the same clear, plain language, Crossman contrasted the tidy countryside beyond the camps and the indifference of the local population with the death and suffering within. He wrote of the dead he had seen abandoned in railway carriages at the camp's boundaries; 'we found them like this, frozen stiff in the snow, alongside a public road'. He was careful with the detail: seventeen of the people in the railway carriages had still been alive, 3,000 were dead. As his script said, 'Germans knew about Dachau, but did not care'.

The original film which Crossman worked on was not shown to the public in its intended form. Most of the footage would not be seen for another forty years. But at the time, the details of the Allied soldiers who spoke to camera, describing what they had encountered, were recorded, with each interviewee holding up a placard giving their army number, as well as them announcing their names, ages and places of birth. The film was shown at a small private screening to a select audience. Among that audience was Solly Zuckerman, the scientific adviser to the British combined operations headquarters. Zuckerman, who described the images in the film as 'more horrible than the worst kind of nightmare', asked

Crossman after the showing why he had recorded those details. Crossman's answer, Zuckerman said, was simple: 'Those films are going into archives. One day there will be people who will stand up and say that there were no such things as concentration camps, and that the whole story was a frame-up by Hitler's enemies. We can't be too careful.'[37]

Crossman made a prescient point. This was probably the strongest argument that existed against the use of black propaganda then or in the future: if it became known that Britain and her Allies had deliberately lied about certain events during the course of the war, why should they then be believed when it came to revealing the terrible truth of the Holocaust?

This harrowing visit made Crossman aware of the failure of British propaganda to address, or even to realise, the full reality of what had happened to the Jews and other victims. As he wrote after his visit to Palestine in 1946, 'though we had heard and reported many stories of Nazi massacres of Jews and Slavs, we had never believed in the possibility of "genocide". We had interrogated countless SS men: we had reported their brutality and corruption: we had known that, theoretically, they were in favour of extermination, but until we saw the concentration camps and the gas chambers, we only believed it with our brains. Now we were to realize that our propaganda had fallen far behind the truth.'[38]

Crossman clearly questioned in his own mind, after the fact, whether he and others could have done more to make their propaganda catch up with that truth. The British propagandists had been aware of some of the terrible events across Europe, but they had often chosen not to emphasise them in their messages to Germany and elsewhere. Anthony Eden had made a statement to Parliament on 17 December 1942, in which he spoke of the 'barbarous and inhuman treatment' to which Jews were being subjected in German-occupied Europe. 'From all the occupied countries Jews are being transported, in conditions of appalling horror and brutality, to Eastern Europe.' He reported that the ghettoes were being systematically emptied of Jews and that 'none of those taken away are ever heard from again.' Britain, and the Allied governments who had agreed on this common declaration, condemned the 'bestial policy of cold-blooded extermination'.[39]

During the early part of the war, there had been an aversion to what was seen as 'atrocity propaganda', which was in part a legacy of the First World War, where atrocities had often been seen to be exaggerated. British officials had been wary of criticism that much of their propaganda was created by exiles and refugees, many of whom were Jewish. Later, British diplomats argued that emphasising such crimes might not, however true they were, be effective propaganda. On the contrary, they feared that reports emphasising deportations might have the effect of increasing persecution of the Jews. One Foreign Office telegram to the United States suggested that the international declaration of 1942 had not been a restraining influence on Germany.[40] In December 1944, Bruce Lockhart protested that the PWE had many competing claims on its time, and while it had done everything possible to protect 'refugees and internees', highlighting their plight was 'not only without beneficial effect, but sometimes result[s] in increased maltreatment'.[41] The situation regarding black propaganda was complicated by the fact that black radio stations were supposed to be broadcasting from within Germany, and also supposed to be the voice of those who had initially supported the regime and presumably therefore its antisemitism. Their intended audience might have been even harder to win over with the truth of the atrocities their own superiors were carrying out.

Crossman, though clearly keenly aware of the importance of recording all the details and the testimony of witnesses accurately and in a way that was beyond questioning, did not explicitly draw out the link between what he witnessed at Dachau and the importance of telling the truth. In the many lectures and articles in which he discussed black propaganda after the war, though, he was clear that he felt that at best it was effort wasted and, at worst, it undermined trust in the country issuing the false news. Black propaganda, however, was not allowed to be publicly discussed for many years. In a 1952 lecture to defence experts at the Royal United Services Institute, Crossman talked fairly extensively about the methods of black propaganda, but with the disclaimer that he couldn't really talk about those techniques 'because officially we never did them'.[42] When Delmer published his account of the war, *Black Boomerang*, ten years after that, Crossman wrote a scathing review in the *New Statesman*. Ultimately, Crossman thought, black propaganda could only be used *in extremis*. 'Black propaganda,' he wrote, 'is a secret weapon which can only be tolerated – if at all – in total war. Like strategic bombing, it is nihilistic in purpose and solely destructive in effect.'[43]

Nor did Crossman believe that black propaganda could be justified by its results. It had not shortened the war or saved lives. Answering the rhetorical question of whether victory would have been delayed for a day if black propaganda had been forbidden, Crossman's answer was 'no'. Despite praising Delmer's 'extraordinary personal achievement' – a backhanded compliment – Crossman was, he concluded, 'more doubtful than ever whether this decision to plunge far below the Nazis' own level of lying, half-lying and news perversion was justified even by its undoubted results'.

After Crossman left Dachau, he continued his journey in order to fulfil a promise to one of the German staff who had worked on propaganda alongside him, an encounter that impressed upon him another way in which propaganda had consequences in the real world. In Rosenheim, Crossman and Paley met a woman Crossman named only as 'Mrs A', the mother of his German colleague. She wasn't easy to find.

Arriving at the town hall, the pair experienced a sense of 'overt hostility' for the first time since their return to Germany. A clerk behind the counter at the town hall was unwilling to help them find Mrs A's address, seemingly because she was a 'notorious anti-Nazi'. At first, Crossman feared she might be dead until one of the crowd of local people also seeking help told him where to find her.

Mrs A welcomed the men into her house, where she was flying the blue-and-white flag of Bavaria. She was anxious to know how soon her son would be coming back home. Within minutes, Crossman felt as if he had known his colleague's mother for years. She had suffered during the war because of the work her son had been doing. If Crossman had always known in theory the potential consequences for the German staff working alongside the British, what Mrs A told him made it clear. 'Because A's voice had been recognised on the radio, she had suffered 29 Gestapo interrogations and all her property had been confiscated: fortunately a week afterwards, an air raid on Berlin had destroyed all the documents so she still lived in the house.'[44]

As Crossman and Mrs A spoke, with Crossman bringing news of her son, Paley observed the conversation, not understanding much German. She told Crossman that although she didn't share her son's political views, she had been persecuted for twelve years for his socialism and had also taken in other socialists in Germany who had fled their homes. At first, Paley thought that Mrs A was relaxed and unmoved, despite hearing for the first time about the son she hadn't seen in years. Then he looked more closely. As she and Crossman talked, Mrs A's hands were bleeding. Paley noticed, 'she had dug her nails into her hands, so intense were her feelings'.

Crossman left the A family's home with a revival of the belief he had long held and argued for since the 1930s: that there were some good Germans who had opposed the regime, no matter how few. People like Mrs A should be supported if

Germany were to be handled in a constructive way – or the Allies risked losing the peace. She and others like her deserved help. 'These people feel the guilt of Germany in their bones and out of that sense of guilt have become as heroic human beings as one can meet anywhere.'

But the lesson that Crossman drew more broadly – both for propaganda and for politics – was summed up in the last line of the powerful script he had written about the concentration camps. 'Unless the world learns the lessons these pictures teach, night will fall. But, by God's grace, we who live will learn.'

Conclusion
The Afterlife of Political Warfare

Political warfare, and even black propaganda, did not die with the end of the war; it had merely been resting for a couple of years. Although the Political Warfare Executive was wound down once peace arrived, in the hope it would no longer be needed, this security was short-lived. The foreign secretary in the post-war Labour government, Ernest Bevin, decided to revive political warfare against the background of increasing communist control of central and eastern Europe. He was afraid that Soviet tactics could be used in western Europe – in France and Italy, for instance – and wanted to strengthen the West's political response. Propaganda was part of the means to do this. His junior minister, Christopher Mayhew, returned from the United Nations General Assembly in New York in 1947 appalled by the way that the Soviet Union was mobilising its propaganda far more efficiently than the West. Mayhew spent his voyage home on the *Queen Elizabeth* writing a memo to the foreign secretary. 'Soviet propaganda was having an impact, especially in the Third World, and needed to be answered,' Mayhew thought, 'and if the answer was to be effective, it must go beyond self-defence and carry the propaganda war into the enemy's camp.'[1] He wrote to Bevin to argue that if Britain was going to launch a propaganda offensive against foreign countries, the government needed to justify it by showing that 'our campaign would take the form of a defence of Britain, the British Commonwealth and Empire, and British social democracy against communist propaganda attack'.[2] Bevin took up the idea and, in November 1947, Mayhew was able to discuss it with senior officials.

Mayhew, a new MP elected in the Labour landslide of 1945, had been one of Hugh Dalton's proteges before and during the war. He was familiar with political warfare in the Woburn era as one of the enthusiastic young aides who accompanied Dalton on his brisk visits to the Country HQ. Dalton found Mayhew suitably keen and eager, describing him as 'bouncing about like a young sheep dog'.[3] Mayhew worked with Dalton at the Ministry of Economic Warfare as his 'black' private secretary and had then gone on to serve in SOE, running agents in France after D-Day. Bevin agreed that the new section should be created, telling the Cabinet that it would pursue 'vital and progressive ideas' and play on 'the weakness of Communism rather than its strength'.[4] One of his concerns, however, was that an overt unit to counter communist propaganda would not be welcomed by Labour's left.

Bevin's proposals on future 'foreign publicity policy' argued that British propaganda should show that British social democracy and western European civilisation represented 'the best and most efficient way of life'. He thought this message should be primarily directed towards 'the broad masses of workers and peasants in Europe and the Middle East', using arguments that would appeal to this audience. Bevin believed they should be told that the standard of living was higher in the West and that Russia's pretence to be a workers' paradise was a 'gigantic hoax'. There would also be an appeal to deeper values based in Christianity, stressing civil liberties, making analogies between the 'Hitlerite' and communist systems, and offering 'a positive rival ideology'.[5]

There was a lively debate within the Cabinet about whether black propaganda should be revived. These arguments echoed those that had gone on throughout the war, but with the added question of whether black propaganda could be justified when the war the politicians were fighting was cold rather than hot. The cabinet secretary, Norman Brook, was worried about this question. They discussed whether the communist takeovers could be compared to the wartime German occupations. 'Is it not dangerous to use that analogy to imply that the wartime techniques of "political warfare" are generally applicable to the circumstances of to-day?' Brook asked Attlee.[6] One of Brook's main objections was one that had been familiar to Crossman and others early in the war: if Britain was not willing to help the people who opposed the regimes to rise up against them, it was morally wrong to urge them to resist. As Brook put it, 'it is useless to stir up resistance to the existing regime unless we can see a practical prospect of its being overthrown'. Then, and for the next forty years, there was little such prospect.

Some in Cabinet also argued that what was needed was a new Political Warfare Executive. Brook was sceptical here too. He advised the prime minister that ministerial responsibility was no longer as divided as it had been during the war. Brook, who had been private secretary to Sir John Anderson in the early part of the war, would have experienced at first hand the fights between Hugh Dalton and Brendan Bracken. And as he also insisted, recreating the PWE would only make sense if the government knew what it would be for, including whether that involved black propaganda. He told Attlee that 'until we have decided precisely what it is we want to do, we cannot sensibly decide what organisation is required for getting it done'.

The inner circle of the Cabinet – Attlee, Bevin, Sir Stafford Cripps (who had objected so fervently to the obscene nature of Delmer's black propaganda and was now the chancellor) and the defence secretary A.V. Alexander – made the final decisions on the matter. They came up with a set of ground rules. Firstly, even if political warfare itself was not dead, its name was. They decided 'the term "political warfare" should not be used in any description of our publicity policy'. There was, further, 'no occasion' to create anything like the wartime PWE. The foreign secretary would be given sole ministerial responsibility for propaganda policy and he would decide the 'extent to which "black" propaganda methods were to be applied in particular countries'. 'Some machinery' would be required on both white and black sides to put that policy into practice.[7]

These decisions, though, were to be kept in a very tight circle. Not even all the Cabinet were included in the discussions about what was really going on. Brook had to avert an awkward situation when the lord president of the council, Herbert Morrison, was enthusiastically making the case for reviving black propaganda and had to be told by the cabinet secretary, in confidence, that it was already happening, that 'black activities were in fact going on to a limited extent', but only a small circle of ministers had been informed.

Even before the Cabinet had fully agreed on what kind of organisation was required, veteran political warriors were being approached to see if they would be willing to serve again. The new department would be called the Information Research Department – a name designed to sound innocuous to anyone who might accidentally hear of it. Robert Bruce Lockhart was invited to dinner in early February 1948 by Christopher Warner, who had taken over from Ivone Kirkpatrick in running Information Services at the Foreign Office. Bruce Lockhart, who had returned to journalism and writing since the end of the war, had been rather sceptical, advising Warner that there were dangers to trying to carry out such operations in peacetime. 'Much of what was done by a secret organisation in war becomes impossible even in the peacetime in which we live,' Bruce Lockhart told him.[8]

Bruce Lockhart was informed that Ralph Murray had already been recruited to the new organisation – and also that they wanted to hire Elisabeth Barker. She was likely to refuse, he said, as she was 'unwilling to lend herself to propaganda'.

Barker herself said that she was minded to turn down the Foreign Office's offer, which she described as dealing with 'slightly undercover information work'. She told them that no, she 'wanted to go straight, as you might say, and not get back into propaganda'.[9] Her situation, however, was more complicated than Bruce Lockhart, her former boss, might have realised.

Barker had resigned as head of the PWE Balkan Region in December 1944. When she went to see Bruce Lockhart to tell him of her decision, he didn't want to lose her. She was 'a remarkably young woman who knew her job thoroughly, handled the somewhat unruly Balkan members of the BBC with tact and skill, and was *persona grata* with the Foreign Office'. Although Barker had been offered a BBC job after the war that came with security and a pension – she had been told she could return to the BBC as Balkan editor – this wasn't what she wanted. She told Bruce Lockhart she wanted adventure and she wished to go to the Balkans. Bruce Lockhart told her she was crazy, but she had an unanswerable response. 'She looked at me for a moment and said quietly, "I have read your books. What would you have done at my age?"'[10]

And that, Bruce Lockhart said, was that. Barker, now thirty-four, had been making her plans for some time. 'My one idea,' she said later, was to 'get away from everything I had done during the war and see what was actually happening in the Balkans.'[11] She had applied for a job at Reuters on 28 September, even before Russian and Yugoslav troops entered Belgrade, saying that she would like to be considered for a job as a foreign correspondent in the Balkans, preferably in Yugoslavia. Although, she wrote, she had never been on the staff of a newspaper or news agency, she thought she had 'sufficient experience of handling news' to enable her to be an efficient correspondent. As ever, Barker was unduly modest in her estimation of what she had done and what she could do. In her letter to Reuters's chief editor, she said that particularly as a result of her war job, she had 'a good and up-to-date knowledge of Balkan affairs' and 'a fair number of Balkan contacts' who might be able to help her in the work. She did not mention that she had been running a department and managing the output of radio stations in multiple languages; this had, of course, been secret work, but her responsibilities had been at a high level.[12] She gave Bruce Lockhart as one of her referees. Reuters offered her a job once she could be released from her war work.

It wasn't until July 1945, after the war in Europe was over, that Barker actually set out as a foreign correspondent, with the *Newspaper World* noting that she was being sent to Istanbul as Reuters's special correspondent in Turkey, the first woman to be sent by the agency on a special assignment in Europe since VE Day. Over the following months, she travelled and reported from the region, spending the autumn of 1945 in Bulgaria, the winter in Romania and the spring of 1946 in Greece. Barker spent the second half of 1946 based in Trieste, where the conflict between Italy and Yugoslavia over their border threatened to spill over into war again. But she wasn't able to visit the one place she really wanted to go – Yugoslavia.[13] Barker attempted to get a visa to cover the Belgrade trial of General Mihailović, the Serb leader who Britain had supported before switching to backing Tito and the Partisans and who was charged with treason, war crimes and collaboration. When Barker was turned down for a visa to enter the country, she managed to secure a place on a trip organised by the UN relief organisation UNRRA, which would have taken her into Yugoslavia. But she only got as far as the airport in Belgrade before being stopped and sent back. Diplomatic protests from Reuters via the Foreign Office didn't help; Reuters in general and Barker in particular were deemed to be undesirable by the Yugoslav authorities. Mihailović was convicted and sentenced to death by the court. He was reported to have been shot, but his body has never been found.

Towards the end of 1946, Barker was finding she was unwelcome in other parts of the Balkans as well, with Bulgaria and Romania also blocking her visas because they had disliked her reporting that was critical of their countries. She found this frustrating and, in December, came back to London on leave. It must have been then, some time in the New Year of 1947, that her circumstances changed. In the spring, she realised that she would not be able to return to the Balkans and had begun writing a book about her experiences there. By late in the summer, she was reluctant to travel but keen to earn more money. And, though she didn't refer to this directly in public, she was pregnant.

Barker's daughter, Dinah, was born on 7 October 1947. Dinah's father was Ralph Murray, Barker's former boss at both the BBC and the PWE. He was married and already, at that time, the father of three children.[14] Despite this, they had had a long relationship which went back to before the war. They had certainly worked together at the BBC since the mid-1930s, though they may even have met before that in Vienna. The relationship had become one that went beyond the professional by the outbreak of war, as they were writing each other personal letters at the time of the visit of Joachim von Ribbentrop, the German foreign affairs minister, to Moscow in August 1939.[15] It must have become a more intermittent affair during the war, since Murray was posted to Cairo by 1943, when Barker took over his job. After the war, he had been based in both Vienna and Singapore.

Murray did not want Barker to have his child. He suggested that she have an abortion, but she refused, and the two of them fell out over the decision. It was, her daughter says, a positive decision to have the baby. Life as a single working mother in 1947 was not likely to be easy. Some of Barker's own family – her father and brother – were also unhappy about her choice, although when the baby was born, she went to live with her divorced sister near Henley in Oxfordshire. Barker

changed her surname by deed poll to 'Collins' and gave that
name to her daughter, probably to give the impression
that there was, or had been, a Mr Collins.[16] She continued to
use her own name for work.

Reuters appear to have allowed Barker a leave of absence.
In correspondence about publication of her book, she mentioned that her flat in London, where there was a copy of
the manuscript, was currently empty, but she didn't talk about
why she was living in the country. Barker was typically self-
deprecating about the book. As she discussed its contents with
Reuters, she said that it was 'non-sensational and impersonal',
so that the agency shouldn't be worried about how it would
reflect on them as her employer. In fact, she believed, people
might find it 'irritatingly "middle of the road" and fence-
sitting', although she also acknowledged that it might 'alienate
certain extremist personal friends of mine in both camps'.

It's not surprising that Barker was in two minds about
what she should do next. In February, a few days after Bruce
Lockhart had been sounded out about whether she might
want to rejoin political warfare, she was offered a well-paid
job by the Foreign Office in the new Information Research
Department. In principle, she might have wanted to remain a
journalist rather than a civil servant, but financially the offer
was tempting.

One factor, though, which must have weighed on her
mind, was that she would again have had to work closely with
Murray, Dinah's father, even though they were no longer in
a relationship. The Information Research Department began
as a very small organisation, based in a few rooms in old
servants' quarters on Carlton House Terrace. At the outset,
there were only ten members of staff, four of whom were
clerical personnel.[17] Barker would therefore have been one
of only six senior employees. In such close confines, there
would have been no chance of the two avoiding each other.
It's surprising that she was even approached under these

circumstances. It seems she had been contacted by a friend in Downing Street – Philip Jordan, a former journalist who was Attlee's public relations adviser. Jordan knew the Balkans. He had been on the ill-fated plane flight with Evelyn Waugh and Randolph Churchill which crashed in Yugoslavia in 1944. It was perhaps a sign of how valuable Barker's expertise was, as one of the few people who had good contacts in eastern Europe on all political sides, as well as knowing how government and propaganda worked.

In the end, she returned to work at Reuters on the diplomatic desk in London in May 1948, seven months after the birth of her daughter. In 1949, she went back to the BBC and later became the corporation's first female diplomatic correspondent. It was a remarkable achievement for its time and even more so considering that she remained a single mother. Her daughter described her as a wonderful mother who loved travel and the outdoors and was a loyal friend. She kept in touch with many of the people she had worked with during the war for the rest of her life. In retirement, she studied the history that she had experienced at first hand and wrote many books which used the documents that were just beginning to be released. She remained, however, discreet and self-effacing; the books do not reveal the extent of her own personal involvement in the events she described. There were many stories, both official and personal, that she chose not to tell.

Elisabeth Barker died in 1986, at the age of seventy-five. Her obituary in *The Times* talked of her beauty and 'the quick elegance with which she moved'. It observed that 'with ambition, she could have risen far higher in the world', but that 'if she had a fault, it was too modest a view of her own abilities. But she knew what she wanted to do and did it.'[18]

One of the reasons that the existence of the Information Research Department was kept so secret was that the Labour government was worried about what many of its own MPs would think about this kind of propaganda. The IRD was kept under wraps until after it was officially closed down by the Labour government of the 1970s and its files were not disclosed until the 1990s. Christopher Mayhew was particularly worried about what Richard Crossman would think of the idea of creating a department which produced anti-communist propaganda. He thought the department could be 'seriously undermined by hostile speeches in Parliament from Dick Crossman and others'.[19]

Crossman was now a Labour MP but not yet a minister. He was someone Bevin and Mayhew wanted kept out of the loop, since he would have objected to the revival of black propaganda in particular. On 22 May 1945, Crossman had gone to see Bruce Lockhart to let him know that he was planning to fight the forthcoming general election. He would formally have to be re-adopted as the candidate for the Coventry seat he'd first been selected for before the war, but Crossman was confident both of his selection and of his imminent victory. Despite that, he asked Bruce Lockhart whether he could keep his options open. Under the government rules, a resignation in order to stand for Parliament was final – Crossman couldn't just walk back into his old job if he lost. Always keen to push things a bit further than his bosses were comfortable with, he sounded out Bruce Lockhart about whether he would be able to rejoin as a temporary civil servant were there another war, and whether he would be able to work for the *New Statesman* at the same time. It seems that his experiences in Germany had left him worried that war was again likely.

But if Crossman wanted to keep Bruce Lockhart on his side, their conversation that afternoon managed at first to rub his boss up the wrong way. Bruce Lockhart called the rant that followed 'a typical Crossman act, that is, the justification of himself and a hot attack on PWE'.[20] Crossman felt that he had been badly treated by the organisation. But the job of propaganda, he believed, was over and 'the whole organisation was crazy'. He was already looking ahead. In another war, he told Bruce Lockhart, 'propaganda should be given to the military and to the people in the front line'. Bruce Lockhart pointed out, quite reasonably, that this only worked under certain conditions – 'when we had conquered the enemy country. It obviously could not apply when both the military and civilian agencies were outside the territory of the enemy.' Crossman calmed down after he had got some of his points off his chest, but the meeting left Bruce Lockhart feeling out of sorts. He complained to his diary: 'typically Crossman was the fact that, although I had been away on two months' painful sick-leave, he never asked once how I was.'

Bruce Lockhart found it in himself, however, to write an only slightly double-edged letter of praise to Anthony Eden when Crossman's resignation took effect. Crossman, he wrote, had been praised by his American colleagues, with General McClure describing his work as 'the most notable achievement in the whole field of political warfare'. But in British eyes, Crossman was 'somewhat lacking in team spirit'. His 'restless ambition' had led him 'not only to take unjustifiable risks but to defy regulations'. But, on the other hand, 'with his agile mind, his almost daemonic energy, his considerable skill in broadcasting and in leaflet-writing, he has made a remarkable contribution to the whole technique of political warfare'. Crossman's virtues, Bruce Lockhart concluded, greatly outweighed his faults.[21]

The two men met again in February 1952. Crossman had been invited to give that lecture on political warfare at the Royal United Services Institute to an audience of senior officers. Bruce Lockhart, who was to chair the gathering, worried that this would be a hostile audience for the left-wing, often pro-Germany Crossman. He invited Crossman to lunch at the Carlton Grill, on 'a lovely sunny day with the first breath of spring in the wind'. Crossman was in bullish form as they lunched, drinking German wine together. He won both Bruce Lockhart and the assembled generals over with his lecture, even almost persuading his former boss that 'PWE was the most peaceful and best-run organisation in the war and that I myself was Dick's greatest friend'.[22] In the lecture, Crossman elaborated on the arguments in favour of white propaganda and against black propaganda, as he had done throughout the war. Although black was 'vastly entertaining', he argued, 'it does not directly assist the job of making [the enemy] surrender more easily'. Trust in propaganda needed to be built up over time. Crossman concluded, as he had worked out in Algiers regarding Tunis and Italy, that 'when morale is breaking, it will break that much quicker because the audience has already submitted to the extent of believing what you say and listening to your instructions'.[23] As he left the lecture, Bruce Lockhart pondered on why Crossman's charm didn't always work so effectively and why he had not been a minister in the last Labour government. Reflecting eight years later, he concluded that Crossman was a 'political lone wolf', but if he could restrain his ambition, he might yet rise high.

In that, Bruce Lockhart was right. When Labour returned to power in 1964, Crossman did become a minister, in charge of housing and local government, going on to hold more Cabinet posts. He returned to the *New Statesman* as editor in 1970 after leaving government and continued to provoke arguments even after his death from liver cancer in April 1974, when he was sixty-six. It was fitting that his final, posthumous battle concerned the publication of his ministerial diaries. He had planned to have his diaries serialised in the *Sunday Times*, wanting to reveal what really went on behind the scenes in government. Once again, Crossman simply did not accept the same set of rules that had always applied to others. The attorney general took his executors to court to try to prevent publication, on the grounds that Cabinet confidentiality should be upheld, but failed. Crossman's indiscretion and his willingness to see every good story as something he could turn to his advantage prevailed. The publication of the diaries changed attitudes to government secrecy and set a precedent that ministers could, in future, give their own versions of events.

The summer of 1945 was a time for farewells. The day after Crossman offered his resignation, Brendan Bracken was also out of his previous ministerial job, though his move was not one of his own choosing. The wartime coalition between Labour and the Conservatives broke apart at the end of the war in Europe, and on 23 May, Churchill offered his resignation to the king. He was immediately reappointed as the head of a caretaker government pending a general election. Bracken had briefly thought he was going to be made president of the Board of Trade, a job where he would at least have had some relevant experience. Following a 'grand old row' between Bracken and Churchill in Eden's presence, late on the evening of the 24th – which left Eden shouting in vain, 'Oh, do be quiet, you two' – Bracken was reshuffled to become first lord of the admiralty.[24] Bracken was 'deeply disappointed', having once hoped to become chancellor. All he had to console him for the next six weeks was an office in a large, beautiful room at the Admiralty, the kind of place about which Bracken loved to wax lyrical.[25] He had been in poor health for the last part of the war, but despite this and his differences with Churchill, he threw himself into the election campaign.

On 6 June, Bruce Lockhart hosted a farewell dinner for his ministerial boss in the Mikado Room at the Savoy. It was a typically boozy occasion – the guest of honour was forty-five minutes late so the fifteen other guests, all members or former members of the PWE, started on the cocktails without him. It was an awkward gathering for many of those present, including the host, who found himself, uncharacteristically, 'too frightened and too nervous even to drink'.[26] Others were not so restrained, with brandy and kümmel flowing round the table at lightning speed. Bracken made a forty-minute after-dinner speech in response to Bruce Lockhart's praise of him that left many of the guests feeling offended. He laid into the fighting services, which Dallas Brooks took as an insult, as well as the Foreign Office and the BBC. As Bruce Lockhart pointed out, though, this was often a Bracken tactic. He told J.B. Clark of the BBC not to worry; if someone else had hosted the dinner, Bracken would have attacked the other institutions and praised his hosts. More troubling to Bruce Lockhart, ever worried about money, was the cost. The dinner came to £61, 'the most expensive dinner I have ever given'.[27] Bracken, drink having been taken, carried on talking 'like a machine-gun firing' before he got into his car and drove off to the Admiralty.

Where Crossman's political star rose with the election, Bracken's fell. He lost his seat in North Paddington and was seen to have tears welling up in his eyes at the count. Although he returned to Parliament after a by-election in Bournemouth later in the year, his political career was effectively over. Bracken was frequently blamed for the nature of the losing election campaign which the Conservatives had fought. His political fortunes had always been closely linked to those of Churchill, and although Churchill persisted despite his poor health, Bracken, also ailing, was losing interest. Bracken wrote to Lord Beaverbrook in late 1946, observing that 'Winston is in very good fettle and is determined to continue to lead the Tory Party until he becomes Prime Minister on earth or Minister of Defence in Heaven'.[28]

Bracken had instead revived his interest in journalism and business, becoming chair of the *Financial Times* when it merged with the *Financial News*. Although he would stay in the House of Commons until 1951, he resigned despite the Conservatives' return to power, with Churchill restored as prime minister on earth. He described being elevated to the Lords as 'translation to the morgue' and declined to use his title of Viscount Bracken or to sit in the upper house. When Bracken died of throat cancer in 1958, he took his secrets with him, having issued that order that all of his personal papers be burned.

Robert Bruce Lockhart struggled on in the PWE until August 1945, describing his last day in Whitehall as 'the most strenuous of the whole war'. He had written to his patron, Beaverbrook, downplaying his own successes but clearly hoping for praise in return. 'I do not know how good a job we have done in PWE,' he wrote, 'but the task has been exacting and has taken a heavy toll of my health and energy. For any personal success that I may have had in managing a large organisation which was something half-way between a newspaper office and a government department I owe a great deal to you and to the training I received from you.'[29] He was grateful for some of his best colleagues, like Tom Delmer and John Rayner, who had come from the Beaverbrook-owned *Express*. His cup of gratitude, he wrote, was full. Beaverbrook's response was as generous as Bruce Lockhart might have hoped, telling him that 'few men can have contributed more vitally to this country's triumph'. His department had 'won the highest praise from all who know how much you achieved, and under what difficulties'. Bruce Lockhart had wanted to leave government sooner, but with the change of administration, he found it hard to get his new political bosses to agree on when he should go. He was still suffering terribly from his skin trouble; on his last day in Westminster he complained of his left leg being swollen like an elephant's, with the skin on both the leg and his arms raw and oozing. His condition was exacerbated by having to shake hands with around 600 staff as he spent an hour and a half saying his goodbyes in the restaurant at Bush House. Bruce Lockhart was particularly keen to thank the women who had worked alongside him, whom he singled out for particular praise in his farewell messages. Praise alone, he acknowledged, wasn't really enough. 'I wished I could have done more for the women who formed by far the larger part of our staff and who had worked long hours with unflagging zeal and without a single complaint.'[30]

Bruce Lockhart's health was toasted at his own farewell dinner at the Dorchester that evening, with Delmer among the guests. His deputy, Ritchie Calder, raised a glass to his boss and praised his 'unique power of inspiring affection'[31] among his team of prima donnas. Despite being prone to frequent bouts of despair, Bruce Lockhart was able to look back on his wartime work with some sense of achievement. They had sent out more than two million words a week on open and secret radio, he estimated. Some may have questioned whether it was worthwhile, but he felt it had been. 'In a world in which truth has been strangled as never before,' he wrote, 'I regard political warfare and propaganda as the most noxious influence. But in war it is a necessary evil.'[32] Propaganda to Germany, he felt, including what he could only refer to shortly after the war as 'our secret propaganda', 'had a very considerable effect in sapping and undermining the efficiency of the Nazi war-machine'.

Bruce Lockhart departed for Scotland, back to the Edinburgh Royal Infirmary, shortly after his fifty-eighth birthday at the beginning of September. He had left the Foreign Office and diplomacy for good and was keen to get back to journalism and other writing. Money, as ever, was a concern and, even in subsequent years, Max Beaverbrook was on hand with subsidies to cover his overdrafts and his tax bills.[33] His first job on leaving government service was as the *Sunday Times* diarist, writing the Atticus column, a role which traded on his love for gossip. Bruce Lockhart's first account of his years with the PWE was published in October 1947 and it was as candid an account as it could be given that much of the PWE's work, in particular in black propaganda, was still secret. He elided some of the details – Delmer, for instance, is never mentioned by name, nor is Crossman – but gave an insight into what it had been like to run the PWE.

More surprisingly, Bruce Lockhart both became a seemingly happily married man and lived a long life. He married the woman who had been his secretary at the PWE throughout the war, Mollie Beck. She was thirty-five when they married, twenty-six years his junior. Her name only creeps into his diaries towards the end of the war, and then only as 'Miss Beck'. At the end of the war, he had still been in a relationship with 'Tommy', his longstanding mistress, the Countess of Rosslyn, but this affair broke down and Bruce Lockhart married Mollie in November 1948. Despite his failing health at the end of the war, he lived for another twenty-five years, writing books on his diverse passions, from angling to Scotch whisky. He died in 1970 at the age of eighty-two. His diaries, which ran to millions of words, were published after his death.

Tom Delmer returned to Germany immediately when the war was over, his official title being 'controller of the German-Austrian Division of the Political Intelligence Department'. What that meant in practical terms was that he was in charge of setting up new, independent news media in occupied Germany. Creating new forms of mass communication for a country that had had no free press for more than a decade was an ambitious task, but Delmer initially threw himself into it. As he had done with black radio broadcasting and leaflets, he wanted to create an accessible, lively style of writing and broadcasting for the German public. It would have a legal framework similar to that in Britain, which would give greater freedom of expression and use British techniques of 'crisp, objective and accurate reporting'.[34] Delmer based himself in the ruined city of Hamburg and recruited many of his former PWE and black propaganda colleagues to his team. The Deutsche Presse Dienst was established and got as far as making dummy copies of a proposed newspaper for the British occupation zone, the *Norddeutsche Zeitung*. Delmer blamed the fact that it was never launched on a combination of British domestic politics – the new Labour government and the absence of Bracken and Eden – and the people he so often placed at the root of his troubles, the left-wing émigré Germans who he believed were motivated by 'petty jealousy'. He decided to resign rather than be transferred to work for the Allied Control Commission, and many of his team left with him.

Instead, he returned to Beaverbrook's fold as the chief foreign affairs reporter of the *Daily Express*. By November 1945, he was applying for permission to return to Germany to report, and also to visit the Soviet Union.[35] Delmer's views of Germany became increasingly bizarre with age. When he wrote his second volume of memoirs, *Black Boomerang*, which covered the war, in 1962, he had become convinced that West Germany was heading in the wrong direction. He argued that dangerous legends were springing up in the new Germany, 'the legend of the good Generals and the good Wehrmacht who were always against Hitler'. At the time, there had been some fears that the far right would rise again in Germany.

Delmer, having revealed many of the secrets of black propaganda in *Black Boomerang*, and having revived his row with Crossman over the issue, promised a third volume of memoirs, which never appeared. He had said that he would, in that book, tell the story of his second marriage. When he and Isabel met in

Paris after their divorce, he said that he was planning to marry again and suggested she do the same. Like Bruce Lockhart, Delmer married one of his female colleagues from the PWE, whom he also only mentioned in passing in his book. She was Peggy Black, the 'pretty driver' who had brought guests to his fancy-dress party. At thirty-five, she was the same age as Bruce Lockhart's second wife, although only nine years younger than her husband. The couple were married in 1948 and had two children. Delmer died in 1979, at the age of seventy-five.

Richard Crossman, looking back at his own work and that of Delmer, said white propaganda was all about building trust. Its function was 'to win the trust of the enemy soldier and civilian by safe, reliable reporting so that when the crack-up comes they will take their orders from the white radio and white leaflets'.[36] While senior ministers in the British government were often prepared to consider lying or at least misleading in their public statements at key points in the war, they often held back from going through with outright lies. They worried that they would be caught out – either internationally, or at home in Parliament. Their leaders discussed in depth the moral and practical value of whether they should use 'a good bouncing lie' and if this could be justified. On a personal level, whatever their own flaws and deceptions, they took the issue seriously.

They still considered the importance of trust as a fundamental part of democracy, particularly when faced with dictatorships which opposed them. The effect of black propaganda, on the other hand, was to destroy trust. There was an argument to be made that undermining trust in hostile and dictatorial regimes was valuable, because it could help to bring them down. One of the risks, though, was provoking revolts that Britain and its Allies could not or would not help succeed.

The deliberate creation of what we would now call 'fake news' set a dangerous precedent. Those who worked on wartime propaganda could not have foreseen how easy it could be, eighty years later, to create the kind of fake stories and images that they produced, nor how simple it would become to spread rumours and conspiracy theories on a huge, global scale and to have them believed.

No matter how carefully Tom Delmer crafted his believable lies, combining them with his detailed truths, he was nonetheless setting those lies loose into the world. The governments of the time could control how that was done to a far greater extent than is possible now. It was far harder to set up a radio station and broadcast, or to print material, particularly under conditions of wartime censorship. The internet has opened this access up to almost everyone. If Delmer wouldn't immediately have understood the internet or social media, he would instantly have recognised the techniques that modern states and other actors use to create and spread disinformation. Having been quick to spot the potential of radio to reach the people he wanted to speak to, he would have been an enthusiast for a technology that goes so much further.

Propagandists in the PWE found it an advantage to be the 'invisible men', the disembodied voices that could spread rumours which penetrated the enemy's defences. It is even harder for us now to find the source of the disembodied identities spreading the rumours and conspiracy theories which can affect what we believe about our security, our health, our elections. They can have direct and tangible effects: untrue stories can be at the root of riots, for instance. Western governments during and since the war were of course not the only ones doing this – both German and Soviet propaganda were trying to create their own versions of events, true or untrue. One of the biggest problems, however, with black propaganda, whether then or now, is that the presence of those untrue rumours calls into question even the most true and trusted stories. Black propaganda, ultimately, was a corrosive weapon of war. Building up the trust with which to counter it is probably even harder today.

Acknowledgements

It has been incredibly rewarding to spend time in so many fascinating archives, and I am grateful to all those who helped me to find my way around, particularly at the National Archives in Kew, the Imperial War Museum, and the Parliamentary Archives. Thanks also to the Beaverbrook Foundation, through the Parliamentary Archives, for permission to quote from Lord Beaverbrook's illuminating letters and other papers.

At the National Library of Scotland in Edinburgh, Alison Metcalfe gave me valuable assistance.

Els Boonen of the BBC's Written Archives Centre at Caversham found a trove of documents for me. BBC copyright content reproduced courtesy of the British Broadcasting Corporation. All rights reserved.

Amy Reytar of the United States National Archives tracked down one significant American document.

Many university archives and the archivists there have been especially generous. I would like to thank the staff of the Churchill Archives Centre at Churchill College, Cambridge, and of the Modern Records Centre at the University of Warwick.

At Lincoln College, Oxford, the current archivist, Alison Ray, and the previous team, archivist Lindsay McCormack and assistant Alice Parkin were very helpful in finding records of Tom Delmer's student days. Oliver Mahony at Lady Margaret Hall, Oxford, likewise helped me to find out more about Elisabeth Barker. The College material is reproduced by kind permission of the Principal and Fellows of Lady Margaret Hall, Oxford.

Quotations from the Isaiah Berlin Virtual Library are used with the permission of the Trustees of the Isaiah Berlin Literary Trust. My thanks go to Henry Hardy and Mark Pottle at Wolfson College, Oxford, for their assistance and for some interesting sidelights on Richard Crossman and his contemporaries.

I began research for this book when many libraries and archives were still under some lockdown restrictions. Many of their staff nonetheless went out of their way to find documents and other information. They include Jacqui Granger at the Royal United Services Institute and David Bates at Chatham House. Rory Carruthers at Reuters, taking over from David Cutler, was particularly persistent and thorough in digging out some very useful information.

I would also like to thank family members of some of those who served in the Political Warfare Executive, including Dinah Elliott, Selina Delmer-Best and the Calder family. I hope I have done justice to their families' stories.

As ever, I owe huge thanks to my agent, Rebecca Carter, for encouraging me to write this book and for her clear-sighted advice on how to tell the story. Amanda Waters has been a brilliant editor to work with, as was Suzanne Connelly, who first took on the book. I am grateful to Jess Anderson and copyeditor Nige Tassell also for their advice and improvements.

Finally, thank you to all my family, including my sister Nicki, and above all to Gareth, Thomas and Maxi for their constant love and support throughout a project that has lasted almost as long as the war itself.

Notes

This book has drawn on a wide variety of published and unpublished sources. Among them, the most important have been the first-hand and contemporary accounts in official documents, as well as personal letters and diaries and newspapers. Documents from the National Archives, the UK government's official archive, are listed below under the reference TNA. Other important archive sources I have consulted include the Parliamentary Archives, which holds Lord Beaverbrook's papers, the Imperial War Museum (IWM), the BBC's Written Archive at Caversham (BBC WAC), the Modern Records Centre at the University of Warwick, which holds Richard Crossman's personal papers, and the Churchill Archives Centre at Churchill College, University of Cambridge. Sir Robert Bruce Lockhart's extensive diaries, which were published in two edited volumes, were also extremely valuable, as were the published wartime diaries of Hugh Dalton and Harold Macmillan.

INTRODUCTION: THE BOYS IN THE BACK ROOM

1. TNA, FO898/547, Walmsley memoir
2. Ellic Howe, *The Black Game* (London, Michael Joseph, 1982)
3. Vernon Bartlett, *And Now, Tomorrow* (London, Chatto & Windus, 1960), p. 56
4. Howe, op. cit., p. 40
5. Thomas Barman, *Diplomatic Correspondent* (London, Hamish Hamilton, 1968), p. 97
6. Robert Bruce Lockhart, *Memoirs of a British Agent* (London, Pan Macmillan, 1982)
7. Robert Bruce Lockhart, *Comes the Reckoning* (London, Putnam, 1947), p. 54
8. Ibid., p. 56

9. Barman, op. cit., p. 97
10. Noël Coward, *Future Indefinite* (London, William Heinemann, 1954), p. 58
11. Parliamentary Archives, Beaverbrook Papers, BBK/D/477
12. Ibid.
13. Bartlett, op. cit., p. 57
14. Denis Sefton Delmer, *Black Boomerang* (London, Secker & Warburg, 1962), p. 40
15. Michael Balfour, *Propaganda in War, 1939–45: Organisations, Policies and Publics in Britain and Germany* (London, Routledge & Kegan Paul, 1979), p. 82
16. Muriel Spark, *Curriculum Vitae* (Manchester, Carcanet, 2009), p. 148 (1st publication Constable 1992)
17. Delmer, op. cit., p. 92
18. Balfour, op. cit., p. 89
19. TNA, FO898/547
20. Sir Campbell Stuart, *Secrets of Crewe House: The Story of a Famous Campaign* (London, Hodder & Stoughton, 1920)
21. Ibid., p. 98
22. Charles Roetter, *Psychological Warfare* (London, B.T. Batsford, 1974), p. 82
23. 'Leaflets dropped in Germany', *The Times*, 8 September 1939, p. 4
24. David Garnett, *The Secret History of PWE* (London, St Ermin's Press, 2002), p. 32
25. Andrew Boyle, *Poor, Dear Brendan* (London, Hutchinson, 1974)

1: THE PRIMA DONNA

1. TNA, FO898/547
2. Letters to Zita Crossman, undated 1939–1940, Richard Crossman archive, Modern Records Centre, University of Warwick, MSS.154/3/2B/786-798
3. Richard Crossman, *Palestine Mission* (London, Hamish Hamilton, 1947), p. 16
4. Letter from Hugh Dalton, 22 September 1936, Richard Crossman archive, MRC, University of Warwick, MSS.154/3/AU/1/70
5. Hugh Dalton, *The Second World War Diary of Hugh Dalton, 1940–1945*, ed. Ben Pimlott (London, Jonathan Cape, 1986), p. 66

6. Tam Dalyell, *Dick Crossman: A Portrait* (London, Weidenfeld & Nicolson, 1989), p. 51

7. Sir Robert Bruce Lockhart, *Giants Cast Long Shadows* (London, Putnam, 1960), p. 94

8. Bruce Page & Tony Clifton, 'Profile: Richard Crossman', *Sunday Times*, 25 May 1969

9. Anthony Howard, *Crossman: The Pursuit of Power* (London, Jonathan Cape, 1990), p. 30

10. Ian Kershaw, *Hitler: 1889–1936: Hubris* (London, Penguin, 1998), p. 333

11. 'Germany Polling To-Morrow', *Manchester Guardian*, 13 September 1930

12. 'Shots fired in Berlin: Rioting in General Elections', *Manchester Guardian*, 15 September 1930

13. 'The German Election', *The Times*, 15 September 1930

14. Crossman, op. cit., p. 15. The Fuld family were cousins of Crossman by marriage.

15. Crossman, ibid., p. 15

16. Page & Clifton, op. cit., 25 May 1969

17. *Sunday Times*, 25 May 1969

18. Birth details via ancestry.co.uk from first and second marriage certificates. Crossman's biographers, Howard and Dalyell, were unclear on Erika's name, calling her either Lansdorf or Landau.

19. Howard, op. cit., p. 36

20. Dalyell, op. cit., p. 29; Howard, op. cit., p. 36. Marriage certificate in divorce file, TNA J77/3316/1299

21. Susan Barnes, 'The Man who Thinks out Loud', *Sunday Times Magazine, Sunday Times*, 29 November 1970

22. Crossman, op. cit., p. 16

23. Page & Clifton, op. cit., 25 May 1969

24. Papers of Richard Crossman, Modern Records Centre, Warwick University MSS.154/4/BR/1/44-47

25. Michael Ignatieff's biographical interviews with Isaiah Berlin, Wolfson College, Oxford (*The Isaiah Berlin Virtual Library*, 2017, https://bit.ly/3qtaB6F, accessed 11 October 2022), MI tape 10, p. 2

26. Michael Ignatieff interviews, *IBVL*, tape 5, p. 24

27. Michael Ignatieff interviews, *IBVL*, tape 5, p. 24 and tape 5, p. 23

28. TNA, J77/3316/1299

29. Bayreuth town archives, https://www.bayreuth.de/rathaus-buergerservice/bildung-wissen/stadtarchiv/

neuigkeiten-aus-dem-archiv/juedisches-leben-in-bayreuth/
herzoghoehe/#1630565415920-09471f86-9d39. Erika survived
the war, remarried several more times and died in Switzerland
in 1979.

30. Richard Crossman, 'Today in Germany', BBC script, 2 July 1934,
Richard Crossman Collection, University of Warwick Digital
Collections, MSS.154/4/BR/1/57

31. BBC Written Archives, Caversham, BBC/R/RCONT/
RCONT1/84/29, Crossman, Richard H.S. MP, Talks 1, 1934–1936,
25 July 1934

32. Ibid., 25 March 1936

33. R.H.S. Crossman, *Plato To-day* (London, George Allen & Unwin, 1959)

34. Baker divorce case, TNA, J/77/3640/2817

35. BBC Written Archives, Caversham, R/RCONT/
RCONT1/84/30, Crossman, Richard H.S. MP, Talks 2, 1937–1942,
8 August 1940

36. TNA, FO898/547

37. Crossman, *Palestine Mission*, op. cit., p. 17

38. TNA, FO898/547

39. Mr R.H.S. Crossman OBE, MP (1952), 'Psychological Warfare',
Royal United Services Institution Journal, 97:587, pp. 319–32

40. Hugh Dalton, *The Fateful Years* (London, Frederick Muller, 1957),
p. 380

41. Conrad Pütter, 'German Refugees and British Propaganda: The
Activities of German Refugees in Secret British Broadcasting
Stations' in Gerhard Hirschfeld (ed.), *Exile in Great Britain: Refugees
from Hitler's Germany* (London, Berg Publishers for the German
Historical Institute, 1984), p. 129

42. Patrick Gordon Walker diaries, 24 July 1940, Churchill Archives
Centre, Churchill College, Cambridge, GNWR 1/3

43. Ibid., 24 September 1940

44. TNA, FO898/191, F.B. Aikin-Sneath, 4 September 1942.
Documents released to files after FOI request.

45. Fritz Eberhard, *Arbeit gegen das Dritte Reich* (Berlin, Gedenkstätte
der Deutsche Widerstand, 1981), p. 28

46. Crossman, Royal United Services Institute lecture, op. cit.

47. Walmsley memoir, TNA FO898/547

48. Barman, op. cit., p. 120

49. Walmsley memoir, TNA, FO898/547

2: THE HUSH-HUSH VILLAGE

1. Imperial War Museum, Peter W memoir, IWM Documents.5038
2. Tam Dalyell, *Dick Crossman: A Portrait*, op. cit., p. 51
3. Mr R.H.S. Crossman OBE, MP (1952), 'Psychological Warfare', op. cit., pp. 319–32
4. Michael Stenton, *Radio London and Resistance in Occupied Europe, 1939–1943* (Oxford, Oxford University Press, 2000), p. 221
5. Imperial War Museum, Audio 5217, Presentation to the King and Queen Elizabeth, November 1941
6. TNA, FO898/35
7. TNA, FO898/60, Report by Ivor Thomas on first year of Italian stations, November 1941
8. TNA, FO898/54, Ralph Murray to Rex Leeper, 30 May 1941
9. Imperial War Museum, Peter W memoir, Documents.5038
10. TNA, FO898/51, Note from Halliday to David Garnett, 1945
11. David Garnett, *The Secret History of PWE*, op. cit., p. 54
12. Ellic Howe, *The Black Game*, op. cit., p. 81; Charles Cruikshank, *The Fourth Arm* (London, Davis-Poynter, 1977), p. 103
13. TNA, FO898/54
14. IWM Audio 5217
15. TNA, FO898/51. There's some confusion in accounts of this story as to which teams were involved.
16. Hugh Dalton, *The Fateful Years*, op. cit., p. 381
17. Ben Pimlott, *Hugh Dalton: A Life* (London, Macmillan, 1985), p. 293
18. Ibid., p. 325
19. Barman, *Diplomatic Correspondent*, op. cit., p. 110
20. Dalton, op. cit., p. 381
21. Delmer, *Black Boomerang*, op. cit., p. 62
22. Dalton, op. cit., p. 378
23. Sir Robert Bruce Lockhart, *The Diaries of Sir Robert Bruce Lockhart, 1939–1965*, ed. by Kenneth Young (London, Macmillan, 1980), p. 78
24. Ibid., p. 78
25. Bruce Lockhart, *Comes the Reckoning*, op. cit., pp. 104–5
26. Dalton, op. cit., p. 370
27. Bruce Lockhart, *Comes the Reckoning*, op. cit., p. 98
28. Bruce Lockhart, *The Diaries of Sir Robert Bruce Lockhart*, op. cit., 29 December 1940, p. 87

29. Sir Robert Vansittart, *Black Record: Germans Past and Present* (London, Hamish Hamilton, 1941), p. 19. Vansittart left the Diplomatic Service in July 1941 and joined the House of Lords, where he could continue to intervene in public affairs.

30. TNA, FO898/178, 3 February 1941

31. TNA, FO898/178

32. 'An Appreciation', *Manchester Guardian*, 9 January 1957

33. 'Obituary: Mr. F.A. Voigt', *The Times*, 9 January 1957, p. 10. Accessed via *The Times* Digital Archive

34. Philip Oltermann, 'Nazis, Fear and Violence: When Reporting From Berlin was Dangerous', *Guardian*, 12 July 2021

35. BBC WAC, BBC/R/RCONT/RCONT1/37/679

36. 'An Appreciation', *Manchester Guardian*, op. cit.

37. FO898/547. Walmsley remembers Delmer as having been at these meetings, but Delmer did not join Woburn until May 1941, by which time Voigt had already resigned.

38. TNA, FO898/9

39. TNA, FO898/181

40. TNA, FO898/547

41. TNA, FO898/9, 11/10/1940. Crossman asked Hugh Gaitskell to hire O'Neill and get him released from the military.

42. Bruce Lockhart, *Giants Cast Long Shadows*, op. cit., p. 92

3: WARFARE BY WORDS

1. Elisabeth Barker, BBC Oral History interview, BBC WAC R143/266/1, Barker, Elisabeth interviewed by Miall, Leonard

2. Elisabeth Barker interview, via ina.fr

3. Julian Jackson, *A Certain Idea of France: The Life of Charles de Gaulle* (London, Penguin, 2019), p. 121

4. Sudhir Hazareesingh, *In the Shadow of the General: Modern France and the Myth of de Gaulle* (Oxford, Oxford University Press, 2012)

5. Hansard, HC Deb, vol. 362, col. 51–61, 18 June 1940

6. Asa Briggs, *The History of Broadcasting in the United Kingdom, vol. 3: The War of Words, 1939–1945* (Oxford, Oxford University Press, 1970), p. 242

7. David Hendy, *The BBC: A People's History* (London, Profile Books, 2022), p. 224

8. Obituary by Margaret Bottrall, *The Brown Book* (Lady Margaret Hall, Oxford, 1986)

9. Anthony Powell, *Journals 1982–1986* (London, Heinemann, 1995), p. 273

10. Anthony Powell, *To Keep the Ball Rolling: The Memoirs of Anthony Powell, volume 3* (London, Heinemann, 1980), p. 113

11. Hendy, op. cit., p. 223

12. Via Hendy, op. cit., but originally from Briggs, op. cit.

13. Noel Newsome, *Giant at Bush House: At the Heart of the Radio War, the Autobiography of Noel Newsome* (The Real Press, 2018), p. 200

14. Reuters's personnel file, E. Barker, 28 September 1944

15. Account by Alan Bullock of wartime broadcasting, Papers of Douglas Ritchie and Noel Newsome, NERI 3/10, Churchill Archives Centre, Churchill College, Cambridge

16. Newsome, op. cit., p. 277

17. Bullock, NERI 3/10, Churchill Archives Centre

18. Tribute to Victor de Laveleye, 15 December 1945, Newsome/ Ritchie papers, NERI 3/10, Churchill Archives Centre

19. V Committee meeting, 26 May 1941, NERI 2/1/2, Churchill Archives Centre

20. V Committee, 7 July 1941, NERI, 2/1/2, Churchill Archives Centre

21. Memo, E. Barker to Ritchie, 7 May 1941 cited in Briggs, op. cit., p. 377

22. 'Victory and Freedom', *The Times*, 21 July 1941, p. 4. Accessed via *The Times* Digital Archive

23. NERI 2/1/2, Monitoring 21 July 1941

24. Hansard, HC Deb, vol. 373, col. 787, 22 July 1941

25. NERI 2/1/2

26. NERI 2/1/1

27. Ivor Thomas, *Warfare by Words* (London, Penguin Special, 1942), p. 85

28. R.H.S. Crossman MP, OBE, Royal United Services Institute lecture, 1952

29. Bruce Lockhart, *Diaries*, op. cit., 24 July 1941, p. 111

30. Hugh Dalton, *Diaries*, op. cit., p. 283

31. TNA, FO898/9

32. TNA, FO898/54, 15 July 1941

4: THE SHOOTING WAR IN WHITEHALL

1. Major-General Edward Spears, *Assignment to Catastrophe* (London, William Heinemann, 1954), pp. 152–3

2. John Colville, *Footprints in Time* (London, Collins, 1976), p. 97

3. Ronald Tree, *When the Moon was High, Memoirs of Peace and War 1897–1942* (London, Macmillan, 1975), p. 111

4. Boyle, *Poor, Dear Brendan*, op. cit., p. 101

5. Ibid, p. 104

6. Parliamentary Archives, Beaverbrook papers, BBK/C/56

7. Andrew Roberts, *Eminent Churchillians* (London, Phoenix, 1995), p. 146

8. Ibid., p. 164

9. Ibid., p. 41, citing Martin Gilbert, *Winston S. Churchill, vol 6* (London, Heinemann, 1983), pp. 543–4

10. Winston S. Churchill, *The Second World War: Volume 2, Their Finest Hour* (London, Cassell, 1949), p. 306

11. The Treasury was then housed in what's now the Cabinet Office building on Whitehall.

12. Boyle, op. cit., p. 259. This story is sourced to 'private information' to the author.

13. Charles Edward Lysaght, *Brendan Bracken* (London, Allen Lane, 1979), p. 178

14. John Colville, *The Fringes of Power: 10 Downing Street Diaries, 1939–1955* (London, Hodder & Stoughton, 1985), p. 225

15. Pimlott, *Hugh Dalton*, op. cit., p. 328

16. M.R.D. Foot, 'Major Lawrence Grand', *Oxford Dictionary of National Biography*, 2004

17. Hugh Dalton's diaries, 18 & 25 November 1940, cited in Pimlott, op. cit., p. 306

18. Pimlott, op. cit., p. 326

19. TNA, PREM 7/3 quoted in Pimlott, op. cit., p. 327

20. John Charmley, *Duff Cooper: The Authorized Biography* (London, Weidenfeld & Nicolson, 1986), p. 151

21. Hugh Dalton, *The Fateful Years*, op. cit., p. 378

22. TNA, INF1/894

23. Bruce Lockhart, *Diaries*, 28 January 1941, p. 89

24. Dalton, *Diaries*, op. cit., p. 162

25. TNA, INF1/894, Letter of 11 April 1941

26. TNA, INF1/894, Letter from Duff Cooper to Dalton, 29 April 1941
27. TNA, INF1/894, Letter from Dalton, 15 May 1941
28. Dalton, *Diaries*, op. cit., p. 209
29. Ibid, p. 202
30. Pimlott, op. cit., p. 338

5: THE STRANGE BIRD OF GOOD OMEN

1. Tree, op. cit., p. 130
2. Colville, *Footprints in Time*, op. cit., p. 111
3. Also known as Valentine, Lawford was later Churchill's interpreter at meetings with de Gaulle and attended many wartime conferences.
4. Colville, *Footprints in Time*, op. cit., p. 111
5. TNA, INF1/912
6. Boyle, op. cit., p. 264
7. His account was written for the Ministry of Information, ahead of a trip to the United States in 1945 where it was expected that he would be asked questions by American journalists about Hess's landing.
8. TNA, INF1/912
9. Ivone Kirkpatrick, *The Inner Circle* (London, Macmillan, 1959), p. 172
10. Harman Grisewood, *One Thing at a Time* (London, Hutchinson, 1968), p. 134
11. Kirkpatrick, op. cit., p. 173
12. Sir Alexander Cadogan, *The Diaries of Sir Alexander Cadogan, OM, 1938–1945* (London, Putnam, 1972), p. 377
13. TNA, INF1/912
14. 'Hitler's Deputy Escapes to Britain', *The Times*, 13 May 1941, p. 4
15. Balfour, *Propaganda in War, 1939–1945*, op. cit., p. 217
16. TNA INF1/912, Note to director general of the Ministry of Information, 13 May 1941
17. TNA INF1/912
18. Hansard, HC Deb, vol. 371, col. 1086, 13 May 1941, question from Sir Henry Morris-Jones
19. 'Cabinet and the Hess Affair', *The Times*, 15 May 1941

20. Bruce Lockhart, *Diaries, vol. 2*, op. cit., p. 99
21. Dalton, *Diaries*, op. cit., p. 203
22. Delmer, *Black Boomerang*, op. cit., p. 43
23. Hansard, HC Deb, vol. 371, col. 1262, 15 May 1941
24. *Observer*, 18 May 1941. There's some divergence in the quotes here: an MP in Hansard on 19 June quotes Morrison as saying 'baby panda'. Elsewhere it's 'giant panda'.
25. TNA, INF1/912, 26 May 1941
26. Hansard, HC Deb, vol. 372, col. 888, 19 June 1941
27. TNA, FO1093/7, Report from Con O'Neill, 22 June 1941
28. TNA, FO1093/7, Minute from Alec Cadogan, 29 June 1941
29. TNA, FO1093/7, Minute from Alec Cadogan, 3 July 1941
30. Hansard, HC Deb, vol. 376, col. 297, 19 November 1941
31. Charmley, *Duff Cooper: The Authorized Biography*, op. cit., p. 150

6: PROPAGANDA IN BATTLEDRESS

1. Muriel Spark, *Curriculum Vitae*, op. cit., p. 146
2. TNA, FO898/547, Walmsley memoir
3. https://www.lincolnsinn.org.uk/library-archives/tales-from-the-archive/may-2015-stone-buildings-and-world-war-ii/
4. Delmer, *Black Boomerang*, op. cit., p. 24
5. TNA, Sefton Delmer MI5 file, KV2/2586, copy of letter written 16 November 1940
6. TNA, Sefton Delmer MI5 file, KV2/2586/2
7. Details of Delmer's university education from Lincoln College, Oxford archives.
8. Denis Sefton Delmer, *Trail Sinister* (London, Secker & Warburg, London, 1961), p. 75
9. Ibid., p. 200
10. Isabel even changed her name by deed poll to that of Epstein's wife, Margaret, before the baby's birth to allow the baby to be accepted as theirs and registered under the Epstein name. The story of Isabel's life and art is in Carol Jacobi's biography, *Out of the Cage: The Art of Isabel Rawsthorne* (London, The Estate of Francis Bacon Publishing, in association with Thames & Hudson, 2021).
11. Virginia Cowles, *Looking for Trouble* (New York, The Modern Library, 2021; originally published 1941), p. 20

12. TNA, FO898/9, Meeting of 29–30 March 1941

13. German radio quoted in Briggs, *The History of Broadcasting in the United Kingdom vol. 3: The War of Words*, op. cit., pp. 212–13

14. TNA, FO898/4

15. Delmer, *Black Boomerang*, op. cit., p. 41

16. TNA, FO898/9, Meeting of 26–7 April 1941

17. TNA, FO898/4, 6 May 1941

18. TNA, FO898/4, 10 June 1941

19. TNA, FO898/4, 10 June 1941

20. TNA, FO898/9, 24–5 May 1941

21. Delmer, *Black Boomerang*, op. cit., p. 50

22. Secklmann's name is often spelt elsewhere as 'Seckelmann', but his German birth and marriage certificates have the first spelling. After the war, his family anglicised the spelling of their surname to 'Seckleman'.

23. UK records of alien internees, 1939

24. TNA, Peter Seckelmann MI5 file, KV2/3667

25. Charles Roetter, *Psychological Warfare*, op. cit., p. 172

26. Reinholz is given his real name in Delmer's book, though he was also known as Hanns Reinholz and Hans Holz, and changed his name to John Reynolds after the war.

27. His original name was Franz Josef Leuwer.

28. Imperial War Museum archives, IWM 15085, recording of GS1, July 1943

29. James Holland, *Sicily '43: The First Assault on Fortress Europe* (London, Penguin, 2020)

30. Charles Roetter, originally Karl Friedrich Roetter, was born in Germany, educated in Britain and was a student at the London School of Economics the start of the war.

31. The tune is called 'Üb immer Treu und Redlichkeit' and sounds similar to the song of Papageno's birdcatcher in Mozart's *The Magic Flute*.

32. Roetter, op. cit., p. 173

33. Ellic Howe, *The Black Game*, op. cit., p. 103

34. Delmer, *Black Boomerang*, op. cit., p. 62

35. TNA, FO898/60

36. TNA, FO898/51, 2 August 1941

37. TNA, FO898/547

38. Howe, op. cit., p. 95, citing letter sent from Walmsley to Howe on 15 August 1973

39. Charmian Brinson & Richard Dove, *Working for the War Effort: German-speaking Refugees in British Propaganda during the Second World War* (Portland, Vallentine Mitchell, 2021), p. 143

40. TNA, Ernst Adam MI5 file, KV2/2192/2

41. TNA, KV2/2192/2. Ernst Adam described the suspected agent as a man who had spent time in Moscow but returned to Berlin to help Leni Riefenstahl make her film about the 1936 Olympic Games. The source reported the man's name as Eric Junghans, but the description corresponds to that of Carl Junghans, who had done all of those things.

42. In one of his interviews, Ernst Adam says this conversation happened earlier in May, on the 11th/12th. He also named this man in another interview as 'Major Shrew', though this might have been misunderstood English or a transcription of his accent.

43. Maass biographical info from www.hamburger-persoenlichkeiten. de, site run by Hamburg State Museums

44. Howe, op. cit., p. 135

45. Bernard, Birgit, Alexander Maass, in: Internetportal Rheinische Geschichte, https://www.rheinische-geschichte. lvr.de/Persoenlichkeiten/alexander-maass/DE-2086/ lido/654cc1c3479f78.53285208. Accessed 8 May 2024

46. Peter Ritchie Calder, *The Kerbstone of History*, unpublished autobiography, Dep370/100, National Library of Scotland

47. Peter Ritchie Calder, paper on 'Meaning, Techniques and Methods of Political Warfare', Dep.370/155, National Library of Scotland

7: THE UNQUIET CEMETERY

1. Andrew Boyle, *Poor, Dear Brendan*, op. cit., p. 265

2. Bracken to Lord Wolmer, 23 July 1941, cited in Charmley, *Duff Cooper*, op. cit., p. 151

3. TNA, INF1/894

4. Bruce Lockhart, *Diaries*, op. cit., p. 101

5. Bruce Lockhart, *Comes the Reckoning*, op. cit., p. 117

6. Bruce Lockhart, *Diaries*, op. cit., p. 104

7. Hugh Dalton, *Diaries*, op. cit., p. 229

8. Bruce Lockhart, *Diaries*, op. cit., p. 106

9. Bruce Lockhart, *Comes the Reckoning*, op. cit., p. 118. The correct title of the film is *Dust Be My Destiny*, starring John Garfield.

10. Parliamentary Archives, BBK/C/221. Inflation calculator via Bank of England.

11. Hansard, HC Deb, vol. 372, col. 1537, 3 July 1941

12. Chris Bryant, *The Glamour Boys: The Secret Story of the Rebels Who Fought for Britain to Defeat Hitler* (London, Bloomsbury, 2020)

13. Note to Eden in TNA, FO898/9; another version of the conversation in Bruce Lockhart, *Comes the Reckoning*, op. cit., p. 121

14. Dalton, *Diaries*, op. cit., pp. 252–3

15. Dalton, *The Fateful Years*, op. cit., p. 382

16. 'From Our Parliamentary Correspondent: Ministerial Changes', *The Times*, 21 July 1941, p. 4. Accessed via *The Times* Digital Archive

17. Sir Robert Bruce Lockhart, *The Diaries of Sir Robert Bruce Lockhart, 1915–1938*, vol. 1, ed. Kenneth Young (London, Macmillan, 1973), 4 October 1932, p. 229

18. Parliamentary Archives, Beaverbrook papers, BBK/D/477

19. Boyle, op. cit., p. 63

20. Lysaght, op. cit., p. 144

21. Tree, op. cit., p. 112

22. Boyle, op. cit., p. 94

23. Parliamentary Archives, Beaverbrook papers, BBK/C/56

24. Boyle, op. cit., p. 7

25. Bruce Lockhart, *Diaries*, vol. 2, op. cit., 16 October 1941, p. 122

26. Boyle, op. cit., p. 119

27. Ibid., p. 120

28. Lysaght, op. cit., p. 191

29. Parliamentary Archives, Beaverbrook papers, BBK/C/56

30. Lysaght, op. cit., p. 196

31. Harold Nicolson, *Diaries and Letters 1939–45*, ed. Nigel Nicolson (London, Collins, 1967), p. 183

32. Boyle, op. cit., p. 266

33. Lysaght, op. cit., p. 193

34. TNA, FO898/9

35. Bruce Lockhart, *Diaries*, op. cit., p. 110

36. Copies in both TNA FO898/286 and INF1/894

37. Hugh Dalton, *Diaries*, op. cit., p. 261

8: A NUISANCE TO THE GOVERNMENT

1. Bruce Lockhart, *Diaries*, op. cit., 8 August 1941, p. 113

2. TNA, FO898/9
3. TNA, FO898/9, 11 August 1941
4. Dalton, *Diaries*, op. cit., p. 268. Letter from Dalton papers.
5. TNA, FO898/10
6. TNA, FO898/10, 22 August 1941
7. TNA, FO898/12, Leeper to Bruce Lockhart, 28 August 1941
8. TNA, FO898/286
9. TNA, INF1/894
10. TNA, FO898/9 about PQ
11. Dalton, *Diaries*, op. cit., p. 279
12. Hansard, HC Deb, vol. 374, col. 294, 11 September 1941
13. Hansard, HC Deb, vol. 374, col. 295, 11 September 1941
14. Dalton, *Diaries*, op. cit., p. 282
15. Bruce Lockhart, *Diaries*, op. cit., p. 119
16. Dalton, *Diaries*, op. cit., p. 292
17. Bruce Lockhart, *Diaries*, op. cit., p. 125
18. Cadogan, *Diaries*, op. cit., p. 409
19. TNA, FO954/24A/21, 26/10/1941. This and the following letters were not available to Bracken and Dalton's biographers as they were kept closed for fifty years at the National Archives.
20. TNA, FO954/24A/24, 27 October 1941
21. TNA, FO 954/24A/33
22. TNA, FO954/24A/35
23. Dalton, *Diaries*, op. cit., 14 November 1941, p. 313
24. TNA, FO954/24A/40
25. Dalton, *Diaries*, op. cit., 19 November 1941, p. 319
26. TNA, FO954/24A/54
27. Dalton, *Diaries*, op. cit., p. 329
28. TNA, FO954/24A/101. Released under FOI request, 2023
29. Bruce Lockhart, *Diaries*, op. cit., p. 130

9: ADMIRABLE IN EFFICIENCY AND IN CONDUCT

1. TNA, FO898/35
2. TNA, FO898/10
3. TNA, FO898/35
4. TNA, FO898/12
5. TNA, FO898/4, 6 August 1940

6. Bruce Lockhart, *Comes the Reckoning*, op. cit., p. 157

7. Jacobi, op. cit., p. 138

8. Howe, op. cit., p. 135

9. Delmer, *Black Boomerang*, op. cit., p. 150

10. *Sunday Express*, 17 February 1946, p. 1

11. Bruce Lockhart, *Diaries*, op. cit., p. 152

12. Delmer, *Black Boomerang*, p. 151

13. TNA, FO898/63

14. Jacobi, op. cit., pp. 141–2, citing Lee Richards, *The Black Art: British Clandestine Psychological Warfare* (Psywar, 2010)

15. IWM, Peter W memoir, Documents.5038

16. TNA, FO898/51

17. Howard, op. cit., p. 97

18. TNA, FO 898/51

19. Anne Symonds, 'Obituary: Ruggero Orlando', *Independent*, 3 May 1994

20. TNA, FO898/60

21. TNA, FO898/60, 18 February 1942

22. Bruce Lockhart, *Diaries*, op. cit., p. 121

23. Olday's original name was Arthur William OLDAG. His security service file is at TNA, KV2/3597.

24. Marcus Barnett, 'The Tribunite Who Tried to Kill Hitler', *Tribune*, 27 December 2021

25. Bruce Lockhart, *Comes the Reckoning*, op. cit., p. 156

26. Dilys Powell, *An Affair of the Heart* (London, Eland, 2019; first published London, Hodder & Stoughton, 1957), p. 28

27. George Angeloglou, *This is London, Good Evening: Edo London, Kalispera Sas: the Story of the Greek Section of the BBC, 1939–1957* (Athens, Efstathiadis Group, 2003), p. 126

28. Richard Clogg, 'The Greek Government-in-Exile 1941–44', *International History Review*, July 1979, p. 380

29. Angeloglou, op. cit., p. 130

30. Ibid., p. 131

31. TNA, FO898/547

32. TNA, FO898/547

33. Bruce Lockhart, *Comes the Reckoning*, op. cit., p. 157

34. Spark, op. cit., p. 146

35. Several rectories around Woburn and Aspley Guise were requisitioned, including the Old Rectory at Tingrith, Holton Rectory near Woburn Sands, and Walton Rectory, near the

Simpson studio in what is now Milton Keynes. It's not clear which of these Spark lived in, though it may have been Walton Rectory.

36. Spark, op. cit., p. 158

37. IWM, Peter W memoir, Documents.5038

38. Peter Quennell, *The Marble Foot: An Autobiography, 1905–38* (London, Collins, 1976); Peter Quennell, *The Wanton Chase: An Autobiography from 1939* (London, Collins, 1980), p. 51

39. Spark, op. cit., p. 159

40. Deborah McDonald & Jeremy Dronfield, *A Very Dangerous Woman: The Lives, Loves and Lies of Russia's Most Seductive Spy* (London, Oneworld, 2015), pp. 93–4, 153

41. TNA, Moura Budberg MI5 file, KV2/980

42. https://www.wilsoncenter.org/sites/default/files/media/documents/article/Venona-London-GRU.pdf

43. Robert Service, *Spies and Commissars: Bolshevik Russia and the West* (London, Pan Macmillan, 2011), p. 348, citing Dmitri Collingridge, 'Aunt Moura', *Sunday Times*, 2 May 2010

10: HE OFTEN APPEARS TO TALK COMPLETE NONSENSE

1. *National Review*, no. 703, September 1941, pp. 266–7

2. 'From Our Special Correspondent: The Truth about Nazi Leaders', *The Times*, 21 July 1941, p. 4. Accessed via *The Times* Digital Archive

3. TNA, FO898/12

4. Dalton, *Diaries*, op. cit., p. 351

5. *Sunday Dispatch*, 8 February 1942

6. Delmer, *Black Boomerang*, op. cit., p. 51

7. Quinton Varley, 'They're telling the Germans we respect them!', *Daily Mail*, 5 February 1942, p. 2. Accessed via the *Daily Mail* Historical Archive

8. TNA, FO898/12

9. TNA, FO898/191, Scarlett to Millard

10. Hansard, HC Debate, vol. 377, col. 1707, 17 February 1942

11. J.B. Priestley, *Postscripts* (London, William Heinemann, 1940), p. 98; Hendy, op. cit., p. 198

12. Hansard, HC Debate, vol. 377, col. 1711, 17 February 1942

13. 'A Channel Inquiry', *The Times*, 18 February 1942, p. 5. Accessed via *The Times* Digital Archive

14. Winston Churchill, *The Second World War: Vol. IV, The Hinge of Fate* (London, Cassell, 1948), p. 81

15. Bruce Lockhart, *Comes the Reckoning*, op. cit., p. 152

16. Ibid., p. 153

17. 'More Savings Imperative', *The Times*, 23 February 1942, p. 2. Accessed via *The Times* Digital Archive

18. Dalton, *Diaries*, op. cit., pp. 374–5

19. *National Review*, no. 709, March 1942, p. 222

20. TNA, FO898/60, Delmer to Leeper, 15 March 1942

21. TNA, FO898/60, draft letter, 6 May 1942

22. Bruce Lockhart, *Diaries*, op. cit., 25 March 1942, p. 153

23. Dalton, *Diaries*, op. cit., p. 355.

24. TNA, FO898/60

25. Bruce Lockhart, *Diaries*, op. cit., p. 154

26. Ibid., p. 155

27. Bruce Lockhart, *Comes the Reckoning*, op. cit., p. 170

28. Bruce Lockhart, *Diaries*, op. cit., p. 156

29. Bruce Lockhart, *Comes the Reckoning*, op. cit., p. 163

11: A RARE ARTIST AND
A GOOD FELLOW

1. Letter, Sir Stafford Cripps to Anthony Eden, 12 June 1942, in TNA FO898/60. This letter was only released to the public files in 2006.

2. Bruce Lockhart, *Comes the Reckoning*, op. cit., p. 184

3. Vernon Bartlett, *News Chronicle*, 24 January 1942, cited in Peter Clarke, *The Cripps Version* (London, Allen Lane, 2002), p. 272

4. Bruce Lockhart, *Diaries*, op. cit., 23 June 1942, p. 178

5. Goebbels's diaries cited in Clarke, op. cit., p. 269

6. Bruce Lockhart, *Comes the Reckoning*, op. cit., p. 184

7. Delmer, *Black Boomerang*, op. cit., p. 252

8. TNA, FO898/60, Rex Leeper minute, 16 June 1942

9. TNA, FO898/60, 20 June 1942

10. Bruce Lockhart, *Comes the Reckoning*, op. cit., p. 185

11. TNA, FO898/54, Murray to Leeper, 5 May 1942

12. Bruce Lockhart, *Diaries*, op. cit., p. 180

13. TNA, FO898/60
14. TNA, FO898/60
15. TNA, FO898/60, January 1941
16. Roetter, op. cit., p. 174
17. Ibid., p. 175
18. Ibid., p. 176, citing Ley in *Der Angriff*

12: YOU HAVE NO CHANCE!

1. Balfour, op. cit., p. 97
2. Bruce Lockhart, *Comes the Reckoning*, op. cit., p. 171
3. Bruce Lockhart, *Diaries*, op. cit., p. 160
4. Max Hastings, *Bomber Command* (London, Michael Joseph, 1979), p. 135
5. Daniel Todman, *Britain's War: A New World, 1942–1947* (London, Allen Lane, 2020), p. 168
6. Henry Probert, *Bomber Harris: his Life and Times* (London, Greenhill Books, 2001), p. 185
7. Hastings, op. cit., p. 138
8. BBC WAC, BBC/E/E2/486, 4 June 1942
9. TNA, FO898/317, Air Marshal Harris's script sent to Operational Propaganda Committee, 13 July 1942
10. TNA, FO898/317, 'Why We Bomb You' draft
11. 'You Have No Chance,' *The Times*, 29 July 1942, p. 2. Accessed via *The Times* Digital Archive
12. Bruce Lockhart, *Comes the Reckoning*, op. cit., p. 172
13. TNA, FO898/317, Letter from Sir Archibald Sinclair to Brendan Bracken, minister of information, 29 July 1942
14. Hansard, HL Deb, vol. 124, col. 59, 29 July 1942
15. Bruce Lockhart, *Diaries*, op. cit., p. 185
16. Hansard, HL Deb, vol. 124, col. 181–92, 4 August 1942
17. TNA, FO898/317
18. Clamjamfry is a Scots word meaning rabble or mob.
19. Bruce Lockhart, *Diaries*, op. cit., p. 187
20. TNA, FO898/131, Dallas Brooks diary of events, September 1942
21. Crossman eventually left Foynes air terminal in Ireland on 26 September 1942, arriving in New York via American Export

Airlines flying boat the following day; US immigration records and Foynes Flying Boat Museum website.

22. TNA, FO898/183, 18 September 1942
23. TNA, FO898/458 cited in Richard Overy, 'Making and Breaking Morale: British Political Warfare and Bomber Command in the Second World War', *Twentieth Century History*, vol. 29, issue 3, September 2015, pp. 370–99, Appendix 1

13: THE END OF THE BEGINNING

1. Bruce Lockhart, *Comes the Reckoning*, op. cit., p. 190
2. TNA, FO898/129, telegram from Eisenhower to Marshall, 6 August 1942
3. Bruce Lockhart, *Diaries*, op. cit., p. 190
4. John Baker White, *The Big Lie* (London, Evans Brothers Ltd, 1956), p. 110
5. At the time that Winner wrote (8 June 1942), Donovan was still the co-ordinator of information. On 13 June, Roosevelt would create the OSS – the Office of Strategic Services, the forerunner of the CIA.
6. US National Archives, Records of the Office of War Information, Entry NC148 6J, record group 208, box 3, 8 June 1942
7. Howe, op. cit., p. 167
8. Bruce Lockhart, *Diaries*, op. cit., p. 199
9. Ritchie Calder papers, 'The Meaning, Techniques and Methods of Political Warfare', National Library of Scotland, Dep 370/155
10. TNA, FO898/129, 10 October 1942
11. TNA, FO898/131
12. TNA, PREM3/365/3. Dalton estimated the costs at £165,000 to buy and install the transmitter, plus another £28,000 a year to run it.
13. Imperial War Museum, Audio 5134, Ellic Howe interview with Harold Robin
14. TNA, FO954/23A/145
15. TNA, FO898/131
16. TNA, PREM3/365/3
17. This is because of a phenomenon called ionospheric reflection which allows skywave propagation. See https://www.fcc.gov/media/radio/am-stations-at-night

18. TNA, FO954/18B/372
19. TNA, PREM3/365/3
20. TNA, FO898/129
21. TNA, FO898/131, 26 October 1942
22. TNA, PREM3/365/3 Roosevelt telegram, 10 October 1942
23. TNA, FO898/131
24. TNA, FO898/131, memo of 22 October 1942
25. TNA, FO898/131, Barman memo, 2 November 1942
26. Newsome, op. cit., p. 312
27. Jackson, op. cit., p. 147
28. Bruce Lockhart, *Comes the Reckoning*, op. cit., p. 206
29. Newsome, op. cit., p. 314
30. TNA, FO898/131, RHBL to Eden, 7 November 1942
31. Garnett, op. cit., p. 255
32. TNA, FO898/131
33. Diary of John Martin, Churchill's private secretary, quoted on winstonchurchill.org
34. Bruce Lockhart, *Comes the Reckoning*, op. cit., p. 209

14: CAUGHT AT LAST!

1. Delmer, *Black Boomerang*, op. cit., p. 81
2. Bruce Lockhart, *Diaries*, op. cit., p. 198
3. Imperial War Museum, Peter W memoir, Documents.5038
4. Delmer, *Black Boomerang*, op. cit., p. 78
5. Howe, op. cit., p. 180
6. Brinson & Dove, op. cit.
7. TNA, FO898/51, Delmer to Wilson and Balfour, 13 October 1942
8. Howe, op. cit., p. 140
9. TNA, FO898/61, 9 January 1943
10. TNA, FO898/61, 10 January 1943
11. Howard, op. cit., p. 99
12. Delmer, *Black Boomerang*, op. cit., p. 77
13. TNA, FO898/65
14. TNA, FO898/64, Evidence of reception, June 1943
15. Howe, op. cit., p. 181
16. IWM, Peter W memoir

17. Agnes Bernelle, *The Fun Palace: An Autobiography* (Dublin, The Lilliput Press, 1996)
18. Hendy, op. cit., p. 228
19. TNA, FO898/35
20. Donald McLachlan, *Room 39: Naval Intelligence in Action, 1939–45* (London, Weidenfeld & Nicolson, 1968), p. 166
21. Howe, op. cit., p. 190
22. TNA, KV2/2192
23. Jacobi, op. cit., p. 143; Simon Fenwick, *Joan: Beauty, Rebel, Muse: the Remarkable Life of Joan Leigh Fermor* (London, Macmillan, 2017), p. 111
24. TNA, FO898/61, Howe paper, 26 August 1941
25. TNA, FO898/61, Rayner, 7 October 1941
26. Howe, op. cit., p. 210
27. Delmer, *Black Boomerang*, op. cit., p. 131
28. De Wohl said that he had chosen to be Hungarian in 1919 when his father's birthplace was divided between Hungary and Czechoslovakia. His father had been born in Losoncz, now Lučenec in Slovakia. His mother and sister, however, became Czechs. Although registered as Catholic, he had Jewish ancestry on his mother's side.
29. ancestry.co.uk: Lajos Theodor Kasper Adolf Wohl, born Berlin 24 January 1903
30. TNA, Louis de Wohl MI5 file, KV2/2821
31. TNA, FO898/51, 27/11/42

15: GREEKS IN THIS AMERICAN EMPIRE

1. Letter to Roger Makins, 11/1/44, Richard Crossman archive, Modern Records Centre, University of Warwick, MSS.154/3/AU/1/94
2. Harold Macmillan, *War Diaries: Politics and War in the Mediterranean 1943–1945* (London, Macmillan, 1984), p. 5
3. Lord Egremont, *Wyndham and Children First* (London, Macmillan, 1968), p. 77
4. Diana Cooper, *Trumpets from the Steep* (London, Century, 1984; first published 1960), p. 172
5. TNA, FO898/137

6. Harold Macmillan, *The Blast of War 1939–1945* (London, Macmillan, 1967), pp. 271–2

7. TNA, FO898/137

8. TNA, FO898/139, Macmillan telegram, 1 June 1943

9. Richard Crossman, 'The Making of Macmillan', *Sunday Telegraph*, 9 February 1964

10. Crossman told a similar version of the story to Dalton (Dalton, *Diaries*, January 1944), mentioning the Greeks and the Romans, around six months after the event, but his retelling in the *Sunday Telegraph* twenty years later is more elaborate.

11. Jackson, op. cit., p. 126

12. Macmillan, *War Diaries*, op. cit., p. 100

13. Crossman, 'The Making of Macmillan', op. cit.

14. Macmillan, *War Diaries*, op. cit., p. 167. Anthony Eden would later have cause to disagree with the view of Jackson as 'loyal'; Jackson started an affair with Eden's first wife, Beatrice, who eventually left Anthony for him. Eden himself also had many affairs (D.R. Thorpe, *Eden: The Life and Times of Anthony Eden, First Earl of Avon, 1897–1977* (London, Pimlico, 2004), p. 311).

15. R.H.S. Crossman, Royal United Services Institute lecture, 1952

16. TNA, FO898/349, Propaganda plan, Spring 1943

17. TNA, PREM3/365/2, Telegram of 17 May 1943

18. TNA, PREM3/365/2, Eden memo, 19 May 1943

19. TNA, PREM3/365/2, Eden telegram Alcove 340, 22 May 1943

20. Franklin D. Roosevelt, Excerpts from 'The Joint Press Conference with Prime Minister Churchill', 25 May 1943, The American Presidency Project https://www.presidency.ucsb.edu/node/210084

21. Todman, op. cit., p. 336, citing psywar.org

22. IWM, Documents.395a, Con O'Neill personal papers

23. Evidence of reception report, cited in Howe, op. cit., p. 185

24. Edith C. Rogers, *The Reduction of Pantelleria and adjacent islands*, Air Historical Office, US Air Force Historical Division, May 1947

25. Ibid.

26. 'The landing on Pantelleria', *The Times*, 14 June 1943

27. Sir Robert Bruce Lockhart, 'Propaganda in Wartime', Royal Institute of International Affairs lecture, 10 September 1946

28. Lord Ritchie-Calder, 'Propaganda during the war', Letter to the Editor, *The Times*, 11 June 1973

29. George Martelli, 'Wartime propaganda', Letter to the Editor, *The Times*, 16 June 1973

30. Churchill telegram to Roosevelt, 5 July 1943, in E. Ralph Perkins & N.O. Sappington (eds), *Foreign Relations of the United States, Diplomatic Papers, 1943, Europe, Volume II* (Washington DC, US Government Printing Office, 1964), Document 296

31. TNA, FO898/349, Harrison, 6 May 1943

32. TNA, FO898/349, note on Roosevelt press conference

33. TNA, FO898/349, Eisenhower telegram, 29 July 1943

34. TNA, PREM3/365/2

35. TNA, FO898/349, Delmer to Bruce Lockhart, 3 July 1943

36. TNA, PREM3/365/2, Anthony Bevir to Leslie Hollis, 3 July 1943

37. TNA, FO954/23A/210

38. E. Ralph Perkins & N.O. Sappington, op. cit., Document 297

39. TNA, FO898/60

40. Thomas, op. cit., p. 71

41. Howe, op. cit., p. 170

42. Ibid., p. 171

43. TNA, FO898/65, Ritchie Calder, 21 September 1943

44. First Supplemental National Defense Appropriation Bill for 1944: Hearings Before a Subcommittee of the Committee on Appropriations, United States Senate, Seventy-eighth Congress [12, 15–19, 22–24, 26, 29 November 1943] (United States: U.S. Government Printing Office, 1943)

45. Viscount Cunningham of Hyndhope, *A Sailor's Odyssey* (London, Hutchinson, 1951)

46. Martelli, op. cit.

47. The joint operation was referred to as the Psychological Warfare Branch.

48. TNA, FO898/137, Crossman to Bruce Lockhart, 12 July 1943

49. Dalton, *Diaries*, op. cit., p. 693; Crossman in Daniel Lerner, *Psychological Warfare against Nazi Germany: The Sykewar campaign, D-Day to VE Day* (Cambridge, MA, MIT Press, 1971; first published 1949), p. 328

50. Crossman, 'The Making of Macmillan', op. cit.

51. Ibid.

52. This is likely to have been between 5 and 8 October, when Macmillan briefly visited London. Macmillan, *War Diaries*, op. cit., p. 249

16: IGNORE THE CIVIL WAR

1. Elisabeth Barker, *Truce in the Balkans* (London, Percival Marshall, 1948), p. 10
2. Stevan K. Pawlowitch, 'Out of Context: the Yugoslav government in London 1941–1945', *Journal of Contemporary History*, vol. 16, no. 1, 1981, pp. 89–118
3. *The Times*, 30 June 1941
4. 'King Peter of Yugo-Slavia: Coming-of-Age Service at St Paul's', *Manchester Guardian*, 17 September 1941, p. 8
5. TNA, FO898/54, Leeper to Murray, 18 May 1941
6. Tim Judah, 'Yugoslavia 1918–2003', bbc.co.uk, 2011
7. David Stafford, *Britain and European Resistance, 1940–1945* (London, Macmillan, 1980), p. 96
8. Imperial War Museum, Audio.5217
9. TNA, FO898/51
10. Michael Stenton, *Radio London and Resistance in Occupied Europe: British Political Warfare 1939–1943* (Oxford, Oxford University Press, 2000), p. 334
11. TNA, FO898/54
12. FO898/54, cited in Stenton, op. cit., p. 356
13. Elisabeth Barker, 'Sidelights on British Policy in Yugoslavia 1942–3', *Slavonic and East European Review*, vol. 54, no. 4, October 1976, pp. 572–85
14. BBC Written Archives Centre, Elisabeth Barker Oral History interview, BBC R143/266/1
15. TNA, FO898/146, 6 March 1943
16. TNA, FO898/54, 21 July 1941
17. TNA, FO898/54, 7 March 1943
18. TNA, FO898/54, 5 March 1943
19. TNA, FO898/54
20. TNA, FO898/54
21. TNA, FO898/54, minutes of meeting 27 May 1943; memo 12 May 1943
22. TNA, FO898/157, telegram 1 August 1943
23. Delmer, *Black Boomerang*, op. cit., p. 103
24. Elisabeth Barker, *British Policy in South-East Europe in the Second World War* (London, Macmillan, 1976), p. 161
25. TNA, FO898/157
26. TNA, FO898/157, Murray to Bruce Lockhart, 14 October 1942

27. TNA, FO898/157, Letter from Clutton (for Dixon) to Murray, 31 October 1942

28. FO371/37578 cited in Barker, *British Policy in South-East Europe in the Second World War*, op. cit., p. 163

29. Fitzroy Maclean, *Eastern Approaches* (London, Jonathan Cape, 1949, reprinted by the Reprint Society, 1951), p. 225

30. Ibid., p. 227

31. Ibid, p. 238

32. Barker, *British Policy in South-East Europe in the Second World War*, op. cit., p. 164

33. TNA, FO898/61

34. Maclean, op. cit., p. 320

35. Michael Foot, 'Randolph' in *Debts of Honour* (London, Faber Finds, 2010; first published 1980)

36. Maclean, op. cit., p. 332

37. TNA, FO898/160, telegram of 28 January 1944

38. TNA, FO898/160, letter of 9 May 1944

39. TNA, FO898/160, letter 12 May 1944

40. Bruce Lockhart to Sir Orme Sargent, 4 May 1944, quoted in Bruce Lockhart, *Diaries*, op. cit., p. 302

41. Ibid., p. 310

42. Macmillan, *War Diaries*, op. cit., p. 448

43. Ibid., *War Diaries*, p. 467

44. Evelyn Waugh, *The Diaries of Evelyn Waugh*, ed. Michael Davie (London, Penguin, 1979), p. 573

17: NEAR TO DEATH'S DOOR

1. Letter to Tosco Fyvel, 14 January 1944, Richard Crossman archive, Modern Records Centre, University of Warwick Modern Records Centre, MSS.154/3/AU/1/98

2. Letter to Roger Makins, 18 January 1944, MRC, University of Warwick, MSS.154/3/AU/1/94

3. Letter to Tosco Fyvel, op. cit.

4. Letter to Roger Makins, op. cit.

5. Dalton, *Diaries*, op. cit., p. 692

6. Delmer, *Black Boomerang*, op. cit., p. 108

7. Bruce Lockhart, *Diaries*, op. cit., p. 275

8. R.H.S. Crossman, 'Listening to the BBC 1: Hearing and Listening', *New Statesman and Nation*, 15 January 1944

9. R.H.S. Crossman, 'Listening to the BBC 2: The "Ersatz" programme', *New Statesman and Nation*, 22 January 1944

10. Peter Ritchie Calder, letter to Robert Bruce Lockhart, 2 January 1944, Dep.370/155, National Library of Scotland

11. Letter from Harold Macmillan, 28 December 1943, MRC, University of Warwick MSS.154/3/AU/1/96

12. Letter from Roger Makins, 29 December 1943, MRC, MSS.154/3/AU/1/92

13. Letter to Harold Macmillan, 11 January 1944, MRC, MSS.154/3/AU/1/97

14. Letter to C.D. Jackson, 20 January 1944, MRC, MSS.154/3/AU/1/104

15. Letter to Frank Roberts, 14 January 1944, MRC, MSS.154/3/AU/1/100-103

16. Parliamentary Archives, House of Lords, Beaverbrook Papers, BBK/C/222, letter of 28 October 1943

17. Bruce Lockhart, *Comes the Reckoning*, op. cit., pp. 273–5

18. Bruce Lockhart, *Diaries*, op. cit., 17 March 1944, p. 288

19. Bruce Lockhart, *Comes the Reckoning*, op. cit., p. 290

20. Lysaght, op. cit., p. 231

21. TNA, FO898/160. Neither of Bracken's biographers mention an operation, but Randolph Churchill would have been well placed to know of one.

22. Boyle, op. cit., p. 301

23. D.R. Thorpe, op. cit., p. 292

24. Bruce Lockhart, *Diaries*, op. cit., p. 298

25. Ibid., p. 293

26. Lord Ritchie-Calder, lecture at Edinburgh University, spring 1965, Dep.370/122, National Library of Scotland

27. Delmer, *Black Boomerang*, op. cit., p. 152

28. Boyle, op. cit., pp. 305–6. Boyle sources this to private information from Crossman, which doesn't appear to be corroborated or referenced anywhere else. It's possible that this story was also partly Crossman's own spin.

18: THE PECCANT DOCUMENT

1. Newsome/Ritchie papers, Churchill Archives Centre, NERI 2/2/3

2. Bruce Lockhart, *Comes the Reckoning*, op. cit., p. 306
3. TNA, PREM3/365/5
4. TNA, PREM3/365/5
5. Bruce Lockhart, *Diaries*, op. cit., p. 305
6. Ibid., p. 303
7. Ibid., 22 May 1944, p. 314
8. TNA, CAB66/50/33, draft for a radio script for use in British and American German Radio Service
9. TNA, CAB65/42/28, 31 May 1944
10. Bruce Lockhart, *Diaries*, op. cit., p. 314
11. TNA, FO954/23A/256
12. TNA, FO954/23A/256
13. TNA, FO954/23A/263

19: THE SOUND OF A THOUSAND PLANES

1. Bruce Lockhart, *Comes the Reckoning*, op. cit., p. 300
2. Charles de Gaulle, *Mémoires de Guerre: L'Unité: 1942–1944* (Paris, Plon, 1956), p. 264; Jackson, op. cit., p. 310
3. The Earl of Avon (Anthony Eden), *The Eden Memoirs: The Reckoning* (London, Cassell, 1965), p. 452
4. Lord Ritchie-Calder, University of Edinburgh lectures, spring 1965, Dep.370/122, National Library of Scotland
5. De Gaulle, op. cit., p. 264
6. TNA, PREM3/365/5
7. Jonathan Fenby, *The General: de Gaulle and the France He Saved* (London, Simon & Schuster, 2010), p. 240
8. Although he managed to return to France with de Gaulle after the landings, Pierre Viénot succumbed to the strain of his incessant work during the war and died of a heart attack six weeks after the invasion, aged forty-seven. https://www.ordredelaliberation.fr/fr/compagnons/pierre-vienot
9. Jackson, op. cit., p. 315
10. Bruce Lockhart, *Diaries*, op. cit., p. 318
11. Fenby, op. cit., p. 241
12. TNA, FO954/9A/180, minute to the secretary of state, 6 June 1944
13. Bruce Lockhart, *Diaries*, op. cit., p. 319

14. Newsome, op. cit., p. 360
15. Delmer, *Black Boomerang*, op. cit., p. 163
16. TNA, FO954/9A/172
17. Bruce Lockhart, *Comes the Reckoning*, op. cit., p. 303
18. 'Snubbed again', *TIME* magazine, 19 June 1944
19. De Gaulle, op. cit., p. 269

20: A MOMENT OF WINGED THUNDER

1. William Sansom, *The Blitz: Westminster at War* (Oxford, Oxford University Press, 1990; first published 1947), p. 195
2. Newsome, op. cit., p. 372
3. Lockhart, *Comes the Reckoning*, op. cit., p. 313
4. TNA, FO898/547, Walmsley memoir
5. Delmer, *Black Boomerang*, op. cit., p. 169
6. TNA, FO898/547
7. Delmer, *Black Boomerang*, op. cit., pp. 170–1
8. Ibid., p. 172
9. Ibid., p. 174
10. TNA, War Cabinet minutes, CAB/65/43/10, 20 July 1944
11. Earl of Avon, op. cit., p. 464
12. Bruce Lockhart, *Comes the Reckoning*, op. cit., p. 314
13. TNA, FO954/10B/391, 24 July 1944
14. Boyle, op. cit., p. 307
15. TNA, Otto John MI5 file, KV2/2465, MI5 letter of 20 November 1944
16. Delmer, *Black Boomerang*, op. cit., p. 179
17. TNA, KV2/2465, interrogation report, Oratory School, 13 November 1944. The SD or Sicherheitsdienst was the German intelligence agency.
18. Delmer, *Black Boomerang*, op. cit., p. 183
19. Otto John, *Twice Through the Lines* (London, Macmillan, 1972), pp. 175–6
20. https://www.cia.gov/readingroom/docs/ZECH-NENNTWICH,%20HANS_0001.pdf, released 2001
21. 'Die Karriere eines SS-Offiziers', *Die Zeit*, 1 May 1964
22. Delmer, *Black Boomerang*, op. cit., p. 188
23. TNA, FO898/65

24. De Gaulle, op. cit., p. 353

25. Bruce Lockhart, *Comes the Reckoning*, op. cit., p. 316

26. John Bew, *Citizen Clem: A Biography of Attlee* (London, Riverrun, 2016), pp. 316–17

27. De Gaulle, op. cit., p. 354

28. Bruce Lockhart, *Diaries*, op. cit., p. 346

29. Ibid., p. 351

30. TNA, FO898/65, Delmer memo of 30 October 1944

31. TNA, FO898/65, Delmer memo

21: WE WHO LIVE

1. Delmer, *Black Boomerang*, op. cit., p. 200

2. R.H.S. Crossman, Supplementary essay in Lerner, op. cit.

3. Crossman, *The Making of Macmillan*, op. cit.

4. TNA, FO898/395, Telegram from PWD SHAEF

5. Crossman in Lerner, op. cit., p. 326

6. TNA, FO898/395, McLachlan, 7 March 1945

7. TNA, FO898/395, Political warfare plan, 15 November 1944

8. TNA, FO898/395, Ritchie Calder memo, 12 March 1945

9. TNA, FO898/395, Bishop to Hollis, 7 March 1945

10. Bruce Lockhart, *Diaries*, op. cit., pp. 404–5

11. Ibid., p. 405

12. TNA, FO898/395, draft of political warfare plan to implement SHAEF requirements, 11 March 1945

13. Delmer, *Black Boomerang*, op. cit., p. 201

14. TNA, FO989/395, minutes of meeting of 15 March 1945

15. Delmer, *Black Boomerang*, op. cit., p. 202

16. Imperial War Museum, Audio 5134, Harold Robin interview with Ellic Howe, July 1981

17. TNA, FO898/395, Delmer Draft Black Evacuation Plan, 9 March 1945

18. TNA, FO898/395, transcript of German Forces Radio broadcast, 27 March 1945

19. Crossman in Lerner, op. cit., p. 326

20. Bruce Lockhart, *Diaries*, op. cit., p. 407

21. Bruce Lockhart, *Comes the Reckoning*, op. cit., p. 345

22. Delmer, *Black Boomerang*, op. cit., p. 216

23. Ibid., p. 217

24. Imperial War Museum, Audio 5205
25. Music tracks identified from the audio recording using the Shazam app.
26. Delmer, *Black Boomerang*, op. cit., p. 218. Again, we only have Delmer's account of the farewell meeting with his staff.
27. Ibid., p. 219
28. TNA, FO898/61, letter from General Alec Bishop, 30 April 1945
29. TNA, FO898/61, letter from Rushbrooke to Bishop, 23 May 1945
30. Bruce Lockhart, *Comes the Reckoning*, op. cit., p. 347
31. Bruce Lockhart, *Diaries*, op. cit., p. 430
32. Diary of 7 May 1945, written on 13 May 1945, Modern Records Centre, Warwick University, MSS.154/3/AU/1/106. Some of this material was also published in Crossman's book, *Palestine Mission*.
33. William S. Paley, *As It Happened: A Memoir* (New York, Doubleday, 1979), p. 167
34. Crossman diary, MRC, Warwick University, MSS.154/3/AU/1/110
35. Paley, op. cit., p. 168
36. TNA, INF1/636. The film itself is at Imperial War Museum Gov 41.
37. Solly Zuckerman, *From Apes to Warlords, 1904–1946: An Autobiography* (London, Hamish Hamilton, 1978), p. 331
38. Richard Crossman, *Palestine Mission*, op. cit., p. 18
39. Hansard, HC Deb, vol. 385, col. 2083, 17 December 1942
40. Bernard Wasserstein, *Britain and the Jews of Europe, 1939–1945* (Leicester, Leicester University Press, 1999), p. 267
41. TNA, FO371/42897/25, cited in Wasserstein, op. cit., p. 270
42. R.H.S. Crossman, Royal United Services Institute lecture, 1952
43. Richard Crossman, 'Black Prima Donna' (review of *Black Boomerang*), *New Statesman*, 9 November 1962
44. Richard Crossman papers, MRC, Warwick University, MSS.154/3/AU/1/122

CONCLUSION: THE AFTERLIFE OF POLITICAL WARFARE

1. Christopher Mayhew, *A War of Words: A Cold War Witness* (London, I.B. Tauris, 1998), p. 18
2. Mayhew memo of October 1947, quoted in Mayhew, op. cit., p. 122

3. Dalton, *The Fateful Years*, op. cit., p. 373
4. Bevin, Cabinet paper CAB129/23, January 1948, cited in Mayhew, op. cit.
5. TNA, CAB21/2745, memo by foreign secretary on future foreign publicity policy, 4 January 1948
6. TNA, CAB21/2745, memo from Norman Brook to Attlee, March 1948
7. TNA, CAB21/2745, minutes of meeting of 12 March 1945
8. Robert Bruce Lockhart, *Diaries*, op. cit., 4 February 1948, p. 648
9. BBC WAC, Elisabeth Barker oral history interview, R143/266/1
10. Bruce Lockhart, *Comes the Reckoning*, op. cit., p. 331
11. BBC WAC, oral history interview, R143/266/1
12. Elisabeth Barker, personnel file, Reuters news agency
13. Elisabeth Barker, *Truce in the Balkans*, op. cit., introductory note
14. The fourth child of his marriage was born in 1948.
15. Interview with Elisabeth Barker's daughter, Dinah, April 2022
16. Dinah Collins birth certificate, registered 21 October 1947; Elisabeth Barker deed poll, 25 February 1948, published in *London Gazette*, 23 March 1948
17. Andrew Defty, *Britain, America and Anti-Communist Propaganda 1945–53* (London, Routledge, 2004), p. 77
18. Obituary of Elisabeth Barker, *The Times*, 28 March 1986
19. Mayhew, op. cit., p. 19
20. Bruce Lockhart, *Diaries*, op. cit., p. 436
21. Bruce Lockhart letter, 7 June 1945, quoted in full in Howard, op. cit., pp. 106–7
22. Bruce Lockhart, *Giants Cast Long Shadows*, op. cit., p. 98
23. Crossman, 'Psychological Warfare', op. cit., pp. 319–32
24. Earl of Avon, op. cit., p. 538
25. Boyle, op. cit., p. 309
26. Bruce Lockhart, *Diaries*, op. cit., p. 445
27. This equates to more than £2,000 in 2023 prices (Bank of England inflation calculator)
28. Parliamentary Archives, Beaverbrook Papers, BBK/C/56, 16 October 1946
29. Parliamentary Archives, Beaverbrook Papers, BBK/C/222
30. Bruce Lockhart, *Comes the Reckoning*, op. cit., pp. 371–2
31. Bruce Lockhart, *Diaries*, op. cit., p. 501
32. Bruce Lockhart, *Comes the Reckoning*, op. cit., p. 372
33. Parliamentary Archives, Beaverbrook Papers, BBK/C/222, 1947

34. Delmer, *Black Boomerang*, op. cit., p. 234
35. TNA, Delmer's MI5 file, KV2/2586
36. Crossman, *Black Prima Donna*, op. cit.

Index

Note: page numbers in **bold** refer to illustrations.

Illustration Credits

Page 3: Sir Robert Hamilton Bruce Lockhart, by Walter Stoneman © National Portrait Gallery, London

Page 21: Richard Crossman circa 1940 © Picture Post / Stringer / Getty

Page 61: Elisabeth Barker © BBC Archive

Page 65: General Charles de Gaulle © BBC Archive

Page 120: Brendan Bracken, 1941 © Topical Press Agency / Stringer / Getty

Page 133: Denis 'Tom' Sefton Delmer at Lincoln College, with kind permission from the Rector and Fellows of Lincoln College, Oxford

Page 147: Tom Delmer © BBC Archive

Page 171: Isabel Delmer. Photograph of Isabel Rawsthorne lying in her bed, c. 1936, Sefton Delmer 1904-1979, Tate Archive © The Estate of Sefton (Tom) Delmer

Page 225: Sir Arthur Travers ('Bomber') Harris, 1st Bt, by Howard Coster © National Portrait Gallery, London

Page 351: RAF ground crew loading propaganda leaflets into Vickers Wellington bomber © Trinity Mirror / Mirrorpix / Alamy Stock Photo

Page 367: D-Day edition of the *Nachrichten für die Truppe* © Imperial War Museum, LBY K. AERIAL 3/537

Page 370: Leaflet dropped over Germany on D-Day © Imperial War Museum, LBY K. AERIAL 3/2379

About the Author

Terry Stiastny is an author, journalist and broadcaster on national and international radio. She reports on British politics for Times Radio and is a frequent commentator on Monocle Radio. Her debut non-fiction book, *Believable Lies*, combines her interests in politics, international history and journalism. She has previously published two political thrillers: *Acts of Omission* and *Conflicts of Interest* (John Murray). *Acts of Omission* won Political Fiction Book of the Year at the Political Book Awards in 2015. Before that, Terry was a correspondent at the BBC, where she worked on radio and television, based in Westminster, Brussels and Berlin, and reporting from many other countries. She was educated at Oxford University, earning an M.Phil in International Relations. She lives in north London with her husband, two sons and dog.